G. F. MACDONALD, a graduate of the
University of Witwatersrand, received his
B.Phil. at Oxford University, where he was a
postgraduate pupil of Sir Alfred Ayer. In 1974
he was appointed Lecturer in Philosophy at
the University of Bradford, having previously
taught at the University of Witwatersrand. His
publications include an introductory text
(with R. Lindley and R. Fellows), *What
Philosophy Does*.

SIR ALFRED AYER was, from 1959 to 1978,
Wykeham Professor of Logic at Oxford
University, and a Fellow of New College. He
was previously Grote Professor of the Philosophy
of Mind and Logic at University College, London
University. He was knighted in 1970.

PERCEPTION AND IDENTITY

PERCEPTION
AND IDENTITY

Essays Presented to A. J. Ayer, with His Replies

edited by

G. F. MACDONALD

Cornell University Press
Ithaca, New York

First published 1979 by Cornell University Press.

International Standard Book Number 0–8014–1265–X
Library of Congress Catalog Card Number 79–52503

Printed in Great Britain

Contents

Introduction   GRAHAM MACDONALD   vii

1. Common Sense and Physics   MICHAEL DUMMETT   1
2. Perception and its Objects   P. F. STRAWSON   41
3. A Comparison between Ayer's Views about the Privileges of Sense-Datum Statements and the Views of Russell and Austin   DAVID PEARS   61
4. Perception, Sense Data and Causality   D. M. ARMSTRONG   84
5. Sense Data Revisited   CHARLES TAYLOR   99
6. A Defence of Induction   J. L. MACKIE   113
7. Ayer on Monism, Pluralism and Essence   DAVID WIGGINS   131
8. In *Self*-Defence   JOHN FOSTER   161
9. Memory, Experiential Memory and Personal Identity   RICHARD WOLLHEIM   186
10. I Do Not Exist   PETER UNGER   235
11. Another Time, Another Place, Another Person   BERNARD WILLIAMS   252
12. Ayer on Metaphysics   STEPHAN KÖRNER   262
13. Replies   A. J. AYER   277

The Philosophical Works of A. J. Ayer   334

Bibliography   343

Notes on Contributors   347

Index   349

We are grateful to the *Radio Times* and Don Smith for permission to reproduce the photograph of Sir Alfred Ayer on the frontispiece.

Introduction

GRAHAM MACDONALD

The twelve essays in this volume have been written in honour of Professor A. J. Ayer, who retired from the Wykeham Chair of Logic at the University of Oxford in 1978. Ayer's philosophical career has been well documented in his autobiography, *Part of My Life*, and I shall not repeat the details here. He has, since the publication of *Language, Truth and Logic* in 1936, become internationally renowned for his forceful and rigorous analysis of important topics in philosophy, especially in the areas of epistemology, the philosophical foundations of probability, the philosophy of science, and metaphysics. His writing has consistently exhibited an elegance and clarity attained by very few other philosophers. In addition he has the pedagogic gifts of patience and understanding, as his many students who have received sympathetic guidance will know.

The contributors were invited to write on topics on which Ayer has published. Most of the articles fall in the area of either philosophy of perception or identity and personal identity. Ayer's responses to the comments on, and criticisms of, his work are a unique feature of the book. The most appropriate place for them seemed to us to be alongside the essays themselves. I would like to thank the contributors for their co-operation and scrupulous care at every stage. It is hoped that the result will be seen as a fitting tribute to Ayer and testimony to the immense contribution he has made to philosophy.

1 Common Sense and Physics

MICHAEL DUMMETT

I. THE PROBLEM

In *The Central Questions of Philosophy* (1973), chapter 5, section E, pp. 108–11,* Professor Ayer inquires into the compatibility of 'the scientific view of the nature of physical objects and that which can be attributed to common sense'. We are presented with three alternative answers. One is that physical theory constitutes, in Ramsey's terminology, a secondary system, the primary system being the world as conceived by common sense, or, rather, as we learn later (pp. 142–5), an attenuated version of it, stripped of dispositional and causal properties. The primary system embodies 'the sum total of . . . purely factual propositions' (p. 33); the function of the secondary system is 'purely explanatory', and the entities to which it refers, in so far as they cannot be identified with those figuring in the primary system, are simply conceptual tools serving to arrange the primary facts (pp. 109–10). This, then, is simply a version of instrumentalism: the actual facts, the hard facts, those that we really believe to obtain, are those of the primary system; the statements of scientific theory represent fictions, in which we do not really believe (as Ramsey confessed that he did not really believe in astronomy), but which we devise as a vivid means of encapsulating patterns and regularities detectable amongst the primary facts. Ayer thinks that such a distinction between primary and secondary systems is inescapable; but, in the present instance, he doubts whether it is necessary to relegate so much to the secondary system.

The second possible answer is to transfer 'all the perceptible qualities of things to the observer's account, leaving things, as they are in themselves, to be represented by the necessarily imperceptible objects of physical theory' (p. 110). This is objectionable because it involves locating imperceptible objects in perceptible

---

* All subsequent page references in this essay are cited from the same work. See bibliography.

space; and it is dubious whether the notion of a spatial system of which none of the elements can be observed is even intelligible (p. 86).

The third alternative, and that which Ayer himself favours, is to conceive of physical particles as being the minute parts of perceptible objects, so that their being imperceptible is not a necessary part of their nature, but simply an empirical consequence of their being so minute. On this view, it is simply an empirical fact that particles which are individually colourless compose coloured objects when enough of them come together; it is a further consequence that we are actually in error when we believe that the surfaces of physical objects are continuous.

What is the question to which these are alternative answers? We could, entirely properly, formulate it as 'What are the hard facts concerning the physical world?'; but this is not Ayer's way of framing it, and would lead us into a discussion of the very important, but very general, distinction between hard and soft facts. A formulation more in accordance with Ayer's discussion, and having the right degree of generality, would be, 'How are we to conceive of physical objects as they are in themselves?' And so our first task is to scrutinise the notion of an object 'as it is in itself'.

We might say that the inquiry how things, in general, are in themselves – not just material objects – is *the* metaphysical inquiry. Here, of course, 'as they are in themselves' stands opposed to 'as they appear to us'. This contrast is stated by Ayer in discussing the view (p. 82) that physics falsifies naïve realism. This view he links with the thesis that tables, for example, are not really coloured; and in elucidating this thesis he says (p. 84), of those who hold it, that 'they want to distinguish between things as they are in themselves and things as they can appear to us, and to count as the real properties of physical objects only those properties that they possess independently of our perceiving them'. There is no doubt that this is a correct characterisation of a very strong and very broad current in philosophical thought. We commonly deploy a distinction between how things appear and how they really are; and it is therefore natural to try to push this distinction to the limit. This seems to me the best way in which to view the so-called 'argument from illusion'. If this is regarded as an argument, properly so called, with premises and a conclusion, it is difficult to make out what are the premises and what the conclusion. Rather, it is a *starting point*. We start with the existence of a distinction, or distinctions, between how things appear and how they really are; and we want to take it as far as we can, or, at any rate, to see how far it can be taken. It is, of course, possible to point out that the contrast between how a thing appears and how it really is is not made at one level: the notion of appearance is not applied uniformly, and so the correlative notion of reality is not applied uniformly either. But we might compare this situation with what Wittgenstein said about possibility. Wittgenstein observed that, at least in most contexts, 'can do such-and-such' may be glossed 'can do such-and-such so far as . . . is concerned', where the dots are filled in in some specific way. But, even if we grant this, we may legitimately inquire whether there is any *absolute* sense of 'can' that falls short of 'does', one that is the conjunction of all the relativised senses. In the same way, we may inquire whether there is a way of characterising a thing that will fall on the side of how it really is, or how it is in itself, as opposed to how it appears, *however* that distinction is applied; and it is this concern which powers a great deal of metaphysical inquiry.

II. REALISM

The thesis that tables and the like are not really coloured was, as we saw, attributed by Ayer to the proponents of the view that physics falsifies naïve realism; and, in the passage (pp. 108–11) with which we are chiefly concerned, the second and third of the three possible answers to our question are stated to be alternative means of upholding realism, while the first answer relegates physical theory to the status of a secondary system. The realism in question is 'a realistic view of the status of physical particles' (p. 110). Now it appears to me that the traditional manner of using the philosophical term 'realism', which Ayer follows, blurs an important distinction. Of course, there is no question of anyone's simply being a realist *tout court*: one may be a realist about a certain subject matter, or, as it seems to me better to say, one may adopt a realistic interpretation of a certain class of statements, and not about some other subject matter, or of some other class of statements. Objections to a realistic interpretation of a given class of statements frequently take their rise from a form of reductionism: one says that a statement of the given class cannot be true unless some statement, or perhaps set of statements, of some other class, which I shall call the *reductive* class, is true. For instance, it is said that a statement ascribing a mental state to somebody cannot be true unless some one of a range of statements about his behaviour is true, statements which may be required to be categorical or may be allowed to include subjunctive conditionals. Here the reductive class consists of statements about the person's behaviour; on

another view, it might consist of statements about his neurophysiological condition. Such a thesis is obviously of philosophical interest
in itself: I shall call it a *reductive* thesis. A reductive thesis concerning
statements ascribing mental states to individuals may be said to
be a thesis about that in virtue of which such statements are true,
when they are true; or to offer an answer to the question of
in what mental states consist. The thesis that, for a given class
of statements, there is no other class of statements with respect
to which a reductive thesis holds – that is, that there is no reductive
class – I shall call an *irreducibility* thesis.

Now, although reductive theses are intrinsically interesting (at
least when the given class has been characterised in such a way
as not to make them trivial), it seems to me a mistake to make
rejection or acceptance of such a thesis a touchstone of whether
one adopts or repudiates a realistic interpretation of the given
class. The reason why it can seem so is that the step of propounding
a reductive thesis is very often a preliminary to a further step.
One observes that, for any particular statement of the given class,
there is no guarantee that there will either be true statements of
the reductive class which render that statement true, or be true
statements of the reductive class which render its negation true
(the given class is assumed closed under negation). From this
it is inferred that there is no guarantee that an arbitrary statement
of the given class will be either true or false: such statements
do not satisfy the principle of bivalence, so long as the falsity
of such a statement is equated with the truth of its negation.
And it is in taking this step that a realistic interpretation of the
statements of the given class has been abandoned. That is, the
touchstone of realism ought to be whether it is held that we possess
a notion of truth for statements of the given class relative to
which they satisfy the principle of bivalence – the principle, namely,
that every statement is determinately either true or false.

The advantage of characterising realism in this way lies in two
facts. First, the acceptance of a reductive thesis does not inevitably
lead to the repudiation of realism: one need not take the second
step in the argument. From a reductive thesis it does not in itself
follow that bivalence fails for statements of the given class: one
has to look at the particular reductive thesis proposed to see whether
that consequence is plausible or not. For instance, those who hold
that a statement ascribing a mental state to someone, if true at
all, will be true in virtue of some neuro-physiological condition
of that person are likely to place a realistic interpretation on statements ascribing mental states, by the criterion of realism formulated
above. And, secondly, the repudiation of realism does not require

the prior acceptance of a reductive thesis: that is simply a familiar route to it. One might hold an irreducibility thesis concerning statements of some given class, and yet believe that the idea that we had, for such statements, a conception of truth relative to which bivalence was satisfied was an illusion. I do not pretend that, in using the term 'realism' in the way proposed, we shall be precisely conforming to traditional philosophical practice. On the contrary, the point of the proposal is to enable us to keep clearly in mind a distinction which, under the traditional use of the term, has frequently been blurred. Whether my terminology is happy is a matter of minor importance; what is important is to maintain the distinction.

All four combinations are possible. If one takes a realistic view of a given class of statements, one may nevertheless admit that some reductive thesis holds for that class; or one may regard the class as irreducible. I shall say that a realist of the first kind is a *sophisticated* realist, one of the second kind a *naïve* realist. Equally, if one repudiates realism concerning a class of statements, one may do so on the strength of some reductive thesis to which one adheres; but one may also do so while admitting that class to be irreducible. I shall call the former a *reductive* anti-realist, the latter an *outright* anti-realist (it would be stretching the term too far to call him 'naïve').

I have so far avoided the label 'reductionist'. A reductionist is usually thought of as one who not merely accepts a reductive thesis, but also holds that it is in principle possible to translate statements of the given class into statements of the reductive class; and this is just the way in which Ayer characterises that position (p. 66). Obviously, one may accept a reductive thesis, but deny the truth of reductionism, for any of several reasons. First, one may, without abandoning the reductive thesis, concede that statements of the reductive class are not intelligible independently of statements of the given class. For instance, one may claim that a mathematical statement, if true at all, can be true only in virtue of the truth of a statement to the effect that we are in possession of a proof of it, but admit that it is impossible to frame a vocabulary in which statements of the latter kind can be expressed without thereby introducing a vocabulary adequate for the expression of the mathematical statements themselves. This is emphatically *not* Ayer's ground for denying the possibility of translating statements about physical objects into statements about sense data (see pp. 91–3). Secondly, one may hold that we have no way of effectively identifying, for any statement of the given class, that statement of the reductive class that must be true if it is to be true. This seems to be Donald Davidson's reason for not holding that psychological statements are translatable into neurophysiological ones; but, again, no such suggestion appears in Ayer. Thirdly, one may think that, to ensure the truth of a statement of the given class, the truth of the statements in some infinite subset of the reductive class is needed; or that the truth of a statement of the given class guarantees the truth of only one out of infinitely many statements in the reductive class; or one may combine these views. If our language does not contain the apparatus for forming the necessary infinite conjunctions and disjunctions, actual translation will be impossible. This is one of Ayer's two reasons for not being a reductionist (p. 107). The other is that a translation would necessitate admitting subjunctive conditionals into the reductive class, and Ayer feels uncomfortable about such conditionals. I do not classify this as a distinct ground for rejecting reductionism while accepting a reductive thesis, since it would seem that, where the premiss was cogent, conditionals would have to be admitted to the reductive class if even the reductive thesis was to hold. What is important is that even reductive anti-realism does not require reductionism in this fully fledged sense.

On the strength of his rejection of reductionism, Ayer claims to be a sophisticated realist (p. 108). Now, Ayer's second argument against reductionism tells equally against a reductive thesis. It is this. To find, for an arbitrary statement about material objects, a statement about percepts the truth of which would render the material-object statement true, it would be necessary to allow the statement about percepts to take the form of a subjunctive conditional. But any class of subjunctive conditionals is itself preeminently a reducible class: some reductive thesis must hold good for it (Ayer expresses this by saying that conditionals do not belong to the primary system – see pp. 142–5). The argument, as thus stated, is not cogent: it shows only that the class of statements, including conditional ones, about percepts is not an *ultimate* reductive class for material-object statements, that we can carry out a further reduction. It would become cogent only if it were claimed, in addition, that the truth of a conditional concerning percepts could be explained only in terms of the truth of suitable (categorical) material-object statements, so that the latter formed a reductive class for conditionals about percepts: then, indeed, the class of material-object statements would be effectively irreducible. There is, however, no suggestion of this kind in Ayer's discussion of subjunctive conditionals (pp. 150–5): he says that we accept a conditional on the basis of a generalisation of law, which differs from a generalisation of fact in that we treat it as projectible.

Of course, this calls for a detailed discussion of what induces us to treat a generalisation as projectible; but there is no explicit claim that we should never so treat generalisations concerning percepts without adverting to material-object statements we consider true.

However this may be, it seems clear that Ayer does not accept even a reductive thesis concerning material-object statements. He is therefore not a sophisticated realist in the sense I gave to that term above; if he is a realist at all, he is a naïve realist in my sense. Now, Ayer does say explicitly (p. 152) that the principle of bivalence does not hold for subjunctive conditionals in general; but, since he does not accept a reductive thesis, we cannot infer that he is not a realist, in my sense, about material-object statements. It is very hard to say whether he is or not: he does not appear to be concerned with this issue in respect of material-object statements couched in everyday language. He *is* concerned with it in regard to the statements of physical theory; for instrumentalism – the view that scientific theories form mere 'secondary systems' – does constitute a rejection of realism, in my sense, for scientific statements. The question he raises concerning material-object statements of everyday language, on the other hand, is not whether they may all be considered as determinately true or false independently of our knowledge, but, roughly speaking, whether they may ever be considered true at all: more exactly, the curious question of whether material objects really have perceptible qualities.

In calling himself a sophisticated realist, Ayer is certainly using the term 'sophisticated' in a technical sense. Sophisticated realism stands opposed to naïve realism; and naïve realism, as Ayer characterises it (pp. 65–6), appears to incorporate what I have here called naïve realism, and an epistemological thesis besides. The epistemological thesis Ayer expresses as being that 'we perceive physical objects not through a screen of sense-impressions but directly'. It is clear that this obscure form of words is meant to exclude the possibility of Cartesian doubt concerning reports of observation, but I shall not, in this essay, discuss Cartesian doubt. We shall have a great deal of trouble with the epistemological thesis here attributed to the naïve realist – a thesis which may, again obscurely, be expressed as that, in observing an object under favourable conditions, we know it as it really is.

III. PERCEPTIBLE QUALITIES

Ayer employs the notion of a perceptible quality, but does not define the term; and there are several different possible ways of using it.

(1) The weakest sense is that under which a quality or relation is perceptible provided only that we can frequently judge, with high probability, that an object possesses it, or that it holds between two objects, just by looking at, listening to, feeling, tasting or smelling that object or those objects. Let us call qualities and relations that satisfy this condition *observable* ones. There are obviously a great many observable qualities: being cylindrical, for example.

As soon as we frame stronger requirements, we step into a morass. I shall first list the conditions I wish to consider, and attach labels to the classes of qualities and relations satisfying them, and then make a number of comments.

(2) A very strong requirement is that, whenever it is possible to override a judgement to the effect that an object possesses the quality, or that the relation holds between two objects – that is, based on looking at or otherwise observing the object or objects – then it is possible to override it by appeal to judgements also so based but to the opposite effect, possibly made under different conditions or by a different observer. I shall call qualities and relations satisfying this condition *simple observational* ones.

(3) A requirement stronger than 1 but weaker than 2 is that any judgement that can be made as to whether an object has the quality, or whether the relation holds between two objects, can be made on the basis solely of perceptual comparisons, in the relevant respect, of one object with another, not necessarily the given object or objects, under varying conditions. Qualities and relations satisfying this condition will be called *complex observational* ones.

Simple and complex observational qualities and relations will be taken as together comprising *observational* qualities and relations.

(4) We may require that a characterisation of what it is for an object to possess the quality, or for two objects to stand in the relation, must involve essential reference to human perceptual faculties. I shall call a quality or relation that satisfies this condition *intrinsically perceptual*.

(5) Finally, following Locke, we may say that a quality is a *primary* observable quality if no explanation of our ability

to perceive an object as having that quality can be given that does not expressly appeal to the object's possession of the quality, and similarly for relations. For instance, we do not expect any account to be forthcoming of how we are able to discern by feeling it that a moderately small object is spherical that does not appeal to the object's being spherical. I shall here be very little concerned with this interesting property of certain observable qualities.

The definitions of simple and complex observational qualities and relations were so framed as not to exclude their being vague: it was not required that the possession of the quality or subsistence of the relation be completely determined in every case by any set, finite or infinite, of actual or possible observations, or by anything else. It may be said that there can be no vague qualities or relations, but only vague *expressions*, which, as Frege would say, therefore do not stand for any qualities or relations at all. We might, of course, just define a vague quality to be what a vague predicate stands for; but, it will be said, there can be no vagueness in nature, in the world, only in language. This presumably means that the world cannot be such as to require vague predicates to describe it, although *we* may be, for various reasons, forced to employ them; but I am inclined to suspect that this attitude represents a deep but unwarranted philosophical prejudice.

For all that, there are grounds for thinking that there can be no simple observational *qualities*. The defining condition for such qualities implies a further condition, which I shall call the *indiscernibility condition*: namely that, if one object possesses the quality, and no relevant difference between it and another object can be perceived, then the second object possesses it. It seems indisputable that we do habitually use a number of adjectives – for example, 'red' and 'sweet' – as if standing for a quality subject to this condition. At the same time, in view of the non-transitivity of perceptual indiscernibility, to which Ayer alludes (p. 90), it is incoherent to suppose that there is any quality that always satisfies the condition.

It does not follow, however, that there are no simple observational *relations*. For the indiscernibility condition to apply to a given quality, we must have a suitable notion of perceiving a relevant difference. In the case of colours, tastes and the like, we do: we make judgements, based on observation, that two objects are or are not perceptibly distinct in colour, as well as judging that a single object is, or is not, red. But consider the relation of being perceptibly distinct in colour itself, which may, of course, be viewed as a quality of pairs of objects rather than as a relation between objects. Then we lack any notion of a perception of a relevant difference between two pairs of objects; we cannot say, 'If you judge those two objects to be perceptibly distinct in colour, then you must judge those two other objects to be so also, because there is no perceptible difference, between the two pairs, in the colour distance of the members of the pairs.' Since, therefore, we lack a notion of a perception of a relevant difference, we cannot even state the indiscernibility condition for this relation. Hence, while there is an incoherence in supposing that there is a simple observational quality of redness, there is not the same reason for thinking that there is any incoherence in supposing that there is a simple observational relation of perceptible difference in colour.

An objection might be made as follows. If having a specific shade of colour were a simple observational quality, then, given an object with that quality, it would be a necessary and sufficient condition for another object to have the quality that it be perceptibly indiscriminable in colour from the given object. The indiscernibility condition required only that perceptual indiscernibility from an object having the quality be a *sufficient* condition for possession of the quality. We expect it to be a *necessary* condition also when the quality is not only observational but also specific or cospecific (a cospecific quality is the negation or complement of a specific one). Now let us say that a pair of objects has quality Q just in case those objects are perceptibly distinct in colour. Then our argument that the indiscernibility condition is inapplicable to quality Q amounts to saying that there is no perceptible relation between pairs of objects such that, for any pair having quality Q, another pair will have quality Q if and only if it stands in that relation to the first pair. This is indeed surprising, inasmuch as we should expect quality Q to be a cospecific quality. However (the objection goes), it does not show that the indiscernibility condition is inapplicable: for this, we need only a perceptible relation which yields a *sufficient* condition for the second pair to have quality Q. But the relation that holds between the pair $\{x, y\}$ and the pair $\{u, v\}$ when x is perceptibly indiscriminable in colour from u, and y from v, is such a relation: since we cannot see any relevant difference between x and u, or between y and v, we are forced to say that, if $\{x, y\}$ has quality Q, then so must $\{u, v\}$ have it. But if x, u, v, y is a sequence such that no two adjacent terms are perceptibly distinct in colour, but x and y are, the conclusion will be false: there is therefore no such simple observational relation as being perceptibly distinct in colour.

The argument is fallacious, however. The condition that x be perceptibly indiscriminable in colour from u, and y from v, is *not* sufficient to make us say that the pair $\{x, y\}$ cannot be perceived as differing in a relevant respect from the pair $\{u, v\}$: the mere fact that we perceive x and y as distinct in colour, and do not so perceive u and v, makes the two *pairs* perceptibly different in the relevant respect, even though we can see no relevant difference between the individual *objects* x and u, or between y and v.

A similar fallacious objection would be one based on the possibility of converting a relation into a quality by fixing one of its terms. If, the objection runs, being perceptibly indiscriminable in colour is a simple observational relation, then being perceptibly indiscriminable in colour from the surface s is a simple observational quality. Hence, if t is not perceptibly distinct in colour from u, and t is not perceptibly distinct in colour from s, then u cannot be perceptibly distinct in colour from s, by the indiscernibility condition; and we appear to have proved the transitivity of indiscernibility of colour, which we know to fail. The mistake in this argument lies in the premiss of fixing one term of a simple observational relation need not yield a simple observational quality. A simple observational quality was defined as one to determine the possession of which by an object we did not need to observe more than that object; but, in deciding whether t is perceptibly distinct in colour from s, we shall need to look at s as well as t, and there was nothing in the definition of a simple observational *relation* to make us think otherwise.

Still, it may be said, it is a matter of common experience that there are no simple observational relations, even if we lack an irrefutable argument to show that there can be none. Consider, for instance, perceived equality of length for juxtaposed objects. If I have a metre rule, and am asked to sort lengths of string into those that are more than twenty-nine centimetres long and those that are no more than twenty-nine centimetres long, I shall in some cases be uncertain; but, if perceived equality of length were a simple observational relation, no such uncertainty could arise. Moreover, if I am instructed to sort the lengths of string into those that are *definitely* over twenty-nine centimetres long and those that are not *definitely* so, I shall still sometimes be uncertain. However, all that this argument shows is that, if perceived equality of length is taken to be a simple observational relation, it is irremediably vague; and, as was already noted, this was not ruled out by the definition of a simple observational relation. We did not reject simple observational qualities on the score merely of their exhibiting the very general feature of vagueness of application, but because they had a very special type of vagueness that engendered actual inconsistency. In any case, we have no argument to demonstrate that there are no exact simple observational relations.

If there are, after all, no simple observational relations, there can be no complex observational qualities or relations. Suppose, following Nelson Goodman, that we define x to be *indirectly discriminable* in colour from y just in case, for some z, x is perceptibly distinct in colour from z, but y is not; or conversely. Then, if (direct) perceptible discriminability in colour is a simple observational relation, indirect discriminability is a complex observational one, vague or exact according as the former is vague or exact. Goodman's idea, by allowing us to introduce complex observational colour qualities related to indirect indiscriminability as the simple observational ones were supposed to be related to direct indiscriminability, gets us over the difficulty that there can be no colour qualities satisfying the indiscernibility condition; but such a device works only if direct indiscriminability is a simple observational relation.

In the definitions of simple and complex observational qualities and relations, I have left an uncertainty about whether it is allowable, in making a comparison, to juxtapose the objects, or whether a comparison between non-adjacent objects must be made with them *in situ*. If we allow juxtaposition, we shall of course get a wider class of qualities and relations. For instance, if, in that case, we had a notion of equality of length considered as determined solely by very direct and straightforward methods of measurement, involving only comparison of juxtaposed objects, and not measurement of angles, calculation, and so on, then equality in length would be a simple or a complex observational relation according as we made only direct comparisons or used a yardstick. However, the important fact is that there are many observable qualities which are not observational at all: for instance, shape qualities, the application of which even to objects of the right size and distance for us to be able to judge of their shape by looking may always be checked by measurement (of distances and angles), the result of which overrides the purely perceptual judgement when it disagrees with it. Measurement may reveal that the base of the tin is not circular, and hence that the tin is not cylindrical, even though no observer can detect the deviation from circularity just by looking. Ayer refers to this fact (p. 77); but he rather brushes it aside. Colour qualities have a better claim to be observational. For instance, when presented with one of the familiar kind of optical illusions, we determine that a figure really is a rectangle, and not, as appears, a trapezium, by some crude measurement; but we determine that an area of the figure is really white, and not yellow or grey, by covering up the rest of the figure and seeing how it looks then, and thus by means of a test of the sort allowed for observational qualities. In the former case, we no longer appeal to any perceptual judgement about shape; but, in the latter case, we still rely on a perceptual judgement as to colour, but we change the conditions under which it is made.

There remains some doubt, especially for those who believe that there is no vagueness in nature, whether there are any simple observational relations, and hence whether there are any observational qualities or relations, simple or complex, at all: certainly we use many familiar terms as standing for simple observational qualities the existence of which involves a contradiction. We must suppose that there exist non-observational qualities the extension of which approximately coincides with our application of such terms; and when, in the sequel, I speak of observational qualities, I must, whenever necessary, be taken as referring to such approximately observational ones.

The notion of an intrinsically perceptual quality also calls for some explanation. It is a plausible hypothesis that some or all of the affective qualities – being funny, boring, macabre, eerie, interesting, and so forth – are, in an analogous sense, intrinsically affective. Various people, such as Bergson and Freud, have attempted to say in what being funny, considered objectively, consists: 'considered objectively' means 'formulated without reference to the capacity to evoke amusement in us'. The problem is this. Suppose that we had got as far as being able to feed narrative stories into a computer: it could then answer examination questions about them, of the type, 'What reason did Jane give for returning to Paris?'; or perhaps it could produce on its console a cartoon depicting the sequence of events. We want now to program the computer to give sensible answers to the question, 'Was that story (a) hilarious, (b) mildly amusing or (c) not funny in the least?': what instructions are we to give it? Only if we had a theory of humour of the kind Bergson and Freud so unsuccessfully attempted to construct could we begin to set about this task. And perhaps there is no such theory. Perhaps being funny is incapable of analysis save in terms of reactions evoked in us: perhaps we are the only creatures in the universe who can perceive this quality, so that it is impossible in principle to design an instrument to detect its presence, unless that instrument incorporates one or more human beings. That is the hypothesis that the quality of being funny is intrinsically affective.

What would it be for a quality to be, in a similar way, intrinsically

perceptual? If, in the definition, we replace 'human perceptual faculties' by 'the perceptual faculties of terrestrial animals', we can
imagine that taste qualities had so turned out. Intense research
had wholly failed to uncover the physiological mechanism of taste;
and repeated efforts had established no correlation between the
taste of a substance and its molecular structure or any other feature
of its physical or chemical constitution. Perhaps it was found that
sodium chloride could be separated out, by getting people to taste
minute quantities of it, into two chemically indistinguishable substances – one twice as salt in taste as ordinary table salt, and
the other quite tasteless: we might find ourselves forced to admit
that our impression that chemically identical substances taste alike
was an illusion owing to most samples' having the same mixture
of substances distinguishable only by taste. This would not *prove*
that taste qualities were intrinsically perceptual: that would be
only a hypothesis – the hypothesis, namely, that terrestrial animals
were the only things in the universe that responded differentially
to, and could therefore be used to detect, qualities of taste. It
would then hold good that the *only* characterisation of what it
is for something to be sweet, for example – the only characterisation
we could ever attain – would be that it tastes sweet to human
beings, bears and the like.

IV. THINGS AS THEY ARE IN THEMSELVES

The formulation of Ayer's original question with which we came
up was, 'How are we to conceive of physical objects as they are
in themselves?' We saw that Ayer connected this with the question
of whether the scientific view of the nature of physical objects
is compatible with that attributable to common sense, and, further,
with the question of whether tables are really coloured. Now, as
already remarked, the main question takes its rise from the fact
that we admit a distinction, or distinctions, between how things
really are and how they appear. For there to be a world – that
is, an external environment – that we all inhabit, there must be
a distinction between how things appear to one person and how
they actually are. From this it does not follow that we need admit
any distinction between how things appear to us generally and
how they really are: I may take as correct etiquette what is not
actually correct etiquette, but it is impossible that we should all
take as correct etiquette what is not actually so. Nevertheless,
we do in fact extend the distinction we make between how material
objects appear to one observer and how they really are to a distinction between how they appear to any (human) observer and how

they really are. This is in part a consequence of the fact that the greater part of the predicates that we use as standing for observable qualities do not stand for observational qualities: the results of physical operations, or of mental ones such as counting, provide criteria for their application that override judgements based on unaided observation. But even for predicates standing for observational qualities we admit the distinction. To any normally sighted person who looks up when he is out of doors on a clear day, it undoubtedly looks as though there is something blue overhead; but the only candidate for being something that really is blue is a purely visual object. Equally, if he looks up on a clear night, he will see the stars twinkling; but the stars do not really twinkle: they only appear to twinkle – though, of course, they really do so appear.

But these, after all, are cases of mistakes – very natural mistakes, but still mistakes: unless otherwise instructed, a man will naturally suppose that there is a blue dome above the clouds, and that the light emitted by the stars fluctuates rapidly in intensity. Is there any reason to admit a distinction between how things appear to all of us and how they really are, when no mistake is in question? If such a distinction is admissible at all in cases when no mistake is involved, it cannot be one that requires us to say that the object in question is not as it appears to be; for this would entail that, in taking it to be as it appears, we had made a mistake, when, by hypothesis, no mistake was in question. It does not follow that there is not a legitimate distinction between different ways of characterising the qualities of objects. The contrast is now not between the qualities that things appear to have and those different qualities that they really have: it is between a method of characterising those qualities that they are agreed to have in terms of our own perceptual capacities and one that is independent of our modes of perception; it is therefore not a matter of discovering that they lack certain qualities that we wrongly supposed them to have. The attempt to say what things are like in themselves is an attempt to find a means of characterising them that is independent, not only of the particular position and circumstances of an individual observer, but also, more generally, of the situation of human beings, located on the surface of a certain planet at a particular stage in its history, being of a certain size and having a particular range of sensory faculties. The making of such an attempt in no way involves us in thinking that a description that is not independent of these things, but is given in terms relative to or explained by reference to our own position and observational capacities, is *incorrect* in any way: only that it does not accomplish what is achieved by a description that is independent of these contingent facts.

Thus the distinction between 'how things are in themselves' and 'how they appear to us' bifurcates into two quite different, though related, distinctions: that between what is true of the world and what only appears to be, but is not actually, true of it; and that between what may be called an absolute and what may be called a relative form of description. A description in relative terms may, in itself, be perfectly correct; but, in reflective moods, and, to a considerable extent, for practical purposes, we prefer a description in absolute terms. One of the things that a scientific theory aims to do is to attain an accurate description of things as they are in themselves, or as they really are, in this sense – that is, a description in absolute terms; and such a description need not invalidate, in the sense of showing to be incorrect, the form of description in relative terms that we employ in everyday life.

But, if this is so, why is an impression to the contrary so wide-spread amongst philosophers? Why is it regarded as a problem, as Ayer regards it, whether a scientific description is compatible with a common-sense one, and, if so, how the reconciliation can be effected? Why should Ayer concern himself with those who think that his table is not really brown? Ayer himself does not think that there is good reason to deny that his table is brown; but he treats the matter as a serious problem, one requiring a subtle philosophical theory to meet the challenge. He wants a theory according to which subatomic particles are colourless only as 'an empirical consequence of their being so minute', i.e. smaller than the wavelength of light; and he thinks that he has to work hard to get such a theory, and so escape the rival theory according to which all physical objects, however large, are in principle colour-less. But why cannot we dismiss this rival theory as involving an elementary confusion between the two types of distinction between how things are in themselves and how they appear? Any normally sighted person, we might say, can see at a glance that there are plenty of coloured material objects: the question is not whether the surfaces of objects have colour, but in what their having any given colour consists. Perhaps those who think that all (material) objects are colourless, and those who are frightened that we may, if we do not relegate science to the status of a 'secondary system', in the Ramsey–Ayer terminology, have to allow that material objects are colourless are making the mistake of confusing the adoption of a reductive thesis concerning statements ascribing colours to objects with the repudiation of a realistic view of such statements – when in fact, as we have seen, the two are independent of one another. Indeed, even the rejection of realism concerning a given class of statements does not involve us in saying that no statement in that class is ever *really* true. Someone who takes a constructivist view of mathematical statements has in no way to deny that there are true mathematical statements: he merely rejects the idea that each statement of classical mathematics is determinately true or false, independently of our knowing, or having the means of knowing, its truth value. In any case, the question here at issue is not that of realism concerning statements about material objects, in the sense in which I am using 'realism': it is, rather, the question of whether a reductive thesis holds good for such statements, where the reductive class consists of statements couched in the terms of physical theory. Modern physics does undoubtedly offer many affronts to common sense: but it does not appear that the denial that objects are coloured is one of them.

V. COMMON SENSE

Against this it may be objected that to say that most people can see at a glance that the world contains many coloured objects is an application of the paradigm-case argument. If so, it may be possible to rebut it by the standard means for rebutting paradigm-case arguments: namely, by agreeing that we normally assume that we can tell whether something is brown by looking at it, but contending that, in calling it 'brown', we ordinarily understand ourselves as attributing to it a property which, if physical theory is not a mere secondary system, it does not actually have. To argue thus is, in effect, to reject the claim made earlier that there is a way of construing the distinction between how things are in themselves and how they appear to us that does not involve that the appearance is delusive. On this account, a physicist who agrees that Ayer's table is brown will not be using the word 'brown' in the same sense as that in which it is used by most people in everyday speech; at least, he will not be so using it if he believes that a description of the table in terms of physical theory is a description of it as it really is, rather than just giving a convenient summary of certain regularities we should observe if we subjected the table to a variety of experiments.

Now, without doubt we may properly speak of certain views as forming, at a particular period and within a particular culture, a part of common sense. A common-sense view is a conception on which most of those who belong to that culture at that time habitually rely in their everyday thinking. It is not required that

they should actually hold it to be correct – they, or some of
them, may know, or think, otherwise: what matters is that their
ordinary thinking proceeds *as if* it were correct. It was remarked
above that modern physical theory offers many affronts to common
sense. It has often been remarked that common sense always lags
behind scientific theory, and one thing that common sense has
still not absorbed is relativity theory; it seems reasonable to say
that common sense continues to take temporal intervals and spatial
distances and therefore shapes as absolute.

To speak about common sense in this way, however, as something
that lags behind the advances in scientific theory, is to reject the
picture of it that some philosophers appear to use: the picture
of a single, unified, permanent 'theory of the world', an acceptance
of which, at least as a basis for one's ordinary everyday thinking,
is simply part of what is involved in being a sane adult human
being. There is no such single unchanging theory. It is, for instance,
a mistake to think of anyone, however little educated, in our own
society as entirely ignorant of science or as uninfluenced by it
in his common modes of thought. On the contrary, all are profoundly
affected, in their view of the world and of ordinary things in
it, by the smatterings of scientific knowledge that they possess.
Perhaps the most striking example of this is the way in which
our thought is permeated by the knowledge of the molecular structure of matter, which informs the way we think about mixtures
of liquids. We have learned to think about these on the model
of mixtures of granular solids such as sugar and salt: so much
does this image dominate us that it is virtually impossible to think
oneself back into those conceptions which seemed natural when
a liquid was thought of as homogeneously filling the whole space
it occupied. St Thomas says that, if a small quantity of water
is added to wine, it becomes wine. Even if we prescind from our
knowledge that wine is already a mixture, this seems to us insane;
but that is because we surreptitiously appeal to the granular model
to explain to ourselves what a mixture is. We cannot recapture
the mode of thought natural if a liquid is taken to be completely
homogeneous; we have no idea how, under such a conception,
we are to describe what takes place when one liquid is added
to another and thoroughly stirred.

Again, in assessing the conception that a 'plain man' has of
phenomena of light, it is wrong to think of him as innocent of
the idea of radiation. He has a wireless and a television set; he
has, perhaps, an electric heater, of which one part works by convec-
tion and the other by radiation; he has a camera, and knows
about the exposure of a film to light; he has X-ray pictures taken

at the hospital; he has heard of radio astronomy and perhaps of x-ray astronomy; he has possibly read newspaper articles about the ozone layer and ultra-violet radiation. For a philosopher who believes that there is such a thing as *the* common-sense view of the world, a natural response to remarks such as these is to say that all they show is that there are no plain men in our society. If, he thinks, we could find a society whose members remained uncorrupted by scientific knowledge, those people would retain the pure, unadulterated common-sense view. But this is an error. Even if we find people who have nothing that we should classify as scientific knowledge, they will have some general account of phenomena of their experience, even if a wholly erroneous one, and, even if most of them have only smatterings of this theory, it will colour the way they find it natural to think about the world. The idea of *the* common-sense view of the world is as much a myth as that of the noble savage (or, indeed, that of the savage). Even if a philosopher who believed the myth were to scour the earth and succeed in finding, in some remote corner, a group of people who accepted just what he had described as constituting *the* common-sense view of the world, it would prove nothing to his advantage: it would show only that he had made a lucky guess about one possible conception of reality; but that conception would have no special standing, among all the different conceptions that have prevailed amongst men of different times and places. The belief in a unique common-sense view is contradictory: it postulates a theory that is, somehow, not a *theory*. It has to be a theory, since, in this context, 'view' and 'conception' are mere stylistic variants on 'theory': it has, that is, to be something in which people may be said to believe, or, at least, to think in accordance with, even if they do not suppose it to be true. Creatures who did not have a theory in this, perhaps fairly low-grade, sense of 'theory' would hardly be *men* at all, but only a kind of talking animals; they would lack the curiosity and the capacity for reflection that are essential marks of being human. But, at the same time, the common-sense view has *not* to be a theory, in that, whenever we find people whose view of the world does not coincide with it, we shall be able to say that their view has been distorted by whatever theory is prevalent in their society. There is, however, no view or set of views that has such a privileged status; no view that men would take if only they were left alone by society to form what view was natural to them; for they owe their language, the vehicle of their thought, and their very humanity to being members of a society.

Philosophers of the kind who raise the problem of reconciliation that Ayer is striving to resolve claim to descry a tension not merely between common-sense and particular ingredients of current scientific thought, but between common sense and science as such. Such a tension is not discerned by the 'plain man' in our society. There are not, for him, two distinct realms – one of science, which describes things in peculiar ways for arcane purposes of its own, and the other the world of common sense; rather, the fragments of scientific knowledge that a man possesses enter into his picture of the world without any feeling of their being an alien ingredient that has no business to be there. As technology advances, new things become part of everyday experience. They will not, indeed, be fully understood by most people, just as the purely natural phenomena encountered are not fully understood; but, in so far as they are understood, they are understood in the only way they can be, by incorporating scientific ideas into our picture of the world as a whole.

If common sense is culturally conditioned and subject to historical evolution, if it can itself digest scientific ideas and diverges from scientific theory only because the process of digestion is slow and imperfect, then there cannot be an opposition in principle between it and science; nor can we owe to common sense any duty of accepting it, reconciling it with science or enshrining it as a primary system, with science demoted to secondary status. We can owe it nothing at all: philosophers need make no presumption that the views which, in their particular age, make up the common sense of the day are in some fundamental sense the true ones, subordinate to which any other conception, whether of scientific or of philosophical origin, must find a place if it can.

That is not to say that a philosopher need not pay any special attention to common sense, that he may dismiss it with the brusque remark that, if common sense conflicts with the truth, then so much the worse for common sense. Common-sense views enter into our understanding of the words we use in everyday speech, and it is this that makes them particularly tenacious and makes us at first resist as unintelligible any theory that conflicts with them. I am not among those who hold that it is impossible in principle to draw any distinction between the meanings we attach to our words and our acceptance as true of statements involving them; but it would be absurd to deny that what we take to be true often bears strongly on the way we take the meanings of our words as being given, or that, given the meaning attached to some predicate, the truth of some substantial proposition needs to be assumed if it is to be believed to have an application. An abandonment of a common-sense view may therefore require a certain shift in the understanding of words, a shift rendered more

palatable by a philosopher's effort to bring the common-sense view
to light and to analyse the change of meaning demanded.

VI. 'THE COLOURS ARE IN THE OBJECTS'

We have still to discover just what view is imputed to common
sense by those philosophers who think that a scientific account,
if accepted as part of a primary system, would require us to believe
that Ayer's table is not brown, as common sense understands
'brown'. On the face of it, if the alleged common-sense view is
to be one that conflicts not merely with the particular scientific
account of colour that we have, but with any conceivable such
account, so that common sense is in opposition not merely to
particular scientific theories, but to science as such, it must be
to the effect that colours are intrinsically perceptual qualities, in
the sense in which, in the imaginary situation described above,
taste qualities would be. On reflection, however, it seems doubtful
that this can capture what is alleged to be the common-sense view.
Does anyone credit common sense with the view that no scientific
account of what enables us to perceive any observable, or, perhaps,
any observational, quality will ever be forthcoming? Surely everyone
would agree that common sense is simply indifferent to the feasibility
of such accounts; or, if anything, in our culture, has a prejudice
in favour of it. An expression of the view imputed to common
sense which some philosophers favour is to say that colours (and
other observational qualities) are *in* the objects. Ayer (p. 85) quotes
Locke as asserting that 'colours are nothing in the objects themselves'; and certainly Berkeley made use of a similar form of expression (disagreeing with Locke about his primary qualities – not,
like the self-appointed champion of common sense, about his secondary ones). But this is a very strange form of words, which does
not, at first sight, convey any clear sense whatever. What can
it mean?

If the alleged common-sense view is not that colours are intrinsically perceptual, can it be that they are *primary*, in the sense
explained above – namely, that any explanation of our capacity
to perceive an object as brown must make essential appeal to
its being brown? That hardly seems right as it stands. If we are
told that our ability to distinguish things that taste sweet from
those that do not is owing to some feature of the shapes of the
molecules of sweet substances, it could hardly be maintained that
here was an affront to common sense. But what, then, *is* meant
when it is contended that, for common sense, the colour (or the
taste) is *in* the object? Perhaps we are going astray because we

have not given due weight to the requirement that the scientific account be regarded as part of a *primary* system, ie. that it be claimed that it describes the object as it really is in itself. Perhaps it is not the scientific account itself that is regarded as conflicting with common sense, but this claim on its behalf. Let us see if we can make any progress by viewing the matter in this light.

Could it not be said that the meanings we ordinarily attach to words for observational qualities render those qualities intrinsically perceptual in a weaker sense – one that does not, just because those meanings relate to the observational character of the qualities, rule out a scientific account of the relevant perceptual faculty? We learn the meanings of expressions for observational qualities by learning to recognise those qualities by observation, and learning also the cases in which a judgement as to the possession of such a quality is to be withdrawn as mistaken. Now, an intrinsically perceptual quality was defined to be one that could be characterised only by reference to human perceptual faculties. If we add the requirement that the characterisation be such as to involve no shift in our everyday understanding of an expression for the quality, we obtain a weaker notion, that of being what we may term an *inherently perceptual* quality. Thus, colours of opaque surfaces, as expressed in our everyday vocabulary, are not intrinsically perceptual qualities, because they can be characterised, in a rather complicated way, in terms of propensities to reflect light of certain frequencies. But such characterisations, if taken as ways of giving the meanings of words such as 'brown' and 'red' as applied to opaque surfaces, involve a shift in the way those meanings are given, since they are ordinarily understood as given by reference to our observational capacities. Hence, the qualities for which they stand, though not *intrinsically* perceptual, are *inherently* perceptual. Perhaps the thesis being imputed to common sense is that all observational qualities are inherently perceptual.

Here we seem to have come closer to our goal; but we have not attained it. For the thesis, as now formulated, can hardly be denied: it follows from the simple fact that we normally acquire, and should normally explain, all expressions for observational qualities by reference to our capacity to recognise such qualities by unaided observation. But we can now make the following suggestion. The thesis that is being imputed to common sense, the thesis expressed by saying that colours, tastes and so on are *in* the objects, is that, in describing an object as it is in itself, each quality that we ascribe to it for which there is an expression in everyday speech must be characterised by the use of that expression in a manner that preserves its meaning as ordinarily understood. The fact that this thesis requires so elaborate a statement is, in itself, no objection to its being regarded as implicit in common-sense conceptions: such conceptions may well be confused or inchoate. On the assumption that this, or something very like it, is the thesis which, in the opinion of some philosophers, is embedded in the common-sense view of the world, we have now to ask whether it really is so embedded.

VII. CORRELATION AND NORMAL CONDITIONS

Let me say at the outset that I do not for a moment believe that any such thesis can be attributed to common sense. The question then arises of why, if it cannot, it has appeared to many philosophers that it can. I shall try to answer this question before arguing that the thesis is not attributable to common sense. The mistake made by the philosophers who think otherwise rests on two inaccurate modes of thought. The first consists in conceiving of physical theory as though it had originally come into existence quite independently of our everyday experience of, and reflection upon, observable qualities. According to this picture, a physical and chemical theory had been developed for some reason or other – say for explaining mechanical and chemical interactions and phenomena of electricity and magnetism; then, subsequently, people had the bright idea of connecting this theory with ordinary observable qualities of objects, so as to yield, in conjunction with the findings of physiologists, an explanation of our capacity to observe such qualities. The model here is an explanation of taste qualities in terms of chemical structure (or molecular shape), or, perhaps, the theory of sound in terms of longitudinal waves in the air. The scientific account is, on this picture, viewed as the discovery of a *correlation*: some observable quality is found to be correlated with some property describable in terms of physical or chemical theory, and then the physiologists are called in aid to explain how this property affects our sense organs. Philosophers who see the matter in this way attribute to common sense the idea that, even if an observable, or, at any rate, an observational, quality can in this way be correlated with a physical property, and the latter used to give a causal explanation for our capacity to perceive the former, still there can be no question of *identifying* the one with the other: the object's possessing the observational quality cannot be taken to *consist* in its having that physical property by means of which our capacity to perceive the observational quality can be explained.

This is a picture that fits certain cases, such as taste qualities – and it may seem natural in view of the esoteric character of contemporary physics, with its quarks, collapses of wave packets and black holes; but it is, in general, a false picture. Physical theory was not first constructed to explain phenomena of which we have little direct perceptual experience, and then subsequently applied to give a causal account of our sensory faculties. It has, on the contrary, grown from the effort to formulate laws governing everyday phenomena, describable in terms of observable qualities: there is a continuous development from the steps we are forced to take even in everyday life to frame an adequate description of the world we observe and live in to the abstruse physics of today. In the course of its growth, physical theory has, naturally, come to embrace ever more recondite phenomena, integrating them, sometimes as a first step, sometimes only at a late stage, with the more familiar ones. Thus, for example, the adjective 'heavy' certainly denotes an observable quality; and, from its birth, physics employed the notion of weight. Later, it split off the notion of mass from that of weight, needing the former notion to formulate laws governing mechanical phenomena having nothing to do with falling or pressing downwards. Only when a heliocentric account of the planetary system had liberated us from the idea that 'up' and 'down' denote directions from any point in the universe could the problem of weight be converted into the problem of gravitation – a big generalisation, indeed, but a natural and inevitable one given the altered view of the macrocosm. And, as for weight, so also for light and heat. Physics reached the point it is now at by continuing to explore the world, and to seek an adequate description of it, in a manner wholly continuous with what everyday observation forces upon us.

The second mistaken idea underlying the false conception of what common sense entails is that the use of expressions for observational qualities is properly described by saying that their application depends upon the judgements we make when the observation is conducted 'under normal conditions'. The idea is that we learn to discount judgements made under special conditions known to give rise to error: it has become a cliché, in philosophical discussions of perception, to say that an object has those observational qualities it is judged to have by normal observers under normal conditions. Thus, someone who has been handling ice will overestimate the temperature of things he touches; while anyone is liable to misjudge the colour of a surface if he sees it under, say, a sodium vapour lamp. This gives rise to the conception that we may, quite literally, distinguish between delusive appearances, on the one hand, and, on the other, seeing (hearing, feeling) an object as it really is – for instance, seeing it in its true colours. Of course, we can, and do, make a distinction between circumstances in which we are prone to make incorrect judgements, or unable to make any at all, and ones in which we shall probably judge correctly; and we sometimes draw this distinction by speaking of seeing an object as it really is. But, for a philosopher to place great weight on this form of words is for him to allow no place for a distinction between what I earlier called a description in absolute and one in relative terms, or, at least, for contrasting the two forms of description as a description of the object as it is in itself and as one in terms of how it appears to us: it allows no conception of the object 'as it appears to us' save when a *mistake* is involved. If our perception of an object 'under normal conditions' is a perception of it as it really is, then a description of it as it really is must be a description of it as we then perceive it – that is, by the use of observational predicates, understood as being explicable only by reference to observation.

Only brief reflection is required in order to reveal that the whole terminology of 'normal conditions' involves a crude oversimplification. It is a well known fact that a piece of metal, being a much better conductor, feels much colder to the touch than a piece of wood when both are at room temperature. Are we, then, to say that a thermometer records real – i.e. observational – temperature inaccurately? If not, what are the 'normal conditions' under which we perceive the true temperature of a piece of metal? Common experience familiarises us with the phenomenon of resolution, as when, in driving, a distant blur resolves itself into separate street lights. But what are the 'normal conditions' for viewing an object the surface of which appears to the naked eye, however close, to be uniformly coloured, but resolves into dots under magnification? What are 'normal conditions' for viewing the Milky Way? Or for viewing the sun, an oxyacetylene torch or a nuclear explosion? Is the 'normal' mode of observing a reflecting surface with the eyes focused on that surface or, behind it, on the image? The only general sense that can be given to 'perceiving the object as it really is' is 'perceiving it under conditions in which one is not liable to make an error of judgement'; and the conditions required will vary according to the particular predicate we are judging to apply or not to apply, and, sometimes, cannot be stated at all, if the judgement is to be based on unaided observation. Given a particular predicate – say, a colour predicate such as 'brown', or other predicate, such as 'shiny', characterising the visual appearance of an opaque surface – there will often be a range of conditions under which an observer will probably give a correct judgement: in the case of 'brown' or 'shiny', when the object is illuminated

by a white light giving a degree of illumination between a certain
minimum and a certain maximum. But that does not mean that,
provided that the necessary 'normal' condition holds, a surface
to which such a predicate is correctly applied will present a unique
visual appearance: appearances which will evoke the description
'brown' or 'shiny' will vary enormously in detail, according to
the position and brightness of the light source or sources, the
position of the observer and the focus of his eyes, the placing
of objects which cast shadows or the variously coloured surfaces
of which reflect onto the observed surface, and so on. The notion
of 'normal conditions' is a myth, except in the restricted sense
stated above: anyone accustomed to the use of observational predicates knows at least implicitly, and will recognise on reflection,
that they stand for essentially dispositional properties, for a propensity to present a range of appearances under a variety of conditions.
This is obvious enough in the case of predicates such as 'shiny'
and 'moiré': a shiny surface must glint, from some angles at least,
but where the gleams are seen depends on the position of the
eye and of the light source. But it is fairly obvious for 'yellow',
and the like, also, even as applied to matt surfaces – as only
a moment's contemplation of, say, the walls of a room will normally
suffice to convince anyone not already conscious of the fact.

   To see how much the habit of talking in terms of 'normal conditions' distorts the character of our actual perceptual experience,
let us consider a world in which it would be entirely appropriate:
one in which, under certain conditions of observation, a complete
characterisation of the visual appearance of a surface would be
given in terms invariant under any change in the circumstances
of the observer, provided only that those conditions continued
to obtain. Suppose that there were only colourless transparent
objects and matt opaque ones; and, within quite a wide range
in intensity of illumination, including daylight on the darkest and
on the brightest day, the appearance of an object did not change
(so that there would be no shadows when the light was sufficiently
bright). We may suppose also that we never saw any source of
light – the sky was always clouded, we never rose above the clouds,
and there was no fire or incandescence. In such a world, we could
say that in daylight we saw the real colours of objects, in a sense
much stronger than we can, in our world, give to that phrase:
for, in the daylight, the visual appearance of a surface would be
independent of the position of the observer, provided that he could
see it at all. The description of something as of a particular shade
of green would tell me all about the colour impression that anyone
would get who saw it in daylight: there would be nothing further

to say that would depend on his position or the quality or direction of the light. In such a world, at least in respect of visual surface qualities, the notion of 'normal conditions' could be employed with full appropriateness; but we have only to compare that world with ours to see how very crude and inadequate a notion it is for characterising our use of observational predicates. In the world imagined, it might be natural for people to adopt, as part of their common-sense view of the world, a thesis like that we have taken to be expressed by the odd phrase 'the colours are in the objects'; but our world is very unlike that one.

VIII. A PLAIN MAN'S VIEW OF COLOURS

I have argued that there can be no such thing as a common sense uninfluenced by theory. Nevertheless, it may be worth attempting to describe how a moderately thoughtful person, not given to philosophical speculation, might conceive of the visual qualities of objects if he were quite innocent of scientific knowledge, but relied only on facts of everyday experience. The most obvious fact is that, to be seen, a surface needs to be in a light; and the second most obvious is that light is something positive, darkness a privation – there are sources of light but no sources of darkness. Light can, however, be blocked; and the most elementary observation of shadows suffices to prompt the conception of light as emanating from light sources in straight lines. It would, on the other hand, be wrong in this context to speak of light as travelling, since, to gross observation, the illumination of a surface when a light source is activated is instantaneous. Gross observation does serve to inform us that the eye is the organ of sight: this is a fact known to everybody, and embodied in the everyday use of the verb 'to look'.

Now, how would a scientifically uninstructed person conceive of the mechanism of sight? That there is such a thing as reflected light is apparent from the common experience of shiny and reflecting surfaces; but need he think of matt surfaces as reflecting light? He would know that light has to fall on a surface for it to be visible; but must he think that it is by light entering the eye that we see? Plato indeed suggested a different idea, that rays from the eye strike the illuminated surface; but, actually, the most banal facts speak against such a conception. For one thing, there could, on such a view, be no expectation that the same objects would be opaque both to light and to the eye rays; but it is a fact that everybody takes for granted that an object which, if placed between the light source and the surface, will throw the surface into shadow, will also block our vision if interposed between the surface and the eye. For another thing, we can certainly see light, as we know if we look directly at a light source. It is difficult to think of the light from a source as not being continuously between the source and the surface it illuminates, but as jumping the gap between them, because, if an object is placed between them, it is illuminated. On the other hand, we cannot normally see the light between the source and the surface. There could be other explanations of this fact; but the overwhelmingly most natural thing to think is that the light, transmitted from the source, is not itself a source, but that we see the surface that it strikes only because it is reflected into our eyes. This is reinforced by the fact that a matt surface will affect the apparent colour of an adjacent surface (for example, a cream-coloured wall takes on a blue tinge near a bright blue box); and it is well known that, with the same strength of light, a room panelled in dark though shiny mahogany is darker than one with matt white walls, and that we are dazzled by sunlight on snow. On the strength of all these facts of common experience, even a quite uninstructed person would quite naturally form the idea that we see by light entering the eye, and that even a matt surface reflects.

I have not specifically discussed the colour predicates, our ordinary understanding of which is quite complicated: we grasp the distinguished roles of black and white, so that we should be baffled by the expression 'black light', and know that what is needed, in any case of doubt, to determine the colour of a clear transparent substance is to put a white surface behind it. It was remarked above that, on a quite ordinary understanding of colour predicates, as applied to opaque and transparent objects, they stand for dispositional properties: no one who has ever noticed – and who has not? – the varied appearance of a uniformly coloured surface, from one area to another, as light from different sources strikes it, as parts lie in shadow and other parts are tinged by reflections from nearby objects, could conceive of them otherwise. This does not hold good, indeed, for colour words as applied to light sources; but, then, we do not ascribe colour to light itself in the same sense as we ascribe it to objects considered as retaining their colours in the dark: we can ask, of an opaque surface, what degree of illumination allows us to judge most reliably of its true colour, but the brightness of a light source is an intrinsic feature of its visual appearance. But the foregoing discussion was intended to bring out that the most familiar facts, with which we need to be acquainted for practical purposes, lead us beyond a merely programmatic conception of visual qualities of surfaces as consisting in propensities to display systematic ranges of different appearances under different conditions of observation. They lead us, that is, to an embryonic theory of that in which such propensities consist – namely, in the ability to emit, reflect, absorb or transmit light of different kinds: in view of our capacity to perceive light, if not too intense, as of different colours, by looking at the sources, it is surely not improper here to speak of 'kinds' of light. This illustrates the contention advanced above that physical theory grows out of our everyday understanding of the world and is continuous with it. At the same time, it displays how enormously more sophisticated is the sort of view that is really to be ascribed to common sense than the crude conception of a quality directly recognisable 'under normal conditions'. Were it not that this style of talk has become a fairly venerable philosophical tradition, one would think that philosophers who indulge in it had never seen mirrors, varnished furniture, shot silk, velvet, expanses of water or cups of coffee, and had never really looked at the variety of other surfaces, of diverse textures, which they encounter every day.

IX. KNOWING AN OBJECT AS IT REALLY IS

Now, the thesis expressed by saying such things as that 'the colours are in the objects', the thesis imputed to common sense by many philosophers, we formulated as the thesis that, to characterise an object as it is in itself, we have to attribute to it what observational qualities it has by means of expressions understood as essentially involving reference to our perceptual faculties. It remains unclear to me, however, whether this formulation yet succeeds in capturing all that is intended. For it appears intuitively that the recognition that an observational quality is dispositional in character itself involves a rejection of the imputed thesis. Someone who thinks that being yellow, like being shiny, is a matter of presenting a variety of visual appearances under a variety of conditions surely does not believe that the colour yellow is in the object, or in the surface, in the intended sense. If this is not so, then Ayer's discussion of Locke rests on a phrase wrenched out of context. Ayer quotes (p. 85) Locke's famous remark that the secondary qualities 'are nothing in the objects themselves but powers to produce various sensations in us' (Ayer adds a comma after 'themselves' which is not in my edition of Locke's *Essay*). One would naturally take the 'nothing' as going with the 'but' – that is, construe the sentence as meaning that they are not anything other than such powers; but Ayer, in the very next paragraph, speaks of Locke as 'holding that colour is nothing in the object itself', without

including the phrase introduced by 'but', as if the sentence were
to be construed to mean, 'They are nothing in the objects themselves;
they are, on the other hand, powers to produce sensations in us.'
On the face of it, this is as unwarranted as if someone, told that
he was nothing but a social climber, were to complain, 'He said
that I was nothing.' However, if the idea that colours and the
rest are dispositional qualities – 'powers', in Locke's terminology
– excludes the view that 'colours are in the objects' is intended
to convey, the transition is warranted; and Locke himself slides
easily from one manner of expression to the other, saying (*Essay*,
II. 8. xv), 'they are, in the bodies . . . , only a power to produce
those sensations in us', and, a little later (ibid., xvii), that they
'are no more really in' the bodies than 'sickness or pain is in
manna'.

But, if Ayer is right and Locke is right on this point, then
our formulation was inadequate. Suppose that some predicate is
explained as applying to a surface if it presents a certain kind
of appearance when viewed in certain lights, from certain angles
and certain distances, and other kinds when viewed in other lights,
from other angles and distances, and we regard this form of explanation as essential to its meaning. Then the predicate qualifies as
one that can serve to characterise an object as it is in itself, under
our formulation of the thesis. On the other hand, it has been
explained in a dispositional manner, as a power of producing certain
sensations in us under certain conditions; and it ought not so
to qualify, if Locke and Ayer are right, and as I too feel, if we
are to interpret the thesis correctly. I find it immensely hard to
express that interpretation of it. It is as if it were thought that,
in perception, whenever it is not delusive, we enter into communion
with the object; we know it as it is known by God. Hence the
importance of the conception of 'normal conditions': it does not
matter if there are many conditions under which we do not perceive
the object truly, so long as there is a type of condition under
which we know it as it is; but to explain a predicate as meaning
that it has this appearance under these conditions, that appearance
under those, is to leave no place for a notion of knowing it as
it really is. The appearances have, in such a case, become as extrinsic
to the quality ascribed to the object as is the smarting sensation
to the astringent quality of the lotion. (Why do we actually use
two different words here? Perhaps because the smarting can continue
when all the lotion has been wiped off. But, then, a taste can
linger, too, as can the burning sensation produced by an excessively
hot curry.)

Ayer cannot explain the notion of knowing an object as it really is in terms of knowing it as God knows it, since he does not believe in God (pp. 211–35); and, although I do, I should hesitate to say that we can know the natural world as God knows it, or even approximate to doing so. (It may well be, however, that part of the allure of science and philosophy, considered as attempts to say what the world is really like, lies in just such an idea.) But, if one sets that explanation aside, it is difficult to express the notion except metaphorically.

X. MEANING

However that may be, once the step of regarding a quality as dispositional is taken, it becomes very easy to take the further step of identifying the quality with that feature of the constitution of the object that confers on it the relevant propensity; and that transition, too, Locke of course makes without hesitation. This is because we are naturally prone to regard dispositional properties as resting on non-dispositional ones; whether or not there are irreducibly dispositional properties, whenever we can find a convincing causal explanation of a disposition, we tend to identify having that disposition with the constitution that explains it. Now, in the case of colours and other visual surface qualities, even before we have any actual scientific knowledge, the complex character of our visual experience forces on us an interpretation of such qualities in terms of propensities to affect (different kinds of) light in various ways; and this already carries us beyond an account of those qualities in terms of how a surface appears to us, although the colours of light itself are still explained only in terms of our capacity to recognise them. The stage is thus already set for an identification of colour qualities with physical properties not in any way characterised in terms of our own colour vision; when a workable theory of light is available, we are at once ready to make this identification.

It may be objected that, in making the identification, we shall be being unfaithful to the meanings of our colour words as these were originally given to us. After all, the contention was never that a physicist, speaking as a physicist, had no right to use the form of words 'Ayer's table is brown'; only that, in so far as he interpreted the adjective 'brown' in terms of the spectral reflection curve of the surface of the table, he was not using it in accordance with its ordinary meaning. This is quite true. But the original contention went further than this: it embodied the claim that, on the physicist's account, the table is *not* brown, as 'brown' is ordinarily understood. It is this claim which is false. The idea that we may identify the colour of a surface with a feature of its spectral reflection curve, that that is what its having that colour consists in, is precisely the idea that, as a matter of physical necessity, just those things that are brown in the new sense may correctly be said to be brown in the original sense. Let us consider once more the analogy with affective qualities such as being funny. Someone who wants to devise a 'theory of humour' asks, 'What does being funny consist in?' If someone else answers, 'It consists in the propensity to evoke amusement in us: that is what the word "funny" *means*', he will reply, 'Of course; but I want to know what feature of an event, remark or story, describable in principle by someone devoid of a sense of humour, *makes* it funny in that sense.' If, now, he succeeds in finding such a feature, then, if he henceforward uses the word 'funny' as meaning 'possessing that feature', he will have modified the meaning of 'funny'; but his theory will be acceptable just in case all and only those things that possess the feature are funny in the original sense, i.e. amuse us: hence no one will have any warrant to say to him, 'You are maintaining that nothing really is funny, in the original sense of the word "funny".' Modifications in the meaning of a general term that, as a matter of theoretical necessity, leave the extension of the term unaffected are the easiest for us to accept; indeed, we usually feel no resistance, but a positive attraction, to them. This is particularly true of terms expressing physical concepts, precisely because the process whereby an individual acquires such concepts is itself a complicated and gradual one: as we advanced from the childhood stage of learning to apply colour words to brightly coloured pictures in a book to mastery of the phenomena of light and colour with which we are familiar as adults, we had repeatedly to modify our understanding of those words. Some philosophers have been so impressed by our willingness to accept modifications of meaning that they have rejected the notion of meaning as altogether useless. This is, in my opinion, a mistake: it suggests that everyone is, at any time, free from all constraints on what sentences he may intelligibly propose for acceptance, when in fact the modifications of meaning that we readily accept are those which do not require us to reject as false sentences that we had previously accepted as true; and, when a modification does call for such revision, we shall accept it only when we can obtain a clear view of the principles governing the new meaning of the term and of the theory that makes the modification mandatory or desirable. The process by which meanings undergo modification is a subtle and complicated one, that requires detailed study; there is no easy way to dispense with such study by jettisoning the whole notion

of meaning. But that does not mean, either, that our conception
of the world can be faithfully described by ignoring the considerations that induce us to modify the meanings of our words; still
less does it entitle a philosopher to say that, whenever we are
prompted to accept such a modification, the statements that we
previously made are, by that very fact, rendered false.

XI. ABSOLUTE AND RELATIVE
FORMS OF DESCRIPTION

The notion of a direct apprehension, in perception or by other
means, of an object as it *really* is seems to me a spurious one,
and certainly not an ingredient of a common-sense view of the
world, as the common sense of ordinary people goes: it is a philosophers' notion, going back at least as far as Locke, and falsely
imputed to the plain man by philosophers. On the other hand,
the notion that we have been considering – that of a *description*
of things as they are in themselves – is an entirely different one;
and this really plays an important role in our thinking. Whenever
one can be attained, we give preference to a form of description
that is independent of the particular circumstances and position
of the observer. That is why, to common sense, our vocabulary
for assigning three-dimensional shapes to objects and giving their
location, relative to one another, in three-dimensional space is preeminently one by which things are described as they are in themselves; for, as already remarked, it is a common-sense view that
shape predicates are independent of viewpoint and stand in no
need of relativisation to the circumstances of the observer. The
interpretation of our essentially two-dimensional visual impressions
as three-dimensional, the conception of objects as disposed in a
three-dimensional space in which we also are, is so fundamental
to our ability to form a conception of the world at all and to
engage in any kind of action, and so integrated with our perceptual
experience, that it may be denied that it can serve as a pattern
to be followed in other cases. It does, however, form just such
a pattern: the practice of taking the physical world to admit of
a description independent of viewpoint, and of regarding such a
description as representing it as it actually is, is rooted in our
most primitive experience of it. Imagine, for example, that the
heavenly bodies, while having negligible proper motion, were vastly
nearer to us than in fact they are, so that we could detect appreciable
parallax in moving a few hundred miles over the earth's surface.
Such parallax would not, of course, enter into our immediate visual
experience, like a landscape seen from a train. Nevertheless, we

should regard the resulting representation of the heavenly bodies as disposed in three-dimensional space not merely as a convenient means of summarising the changes in the appearance of the night sky as we moved about the earth, but as depicting the actual state of affairs.

There is no *a priori* reason why the world should admit a description in absolute terms. One can, for instance, imagine a world in which the apparent colours of objects varied, in a totally unsystematic manner, according to the distance from them of the observer. In such a world, we could not describe an object simply as yellow, but only as yellow from within a certain interval of distance from it. But, if, now, we suppose that, although there was no general correlation between the apparent colour of an object from two feet and that from twenty feet, still objects were found to split up into a manageable number of different types, any two objects of the same type behaving in the same way in respect of its apparent colour from varying distances, then a vocabulary for assigning objects to these types would serve the function that, in our language, is served by the vocabulary of colour words as applied to objects. There is no guarantee that we shall be able to devise an observer-independent vocabulary; but we always seek for one, and, the world being as it is, we always find one. As far as colours are concerned, for example, it is far from irrelevant that, although we are liable to make mistakes if we try to estimate the 'true' colours of objects seen under coloured light, we know that the changes induced by such light in their apparent colours are not random, just as the apparent uniform colour of a multicoloured object seen from too great a distance for us to resolve the surface into its components is not random. Knowledge of this kind plays an important part in our conception of colour qualities; and this is a further reason why the conception of 'normal conditions' is so misleading.

Just as, in considering the extraterrestrial cosmos, we extend the procedure of giving spatial descriptions independent of the position of the individual observer to obtain ones independent of our location, as a species, on the surface of this planet, so, as we learn more about physical properties and about the physiology of perception, we attain forms of description that are independent of our particular range of sensory faculties. Even before we have any scientific account of sound, it is natural to think of a sound as something that is given off, its finite velocity being evident to ordinary observation, as in thunderstorms and when we see and hear a distant gun being fired. As with the more complex case of visual surface qualities, this conception prepares us to accept the identification of sounds with waves in the air when the scientific explanation of them becomes available: to resist that identification would be to insist on a pointless duplication. But, even before we know this explanation, we shall be willing to sever the tie between the notion of sound and our own perceptual capacities: the possibility of sounds too high for us to hear cannot be ruled out as contradictory even before we identify sounds with sound waves. Perhaps, until that identification is made, the possibility requires that there be organisms (for instance, dogs) sensitive to such humanly inaudible sounds; but, when it is made, not even that requirement is necessary for the conception to be intelligible. In the same way, the programmatic notion of kinds of light by means of which we may conceive of colour phenomena before we have any actual theory of light gives way to an understanding of those phenomena that reveals the highly contingent character of our colour perception. Not only does it become intelligible to say that insects are sensitive to ultra-violet 'light', which is invisible to us; but, even restricted to the visible spectrum, the colour of an opaque surface, as we discriminate it, is not to be equated to its spectral reflection curve, but stands, rather, in a complicated one–many relation to it. Having arrived at this stage of understanding, we subsume the concept of light under the more general one of electromagnetic radiation, and regard propensity to reflect, absorb or transmit radiation of different wavelengths as a more accurate replacement of the experientially based notion of colour. In doing so, we are not rejecting the lessons taught by our everyday experience: we are simply remaining faithful to that quest for a description of reality in absolute terms that we have from the outset taken as a quest for a description of it as it is in itself.

XII. THE CAUSAL THEORY OF PERCEPTION

I have argued that there is no conflict in principle between science and common sense, and that therefore, contrary to Ayer, no subtle theory is called for to allow each its proper place: though common sense lags behind science, science grows out of common sense and is continuous with it. If I am correct, then Ayer is wrong in what he says (pp. 82–8) about the causal theory of perception. I do not believe that the notion of cause, as such, is integral to the concept of perception: all that is integral to the latter concept is that my perceptions should always afford some ground, even if one that can in some cases be overriden, for supposing things to be as I perceive them. If someone believes, with Malebranche, that the presence of the object and my perception of it are joint effects of some further cause, his belief does not violate the concept of perception, so long as he allows that my perception supplies a reason for taking the object to be there. (I owe this point to Mr John Foster.) But it does not follow from this that there must be more to our perceiving objects than their causing us to have certain perceptual experiences. Ayer argues that, if perception is to be from the outset linked to the causal action of the object on the percipient, there can be no barrier against a total scepticism (p. 87); he is here following Hume, whom he quotes with approval (p. 86) as saying that 'the philosophical system' contains all the difficulties of 'the vulgar system' with others peculiar to itself. The reason is that, if we link perception with cause at the outset, then, Ayer thinks, we shall convert the objects perceived into 'unobservable occupants of an unobservable space'. Hence we have to assume a primitive notion of perception explicable without reference to the notion of causality: a link with causality can be made only at a later, secondary stage in the development of the concept of perception. This supposed primitive notion of perception is presumably that which we earlier found it so difficult to express, one under which perception (when it takes place under normal conditions) is a kind of immediate awareness of the object as it really is, a communion with it in its essential being.

We here see more clearly the genesis of this curious idea; but it is conceived in the womb of philosophy, not of common sense. To conceive of perception, even at the outset, as the causal action of the object – more exactly, for any of the senses that operates at a distance, of something emitted by the object – on the percipient does not reduce the object to an unobservable occupant of an unobservable space: how could it do so, when, by hypothesis, it is the object being observed? We need not postulate the existence, let alone the validity, of any more primitive notion of perception to save the objects of observation from this unfortunate fate. Not only is the observed object by hypothesis observable: it can also perfectly well be described. The only descriptions we can initially frame are expressed by words the meaning of which is given in terms of our own observational capacities; but, as I have argued, that does not make those descriptions incorrect, even though, for greater understanding of the world, we seek descriptions of a different form. The trouble seems to be that, although Ayer starts with a more or less correct delineation of the distinction between a description of things as they are in themselves and one in terms of how they appear to us – that is, between a description in absolute and one in relative terms – he soon forgets the nature of this distinction. He begins (p. 84) by elucidating the statement that physical objects are not really coloured as meaning that being coloured 'is not an intrinsic property of the object', i.e. is not a property that it possesses 'independently of our perceiving' it: this can certainly be understood as meaning that to describe an object as coloured is to use a relative rather than an absolute form of description, in the terminology I have been using; and the statement that physical objects are not really coloured, when understood in this way, will be correct if the term 'coloured' is regarded as explicable only in terms of our faculty of colour vision. But, in what he writes subsequently, it appears that he has forgotten that he has elucidated 'is not really coloured' in this very special sense: he takes it, thenceforward, in the other, more straightforward, sense under which the appearances are delusive – that is, in the sense in which to say that something is coloured, when really it is not is to say something untrue. If we take perception as being, from the outset, linked with causality, then, he thinks, we must regard the object as being, in itself, as it would be described in the causal account of the sensory process. But, then, forgetting that the qualification 'as it is in itself' relates to the form, not to the correctness, of the description, he infers that, on this view of perception, the object will lack colour or any other observable quality, and hence will itself be unobservable. But the dilemma is a spurious one: no such consequence follows.

XIII. INSTRUMENTALISM

So far this essay has read as a wholehearted repudiation of instrumentalism, the view according to which scientific theories have only the status of 'secondary systems'; and I wish to back-pedal somewhat. Science begins by borrowing concepts, such as those of weight, heat, light and force, from everyday discourse, and subjects them to progressive refinement. It has been argued here that this process is continuous with that of forming a coherent picture of the physical world in which we engage in ordinary life, and that, for that reason, we have no option but to take science as revealing what the physical world is like in itself. But, somewhere in the course of scientific development, the character of the theories changes. Properties, such as those of 'colour' and 'strangeness', now attributed to fundamental particles, have no connection with ordinary experience: they are mere labels for ingredients of a purely mathematical model. Now instrumentalism is usually thought of as a doctrine about the ontological status of theoretical entities, or the semantic status of theoretical statements (semantic status, not epistemological status, as is sometimes inaccurately said: the question is what their truth consists in, not how we know them to be true). It is, in effect, the rejection of realism for theoretical statements: there is no objectively existing reality that renders such statements determinately true or false; rather, they are not to be interpreted literally at all, but are to be viewed as pictures that help us to master complicated regularities governing real, i.e. straightforwardly observable, phenomena.

In order to evaluate such a doctrine, it is necessary to gain a clear view of what is to be counted as a theoretical statement, in the relevant sense. For this purpose, a theoretical statement may be considered one on which we have not conferred a definite semantics – that is, the conditions for the truth and falsity of which we have not determined: it functions only as part of a theory which behaves in a Duhemian fashion, forming a sort of coagulated lump within the language; we have means of judging the correctness or incorrectness of the theory as a whole, but not of individual statements belonging to it. To characterise theoretical statements in this way is, indeed, to prejudge the issue between instrumentalism and realism in favour of the former: if theoretical statements are ones on which we have not conferred determinate truth conditions, it must be superstition to believe in an objective reality that determines them as true or as false. But a plausible formulation of instrumentalism must find a convincing way of circumscribing the range of statements to which it applies – those to be regarded, for this purpose, as theoretical. The usual formulations of it either leave this range quite unspecified, or, more often, treat as theoretical any scientific law that rises above the level of a straightforward generalisation (for example, the law of the rectilinear propagation of light). A law may be said to rise above the level of a mere generalisation if it effects some modification of our concepts. Precisely because it does so, it cannot be considered, as can a simple empirical generalisation, as having associated with it in advance determinate conditions under which it holds good. We do not, for example, start with a conception of light as travelling along certain paths, and subsequently notice that, in most cases, the paths in question are straight lines: adoption of the principle of the rectilinear propagation of light is likely to be simultaneous with the introduction of the notion of the path along which light travels. But it is a mistake to infer from that that the statement, once adopted, remains without definite truth conditions: the modification of our concepts once effected, we know what observations will suffice to show that the law does not hold in full generality.

When instrumentalism is in this way applied to every scientific statement that rises above the level of simple generalisation, it becomes utterly implausible, and it is no wonder that it is resisted;

we have here another example of the frequent phenomenon that realism scores too easy a victory, because the alternative to it has been incorrectly formulated. As I have tried to argue, a statement such as that light travels in straight lines is virtually forced on us in the attempt to make sense of our everyday experience; and many other scientific laws are arrived at by a process essentially the same in character as that by which, in ordinary life, we form a picture of the world we live in. Hence, if instrumentalism is to have any claim on our consideration, it must be maintained that the critical line, beyond which we begin to deal in theoretical statements properly so called, is crossed not as soon as anything recognisable as a scientific theory is framed, but at some much later stage in the development of science. Just when this occurs will be very hard to say. It is a problem in the theory of meaning; and the theory of meaning is not yet in a sufficiently well developed state for us to be able to give a ready answer to the question of when we may be considered to have conferred determinate truth conditions upon any given range of statements: that is, indeed, the central question over which the participants in a dispute about whether statements of a given class admit a realistic interpretation disagree with one another. It will be the task of scientific realism to maintain that there are no theoretical statements in the required sense – that, in other words, no line can be drawn: the progress of science is, on a realist view, everywhere continuous with the kind of attempt we make, even before science begins, to understand our world and arrive at a description of it as it is in itself. Earlier in this essay, I did indeed express such a view, but I do not really want to commit myself to it: I wish to remain agnostic about whether it is possible to delineate a range of theoretical statements for which the instrumentalist thesis is plausible. The theses for which I wish to contend are the following: that instrumentalism, if correct at all, is so only for the most rarefied statements of scientific theory; that there is no conflict in principle between scientific truth and a common-sense view of the world, and, therefore, no problem of reconciling them or necessity to opt for one or the other; that there is no legitimate notion of knowing an object, by immediate awareness, as it really is, when this is taken as involving more than that we have not made a mistake; but that there is a legitimate notion of a description of an object as it is in itself, and that we cannot but view science, at least before it transcends some critical level of abstraction, as attempting to arrive at such descriptions.

Instrumentalism constitutes a very special form of reductive thesis, applied to theoretical statements of physical science, the reductive class consisting of non-theoretical statements about the physical world. A thoroughgoing scientific realist needs to refute instrumentalism, presumably by an argument along the lines sketched above. But, when he has done so, he has not thereby established as correct a realistic interpretation of the statements of physical theory: he has merely rebutted one line of criticism. There may be – indeed, there is – a form of argument to show that we should not adopt a realistic interpretation of statements about the physical world in general, whether scientific or everyday statements, theoretical or non-theoretical ones; and the scientific realist has also to meet this more general challenge. There are also quite specific considerations concerning the character of quantum theory which yield a strong case for saying that, so long as physics incorporates that theory, a realistic interpretation is ruled out – this is another very particular attack which the scientific realist has to face. These issues are remote from the topic of the present essay; but, because we tend to have an endemic prejudice in favour of realism, we are always allowing it to score too easy a victory; and I did not want to be guilty of abetting this process.

2 Perception and its Objects

P. F. STRAWSON

Ayer has always given the problem of perception a central place in his thinking. Reasonably so; for a philosopher's views on this question are a key both to his theory of knowledge in general and to his metaphysics. The movement of Ayer's own thought has been from phenomenalism to what he describes in his latest treatment of the topic as 'a sophisticated form of realism'.[1] The epithet is doubly apt. No adequate account of the matter can be simple; and Ayer's account, while distinguished by his accustomed lucidity and economy of style, is notably and subtly responsive to all the complexities inherent in the subject itself and to all the pressures of more or less persuasive argument which have marked the course of its treatment by philosophers. Yet the form of realism he defends has another kind of sophistication about which it is possible to have reservations and doubts; and, though I am conscious of being far from clear on the matter myself, I shall try to make some of my own doubts and reservations as clear as I can. I shall take as my text chapters 4 and 5 of *The Central Questions of Philosophy*; and I shall also consider a different kind of realism – that advocated by J. L. Mackie in his book on Locke.[2] There are points of contact as well as of contrast between Ayer's and Mackie's views. A comparison between them will help to bring out the nature of my reservations about both.

According to Ayer, the starting point of serious thought on the matter of perception consists in the fact that our normal perceptual judgements always 'go beyond' the sensible experience which gives rise to them; for those judgements carry implications which would not be carried by any 'strict account' of that experience.[3] Ayer sees ordinary perceptual judgements as reflecting or embodying what he calls the common-sense view of the physical world, which is, among other things, a realist view; and he sees that view itself as having the character of 'a theory with respect to the immediate

data of perception'.⁴ He devotes some space to an account of
how the theory might be seen as capable of being developed by
an individual observer on the basis of the data available to him;
though he disavows any intention of giving an actual history of
the theory's development. The purpose of the account is, rather,
to bring out those features of sensible experience which make it
possible to employ the theory successfully and which, indeed, justify
acceptance of it. For it is, he holds, by and large an acceptable
theory, even though the discoveries of physical science may require
us to modify it in certain respects.

Evidently no infant is delivered into the world already equipped
with what Ayer calls the common-sense view of it. That view
has to be acquired; and it is open to the psychologist of infant
learning to produce at least a speculative account of the stages
of its acquisition. Ayer insists, as I have remarked, that his own
account of a possible line of development or construction of the
common-sense view is not intended as a speculative contribution
to the theory of infant learning. It is intended, rather, as an analysis
of the nature of mature or adult perceptual experience, an analysis
designed to show just how certain features of mature sensible experience vindicate or sustain the common-sense view which is embodied
or reflected in mature perceptual judgements. Clearly the two aims
here distinguished – the genetic–psychological and the analytic–philosophical – are very different indeed, and it will be of great importance
not to confuse them. In particular it will be important to run
no risk of characterising mature sensible experience in terms adequate at best only for the characterisation of some stage of infantile
experience. It is not clear that Ayer entirely avoids this danger.

What is clear is that if we accept Ayer's starting point, if we
agree that our ordinary perceptual judgements carry implications
not carried by a 'strict account' of the sensible experience which
gives rise to them, then we must make absolutely sure that our
account of that experience, in the form it takes in our mature
life, is indeed strict – in the sense of strictly correct. Only so
can we have any prospect of making a correct estimate of the
further doctrines that the common-sense view of the world has
the status of a *theory* with respect to a type of sensible experience
which provides *data* for the theory; that this experience supplies
the *evidence* on which the theory is based;⁵ that the common-sense
view can be regarded as *inferred* or at least inferrable from this
evidence; and that our ordinary perceptual judgements have the
character of *interpretations*,⁶ in the light of theory, of what sensible
experience actually presents us with.

But can we – and should we – accept Ayer's starting point?

I think that, suitably interpreted, we both can, and should, accept it. Two things will be required of a strict account of our sensible experience or of any particular episode or slice of sensible experience: first, as I have just remarked, that it should in no way distort or misrepresent the character of that experience as we actually enjoy it, i.e. that it should be a true or faithful account; secondly, that its truth, in any particular case, should be independent of the truth of the associated perceptual judgement, i.e. that it should remain true even if the associated perceptual judgement is false. It is the second requirement on which Ayer lays stress when he remarks that those judgements carry implications which would not be carried by any strict account of sensible experience; or, less happily in my opinion, that in making such judgements we take a step beyond what our sensible experience actually presents us with. But it is the first requirement to which I now wish to give some attention.

Suppose a non-philosophical observer gazing idly through a window. To him we address the request, 'Give us a description of your current visual experience', or 'How is it with you, visually, at the moment?' Uncautioned as to exactly what we want, he might reply in some such terms as these: 'I see the red light of the setting sun filtering through the black and thickly clustered branches of the elms; I see the dappled deer grazing in groups on the vivid green grass . . .' and so on. So we explain to him. We explain that we want him to amend his account so that, without any sacrifice of fidelity to the experience as actually enjoyed, it nevertheless sheds all that heavy load of commitment to propositions about the world which was carried by the description he gave. We want an account which confines itself strictly within the limits of the subjective episode, an account which would remain true even if he had seen nothing of what he claimed to see, even if he had been subject to total illusion.

Our observer is quick in the uptake. He does not start talking about lights and colours, patches and patterns. For he sees that to do so would be to falsify the character of the experience he actually enjoyed. He says, instead, 'I understand. I've got to cut out of my report all commitment to propositions about independently existing objects. Well, the simplest way to do this, while remaining faithful to the character of the experience as actually enjoyed, is to put my previous report in inverted commas or oratio obliqua and describe my visual experience as such as it would have been natural to describe in these terms, had I not received this additional instruction. Thus: "I had a visual experience such as it would have been natural to describe by saying that I saw,

etc. . . . [or, to describe in these words, 'I saw . . . etc.'] were it
not for the obligation to exclude commitment to propositions about
independently existing objects." In this way [continues the observer]
I *use* the perceptual claim – the claim it was natural to make
in the circumstances – in order to characterise my experience, without actually making the claim. I render the perceptual judgement
internal to the characterisation of the experience without actually
asserting the content of the judgement. And this is really the best
possible way of characterising the experience. There are perhaps
alternative locutions which might serve the purpose, so long as
they are understood as being to the same effect – on the whole,
the more artificial the better, since their artificiality will help to
make it clearer just to what effect they are intended to be. Thus
we might have: "It sensibly seemed to me just as if I were seeing
such-and-such a scene" or "My visual experience can be characterised by saying that I saw what I saw, supposing I saw anything,
as a scene of the following character. . . ." '

If my observer is right in this – and I think he is – then certain
general conclusions follow. Our perceptual judgements, as Ayer
remarks, embody or reflect a certain view of the world, as containing
objects, variously propertied, located in a common space and continuing in their existence independently of our interrupted and
relatively fleeting perceptions of them. Our making of such judgements implies our possession and application of concepts of such
objects. But now it appears that we cannot give a veridical characterisation even of the sensible experience which these judgements, as
Ayer expresses it, 'go beyond', without reference to those judgements
themselves; that our sensible experience itself is thoroughly permeated with those concepts of objects which figure in such judgements. This does not mean, i.e. it does not follow directly from
this feature of sensible experience, that the general view of the
world which those judgements reflect must be true. That would
be too short a way with scepticism. But it does follow, I think,
that our sensible experience could not have the character it does
have unless – at least before philosophical reflection sets in – we
unquestioningly *took* that general view of the world to be true.
The concepts of the objective which we see to be indispensable
to the veridical characterisation of sensible experience simply would
not be in this way indispensable unless those whose experience
it was initially and unreflectively took such concepts to have application in the world.

This has a further consequence: the consequence that it is quite
inappropriate to represent the general, realist view of the world
which is reflected in our ordinary perceptual judgements as having

the status of a *theory* with respect to sensible experience; that it is inappropriate to represent that experience as supplying the *data* for such a theory or the *evidence* on which it is based or from which it is *inferred* or *inferrable*; that it is inappropriate to speak of our ordinary perceptual judgements as having the character of an *interpretation*, in the light of theory, of the content of our sensible experience. The reason for this is simple. In order for some belief or set of beliefs to be correctly described as a theory in respect of certain data, it must be possible to describe the data on the basis of which the theory is held in terms which do not presuppose the acceptance of the theory on the part of those for whom the data *are* data. But this is just the condition we have seen not to be satisfied in the case where the so-called data are the contents of sensible experience and the so-called theory is a general realist view of the world. The 'data' are laden with the 'theory'. Sensible experience is permeated by concepts unreflective acceptance of the general applicability of which is a condition of its being so permeated, a condition of that experience being what it is; and these concepts are of realistically conceived objects.

I must make it quite clear what I am saying and what I am not saying here. I am talking of the ordinary non-philosophical man. I am talking of us all before we felt, if ever we did feel, any inclination to respond to the solicitations of a general scepticism, to regard it as raising a problem. I am saying that it follows from the character of sensible experience as we all actually enjoy it that a common-sense realist view of the world does not in general have the status of a theory in respect of that experience; while Ayer, as I understand him, holds that it does. But I am not denying that to one who has seen, or thinks he has seen, that sensible experience might have the character it does have and *yet* a realist view of the world be false, to *him* the idea may well present itself that the best way of accounting for sensible experience as having that character is to accept the common realist view of the world or some variant of it. *He* might be said to adopt, as a theory, the doctrine that the common realist view of the world is, at least in some basic essentials, true. But this will be a philosopher's theory, designed to deal with a philosopher's problem. (I shall not here discuss its merits as such.) What I am concerned to dispute is the doctrine that a realist view of the world has, for any man, the status of a theory in relation to his sensible experience, a theory in the light of which he interprets that experience in making his perceptual judgements.

To put the point summarily, whereas Ayer says we take a step beyond our sensible experience in making our perceptual judgements, I say rather that we take a step back (in general) from our perceptual judgements in framing accounts of our sensible experience; for we have (in general) to include a reference to the former in framing a veridical description of the latter.

It may seem, on a superficial reading, that Ayer had anticipated and answered this objection. He introduces, as necessary for the characterisation of our sensible experience, certain concepts of types of pattern, the names for which are borrowed from the names of ordinary physical objects. Thus he speaks of visual leaf patterns, chair patterns, cat patterns, and so on.[7] At the same time, he is careful, if I read him rightly, to guard against the impression that the use of this terminology commits him to the view that the employment of the corresponding physical-object concepts themselves is necessary to the characterisation of our sensible experience.[8] The terminology is appropriate (he holds) simply because those features of sensible experience to which the terminology is applied are the features which govern our identifications of the physical objects we think we see. They are the features, 'implicitly noticed',[9] which provide the main clues on which our everyday judgements of perception are based.

This is ingenious, but I do not think it will do. This we can see more clearly if we use an invented, rather than a derived, terminology for these supposed features and then draw up a table of explicit correlations between the invented names and the physical-object names. Each artificial feature name is set against the name of a type of physical object: our perceptual identifications of seen objects as of that type are held to be governed by implicit noticings of that feature. The nature and significance of the feature names is now quite clearly explained and we have to ask ourselves whether it is these rather than the associated physical-object terms that we ought to use if we are to give a quite strict and faithful account of our sensible experience. I think it is clear that this is not so; that the idea of our ordinary perceptual judgements as being invariably based upon, or invariably issuing from, awareness of such features is a myth. The situation is rather, as I have already argued, that the employment of our ordinary, full-blooded concepts of physical objects is indispensable to a strict, and strictly veridical, account of our sensible experience.

Once again, I must make it clear what I am, and what I am not, saying. I have been speaking of the typical or standard case of mature sensible and perceptual experience. I have no interest at all in denying the thesis that there also occur cases of sensible experience such that the employment of full-blooded concepts of physical objects would not be indispensable, and may be inappropriate, to giving a strict account of the experience. Such cases are of different types, and there is one in particular which is of interest in the present connexion. An observer, gazing through his window, may perhaps, by an effort of will, bring himself to see, or even will-lessly find himself seeing, what he knows to be the branches of the trees no longer *as* branches at all, but as an intricate pattern of dark lines of complex directions and shapes and various sizes against a background of varying shades of grey. The frame of mind in which we enjoy, if we ever do enjoy, this kind of experience is a rare and sophisticated, not a standard or normal, frame of mind. Perhaps the fact, if it is a fact, that we can bring ourselves into this frame of mind when we choose may be held to give a sense to the idea of our 'implicitly noticing' such patterns even when we are not in this frame of mind. If so, it is a sense very far removed from that which Ayer's thesis requires. For that thesis requires not simply the possibility, but the actual occurrence, in all cases of perception, of sensible experience of this kind. One line of retreat may seem to lie open at this point: a retreat to the position of saying that the occurrence of such experiences may be *inferred*, even though we do not, in the hurry of life, generally notice or recall their occurrence. But such a retreat would be the final irony. The items in question would have changed their status radically: instead of data for a common-sense theory of the world, they would appear as consequences of a sophisticated theory of the mind.

This concludes the first stage of my argument. I have argued that mature sensible experience (in general) presents itself as, in Kantian phrase, an *immediate* consciousness of the existence of things outside us. (*Immediate*, of course, does not mean *infallible*.) Hence, the common realist conception of the world does not have the character of a 'theory' in relation to the 'data of sense'. I have not claimed that this fact is of itself sufficient to 'refute' scepticism or to provide a philosophical 'demonstration' of the truth of some form of realism; though I think it does provide the right starting point for reflection upon these enterprises. But that is another story and I shall not try to tell it here. My point so far is that the ordinary human commitment to a conceptual scheme of a realist character is not properly described, even in a stretched sense of the words, as a theoretical commitment. It is, rather, something given with the given.

II

But we are philosophers as well as men; and so must examine more closely the nature of the realist scheme to which we are pre-theoretically committed and then consider whether we are not rationally constrained, as Locke and Mackie would maintain we are, to modify it quite radically in the light of our knowledge of physics and physiology. Should we not also, as philosophers, consider the question of whether we can rationally maintain any form of realism at all? Perhaps we should; but, as already remarked, that is a question I shall not consider here. My main object, in the present section, is to get a clear view of the main features of our pre-theoretical scheme before considering whether it is defensible, as it stands, or not. I go in a somewhat roundabout way to work.

I have spoken of our pre-theoretical scheme as realist in character. Philosophers who treat of these questions commonly distinguish different forms of realism. So do both Ayer and Mackie. They both mention, at one extreme, a form of realism which Mackie calls 'naïve' and even 'very naïve', but which might more appropriately be called 'confused realism'. A sufferer from confused realism fails to draw any distinction between sensible experiences (or 'perceptions') and independently existing things (or 'objects perceived') but is said (by Mackie expounding Hume) to credit the former with persistent unobserved existence.[10] It should be remarked that, if this is an accurate way of describing the naïve realist's conception of the matter, he must be very confused indeed, since the expression 'unobserved' already implies the distinction which he is said to fail to make. Speaking in his own person, Mackie gives no positive account of the naïve realist's view of things, but simply says that there is, historically, in the thought of each of us, a phase in which we fail to make the distinction in question.[11] It may indeed be so. The point is one to be referred to the experts on infantile development. But in any case the matter is not here of any consequence. For we are concerned with mature perceptual experience and with the character of the scheme to which those who enjoy such experience are pre-theoretically committed. And it seems to me as certain as anything can be that, as an integral part of that scheme, we distinguish, naturally and unreflectively, between our seeings and hearings and feelings – our perceivings – of objects and the objects we see and hear and feel; and hence quite consistently accept both the interruptedness of the former and the continuance in existence, unobserved, of the latter.

At the opposite extreme from naïve realism stands what may be called scientific or Lockian realism. This form of realism credits physical objects only with those of their properties which are mentioned in physical theory and physical explanation, including the causal explanation of our enjoyment of the kind of perceptual experience we in fact enjoy. It has the consequence that we do not, and indeed cannot, perceive objects as they really are. It might be said that this consequence does not hold in an unqualified form. For we perceive (or seem to perceive) objects as having shape, size and position; and they really do have shape, size and position and more or less such shape, size and position as we seem to perceive them as having. But this reply misconstrues the intended force of the alleged consequence. We cannot in sense perception – the point is an old one – become aware of the shape, size and position of physical objects except by way of awareness of boundaries defined in some sensory mode – for example, by visual and tactile qualities such as scientific realism denies to the objects themselves; and no change in, or addition to, our sensory equipment could alter this fact. To perceive physical objects as, according to scientific realism, they really are would be to perceive them as lacking any such qualities. But this notion is self-contradictory. So it is a necessary consequence of this form of realism that we do not perceive objects as they really are. Indeed, in the sense of the pre-theoretical notion of perceiving – that is, of immediate awareness of things outside us – we do not, on the scientific-realist view, perceive physical objects at all. We are, rather, the victims of a systematic illusion which obstinately clings to us even if we embrace scientific realism. For we continue to enjoy experience *as of* physical objects in space, objects of which the spatial characteristics and relations are defined by the sensible qualities we perceive them as having; but there are no such physical objects as these. The only true physical objects are items systematically correlated with and causally responsible for that experience; and the only sense in which we *can* be said to perceive them is just that they cause us to enjoy that experience.

These remarks are intended only as a *description* of scientific realism. I do not claim that they show it to be untenable. I shall return to the topic later.

In between the 'naïve' and the 'scientific' varieties, Ayer and Mackie each recognise another form of realism, which they each ascribe to 'common sense'. But there is a difference between Ayer's version of common-sense realism and Mackie's. For Mackie's version, unlike Ayer's, shares one crucial feature with scientific realism.

The theory of perception associated with scientific or Lockian realism is commonly and reasonably described as a representative theory. Each of us seems to himself to be perceptually aware of objects of a certain kind: objects in space outside us with visual and tactile qualities. There are in fact, on this view, no such objects; but these object appearances can in a broad sense be said to be representative of those actual objects in space outside us which are systematically correlated with the appearances and causally responsible for them. The interesting feature of Mackie's version of common-sense realism is that the theory of perception associated with it is no less a representative theory than that associated with Lockian realism. The difference is simply that common sense, according to Mackie, views object appearances as more faithful representatives of actual physical objects than the Lockian allows: in that common sense, gratuitously by scientific standards, credits actual objects in space outside us with visual and tactile as well as primary qualities. As Mackie puts it, common sense allows 'colours-as-we-see-them to be *resemblances* of qualities actually in the things'.[12] On both views, sensible experience has its own, sensible objects; but the common-sense view, according to Mackie, allows a kind of resemblance between sensible and physical objects which the scientific view does not.

I hope it is already clear that this version of common-sense realism is quite different from what I have called our pre-theoretical scheme. What we ordinarily take ourselves to be aware of in perception are not resemblances of physical things but the physical things themselves. This does not mean, as already remarked, that we have any difficulty in distinguishing between our experiences of seeing, hearing and feeling objects and the objects themselves. That distinction is as firmly a part of our pre-theoretical scheme as is our taking ourselves, in general, to be immediately aware of those objects. Nor does it mean that we take ourselves to be immune from illusion, hallucination or mistake. We can, and do, perfectly adequately describe such cases without what is, from the point of view of the pre-theoretical scheme, the quite gratuitous introduction of sensible objects interposed between us and the actual physical objects they are supposed to represent.

The odd thing about Mackie's presentation is that at one point he shows himself to be perfectly well aware of this feature of the real realism of common sense; for he writes, 'What we seem to see, feel, hear and so on ... *are seen as real things without us* – that is, outside us. We just see things as being simply there, of such-and-such sorts, in such-and-such relations. ...'[13] He goes on, of course, to say that 'our seeing them so is logically distinct from their being so', that we might be, and indeed are, wrong. But he would scarcely dispute that what is thus *seen as* real and outside us is also *seen as* coloured, as possessing visual qualities; that what is *felt as* a real thing outside us is also felt as hard or soft, smooth or rough-surfaced – as possessing tactile qualities. The real realism of common sense, then, does indeed credit physical things with visual and tactile properties; but it does so not in the spirit of a notion of representative perception, but in the spirit of a notion of direct or immediate perception.

Mackie's version of common-sense realism is, then, I maintain, a distortion of the actual pre-theoretical realism of common sense, a distortion which wrongly assimilates it, in a fundamental respect, to the Lockian realism he espouses. I do not find any comparable distortion in Ayer's version. He aptly describes the physical objects we seem to ourselves, and take ourselves, to perceive as 'visuo-tactual continuants'. The scheme as he presents it allows for the distinction between these items and the experiences of perceiving them and for the causal dependence of the latter on the former; and does so, as far as I can see, without introducing the alien features I have discerned in Mackie's account. It is perhaps debatable whether Ayer can consistently maintain the scheme's freedom from such alien elements while continuing to represent it as having the status of a 'theory' in relation to the 'data' of sensible experience. But, having already set out my objections to that doctrine, I shall not pursue the point.

Something more must be said, however, about the position, in the common-sense scheme, of the causal relation between physical object and the experience of perceiving it. Although Ayer admits the relation to a place in the scheme, he seems to regard it as a somewhat sophisticated addition to the latter, a latecomer, as it were, for which room has to be made in an already settled arrangement.[14] This seems to me wrong. The idea of the presence of the thing as accounting for, or being responsible for, our perceptual awareness of it is implicit in the pre-theoretical scheme from the very start. For we think of perception as a way, indeed the basic way, of informing ourselves about the world of independently existing things: we assume, that is to say, the general reliability of our perceptual experiences; and that assumption is the same as the assumption of a general causal dependence of our perceptual experiences on the independently existing things we take them to be of. The thought of my fleeting perception as a *perception* of a continuously and independently existing thing implicitly contains the thought that if the thing had not been there, I should not even have *seemed* to perceive it. It really should be obvious that with the distinction between independently existing objects and perceptual awareness of objects we already have the general notion of causal dependence of the latter on the former, even if this is not a matter to which we give much reflective attention in our pre-theoretical days.

Two things seem to have impeded recognition of this point. One is the fact that the correctness of the description of a perceptual experience as the perception of a certain physical thing *logically* requires the existence of that thing; and the *logical* is thought to exclude the *causal* connection, since only logically distinct existences can be causally related. This is not a serious difficulty. The situation has many parallels. Gibbon would not be the historian of the decline and fall of the Roman Empire unless there had occurred some actual sequence of events more or less corresponding to his narrative. But it is not enough, for him to merit that description, that such a sequence of events should have occurred and he should have written the sentences he did write. For him to qualify as the *historian* of these events, there must be a causal chain connecting them with the writing of the sentences. Similarly, the memory of an event's occurrence does not count as such unless it has its causal origin in that event. And the recently much canvassed 'causal theory of reference' merely calls attention to another instance of the causal link which obtains between thought and independently (and anteriorly) existing thing when the former is rightly said to have the latter as its object.

The second impediment is slightly more subtle. We are philosophically accustomed – it is a Humian legacy – to thinking of the simplest and most obvious kind of causal relation as holding between types of item such that items of both types are observable or experienceable and such that observation or experience of either term of the relation is distinct from observation or experience of the other: i.e. the causally related items are not only distinct existences, but also the objects of distinct observations or experiences. We may then come to think of these conditions as constituting a requirement on all primitive belief in causal relations, a requirement which could be modified or abandoned only in the interests of theory. Since we obviously cannot distinguish the observation of a physical object from the experience of observing it – for they are the same thing – we shall then be led to conclude that the idea of the causal dependence of perceptual experience on the perceived object cannot be even an implicit part of our pretheoretical scheme, but must be at best an essentially theoretical addition to it.

But the difficulty is spurious. By directing our attention to causal relations between *objects* of perception, we have simply been led to overlook the special character of perception itself. Of course, the requirement holds for causal relations between distinct objects of perception; but not for the relation between perception and its object. When x is a physical object and y is a perception of x, then x is *observed* and y is *enjoyed*. And in taking the enjoyment of y to be a perception of x, we *are* implicitly taking it to be caused by x.

This concludes the second phase of my argument. I have tried to bring out some main features of the real realism of common sense and of the associated notion of perception. From the standpoint of common-sense realism we take ourselves to be immediately aware of real, enduring physical things in space, things endowed with visual and tactile properties; and we take it for granted that these enduring things are causally responsible for our interrupted perceptions of them. The immediacy which common sense attributes to perceptual awareness is in no way inconsistent either with the distinction between perceptual experience and thing perceived or with the causal dependence of the former on the latter or the existence of other causally necessary conditions of its occurrence. Neither is it inconsistent with the occurrence of perceptual mistake or illusion – a point, like so many others of importance, which is explicitly made by Kant.[15] Both Ayer and Mackie, explicitly or implicitly, acknowledge that the common-sense scheme includes this assumption of immediacy – Mackie in a passage I have quoted, Ayer in his description of the common-sense scheme. Unfortunately, Mackie's acknowledgment of the fact is belied by his describing common-sense realism as representative in character and Ayer's acknowledgment of it is put in doubt by his describing the common-sense scheme as having the status of a theory in relation to sensible experience.

III

It is one thing to describe the scheme of common sense; it is another to subject it to critical examination. This is the third and most difficult part of my task. The main question to be considered, as already indicated, is whether we are rationally bound to abandon, or radically to modify, the scheme in the light of scientific knowledge.

Before addressing ourselves directly to this question, it is worth stressing – indeed, it is essential to stress – the grip that common-sense non-representative realism has on our ordinary thinking. It is a view of the world which so thoroughly permeates our consciousness that even those who are intellectually convinced of its falsity remain subject to its power. Mackie admits as much, saying that, even when we are trying to entertain a Lockian or scientific realism, 'our language and our natural ways of thinking keep pulling us back' to a more primitive view.[16] Consider the character of those ordinary concepts of objects on the employment of which our lives, our transactions with each other and the world, depend: our concepts of cabbages, roads, tweed coats, horses, the lips and hair of the beloved. In using these terms we certainly intend to be talking of independent existences and we certainly intend to be talking of immediately perceptible things, bearers of phenomenal (visuo-tactile) properties. If scientific or Lockian realism is correct, we cannot be doing both at once; it is confusion or illusion to suppose we can. If the things we talk of really have phenomenal properties, then they cannot, on this view, be physical things continuously existing in physical space. Nothing perceptible – I here drop the qualification 'immediately', for my use of it should now be clear – is a physically real, independent existence. No two persons can ever, in this sense, perceive the same item: nothing at all is publicly perceptible.

But how deep the confusion or the illusion must go! How radically it infects our concepts! Surely we mean by a cabbage a kind of thing of which most of the specimens we have encountered have a characteristic range of colours and visual shapes and felt textures; and not something unobservable, mentally represented by a complex of sensible experiences which it causes. The common consciousness is not to be fobbed off with the concession that, after all, the physical thing has – in a way – a shape. The way in which scientific realism concedes a shape is altogether the wrong way for the common consciousness. The lover who admires the curve of his mistress's lips or the lover of architecture who admires the lines of a building takes himself to be admiring features of those very objects themselves; but it is the visual shape, the visually defined shape, that he admires. Mackie suggests that there is a genuine *resemblance* between subjective representation and objective reality as far as shape is concerned;[17] but this suggestion is quite unacceptable. It makes no sense to speak of a phenomenal property as *resembling* a non-phenomenal, abstract property such as physical shape is conceived to be by scientific realism. The property of looking square or round can no more resemble the property, so conceived, of being physically square or round than the property of looking intelligent or looking ill can resemble the property of being intelligent or being ill. If it seems to make sense to speak of a resemblance between phenomenal properties and physical properties, so conceived, it is only because we give ourselves pictures – phenomenal pictures – of the latter. The resemblance is with the picture, not the pictured.

So, then, the common consciousness lives, or has the illusion of living, in a phenomenally propertied world of perceptible things in space. We might call it the lived world. It is also the public world, accessible to observation by all: the world in which one man, following another's pointing finger, can see the very thing that the other sees. (Even in our philosophical moments we habitually contrast the colours and visual shapes of things, as being publicly observable, with the subjective contents of consciousness, private to each of us, though not thereby unknowable to others.)

Such a reminder of the depth and reality of our habitual commitment to the common-sense scheme does not, by itself, amount to a demonstration of that scheme's immunity from philosophical criticism. The scientific realist, though no Kantian, may be ready, by way of making his maximum concession, with a reply modelled on Kant's combination of empirical realism with transcendental idealism. He may distinguish between the uncritical standpoint of ordinary living and the critical standpoint of philosophy informed by science. We are humanly, or naturally – he may say – constrained to 'see the world' in one way (i.e. to think of it as we seem to perceive it) and rationally, or critically, constrained to think of it in quite another. The first way (being itself a causal product of physical reality) has a kind of validity at its own level; but it is, critically and rationally speaking, an inferior level. The second way really is a correction of the first.

The authentically Kantian combination is open to objection in many ways; but, by reason of its very extravagance, it escapes one specific form of difficulty to which the scientific realist's soberer variant remains exposed. Kant uncompromisingly declares that space is in us; that it is 'solely from the human standpoint that we can speak of space, of extended things etc.';[18] that things as they are in themselves are not spatial at all. This will not do for the scientific realist. The phenomenally propertied items which we take ourselves to perceive and the apparent relations between which yield (or contribute vitally to yielding) our notion of space, are indeed declared to have no independent reality; but, when they are banished from the realm of the real, they are supposed to leave behind them – as occupants, so to speak, of the evacuated territory – those spatially related items which, though necessarily unobservable, nevertheless constitute the whole of physical reality. Ayer refers in several places to this consequence; and questions its coherence.[19] He writes, for example, 'I doubt whether the notion of a spatial system of which none of the elements can be observed is even intelligible.'

It is not clear that this difficulty is insuperable. The scientific realist will claim to be able to abstract the notion of a position in physical space from the phenomenal integuments with which it is originally and deceptively associated; and it is hard to think of a conclusive reason for denying him this power. He will say that the places where the phenomenally propertied things we seem to perceive seem to be are, often enough, places at which the correlated physically real items really are. Such a claim may make us uneasy; but it is not obvious nonsense.

Still, to say that a difficulty is not clearly insuperable is not to say that it is clearly not insuperable. It would be better to avoid it if we can. We cannot avoid it if we embrace unadulterated scientific realism and incidentally announce ourselves thereby as the sufferers from persistent illusion, however natural. We can avoid it, perhaps, if we can succeed in combining elements of the scientific story with our common-sense scheme without downgrading the latter. This is the course that Ayer recommends[20] and, I suspect, the course that most of us semi-reflectively follow. The question is whether it is a consistent or coherent course. And at bottom this question is one of identity. Can we coherently identify the phenomenally propertied, immediately perceptible things which common sense supposes to occupy physical space with the configurations of unobservable ultimate particulars by which an unqualified scientific realism purports to replace them?

I approach the question indirectly, by considering once again Mackie's version of common-sense realism. According to this version, it will be remembered, physical things, though not directly perceived, really possess visual and tactile qualities which resemble those we seem to perceive them as possessing; so that if, *per impossibile*, the veil of perception were drawn aside and we saw things in their true colours, these would turn out to be colours indeed and, on the whole, just the colours with which we were naïvely inclined to credit them. Mackie does not represent this view as absurd or incoherent. He just thinks that it is, as a matter of fact, false. Things *could* really be coloured; but, since there is no scientific reason for supposing they are, it is gratuitous to make any such supposition.

Mackie is surely too lenient to his version of common-sense realism. That version effects a complete logical divorce between a thing's being red and its being red-looking. Although it is a part of the theory that a thing which is, in itself, red has the power to cause us to seem to see a red thing, the logical divorce between these two properties is absolute. And, as far as I can see, that divorce really produces nonsense. The ascription of colours to things becomes not merely gratuitous, but senseless. Whatever may be the case with shape and position, colours are visibilia or they are nothing. I have already pointed out that this version of common-sense realism is not the real realism of common sense: *that* realism effects no logical divorce between being red and being red-looking; for it is a perceptually direct and not a perceptually representative realism. The things seen as coloured are the things themselves. There is no 'veil past which we cannot see'; for there is no veil.

But this does not mean that a thing which is red, i.e. red-looking, has to look red all the time and in all circumstances and to all observers. There is an irreducible relativity, a relativity to what in the broadest sense may be called the perceptual point of view, built in to our ascriptions of particular visual properties to things. The mountains are red-looking at this distance in this light; blue-looking at that distance at that light; and, when we are clambering up them, perhaps neither. Such-and-such a surface looks pink and smooth from a distance; mottled and grainy when closely examined; different again, perhaps, under the microscope.

We absorb this relativity easily enough for ordinary purposes in our ordinary talk, tacitly taking some range of perceptual conditions, some perceptual point of view (in the broad sense) as standard or normal, and introducing an explicit acknowledgement of relativity only in cases which deviate from the standard. 'It looks purple in this light', we say, 'but take it to the door and you will see that it's really green.' But sometimes we do something else. We shift the standard. Magnified, the fabric appears as printed with tiny blue and yellow dots. So those are the colours it really is. Does this ascription contradict 'it's really green'? No; for the standard has shifted. Looking at photographs, in journals of popular science, of patches of human skin, vastly magnified, we say, 'How fantastically uneven and ridgy it really is.' We study a sample of blood through a microscope and say, 'It's mostly colourless.' But skin can still be smooth and blood be red; for in another context we shift our standard back. Such shifts do not convict us of volatility or condemn us to internal conflict. The appearance of both volatility and conflict vanishes when we acknowledge the relativity of our 'reallys'.

My examples are banal. But perhaps they suggest a way of resolving the apparent conflict between scientific and common-sense realism. We can shift our point of view within the general framework of perception, whether aided or unaided by artificial means; and the different sensible-quality ascriptions we then make to the same object are not seen as conflicting once their relativity is recognised. Can we not see the adoption of the viewpoint of scientific realism as simply a more radical shift – a shift to a viewpoint from which no characteristics are to be ascribed to things except those which figure in the physical theories of science and in 'the explanation of what goes on in the physical world in the processes which lead to our having the sensations and perceptions that we have'?[21]

We can say that this is how things really are so long as the relativity of this 'really' is recognised as well; and, when it is recognised, the scientific account will no more conflict with the ascription to things of visual and tactile qualities than the assertion that blood is really a mainly colourless fluid conflicts with the assertion that it is bright red in colour. Of course, the scientific point of view is not, in one sense, a point of *view* at all. It is an intellectual, not a perceptual, standpoint. We could not occupy it at all, did we not first occupy the other. But we can perfectly well occupy both at once, so long as we realise what we are doing.

This method of reconciling scientific and common-sense realism requires us to recognise a certain relativity in our conception of the real properties of physical objects. Relative to the human perceptual standpoint the grosser physical objects are visuo-tactile continuants (and within that standpoint the phenomenal properties they possess are relative to particular perceptual viewpoints, taken as standard). Relative to the scientific standpoint, they have no properties but those which figure in the physical theories of science. Such a relativistic conception will not please the absolute-minded. Ayer recommends a different procedure. He suggests that we should conceive of perceptible objects (i.e. objects perceptible in the sense of the common-sense scheme) as being literally composed of the ultimate particles of physical theory, the latter being imperceptible, not in principle, but only empirically, as a consequence of their being so minute.[22] I doubt, however, whether this proposal, which Ayer rightly describes as an attempt to *blend* the two schemes can be regarded as satisfactory. If the impossibility of perceiving the ultimate components is to be viewed as merely empirical, we can sensibly ask what the conceptual consequences would be of supposing that impossibility not to exist. The answer is clear. Even if there were something which we counted as perceiving the ultimate particles, this would still not, from the point of view of scientific realism, count as perceiving them as they really are. And nothing could so count; for no phenomenal properties we seemed to perceive them as having would figure in the physical explanation of the causal mechanisms of our success. But, so long as we stay at this point of view, what goes for the parts goes for any wholes they compose. However gross those wholes, they remain, from this point of view, imperceptible in the sense of common sense.

Ayer attempts to form one viewpoint out of two discrepant viewpoints; to form a single, unified description of physical reality by blending features of two discrepant descriptions, each valid from its own viewpoint. He can seem to succeed only by doing violence to one of the two viewpoints, the scientific. I acknowledge the discrepancy of the two descriptions, but claim that, once we recognise the relativity in our conception of the real, they need not be seen as in contradiction with each other. Those very things which from one standpoint we conceive as phenomenally propertied we conceive from another as constituted in a way which can only be described in what are, from the phenomenal point of view, abstract terms. 'This smooth, green, leather table-top', we say, 'is, considered scientifically, nothing but a congeries of electric charges widely separated and in rapid motion.' Thus we combine the two standpoints in a single sentence. The standpoint of common-sense realism, not explicitly signalled as such, is reflected in the sentence's grammatical subject phrase, of which the words are employed in no esoteric sense. The standpoint of physical science, explicitly signalled as such, is reflected in the predicate. Once relativity of description to standpoint is recognised, the sentence is seen to contain no contradiction; and, if it contains no contradiction, the problem of identification is solved.

I recognise that this position is unlikely to satisfy the determined scientific realist. If he is only moderately determined, he may be partially satisfied, and may content himself with saying that the scientific viewpoint is *superior* to that of common sense. He will then simply be expressing a preference, which he will not expect the artist, for example, to share. But, if he is a hard-liner, he will insist that the common-sense view is wholly undermined by science; that it is shown to be false; that the visual and tactile properties we ascribe to things are nowhere but in our minds; that we do not live in a world of perceptible objects, as understood by common sense, at all. He must then accept the consequence that each of us is a sufferer from a persistent and inescapable illusion and that it is fortunate that this is so, since, if it were not, we should be unable to pursue the scientific enterprise itself. Without the illusion of perceiving objects as bearers of sensible qualities, we should not have the illusion of perceiving them as space-occupiers at all; and without that we should have no concept of space and no power to pursue our researches into the nature of its occupants. Science is not only the offspring of common sense; it remains its dependant. For this reason, and for others touched on earlier, the scientific realist must, however ruefully, admit that the ascription to objects of sensible qualities, the standard of correctness of such ascription being (what we take to be) intersubjective agreement, is something quite securely rooted in our conceptual scheme. If this means, as he must maintain it does, that our thought is condemned to incoherence, then we can only conclude that incoherence is something we can perfectly well live with and could not perfectly well live without.

NOTES

1. A. J. Ayer, *The Central Questions of Philosophy* (London: Weidenfeld and Nicolson, 1973) chs 4 and 5, pp. 68–111.
2. J. L. Mackie, *Problems from Locke* (Oxford: Clarendon Press, 1976) chs 1 and 2, pp. 7–71.
3. Ayer, *Central Questions*, pp. 81, 89.
4. Ibid., p. 88.
5. Ibid., p. 89.
6. Ibid., p. 81.
7. Ibid., p. 91.
8. Ibid., p. 96.
9. Ibid., p. 91.
10. Mackie, *Problems*, p. 67.
11. Ibid., p. 68.
12. Ibid., p. 64.
13. Ibid., p. 61.
14. Ayer, *Central Questions*, pp. 87–8.
15. Kant, 'The Refutation of Idealism', in *Critique of Pure Reason*, B274–9.
16. Mackie, *Problems*, p. 68.
17. Ibid., chs 1 and 2, *passim*.
18. Kant, 'Refutation of Idealism', in *Critique*, B42.
19. Ayer, *Central Questions*, pp. 84, 86–7, 110.
20. Ibid., pp. 110–11.
21. Mackie, *Problems*, p. 18.
22. Ayer, *Central Questions*, p. 110.

3 A Comparison between Ayer's Views about the Privileges of Sense-Datum Statements and the Views of Russell and Austin

DAVID PEARS

Russell and Ayer have both written extensively about the nature and privileges of sense-datum statements. Austin too dealt with their privileges, but his main concern was with the question of whether there is any basic class of empirical statements. A good way of approaching the question of the privileges of sense-datum statements is to compare the views of the three philosophers. This will help to isolate some of the problems and it may suggest promising ways of solving them.

Sense-datum statements form a loosely knit group. They include statements about the location, intensity and qualities of bodily sensations, and a large variety of statements based on the use of an outward-facing sense but non-committal about the existence or character of the external object. Two privileges have been assigned to them, infallibility and incorrigibility. An extreme verificationist would deny that these are two different things, on the ground that it is meaningless to speak of an error that could never be discovered or corrected. But I shall assume that there is a difference, most clearly exhibited by reports of dreams.

Russell's theory of knowledge by acquaintance shaped his early account of the privileges of sense-datum statements, and the account that he gave after 1919, when he abandoned acquaintance, was quite different. The theory of acquaintance, while he still held it, was threatened by an internal tension, which he later diagnosed in *The Analysis of Mind*.[1] The theory treated acquaintance as a

kind of knowledge, but defined it as a direct relation between
subject and object not necessarily involving knowledge of any truth
about the object.[2] So perceiving and sensing, which are examples
of this direct relation, are treated extensionally. True, Russell assures
us that it rarely, if ever, happens that a subject is acquainted
with an object without knowing any truth about it.[3] But that
is not the same as construing acquaintance intensionally. There
appears to be only one passage which implies that acquaintance
is intensional.[4] His settled view is that it is extensional, and yet
he treats it as a kind of knowledge.

When Russell interpreted perceiving and sensing as instances of
acquaintance, the result was likely to be an exaggeration of the
immunity from error enjoyed by sense-datum statements. For the
theory of acquaintance seemed to offer the possibility of knowledge
without the risks attending the description of what is known. 'Uncritical use of the direct object after *know* seems to be one thing
that leads to the view that (or to talking as though) sensa, that
is things, colours, noises and the rest, speak or are labelled by
nature, so that I can literally *say* what (that which) I *see*: it pipes
up, or I read it off.'[5] However, though Russell did sometimes
imply that sense-datum statements are infallible, the reasoning that
led him in that direction was complicated. If it involved the confusion
between the relative pronoun and the interrogative pronoun 'what',
the confusion was part of an elaborate theory about the way in
which a person comes to make a statement about a sense datum.

The implication that sense-datum statements are infallible is
clearly contained in a passage in *The Problems of Philosophy*:

> This problem [i.e. that some of our beliefs turn out to be
> erroneous] does not arise with regard to knowledge by acquaint-
> ance, for, whatever may be the object of acquaintance, even
> in dreams and hallucinations, there is no error involved so long
> as we do not go beyond the immediate object: error can only
> arise when we regard the immediate object, i.e. the sense-datum,
> as a mark of some physical object.[6]

Here Russell is evidently assuming that there is only one way
of going beyond the immediate object – namely, treating it as
a sign of some other object. But other remarks made by him
in this period give a different impression.

> An observed complex fact, such as that this patch of red is
> to the left of that patch of blue, is also to be regarded as
> a datum from our point of view: epistemologically it does not
> differ greatly from a simple sense-datum as regards its function

in giving knowledge. Its *logical* structure is very different, however, from that of sense: *sense* gives acquaintance with particulars, and is thus a two-term relation in which an object can be *named* but not *asserted*, and is inherently incapable of truth or falsehood, whereas the observation of a complex fact, which may be suitably called 'perception' is not a two-term relation, but involves the propositional form on the object side, and gives knowledge of a truth, not mere acquaintance with a particular.[7]

The immediate object in this case is a complex sense datum – namely, one with the structure '*a-in-the-relation-R-to b*', rather than '*a-with-the-property-$\varnothing$*'. Russell does not go so far as to say that a subject who merely analyses and describes this object without treating it as a sign of some other object may nevertheless go beyond it. But he does maintain a firm distinction between acquaintance with its constituents and knowledge of the true analysis of its structure. So the subject has to do something in order to move from mere acquaintance to knowledge of the truth. May he not make a mistake in what he does?

In the Introduction to *Principia Mathematica* Russell answers this question more cautiously than in the passage quoted from *The Problems of Philosophy*:

> Let us consider a complex object composed of two parts *a* and *b* standing to each other in the relation *R*. The complex object *a*-in-the-relation-*R*-to-*b* may be capable of being *perceived*; when it is perceived, it is perceived as one object. Attention may then show that it is complex; we then *judge* that *a* and *b* stand in the relation *R*. Such a judgement, being derived from perception by mere attention, may be called a judgement of perception. This judgement of perception, considered as an actual occurrence, is a relation of four terms, namely *a* and *b* and *R* and the percipient. The perception, on the other hand, is a relation of two terms, namely *a*-in-the-relation-*R*-to-*b* and the percipient.[8]

This tells us what the percipient has to do, in order to arrive at his judgement: he must attend to what he perceives. It also tells us that he is acquainted with the complex object *a*-in-relation-*R*-to-*b* as well as with its parts.

But is his judgement of perception immune from error? Russell continues,

> Since an object of perception cannot be nothing, we cannot perceive *a*-in-the-relation-*R*-to-*b* unless *a* is in the relation *R* to *b*. Hence a judgement of perception, according to the above

definition, must be true. This does not mean that in a judgement which *appears* to us to be one of perception we are sure of not being in error, since we may err in thinking that our judgement has really been derived merely by analysis of what was perceived.

What sort of error is Russell contemplating? If the complex object is a sense datum, it can hardly be the error of treating it as a sign of a non-existent physical object. For, if we did make such a mistake, we could not fail to realise that we were taking that particular risk, and so we could not believe that we were merely attending to the complex sense datum and trying to analyse it. Incidentally, it is not really necessary to qualify the sense datum in this case as 'complex', because a-with-the-property-$\emptyset$ is also complex, albeit in a simpler way.

If the error that Russell has in mind cannot be the error of treating the sense datum as a sign of a non-existent physical object, it must lie in the sense-datum statement itself. It is then no consolation to be told that in that case the sense-datum statement was not really a judgement of perception. We need to know what we did wrong. But this is something that he does not explain.

The reason why he left this gap in his theory is that it seemed to him to be, at the worst, a small one, because he believed the fallibility of sense-datum statements to be marginal or non-existent. But was he right in this belief? He certainly does not argue for it, or even raise the question of whether someone who simply describes a sense datum without treating it as a sign of any other object may be going beyond the sense datum in some other way.

These deficiencies are consequences of his theory of knowledge by acquaintance, but they were produced in more than one way. First, it is evident that his extensional treatment of acquaintance obscured the fact that the subject has to identify the parts of the complex object, and may even have suggested that there was nothing of this kind for him to do, or at least nothing that he might get wrong. In the example used by Russell, two of the parts really are supposed to make no demands on the subject's skill, because they are given the logically proper names a and b. But the relation, R, is another matter, and Russell ought to have pointed out that it is possible to misidentify it, or to misconstrue its direction if it is asymmetrical. So at this point his theory really is affected by something like the confusion described by Austin. The confusion is encouraged by his idea that all that the subject has to do to the sense datum is to analyse it or cut it up, in the right way. For it is easy to overlook the fact that this action is in the mind and must be interpreted intensionally. It is not like cutting a cake in half, which can be done without the belief that the two pieces will be the same size.

There is also another way in which Russell's theory of acquaintance produced the deficiencies in his account of sense-datum statements. In the passage quoted from *Principia Mathematica* he says that the subject is acquainted with the complex object 'a-in-the-relation-R-to-b'. But in *The Problems of Philosophy* he implies[9] that, when the subject makes a judgement of perception, he is acquainted with the (complex) fact that *aRb*, and he observes that acquaintance with a complex fact 'gives us the complex whole, and is therefore only possible when its parts do actually have that relation which makes them combine to form such a complex'. This last point depends on the meaning of the word 'fact', and is, like all such points, unhelpful. What makes the passage interesting is that it identifies the complex object 'a-in-the-relation-R-to-b' with the fact that *aRb*, or at least comes perilously near to doing so.

Now, Russell's thesis, that acquaintance is extensional, entails that the subject may be acquainted with the complex object a-in-the-relation-R-to-b without knowing that that is what it is, and so without any inclination to claim that *aRb*. But, if he is acquainted with the fact that *aRb*, his acquaintance cannot be extensional. For it does not make sense to say of him that he is acquainted with the fact that *aRb* but is not in a position to make any claim about it, or is, perhaps, inclined to claim that it is some other fact. There are, of course, other obstacles to the identification of complex objects with facts, but this one ought to have been enough to prevent Russell from identifying them with one another. If, as appears very probable, he did identify them with one another, the reason must have been that he did not clearly realise that acquaintance with facts can only be intensional. But, though he never acknowledged the intensionality of acquaintance with facts, he did tacitly exploit it. For his remark that the subject is acquainted with the fact that *aRb* immediately suggests that he must be inclined to make the claim that *aRb*. In this way extensional acquaintance with a complex object acquires a logic that is not its own.

This is not a criticism of Russell's unhelpful point about the meaning of the word 'fact'. The target is the suggestion that extensional acquaintance with a complex object involves the inclination to make any claim at all, correct or incorrect, about it. However, the criticism may seem to be no more than an application of Austin's point to complex objects. But it does bring in an additional factor – namely, the effect of the tension between the following three theses: (1) acquaintance is extensional, (2) complex objects are facts, and (3) we are acquainted with complex objects.

When Russell abandoned the theory of knowledge by acquaintance, he could no longer analyse perception as a transaction in which a subject is given something, i.e. a sense datum. So in *An Inquiry into Meaning and Truth* he speaks[10] of 'basic' propositions or statements, rather than sense-datum statements, adopting Ayer's translation of *Protokollsätze*. The account that he gives of them is brief. The elaborate epistemology has gone, and the old intuition, that they are infallible, or almost infallible, is expressed in a rather perfunctory theory about the way in which they achieve a match with their causes.

Russell defines basic propositions as those which are caused as immediately as possible by perceptive experiences.[11] Naturally, all statements that are caused by perceptive experiences have to match them: ' "This is blue" is true if it is caused by what "blue" means'.[12] The peculiarity of basic statements is that 'they do not imply anything beyond an experience private to me',[13] and so the only possibility of error is 'ignorance of the language, leading me to call "blue" what others call "violet". This is social error, not intellectual error; what I am believing is true, but my words are ill chosen'.[14]

But, we may ask, in such cases how is it that a person is able to avoid all but linguistic errors? Russell only maintains that 'the truth of what he says, given the meaning of his words, can, given adequate care, be wholly dependent on the character of one occurrence that he is noticing'.[15] This cautious statement contains two points. First, the possibility of linguistic error is allowed for and set on one side by the phrase 'given the meaning of his words'. Secondly 'adequate care' is then said to be enough to secure a certain happy result. But Russell does not actually specify this happy result as match or truth. He specifies it only as *exclusive causal dependence on the experience*. Now, as Ayer observes, that is not the same thing as truth.[16] However, this is not an oversight of Russell's. For he does not go on to draw the conclusion that only linguistic error is possible, as he does in his later treatment of this subject in *Human Knowledge*.[17] His conclusion is only that a basic statement cannot be corrected with certainty:

> It is true that, in the sense in which we infer eclipses, there can be evidence against a present judgement of perception, but this evidence is inductive and merely probable, and cannot stand against 'the evidence of the senses'. When we have analyzed a judgement of perception in this way, we are left with something which cannot be *proved* to be false.[18]

These brief remarks contain some interesting points. Russell takes the exigencies of describing more seriously than he did before 1919, when extensional acquaintance was supposed to do so much of the work. But he is inclined to think that error in basic statements is always linguistic, i.e. unintentional error in what the person says, rather than in what he believes. There is also an implicit distinction between fallibility and corrigibility in his more cautious discussion in *Inquiry into Meaning and Truth*. However, the distinction between linguistic errors and other errors had already been used by Ayer in *Language, Truth and Logic*, and Ayer's development of it, like his development of the distinction between fallibility and corrigibility, is more detailed than Russell's. So the points made by Russell in this period are best examined in the form that Ayer gave them.

Ayer's first contribution to the subject is a powerful attack on the thesis that sense-datum statements point without describing. An attempted statement that was purely ostensive would consist entirely of demonstrative symbols, and so it would not convey any information. 'If a sentence is to express a proposition, it cannot merely name a situation; it must say something about it. And in describing a situation one is not merely registering a sense-content; one is classifying it in some way or other, and this means going beyond what is immediately given.'[19] This is directed against the theories of Schlick and von Juhos, but the adversary could have been Russell's suggestion that there is only one way of going beyond the immediate object – namely, treating it as a sign of some other object.[20] Ayer even says that sense-datum statements may be mistaken.[21]

In the Introduction to the second edition of *Language, Truth and Logic* (1946) he moves back from this position in the direction of the position that he had attacked in 1935. But it is difficult to be sure how far he retreats. He now says that 'the form of words that is used to express a basic proposition' may be understood in two different ways: 'It may be understood to express something that is informative both to another person and to oneself', or 'it may refer solely to the content of a single experience'. In the first case, 'it no longer expresses a basic proposition', but, since it would still be a report of a sense datum, it would presumably be a sense-datum statement which was non-basic and perhaps not immune from error. This is an inconspicuous but important complication, but, once noticed, it is easy to understand.

What is less easy to understand is Ayer's account of the second alternative, i.e. the case in which the same form of words is used to refer solely to the content of a single experience. In such a case, he says, the words still express a proposition, and the proposition is conclusively verified by the occurrence of the experience and is immune from all but verbal error.

> In a verbal sense, indeed, it is always possible to misdescribe one's experience; but if one intends to do no more than record what is experienced without relating it to anything else, it is not possible to be factually mistaken; and the reason for this is that one is making no claim that any further fact could confute. It is, in short, a case of 'nothing venture, nothing lose'. It is, however, equally a case of 'nothing venture, nothing win', since the mere recording of one's present experience does not serve to convey any information either to any other person or indeed to oneself; for in knowing a basic proposition to be true one attains no further knowledge than what is already afforded by the occurrence of the relevant experience.[22]

In this passage a number of ideas are held together in uneasy association. The result is that the better ones suffer from their contact with the others, and should be examined in the less cramping context of Ayer's later writings. The trouble lies in the second alternative described here – namely, the use of a sentence to express a basic proposition 'referring solely to the content of a single experience'. If such propositions are conclusively verifiable, it must be possible for them to be false, even if only because the speaker intends them to be false. But the two alternatives, true and false, are possible only if the meaning of the proposition is fixed independently of the character of the sense datum to which it refers. Otherwise there will be no question of match or mismatch. It follows that even a basic proposition will be informative both to others and to the speaker, except in the sense that it will not be news to him at the time. If this were not so, it would be immune from verbal error as well as from factual error. In short, basic propositions cannot be purely ostensive.

However, it is not clear that Ayer really is going back to the position that he attacked in 1935. For he also allows sentences that might express basic propositions to be used in another, non-basic way, to convey information both to the speaker and to others. Now the form of words would be the same, and so, as already noted, these non-basic propositions would also be about sense data. But they would not be conclusively verifiable. However, that is no disadvantage. For, according to Ayer, if they had been conclusively verifiable, they would have been purely ostensive and uninformative, and in that case they could hardly have served as the foundations of empirical knowledge. If you dig your foundations too deep they disappear.

There is some reason for thinking that Ayer realised that non-basic sense-datum propositions would be the important ones. But his main concern in this part of the Introduction to the 1946 edition was with a side issue – namely, making room for conclusively verifiable propositions, even if they are of little use. Nevertheless, his account of them ought to have allowed for the possibility of match or mismatch. So it is worth asking what impelled him towards purely ostensive propositions, which are beyond match and mismatch.

The answer is implicit in his claim that basic propositions 'refer solely to the content of a single experience'. This implies that, in Russell's words, 'we do not go beyond the immediate object'. But treating the sense datum as a sign of something in the external world does not seem to be the only way of going beyond it. It may be that the meaning of the proposition cannot be fixed independently of the character of the immediate object unless one goes beyond it in some other way. But how? If we say that the speaker implies that his sense datum is in a certain respect like another that he has had previously, we rule out the possibility that it is the first sense datum of the kind experienced by him, and that cannot be right, because it could be the first, and his basic proposition would surely not be *false* if it were the first. It seems probable that in 1946 Ayer did not see how a report of a sense datum which was non-committal about the existence or character of anything in the external world could go beyond the immediate object, and that this drove him towards purely ostensive propositions. Certainly this problem is his main concern in his next contribution to the subject, 'Basic Propositions'.[23]

There is also something else that was pushing him in the same direction. He says that 'if one intends to do no more than record what is experienced without relating it to anything else, it is not possible to be factually mistaken; and the reason for this is that one is making no claim that any further fact could confute'. This implies that a factual mistake (as opposed to a verbal one) would have to be *confutable* by a further fact. But factual error may not always be corrigible, and, when it is, the correction may not be knockdown. However, Ayer's account of the precise connection between fallibility and corrigibility was not developed until 1959,[24] and so exaggeration of the tightness of this connection and of the force of the correction may have helped to push him in the direction of purely ostensive propositions in 1946. For, if the factual fallibility of sense-datum propositions did entail knockdown corrigibility, it would be natural to argue that they are not factually fallible.

So this passage in the 1946 Introduction marks out two problems for later investigation. How can a sense-datum statement 'go beyond the immediate object'? And what is the precise connection between fallibility and corrigibility? But a realistic discussion of these two problems evidently requires a prior distinction between verbal and factual mistakes. Ayer alludes to the distinction in this passage, but he does not draw it, and this is a deficiency in his theory of sense-datum statements which he did not really make good later. In fact, one of the things that make it difficult to assess the controversy between Austin and him about the fallibility and corrigibility of sense-datum statements is the lack of a clear distinction between verbal and factual error. Unless the concept of verbal error is given a definite limit, it threatens to engulf all examples of error in a totally uninteresting way.

One last question needs to be raised about the 1946 Introduction before we move on to Ayer's later contributions to this subject. Does he really mean that non-basic sense-datum statements can be factually mistaken? The text suggests that he does mean this, because his reason for denying that basic sense-datum statements can be factually mistaken is that, unlike non-basic ones, they refer solely to the content of a single experience and so are uninformative. But it may be doubted whether he really took himself to be committed to the implication that non-basic sense-datum statements can be factually mistaken. Certainly, his later discussions of this problem read as if he is now not so sure as he had been that non-basic sense-datum statements are immune from factual error. It must be remembered that his main concern in this part of the 1946 Introduction is to establish the possibility of conclusively verifiable propositions. This leads him to explore again what is in fact a cul-de-sac, and to say very little about what later turned out to be the main road.

In the end, Ayer himself admits that he is not sure whether Austin established that factual error is a possibility for sense-datum statements.

> On this point I am not sure whether he is right or wrong. There is no doubt that it is possible to misdescribe the way things appear to one, but it is not clear whether there are any cases in which a mistake of this kind ought to count as factual rather than verbal. Since I am on the whole inclined to think that there are, I do not wish to commit myself to the view that my experiential statements are incorrigible.[25]

These experiential statements are the non-basic sense-datum statements of 1946, but from now on they will be called 'sense-datum statements', without qualification, because after 1946 Ayer did not require basic statements to be purely ostensive. In this passage his point is that sense-datum statements may be factually corrigible. But factual corrigibility is a sufficient but not necessary condition of factual fallibility, and it is better to examine the latter first.

The hard task is to find the distinguishing mark of purely verbal mistakes. There is no doubt about the central case, misdescription by a slip of the tongue. But suppose that someone is really uncertain what word to apply to his sense datum. In such a case the explanation will not always be that he knows how the thing looks or tastes to him at the moment but unfortunately cannot think of the right word for it. It is true that, when that is the explanation, a mistake, if he made one, would be purely verbal. But even in this case the speaker may mislead himself, because his later memory may not reach back behind his words to the actual experience. So here is an example of verbal error with one of the features that is often taken to be distinctive of factual error.

It may be objected that the speaker is not misled at the time, and that it is irrelevant what happens later. But that would be a strange view to take of the acquisition and preservation of knowledge. For unrecorded facts are inaccessible to others and eventually to the person himself. It is true that there is a sense in which the person himself is not misled at the time. But there will come a time when, looking back on his privilege, he can only describe it as the opportunity to get the record right. But if he could not get it right on the first occasion, then later, even if his memory does still reach back to the actual experience, he will only have another opportunity not quite so good as the original one, which he was unable to exploit. Now the original opportunity was a case of extensional acquaintance: he had the sense datum. Such cases form the fringe of the corpus of knowledge as it expands. But they do not quite count as knowledge. No doubt, if we never recorded acquired knowledge, we should take a different view of this fringe. But our standard of knowledge is set by the fact that we have to record it in order to preserve it, and verbal error, which is an error in the record, is from the beginning potentially misleading, and eventually necessarily misleading, about the fact.

Considerations of this sort led Austin to arrange cases of verbal error in a sequence exhibiting more and more of the features usually ascribed to factual error. Suppose next that it is not the case that the speaker knows how the thing looks or tastes to him at the moment but unfortunately cannot think of the right word for it. In this area Austin distinguishes several types of example. In one 'I can find nothing in my past experience with which to compare the current case .... This case, though distinguishable enough, shades off into the more common type of case where I'm not quite certain, or only fairly certain, or practically certain, that it's the taste of, say, laurel.' There is also a third case, which

> is different, though it very naturally combines itself with the first. Here what I try to do is to *savour* the current experience, to *peer* at it, to sense it vividly. I'm not sure that it *is* the taste of pineapple: isn't there perhaps just something about it, a tang, a bite, a lack of bite, a cloying sensation, which isn't quite right for pineapple? Isn't there perhaps just a peculiar hint of green, which would rule out mauve and would hardly do for heliotrope?[26]

Austin's strategy is understandable. He does not draw a distinction between verbal and factual error, because he thinks that, if the distinction is supposed to produce the consequences usually attributed to it, there is no such distinction to be drawn. However, the impact of his examples would have been clearer if he had gone on to draw a non-tendentious distinction between purely verbal mistakes (no longer claimed to be necessarily non-misleading) and others, and then argued that sense-datum statements are not immune from all but purely verbal mistakes.

The general idea of purely verbal error is, in Russell's words, that it is 'not intellectual error: what I am believing is true, but my words are ill chosen'.[27] In such a case the character that I believe my sense datum to possess is the same as its actual character, but, unfortunately, my description does not match the character that I believe it to possess, and therefore does not match its actual character. Given this criterion of purely verbal error, it is an empirical question whether sense-datum statements are open to any other kind.

First it would be necessary to sharpen the criterion more than I can sharpen it here. For restrictions need to be imposed both on the content of the correct belief that the speaker claims to hold, and on the tests that would establish that he really did hold it, and really was trying to express it in his ill chosen words. Obviously, the content of his correct belief must be more than that his sense datum has '*this* character' (and here he attends to it again). But must it be that it is $\emptyset$, when $\emptyset$ is a predicate belonging to the same level as his ill chosen predicate ψ? Suppose that someone says, 'This looks magenta to me now', when what it actually looks to him is vermilion, and then claims that his mistake was purely verbal on the ground that he was expressing, in the wrong way as it turned out, the correct belief that it looked red, or, at least, coloured. If he really was trying to express one of these less specific beliefs, we should allow that his mistake was purely verbal. But he might have held one of them without trying to express it, and what he was trying to express might have been a more specific claim. Or he might not know quite what he was trying to express, and in that case, when we asked for his correct underlying belief, we might insist that it should contain the predicate 'vermilion', on the ground that a discrepancy of level between the predicate in the expression and the predicate in the thought is not, in general, likely.

The tests for establishing actual possession of the correct underlying belief raise familiar problems. It would have to be decided how much questioning, prompting and exposure to further examples was allowable. The difficulty is that such tests run a risk of creating a new belief that is back-dated instead of revealing an actual earlier belief.[28] Only a slip of the tongue, instantly corrected by the speaker, is completely free from this risk.

There is another point that should be mentioned here in order to prevent misunderstanding. When we ask whether sense-datum statements are immune from all but purely verbal error, we are asking the question about such statements as 'This tastes like tarragon to me now', and not about such statements as 'This tastes to me like what I am now inclined to call "tarragon".' A person who makes the first statement avoids knockdown falsification when there is no tarragon in the sauce. This is a cautious move, but he would have been even more cautious had he made the second statement instead. For in that case he would have avoided knockdown falsification even when the sauce did not actually taste to him of tarragon. When he uses the first form of words he hedges his bet against the possibility that the sauce is not matched by its taste to him, but when he uses the second form of words he also hedges his bet against the possibility that its taste to him is not matched by his chosen words.

It is important to distinguish the two types of statement, and to focus the inquiry onto the first type, because they are easily confused. If, for example, someone says, 'It seems like tarragon to me', it is not clear whether he is hedging against the second possibility as well as against the first. Moreover, the effect of the second hedge may be quite different in different kinds of case. For example, in philosophical discussions of the privileges of sense-datum statements it is often assumed that they will be the same as the privileges of such statements as 'I am thinking about Christmas'.[29] But this may lead us to argue in a way which is, if Austin is right, fallacious. First, we realise that a thought is not something that I can have difficulty in identifying at the time, because it does not even present me with a problem of identification. (My intentions sometimes do present me with this problem: e.g. as already noted, I might not know exactly what belief I had been trying to express in my ill-chosen words.) So if I hedge against the second possibility and say 'It seems to me that I am thinking about Christmas', this can only be intended to neutralise the effect of some purely verbal error, such as making the slip of substituting 'Christmas' for 'Easter'. We may then argue that the same applies to the statement 'This tastes to me like what I am now inclined to call "tarragon".' But the analogy seems to break down at the very point at which this inference relies on it. For Austin seems to be right in thinking that the character of my gustatory sensation is something that I may have difficulty in identifying at the time, so that in this case the second hedge will also neutralise the effect of error that is not purely verbal. The example of pain is often used to ease the transition from the first kind of case to the second.

It is worth observing that the second hedge does not reduce the information conveyed about the speaker's sense datum to zero, so that the more cautious of the two statements about the taste is not like a purely ostensive statement. This may seem surprising given that it has a negligible possibility of error, i.e. error about the inclination to apply the word 'tarragon' now. The explanation is that, although the truth conditions of the more cautious statement do not include the fact that the sauce actually does taste of tarragon to the speaker, it is a probable inference that it does, and such inferences are included in the information conveyed by the statement when it is made by this speaker. We argue from this speaker's powers of discrimination to the actual character of his sense datum, even when he himself uses the second hedge.

But my inquiry is concerned with the less cautious statement, 'It tastes like tarragon to me now.' Is this really immune from all but purely verbal error? So far, my argument has been only that, if Austin is right, it is not, and therefore that, if the second hedge had been added in this case, it would have neutralised the effect not only of purely verbal error but also of error that is not purely verbal. But is Austin right? There are really two distinguishable questions here. Is it sometimes difficult to identify the character of a sense datum, quite apart from finding the right word for its character? And, if so, does that difficulty sometimes cause actual error? I am, of course, presenting the problem in a way that differs from Austin's way of presenting it, for he thought that sense-datum statements are a motley crowd not deserving a single name, and he did not mark off any class of purely verbal errors, because he believed that wrong ideas had become too firmly associated with this distinction. I, though, have picked out a sub-class of sense-datum statements from the motley crowd, and have drawn a non-tendentious distinction between purely verbal errors and others.

Austin's view is that I may find it difficult to identify the character of a so-called 'sense datum', quite apart from finding the right word for its character. He suggests two main ways in which this may come about. My past experience may not have equipped me to identify its character at a specific level, and it may happen to be an especially difficult case. Ayer gives a convincing example of the second kind in *The Problem of Knowledge*:

> Suppose that two lines of approximately the same length are drawn so that they both come within my field of vision, and I am then asked to say whether either of them looks to me to be the longer, and if so which. I think I might well be uncertain how to answer. But it seems very strange to say that what, in such a case, I should be uncertain about would be the meaning of the English expression 'looks longer than'. . . . I know quite well how the words 'looks longer than' are used in English. It is just that in the present instance I am not sure whether, as a matter of fact, either of the lines does look longer to me than the other.[30]

Cases of the first kind, in which my previous experience has been deficient, are more various. I may never have encountered a particular shade of colour or a precise taste, or I may never have had to locate a pain precisely in a particular part of my body. (In the latter case, the tendency to confuse the two hedges is very strong, and it must be resisted.) Or, as Austin implies, my previous experience may have been deficient not in its range but in its volume, so that I have not had enough practice in such fine discriminations. It is clear that in this kind of case too I may be uncertain about the truth, quite apart from finding the right words to express it.

However, this is not enough to prove that such statements are liable to error that is not purely verbal. For it may be objected that, although uncertainty and doubt are possible in these cases, it does not follow that actual error is possible, because the speaker may always use the second hedge when in doubt. There is also another, quite different objection that may be made at this point. I have argued that it is a necessary condition of purely verbal error that the speaker should have been expressing in the wrong way a correct belief about his sense datum – a condition that clearly would not be fulfilled in the cases that have just been mentioned, if he ended by making a statement without the second hedge. But the necessity for this condition may be challenged on the ground that, even when it is not fulfilled, the speaker is still misapplying his chosen predicate ψ, and so is revealing that he does not know its meaning. This objection is the one against which Ayer is arguing in the passage just quoted from *The Problem of Knowledge*.

Let us first inquire whether the fact of uncertainty is associated with the possibility of error that is not purely verbal. Austin assumes that it is,[31] but an argument is needed. Of course, no argument will prove that all sense-datum statements, however unspecific, run an appreciable risk of error that is not purely verbal. For decrease in this risk is, in part, a function of decrease in specificity. But the following argument shows that some sense-datum statements run an appreciable risk of this kind. Suppose that a person is asked to make a sequence of reports on his sense-data, all of the same general kind, but each more difficult than the preceding one. For example, he is given a sequence of pairs of artificially produced bodily sensations and asked to report the relative positions of the members of each pair, or he is asked to say how various substances taste to him at the moment. As the difficulty increases, he will become more and more liable to error, if he makes unguarded statements about his sense-data, and so his statements will become more guarded. But the increase in his caution will not be the right function of the increase in the difficulty of the task except in those areas in which experience has taught him the limits of his powers of discrimination, and even then the lesson is not always easy to apply. Therefore such sequences will include cases in which he hazards a statement about his sense datum without the second hedge, and gets it wrong, but not in a purely verbal way.

This is not a demonstrative argument. It offers general grounds for expecting a certain result from a certain experiment. But, unless we carry out the experiment, that is the best that we can do, because the question is an empirical one, and the result cannot be deduced with certainty from a theory of language. Those who reject this argument assume that, whenever a person does not know the character of his sense datum, he will know that he does not know it, and so will use the second hedge. But I have found this empirically false.

Next consider the objection that in all such cases the speaker is misapplying his ill chosen predicate, ψ, and therefore does not know its meaning. The plausibility of this objection depends on the type of ψ. If ψ is a complex sortal, knowledge of its meaning will not necessarily include the ability to recognise instances, even when the instances are not unusually difficult instances of ψs. But if ψ signifies a sensory quality, knowlege of its meaning will some-times include this ability. For example, if someone said that he did not know whether he had a pain or not, it would be natural to retort that in that case he did not know the meaning of the word 'pain'. However, it would be a mistake to generalise this to all words signifying sensory qualities. For the reason why we take this line about pain is only that there is no difficulty in identifying it, except, perhaps, in a few marginal types of case. Consequently, when someone says that he does not know whether he has a pain, we infer that he knows what he has but does not know the name for it, perhaps because he is too young. But this will not always be true of a person who is uncertain whether the sauce tastes of tarragon to him at the moment. So the attempt to enlarge the class of verbal errors to include unintentionally false statements collapses, and it is better to return to the criterion of purely verbal error that was proposed earlier.

The advantage of the criterion is clear. It limits the class of purely verbal errors so that it does not engulf all instances of error in a totally uninteresting way. The method of fixing the limit is to distinguish between three things – the actual character of the sense datum, its believed character and its stated character – and so to distinguish two reasons why the third thing may fail to match the first: namely, the second may fail to match the first or the third may fail to match the second. If someone rejects this criterion and prefers to say that all mismatches between the third thing and the first are cases of purely verbal error, what he says is uninteresting. It is against this position that Austin's strategy is most effective: if all such mistakes are qualified as 'merely verbal', we cannot 'laugh this off as a quite trivial qualification'.[32]

If sense-datum statements are liable to error, of whatever kind, we need answers to the two questions that were posed earlier only to be postponed. How does a sense-datum statement go beyond the immediate object? And what is the precise connection between fallibility and corrigibility? Ayer discusses the first question in 'Basic Propositions'[33] and the second in 'Privacy'.[34]

In 'Basic Propositions' he argues convincingly that 'This sense-datum is ψ' does not entail that anything else is like it, and so does not entail that anything else is ψ. But if it does not entail that another ψ sense datum was previously had by me, how can it be a description? For surely 'to describe something is to relate it ... at least to something one has experienced in the past'.³⁵ One reaction to this problem would be to narrow the focus of a sense-datum statement, and to maintain that it 'refers solely to the content of a single experience' and does not 'go beyond the immediate object' in any way at all. But this leads to an *impasse* which has already been explored. Ayer's new solution is that, though ψ is a description of the sense datum, its truth or falsity depends on whether its application conforms to a meaning rule. The merit of this solution is that it treats the meaning of the sense-datum statement as something that is fixed independently of the character of the sense datum to which it refers, and so allows for a real possibility of mismatch, and that it does this without loading the statement with an entailment that evidently does not belong to it.

However, it is not a complete solution to the problem. For the concept of a purely ostensive meaning rule linking a word with a class of instances needs further elucidation. Moreover, in a particular case the audience will hardly be satisfied with the mere assumption that the speaker is following the relevant meaning rule correctly. They will require evidence that he is doing so, and often the only convincing evidence will be that he has had previous ψ sense data. This is connected with a point that was made earlier. It is obvious that the truth condition of 'This tastes like tarragon to me now' is that it should taste like tarragon to me now. But when I make the statement, my audience want to know whether it really does taste like tarragon to me now, because that is the fact that they will use, once it is established. But their inference from my statement to the fact will depend on their conviction that my powers of discrimination are sufficiently great, and that, in its turn, will depend on what they believe my past experience to have been. So, although Ayer correctly excludes a reference to the past from the truth conditions of what I say, the credibility of what I say brings it in again.

Finally, there is the question how fallibility and corrigibility are connected with one another. This question is conjured off the scene by those who use 'incorrigible' to mean 'infallible', but when the two things are distinguished it is evident that fallibility does not always have to be corrigible, because some mistakes may go undetected. Indeed, when we hesitate to accept someone's apparently honest sense-datum statement, we seldom have such strong independent evidence about the character of his sense datum that we are prepared to override him, and we usually remain hesitant until he accepts our correction. So Russell says in a passage already quoted.

It is true that, in the sense in which we infer eclipses, there can be evidence against a present judgement of perception, but this evidence is inductive and merely probable, and cannot stand against 'the evidence of the senses'. When we have analyzed a judgement of perception in this way, we are left with something which cannot be *proved* to be false.[36]

In 'Privacy' Ayer seems to go further in this direction. He begins by conceding that, when someone makes a sense-datum statement, he may make a mistake that is not purely verbal. (He is not sure that this ever happens, partly because he uses a mixed set of examples, which include expressions of thoughts as well as descriptions of feelings. See p. 14.) Then he argues that, though he

> may not be infallible ... still his word is sovereign. If he is not infallible, others may be right when he is wrong. Even so their testimony is subordinate to his in the same way and for the same reason as the testimony of clairvoyants is subordinate to that of eyewitnesses. If his reports are corrigible, it must be that he himself is ready to correct them, not after an interval of time in which a lapse of memory would rob him of his authority, but as it were in the same breath.[37]

This looks like Russell's thesis, that the speaker cannot be proved wrong in cases where he rejects the correction. But in fact Ayer may be going further than this. For, when he is arguing for the analogy with eyewitnesses and clairvoyants, he says that 'it enters into the logic of statements about perceptible physical events that the eyewitnesses have the final say in deciding whether they are true or false'.[38] This suggests that in a case of unresolvable conflict the authority of an eyewitness is enough to support the verdict that what he said was true, rather than not proven false. On the other hand, when he summarises his thesis about sense-datum statements, he says that 'the logic of these statements is such that, if others were to contradict him [i.e. the speaker], we should not be entitled to say that they were right, so long as he honestly maintained his stand against them'.[39] However, when he first introduces the thesis, he puts it in a way that suggests the more extreme interpretation 'One may be the last authority with regard to one's own present thoughts and feelings, even though one's reports of them are not infallible'.[40] Moreover, he finds the speaker's privilege mysterious, and though both versions make it mysterious, the extreme one makes it more so: '... it is obvious that having a private method of detecting something is not sufficient to make one a final authority concerning it. ... Why indeed such a privilege should exist in the cases where it does is a question to which I have not found an answer. We may just have to take it for a fact for which no further reasons can be given.'[41]

The fundamental question here is about the source of the speaker's authority. In a particular case we should prefer the testimony of an eye-witness to that of a clairvoyant, not because clairvoyants can establish their powers only with the help of eyewitnesses (though this is true), but because eyewitnesses are, in general, more likely to be right. But, if this is the source of the authority of the person who has the sense datum, even the moderate thesis is wrong. For consider a particular case in which error, if it occurred, would not be purely verbal. Surely the circumstantial evidence against the speaker's report might well carry the day. For example, it might lead us to reject his statement about the relative positions of two artificially produced bodily sensations, provided that he did not use the second hedge.

The case against the extreme thesis is similar, but stronger; for all that is required against it is that circumstantial evidence against a sense-datum statement should sometimes lead us to say 'Not proven.' Moreover, given that the source of the speaker's authority is only that he is more likely to be right, it would be utterly mysterious if we allowed his say-so to be sufficient condition of truth in all cases. Here the analogy with eyewitnesses and clairvoyants may be misleading. It is true that the best evidence is generally that provided by eyewitnesses, and that whatever confidence we place in clairvoyants' reports is based on their general agreement with those of eyewitnesses. But that does not prevent us from concluding in a particular case that what the eyewitness said was false and what the clairvoyant said was true. If that seems to be an unlikely outcome, the reason is only that we put less trust in the reports of clairvoyants than in carefully collected circumstantial evidence about the character of another person's sense datum.

However, there is also another, quite different source of the speaker's authority. In real life the character of his sense datum is usually unimportant, and it is politeness that leads us to speak as if his say-so were a sufficient condition of the truth of his statement about it. For example, a chef would be interested in a diner's sense datum only if he had been labouring to produce a sensory effect in him, or, more rarely, if his sense datum provided the only evidence of the taste of the sauce. (Another example: he was drinking the last surviving bottle of a particular wine dating from the nineteenth century.) Otherwise, the character of his sense data would not be sufficiently important for his statement to be worth challenging or testing, and so social reasons for letting him have the last word would begin to operate.

This trivial fact is worth stating explicitly, because it is part of the basis of the common intuition that the speaker is the final authority on the character of his sense datum. Indeed, it was always evident that the intuition would have to be explained in some such way. For, if we allow that the speaker may make a mistake that is not purely verbal, and if we say that nevertheless circumstantial evidence would never convince us that he had made a mistake, there is a mystery. Why should we *never* conclude that his statement was false?

If the reason is social, the mystery is dispelled. But then it is imperative not to retain the intuition in the context of a philosophical theory that removes its support by treating the truth or falsity of all sense-datum statements as an important scientific question. If a person describes a pain that he has, he expects different reactions from his doctor and from a bored travelling companion. At this point other small biases contribute to what in the end becomes a substantially mistaken philosphical theory. Perhaps we concentrate with obsessive enthusiasm on the special case of pain outside a clinical context. Or perhaps we overlook the difference between making a sense-datum statement with and making it without the second hedge. There are many ways in which a philosopher may come to exaggerate the privileges of sense-datum statements. It is even important that he asks, 'How can *I* be wrong about *my* sense data?'

In the end, Ayer's exaggeration of their incorrigibility is slight, because he does not definitely opt for the more extreme thesis, but is nevertheless committed at least to the moderate thesis. His final position on the question of whether sense-datum statements are immune from all but verbal error is equally cautious, but more explicit – namely, agnosticism with an inclination to a negative answer. In general, what makes his contributions to this topic so interesting is the complexity and judiciousness of his arguments. He gives due weight to many conflicting considerations, and, though he does not always arrive at definitive solutions, his investigations are more successful than many that do reach them.

NOTES

1. Bertrand Russell, *The Analysis of Mind* (London; Allen and Unwin, 1921) pp. 141–2.
2. Bertrand Russell, *The Problems of Philosophy* (London: Oxford University Press, 1912) p. 47.
3. Ibid., p. 46.
4. Bertrand Russell, 'Knowledge by Acquaintance, Knowledge by Description', in *Mysticism and Logic*, 2nd edn (London: Allen and Unwin, 1917) p. 215.
5. J. L. Austin, 'Other Minds', in *Philosophical Papers*, ed. J. O. Urmson and G. Warnock, 2nd edn (Oxford: Clarendon Press, 1970) p. 65.
6. Russell, *Problems*, p. 110.
7. Bertrand Russell, 'The Relation of Sense-data to Physics', in *Mysticism and Logic*, p. 147.
8. Bertrand Russell, *Principia Mathematica* (Cambridge: Cambridge U. P., 1910) vol. I, p. 43.
9. Russell, *Problems*, p. 136.
10. Bertrand Russell, *An Inquiry into Meaning and Truth* (London: Allen and Unwin, 1940) p. 137.
11. Ibid.
12. Bertrand Russell, *Human Knowledge, its Scope and Limits* (London: Allen and Unwin, 1948) p. 133.
13. Ibid.
14. Ibid.
15. Russell, *Inquiry*, pp. 137–8.
16. A. J. Ayer, *Russell and Moore: The Analytical Heritage* (Cambridge, Mass.: Harvard University Press, 1971) pp. 108–9.
17. Russell, *Human Knowledge*, p. 133.
18. Russell, *Inquiry*, p. 139.
19. A. J. Ayer, *Language, Truth and Logic*, 1st edn (London: Gollancz, 1936) ch. 5. In the 2nd edn (London: Gollancz, 1946) this passage is on p. 91.
20. Russell, *Problems*, p. 110 (quoted earlier – see note 6).
21. Ayer, *Language, Truth and Logic*, 2nd edn, p. 92.
22. Ibid., pp. 10–11.
23. A. J. Ayer, 'Basic Propositions', in *Problems of Analysis*, ed. Max Black (London: Routledge, 1954); repr. in A. J. Ayer, *Philosophical Essays* (London: Macmillan, 1954).
24. A. J. Ayer, 'Privacy', in *Proceedings of the British Academy*, XLV (1959).
25. A. J. Ayer, 'Has Austin Refuted Sense-data?', in *Symposium on J. L. Austin*, ed. K. T. Fann (London: Routledge and Kegan Paul, 1969) p. 305.
26. Austin, in *Philosophical Papers*, ed. Urmson and Warnock, pp. 60–1.
27. Russell, *Human Knowledge*, p. 133 (quoted earlier – see note 17).
28. Similar difficulties are discussed by C. B. Martin and Max Deutscher in 'The Causal Theory of Memory', *Philosophical Review*, LXXV (1966), 161–96.
29. Ayer, in *Proceedings of the British Academy*, XLV, 56–7.
30. A. J. Ayer, *The Problem of Knowledge* (Harmondsworth: Penguin, 1956) p. 65.
31. Austin, in *Philosophical Papers*, ed. Urmson and Warnock, pp. 60–1. Cf. J. L. Austin, *Sense and Sensibilia* (Oxford: Clarendon Press, 1962) pp. 42–3.
32. Ibid., p. 112.
33. See note 23.
34. See note 24.
35. Ayer, in *Philosophical Essays*, pp. 116–17.

36. Russell, *Inquiry*, p. 139.
37. Ayer, in *Proceedings of the British Academy*, xlv, 59.
38. Ibid.
39. Ibid.
40. Ibid., p. 57.
41. Ibid., pp. 64–5.

4 Perception, Sense Data and Causality

D. M. ARMSTRONG

I suppose that every beginner in philosophy is attracted to the representative theory of perception. Certainly I was. However, John Anderson, my teacher at Sydney University, held a direct realist theory. He quickly convinced me of the general plausibility of his position, but I saw, or thought I saw, considerable difficulties of detail. One of the first philosophical tasks which I set myself was to work out a detailed defence of direct realism.

I am very grateful to Professor Ayer, because in the early stages of this enterprise he encouraged me to proceed with it. This encouragement was, of course, entirely disinterested, because Ayer rejected and still rejects direct realism. For my own part, I greatly admire, and have learnt much from, long consideration and reconsideration of the problems of the philosophy of perception. Indeed, all students of these problems have reason to be grateful for his work. He will not agree with the views put forward in this paper, but will know that my voicing of disagreement with him springs from no spirit of contention.

I

It is customary, and I think it is useful, to classify philosophical theories of perception as direct realist, representative (representative realist) and phenomenalist. Ayer now definitely rejects phenomenalism, as may be seen from his *The Central Questions of Philosophy*.[1] His reason for this is that phenomenalism must give an account of the physical world largely in terms of unfulfilled conditional statements, but that such statements are not adequate to this task. He would therefore perhaps agree that we should look either to some form of direct realist or else to some form of representative theory. He, at any rate, now favours a version of the representative theory.[2]

If we do reject phenomenalism, and so take a realistic view of the physical world, we must think of the world as acting causally upon our minds, *via* a certain causal chain, to produce perceptual awareness of the world. If we also postulate entities such as sense data intermediate between the physical world and perceptual awareness of the world, then it is natural to consider what place they have, or do not have, in this causal chain. In this essay I shall try to show that this question involves a good deal of difficulty for representative theories, difficulty which does not arise for direct realism. At the same time, however, I shall indicate one problem where the representative theory may perhaps have an advantage over direct realism.

I begin by considering the notion of perception of a physical object and the causal role which the object plays in such a perception.

II

It is clear that many perceptual statements assert that a *relation* of perception holds between a perceiver, on the one hand, and a physical object, event or state of affairs, on the other. This is not the case for all perceptual statements. If somebody looks down a kaleidoscope, it can be said that he sees a symmetrical arrangement of coloured objects. Together with many other philosophers, Ayer used to, and I take it still does, say that this situation involves a relation holding between the perceiver and a symmetrical arrangement of coloured objects. But everybody would agree that these coloured objects are not *physical* objects. It can be said truly that the perceiver *seems to see* a symmetrical arrangement of coloured physical objects. But *seeming to see* cannot be a relation in this context, because one term of the 'relation' – the physical objects which seem to be seen – does not exist. However, it can truly be said that in this situation the perceiver sees a number of irregularly disposed pieces of coloured glass. This *is* a relation of perception holding between the perceiver and something physical which is perceived.

What is the nature of the relation which holds when a perceiver perceives something physical? If we abstract from the non-relational nature of the terms related, it is hard to discern anything except a particular case of *causation*. The physical object, event or whatever, acts upon the sense organs of the perceiver and produces certain perceptions in the perceiver's mind. These perceptions are said to be perceptions of the object. But they can be characterised, and characterised *as* perceptions, in a way which does not entail the existence of the physical object.[3]

It seems clear, at the very least, that a causal relation is a necessary condition for this relation of perception. This is shown by considering cases where a physical object does not act to produce perception in a perceiver. In no such case will we admit that that object is perceived. Suppose that a perceiver's eyes are directed towards a mirror and, as a result, he is having certain visual perceptions. Suppose that, behind the surface of the glass, the physical scene exists exactly as these perceptions present it. The perceiver's mirror double, his identical twin except for left–right reversal, is as far behind the surface of the glass as the perceiver is in front of it, and so for everything else 'seen in the mirror'. It is clear that the perceiver is not perceiving these objects. Rather, he is perceiving his own body and other objects in front of the surface of the glass. These objects visually appear to him to be in a place where they are not and are subject to left–right distortion. Suppose, now, that the mirror is a 'distorting' one (that is, suppose it distorts still further) and suppose that the physical objects behind the mirror faithfully copy these distortions. It is still the undistorted objects in front of the mirror which the perceiver is perceiving.

It is clear why the objects in front of the mirror are said to be perceived and the objects behind the surface are not said to be perceived. The objects in front are acting upon the perceiver to produce his perceptions, the objects behind are not. A particularly striking case is the perception of stars. The perception we have of a star almost completely fails to represent the nature of the physical object which, years before, set in train the process by which we come to have the perception. Yet we are prepared to say that we see the star, because the star is the cause of our perception.[4]

Once it is granted that causation is necessary for this relation of perception, it may be asked what more is required to yield sufficiency. It is clear, of course, that not every case where a physical object causes perception in a perceiver is a case where the perceiver perceives that object. A brain probe might bring about a visual perception, but we would not say that we saw the probe. Even if it be added that the physical object must act by stimulating sense organs, it is not the case that every object which produces perceptions in this way is perceived. However, all that seems further required to yield necessary and sufficient conditions for the relation of perception is (1) a condition which ensures that the perception in some way reflects, however distortedly, the nature of the object perceived, and (2) some restrictions upon the nature of the causal chain which brings the perception to be. I do not know how to spell out these restrictions in detail, but it seems that nothing more than such restrictions are required. If so, the relation of perception which holds when a perceiver perceives a physical object is fundamentally a causal relation.

So far, nothing very new. But I think it is possible to make a little further progress in explicating this relation of perception by reflecting upon the nature of causation. When one object acts upon another to produce in the latter an effect of a certain nature, it does not act as an undifferentiated whole but rather in virtue of certain of its properties. In depressing a scale, for instance, an object acts solely, or almost solely, in virtue of its mass. Anything closely similar in mass, acting in the same causal context, would produce the same, or almost the same, effect.

This trite reflection may be applied to the relation of perception. Consider seeing an apple. Whether the perceptions produced by the apple be veridical or illusory, it is clear that it is not the apple as a whole which acts upon the eyes to produce these perceptions. If, for example, the back half of the apple had been cut away, this would have had no effect upon the resultant perception. Although by hypothesis we are seeing a *whole* apple, the back half of the apple is playing no causal role in the perceptual situation. Furthermore, we could obviously pare away a good deal more of the apple and yet the object left might still have exactly the same perceptual effect. All that is required for that effect is that a portion of the apple's surface have certain properties. (They will in fact be reflectional properties.) Only certain parts of the apple, and certain properties of these parts, will play any role in bestowing these properties.

If we consider these facts, there seems to be a clear sense in which when, as we say, somebody sees an apple, then 'in truth and strictness', as Berkeley would put it, they see something far less. They see a much smaller object and see only a selection of the properties of that smaller object. (Note, once again, that this reduced object does not have to create *veridical* perceptions in the apple-seer, even veridical perceptions of the facing surface.) Or, to put the point as Frank Jackson has put the point in a similar context (unpublished work), when it is true that somebody sees an apple, then they see it *in virtue of* seeing very much less than the apple. To use Jackson's illustration, a car may touch the kerb in virtue of the fact that a portion of the surface of one of its wheels is touching the kerb. If we remember that perceiving a physical object is a causal relation, and that things do not act causally as undifferentiated wholes, we see that an apple is seen in virtue of seeing much less than the apple.[5]

III

So much for the relation of perception which holds between perceiver and physical objects. I now wish to see whether the results obtained so far can be applied in criticism of the representative theory of perception. In a representative theory, no physical object or state of affairs is ever immediately perceived. What are immediately perceived (or, perhaps, 'sensed') are representative or immediate entities variously named. I shall speak of sense data. The perceived table, or whatever, stands in a certain relation to a sense datum. This is a causal relation. The table brings the sense datum into existence. But the sense datum also stands in some relation to the perceiving mind or, if the sense datum is held to be within the mind, to the rest of the mind. That a *relation* is involved becomes clear when we note that there is never any question for sense-datum theorists of the sense datum's being perceived (or immediately perceived, or sensed) yet not existing. We noted at the beginning of the previous section that 'perceive' may sometimes have the force of 'seem to perceive', and that what the perceiver seems to perceive need not exist. But such a possibility is never admitted in the case of sense data. If the sense data always exist, then they must always stand in some relation or other to the mind or the rest of the mind. For the representative theory, then, perception of a physical object involves *two* relations, a relation of the object to the sense datum and a relation of the sense datum to the mind or the rest of the mind.

What is the nature of this second relation? It seems clear that, however unconsciously, the relation between perceiver and sense datum has been modelled on the relation between perceiver and physical object. If so, then the relation between perceiver and sense datum should be a causal one. But in any case it is a natural hypothesis that the sense datum, epistemologically intermediate as it is between physical object and perceiving mind, is also causally intermediate. Let us therefore explore the consequences of this hypothesis. We shall afterwards explore the consequences of denying that sense data play this causal role. My contention is that both hypotheses involve great difficulties for the representative theory.

First, then, let us take it that sense data are causal intermediates. Physical objects act upon the perceiver's sense organs, which in turn act upon some portion of his central nervous system. As a result of this action, sense data are brought into existence. (There may be mixed theories according to which *in some cases* the physical object causes perception of the physical object in the perceiver without the causal chain's involving intermediate sense data.) The sense data act upon the perceiver's mind.[6] As a result, the perceiver is caused to have perceptions of (or to sense) the sense data. These perceptions in turn bring about perceptions of the physical object.

We have noted that the perception *of* a physical object, although caused by that object, can be characterised, and characterised as a perception, independently of the existence of that physical object. In the same way, if the relation between the sense datum and the perception of the sense datum is causal, then it should be possible to characterise the perception of that sense datum, and characterise it as a perception, independently of the existence of the sense datum.

Sense data are generally credited with having certain *sensible qualities* and *sensible relations* (to other sense data): sensible redness, sensible adjacency and so on. We have noted that a thing acting as a cause produces its effect in virtue of some, and only some, of its properties. A natural hypothesis, therefore, is that the sense data act upon the perceiver to bring about perceptions of the sense data in virtue of their sensible qualities and relations. The perception of a sense datum as having a certain sensible quality will presumably occur as a causal result of the sense datum's possession of that sensible quality. Or, at least, this may be presumed to be the normal case.

Cause and effect, however, are 'distinct existences'. It must therefore be logically possible for the cause to exist, but not its customary effect or, indeed, any effect at all. It follows that the perceiver's perception or sensing of the sense datum does not have to be a *veridical* perception or sensing. Just as a perceiver may perceive a physical object, but not perceive the object as it is, so the perceiver's perception of the sense datum may misrepresent the sense datum. It is true that an effect may be described in such a way (for instance, as an effect) that it entails the existence of a cause. But the perception of a sense datum, described as a certain perceptual happening in the mind, does not entail the existence of its sense-datum cause. It follows that the perception of the sense datum need not be incorrigible. Still less need the perception of it be comprehensive, embracing every feature of it.

This result is immensely important. Once it is granted that the perception of the sense datum need not be veridical, it can be questioned whether there is any particular reason to postulate sense data. Historically, one of the major reasons for postulating them has been to provide a non-physical object which is veridically perceived in the case of non-veridical perception of physical objects. When Macbeth seems to see a physical dagger which is not there, many theorists have thought that a non-physical dagger-like object must be postulated to be the thing which *is* veridically perceived. But if it is possible that even the sense datum should not be veridically perceived, then this traditional motivation for postulating sense data is removed. This is not to say that the postulation is incoherent, simply that a major reason for making it is gone.

IV

If we accept the above sketch of the causal role of sense data in perception – a role which, it seems to me, it is natural to give them – then I can find only one argument for postulating sense data which seems to have any force. A case can be made for postulating them as *the bearers of the secondary qualities.*

Colour, sound, taste, smell and so on certainly seem to be *perceived* qualities. If they are qualities, then it is reasonable to say that they are qualities of something. They perceptually *appear* to be qualities of physical objects, or physical states of affairs, or both. But there is a line of argument, based upon reasonably plausible premises, which suggests that they cannot be qualities of physical objects. Sense data are then introduced as alternative bearers.

There is one view, which I favour myself, according to which the secondary qualities are nothing but – that is, are identical with – their physical correlates. Colours, and this means *perceived* colours, the colours which persons blind from birth are supposed to lack acquaintance with, can, I believe, be identified with light-waves, felt heat can be identified with mean kinetic energy, heard sound can be identified with certain sorts of vibration in the air or other medium. This view is, of course, phenomenologically im-plausible, but I do not think that phenomenological considerations should weigh heavily when faced with the systematic considerations in favour of the identification. The identification is the natural view to take if we want to respect what is known, or plausibly believed, about the causal order of nature, and yet at the same time want to allow that the secondary qualities bestow causal efficacy upon the particulars which they qualify. (An important reason for accepting the second of these propositions is that it is hard to see how we could ever come to know of the existence of causally idle properties.)

If this 'realistic reduction' of the secondary qualities can be carried through, then I can find no argument for inserting sense data into the perceptual causal chain. Suppose, however, as Ayer and many others would maintain, that the reduction cannot be carried through. Can *irreducible* secondary qualities be plausibly thought to qualify physical objects?

If physical objects are conceived of as they are conceived of in what Wilfrid Sellars calls the 'manifest image' of the world, then there is no particular problem in attributing the secondary qualities to them. However, the natural sciences, and in particular physics, have now given us a 'scientific image' of the world which is in certain respects incompatible with the manifest image. For instance, in the scientific image, the ordinary continuously solid physical objects of the manifest image are replaced by swarms of 'fundamental particles' in what is, however, largely empty space. The conflict between manifest and scientific image would be resolved in favour of the former if an operationalistic or instrumentalistic view of physics could be accepted. However, with Sellars and many others, I believe that this strategy is hopelessly implausible. (A position more cautiously taken up by Ayer in the *Central Questions*, p. 110.) In the conflict of the images, the manifest must give way to the scientific.

It is, however, difficult to hold simultaneously that (1) the scientific image of the world is broadly correct; (2) the secondary qualities are irreducible; and yet (3) the secondary qualities are qualities of physical objects. Granted (1) and (2), the secondary qualities are additional properties to those which appear in the theories and explanations of physics. Proposition (3) then becomes difficult to maintain. First, as J. J. C. Smart has repeatedly emphasised, we should need to postulate highly implausible bridge laws which link the simple or relatively simple secondary qualities with incredible physical complexities. Secondly, there is no evidence that the secondary qualities *so conceived* make any contribution to what G. F. Stout called 'the executive order of nature'. As already mentioned, it is difficult to see how we could ever become aware of causally idle properties of physical objects. In particular, our perceptions would be the same whether or not the properties existed. In the light of these two difficulties, it seems plausible to postulate sense data to be bearers of the secondary qualities, and further to make such qualities causally efficacious in the production of perceptions of the sense data.[7]

I have suggested that the argument of the previous paragraph is the only plausible reason for inserting sense data into the perceptual causal chain. I re-emphasise that the argument depends upon premises one of which I do not accept, although I admit its phenomenological plausibility: that of the irreducibility of the secondary qualities. Suppose, however, that all the premises of the argument are accepted. Are there other ways, besides the postulation of sense data, to deal with the problem of the location of the secondary qualities? Two suggestions come to mind.

First, it might be maintained that the secondary qualities do not exist, that they are, in Berkeley's phrase, 'a false imaginary glare'. It is clear that the secondary qualities *appear* to qualify physical things. It is granted, for the sake of the argument, that it is impossible that they should be identical with complex physical properties of these objects. But why must it be assumed that they qualify *something*? Perhaps they appear to qualify physical objects, do not qualify these objects, *and do not qualify anything else*. This would be a 'disappearance' theory of the secondary qualities parallel to the 'disappearance' theory of the mind advocated by Richard Rorty and Paul Feyerabend.

I think that it would be freely granted that we can form the conception of complex, analysable properties which certain objects appear to possess but which in fact nothing possesses. Following what might be called an 'Aristotelian' tradition, I should argue that such properties do not exist. In the realm of properties, they resemble the present King of France in the realm of particulars. A more 'Platonic' point of view is that such properties do have some sort of existence. But it would be generally granted, I take it, that such complex properties need not be *instantiated* (at any time). Why then should we not form the conception of an *unanalysable* property which objects appear to possess (we have perceptions as of objects having that property) but which in fact nothing possesses? There are deep prejudices here, or, perhaps I should more fairly say, deep intuitions. There are philosophies such as logical atomism which enshrine these intuitions ('at least the simple elements must be real'). But it is not clear to me that these intuitions are sacrosanct. I suspect that they involve confusions of meaning with reference and intentional objects with real ones.

Suppose, however, that this solution is unacceptable on the ground that, although the secondary qualities cannot be qualities of the objects which they appear to be qualities of, they must be qualities of some particulars. Are we forced to postulate sense data to be these particulars?

A possibility is that these qualities should be associated, not with the things perceived, be they sense data or physical objects, but with the perceptions themselves, the perceivings rather than the perceived. It seems implausible to say that perceptions are particulars. They are, rather, states of particulars, states of minds or portions of minds. But it might be suggested that the secondary qualities really qualify these particulars, yet perceptually appear to qualify the (physical) things which the perceptions are perceptions *of*. If I understand him, a view of this sort is favoured by Wilfrid Sellars.[8]

It is possible for there to be unconscious perceptions, perceptions which we have but are unaware of having. Normally, however, we not merely have perceptions but are introspectively (if unselfconsciously) aware that we are having the perceptions. The present hypothesis is that in being aware of our perceptions we are aware of the secondary qualities. But, by a phenomenological mistake, the secondary qualities appear to be qualities of the objects *perceived*.

The upholder of sense data can hardly object in principle to this wholesale mislocation of properties. For he himself maintains something very similar. For consider our hypothetical perceptions (sensings) of sense data. Phenomenologically, they appear to be perceptions not of sense data but of physical things. Hence the sense-datum theorist must admit that the secondary qualities, which he takes to qualify sense data, *appear* to qualify physical things. How, then, can he refuse to consider the hypothesis that they qualify not sense data or physical things, but minds?

W. D. Joske has raised an objection to this suggestion. Consider the particular case of colour. In visually perceiving a surface, it is perceived as coloured. Furthermore, if the colour is not perceived, then the spatial properties of the surface are not perceived. How is this possible if the colour is merely wrongly attributed to the surface, while the spatial properties are rightly attributed?

I do not think that the objection is insuperable. It may be noted, first, that it seems not to be a necessary proposition that visual perception of spatial properties demands that the objects having the spatial properties be perceived as coloured. Motion and, in some degree, size may be perceived out of the corner of the eye without any perception of colour, or even, perhaps, light and shade. It is a fact that objects in the centre of the visual field are perceived as coloured. It is also a fact that, if no colour differences are perceived in this centre, no spatial properties are perceived. But this might be explained by saying that the perception has an internal structure corresponding to the objects which seem to be perceived and that this structure is a colour structure. A change in the light-waves reflected by the thing perceived is represented *in the perception* as a change of colour. When we perceive 'the colour of a surface' we are really aware of the colour structure of our perceptions. We wrongly 'project' the colour onto the (genuinely perceived) surface. The changes induced in perception by coloured spectacles may furnish some sort of model. Our perceptions themselves act as permanent coloured spectacles. A consequence of this hypothesis would be that unconscious perception would not involve attribution of the secondary qualities to objects.

This second suggestion for dealing with irreducible secondary

qualities without postulating sense data has a truly epicyclic character, particularly when Joske's objection is taken into account. But
perhaps a small epicycle which gets rid of the great epicycle of
sense data may be justified. If it is unacceptable, a 'disappearance'
account of the secondary qualities may still be attempted.

v

In section III I tried to spell out the causal role which it seems
natural to attribute to sense data if we postulate them at all.
In this section I consider alternative accounts of this causal role.

I argued that, if sense data cause perceptions (sensings) of the
sense data, then it must be possible to characterise the perceptions
or sensings *as* perceptions or sensings, independently of the existence
of the sense data. It was this that seemed to make postulation
of sense data redundant, unless indeed they are required to be
bearers of the secondary qualities.

To get around this, it might be suggested that such perceptions
are 'transparent' or 'diaphanous'. Brought into existence by the
sense data, the perceptions are differentiated from each other in
nature solely by the differences of the sense data which are their
causes.

The problem about this suggestion is that perceptions of different
sense data must have different effects in the economy of the mind.
If traffic lights are to work, the perception of a green sense datum
must, in general at least, have a different effect upon the mind
from the perception of a red sense datum, yet this differentiation
cannot be achieved by perceptions which differ numerically only.
It is clear that the thing with causal effect must therefore be green
sense datum + perception of it, red sense datum + perception of
it, and so on. But then the perception is seen to be an idle wheel.
Why not, like the neutral monists, identify perception and sense
datum, although, unlike the neutral monists, retaining a physical
cause of the sense datum?[9] I believe that the position then reached,
if thought through just a little further, turns out to be the true
theory of perception: direct realism. But I shall leave this identification of perception and sense datum aside for the moment, because
we shall shortly reach it by another route.

Let us now consider the suggestion that sense datum and perception are related by some relation which does not involve the relation
of causation. I shall first argue against the hypothesis that the
related things are 'distinct existences', logically capable of existing
in independence of each other *as* sense data and perceptions, and
then consider the alternative.

If such distinct existence is assumed, then it seems that the logical corrigibility of the perception must be granted also. For it must be logically possible for the perception to exist while the sense datum does not. Once this is granted, we have the same reason for eliminating the sense datum that we had when considering the causal version of the theory.

There is also a further difficulty. According to the view now being criticised, stimulation of the sense organs brings into existence both the sense datum and the perception of the sense datum, but the two are brought into existence independently. But if the sense datum plays no part in bringing the perception into existence, what reason is there to think that the sense datum exists? In the causal version, the sense datum was criticised as an unnecessary link in the chain. But now it is even less. It is a causal by-product of the process which produces the perception. What reason can there be to postulate such a by-product? It might be different if there were *independent* reasons to postulate the sense datum – for instance, because it gave rise to further effects which had to be explained. But the only reason that has ever actually been offered for postulating the sense datum is the perception itself.

Once again, of course, the upholder of sense data may appeal to the special problem of the secondary qualities. But it does not seem that his position has been strengthened in any way by rejecting the causal relation. Rather, his position is weakened. If sense data are causally impotent, and if the secondary qualities qualify only sense data, then the secondary qualities bestow no causal potence. But, if a property bestows no powers, how can it be known?

Perhaps, then, the defender of sense data who nevertheless denies that they bring the perceptions of sense data into existence ought to maintain that the two are necessarily connected? The natural way to develop this hypothesis will be to maintain that the existence of a perception entails the existence of a sense datum corresponding to the content of the perception. (We can leave unanswered the question of whether the existence of a sense datum entails the existence of a perception of it: the problem of unsensed sensibilia.) The stimulation of sense organs may then be thought of as bringing into existence the following complex: perception necessarily connected with the corresponding sense datum.

Once again, however, the question arises of whether we have any reason to postulate the sense data. The problem is not evaded by invoking a necessary connection between the perceptions of the sense data and the sense data themselves. There is an old link in philosophical thinking between necessity and self-evidence. But it is now sufficiently appreciated that necessary truths need not be self-evident and that the existence of a necessary connection needs to be argued for. In this particular case, there seems no necessity to postulate the necessary connection. Why not simply postulate the perception, and make it a perception of what it appears to be a perception of, a perception of the physical world? Since, by hypothesis, the sense datum is causally inoperative, the perception of it cannot be 'transparent' or 'diaphanous'. For, if the perceptions are transparent and sense data causally inoperative, the different causal powers of different perceptions will be inexplicable. The perception must therefore have a content which reflects the nature of the sense datum. If so, why not let the perception do the whole work? Appeal may still be made to the problem of the location of the secondary qualities. But it does not seem that the necessary connection does anything to ease the problems raised by these qualities.

The hypothesis that perception and sense data are necessarily connected leads on to a final modification of the theory. Necessary connection suggests identity. The final hypothesis we might try is that perception and sense datum are necessarily connected because the sense datum *is* the perception.

I think that this is pretty nearly correct. But now the theory is no longer a representative theory, but a direct realist one. For, if the sense datum is the perception, it cannot simultaneously be the object of this perception. The perception must indeed have a content or intentional object: what seems to be perceived. Further-more, it should perhaps be said of sense data that they are not strictly identical with the perception, but are really the content or intentional objects of perceptions wrongly turned into real objects.[10] But, whether sense data are perceptions or the content of perceptions, they are *not* something perceived.

So in the end, I think, we arrive at a simple direct-realist theory. Physical objects stimulate the sense organs, giving rise to what may indifferently be called sensations, sensory states, perceivings or perceptions. They are not something perceived, although we may be, and regularly are, introspectively aware of them. They are perceptions of physical objects, perceived as having certain properties and relations. But the perceptions need not be veridical any more than our beliefs need all be true. If what a perception is a perception *of* is reified into an object, then we get a sense-datum theory, in just the same way that, if the content of a belief is reified into an object, we get subsistent propositions. Insoluble problems then arise about the causal role of these objects.

VI

I have tried to criticise representative theories of perception by asking what role is played in the causal process by the epistemological intermediates postulated by such theories. This line of thought may be intellectually unattractive to Professor Ayer on the grounds that, in his view, causal connections are not to be found within what, following F. P. Ramsey, he calls 'the primary system'.[11] If this ground is taken, I can only say that I believe that causal connection is as bed-rock a fact as any in the world, and that any theory of the world must give an account of how things are causally interrelated. In particular, I think that causal connection can be as directly, that is, non-inferentially, perceived as, say, colour, shape or heat. To introduce sense data, or similar objects, but not to raise questions about their place in the causal nexus seems to me to be quite arbitrary. I do, however, find a Humian view of causality quite incredible. One who, like Ayer, accepts a Humian view may find it easier to exclude causality from the primary system.

NOTES

1. A. J. Ayer, *The Central Questions of Philosophy* (London: Weidenfeld and Nicolson, 1973) ch. 5, section D.

2. Ibid., section E.

3. Whatever the argument from illusion may fail to prove, I take it that it does prove this. Whether the perceptions can be characterised as perceptions without using a *physical-object vocabulary* is a further question and one which will not be examined here.

4. The necessity for a causal relation if there is to be perception of a physical object is now widely granted. It is granted by Ayer in the *Central Questions*, ch. 5, section D, p. 87, although he does maintain that 'there must be a primitive account of perception which makes no reference to any causal relation between the percipient and the objects which he perceives'. But, if these 'objects' are physical objects, the objects which we are ordinarily said to perceive, then, I maintain, it is not possible to have a relation of perception without a relation of causation.

5. It seems to me that this point helps to give further support to Ayer's support for Russell's claim that ordinary judgements of perception such as 'This is a table' entail an inference (*Central Questions*, p. 80). If only a small portion of the table is actually causally responsible for the perception produced in the perceiver, it is reasonable to think that the *non-inferential* component of the perception, or the judgement based on the perception, is far less than 'This is a table.' If this is correct, then even a direct realist ought to maintain that most ordinary judgements of perception involve inference.

The point may also remind us of the hypothesis that G. E. Moore was forever considering: that visual sense data are identical with the facing portions of the surface of physical objects.

6. Some philosophers will demand that all talk of objects acting as causes be cashed in terms of events (events involving these objects), which are the true causes.

They may be right in this demand. If so, the event in question here would appear to be the coming-to-be of the sense datum or the monotonous event of the sense datum persisting.

7. It seems that Ayer does not think that the sort of considerations advanced in this paragraph are very weighty. At any rate, he expresses some preference for the view that the secondary qualities qualify macroscopic, but not microscopic, collections of the particles of physics (*Central Questions*, p. 110). I suggest that, if his view is correct, he thereby destroys the most plausible argument for sense data!

8. See Wilfrid Sellars, 'Empiricism and the Philosophy of Mind', repr. in his *Science, Perception and Reality* (London: Routledge and Kegan Paul, 1963) p. 194.

9. Frank Jackson, to whom I am greatly indebted for commenting on a draft of this paper, has objected that the perception need not be an idle wheel because it may be causally necessary for any sense datum to have its usual effect. It would not contribute to the difference of effect associated with the difference between a green and a red sense datum, but without it neither could bring about anything in the mind. My reply to this is to agree that this is a logical possibility. But there would seem to be no reason to believe that the perception was playing this role. In default of further evidence that the perception is playing this 'catalytic' role, we should therefore identify it with the sense datum. It is perhaps important to say here that I am not arguing that the various forms of the representative theory of perception which I have been examining are logically incoherent. I do not think that they are. I am simply arguing that we have no good reason to adopt them.

10. As argued by G. E. M. Anscombe, 'The Intentionality of Sensation: A Grammatical Feature', in *Analytical Philosophy*, 2nd ser., ed. R. J. Butler (Oxford: Blackwell, 1965).

11. Ayer, *Central Questions*, ch. 8, section B.

5 Sense Data Revisited

CHARLES TAYLOR

I want in this paper to return to a subject which has been out of fashion now for about two decades, the subject of sense data. I want to argue that there is something incoherent and in principle unacceptable about any account of experience which makes use of this notion.

But first I feel bound to say a few words in defence of this odd choice of topic. It may well be felt today that the issue of sense data is dead and buried; that phenomenalism succumbed under the weight of the many objections which were put up against it, and that it has passed from fashion not just following some collective caprice but for the good reason that it was solidly refuted. Why rake over these old coals; or, put less kindly, why flog this dead horse?

My first answer is that in philosophy dead horses have a tendency to ride again, sometimes after a suitable interval. A theory of knowledge based on sense data goes back at least to Locke, with intermittences and other different names; and we might also claim ascent to Descartes. Something which kept coming back for that long will probably return again one of these decades. Nor can one argue that it only returned in the past because it was not adequately refuted until contemporary times. For, as I should like to claim in the following pages, Kant dealt it what ought to have been a death blow.

But, more importantly, I believe that something interesting can be learned from a reflection on why sense-datum theories do not work, which we lose if they just slip from the agenda, vaguely discredited by their supposed conceptual confusions.

My argument, put briefly, will be this: that the sense datum is an impossible entity, that anything which could fulfil the requirements of a sense-datum theory could not be a (part of) perceptual experience.

The place to start this argument would be with an account of what sense data are. But an embarrassment arises immediately, in that impossible entities are, to say the least, difficult to characterise.

From the standpoint of the thesis I am defending, it is not at all surprising that the notion has been very difficult to pin down. But this very difficulty seems to block the kind of argument I want to make against it.

However, what one can do is to identify the characteristics which sense data are meant to have according to the theory, and then see if anything could have these and be part of experience. This involves approaching the question from the philosophical motives behind the introduction of the notion.

The motivation is in fact complex – I believe, part epistemological, and partly arising from a certain mechanistic psychology. I want to focus at first on the epistemological considerations. Why introduce sense data into one's theory of knowledge?

I should like to follow here one of the last discussions of this question before the whole issue slipped away: that in chapter 3 of Professor Ayer's *The Problem of Knowledge*.[1] This is not only an admirably clear treatment of the subject, but also has the advantage of taking into account many of the objections which had been made.

We might say that the main reason for introducing sense data is to answer the need for hard data, data of which one can be certain. It would appear that perceptual claims can turn out to be mistaken. Yet these are never totally gratuitous; they are made on the basis of perceptual experience. When the stronger claim about what I perceive turns out to be wrong, can I not still make a less sweeping claim, one which goes no further than the perceptual experience on the basis of which I made the original (as it turns out mistaken) claim? And is not this smaller claim in the nature of things very strongly established? In the limiting case it would go no farther than the perceptual experience itself, and surely there can be no doubt that *this* occurred. And, even if we cannot cash this rock-bottom certainty in a range of incorrigible statements,[2] we must surely admit that I have isolated a maximally 'hard' datum. As Ayer puts it,

> If I can be undergoing an illusion when, on the basis of my present experience, I judge, for example, that my cigarette case is lying on the table in front of me, I may, in saying that I see the cigarette case, be claiming more than the experience strictly warrants. ... It may be suggested, therefore, that if I wish to give a strict account of my present visual experience, I must make a more cautious statement.[3]

At the limit there ought to be a statement which would say no more than the experience 'strictly warrants', a statement which gives us an account of the experience itself without going beyond to any statements which would 'serve as descriptions of the contents of our sense-experiences, irrespective of any larger claims that these experiences may normally induce us to make'.[4] We are already familiar with this in ordinary life, where on being challenged, we scale down a perceptual claim in order to have something we can really vouch for. 'Did you really see the accused stab the victim?' 'Well, no, not really, but I saw him take out his knife, and gesture threateningly, and just then my attention was distracted, but I heard a cry, and there was the victim, lying on the ground', and so on. But, of course, in these cases the stripped-down claim is still a 'material-object' claim; it deals with certain objects seen, not just with the experience of seeing. Can we extend this scaling-down procedure beyond the limit of claims about objects in the world? At first blush, there would seem to be no difficulty here. Can we not imagine someone who is really pressed, faced with all sorts of evidence that his experience was really illusory, falling back on some such statement as, 'Well, it *seemed* to me that *x*' or 'You may not believe it, but at that moment it *looked* to me just as though . . .'? And we could imagine causes where this would be beyond challenge.

But there is still a difficulty in the way of the sense-datum theory, which Ayer goes on to elaborate in this chapter. We can quite well understand such scaled-down experience claims' taking the form 'It seemed to me that . . . .' But sense data are meant to be objects of which I am immediately aware in this perceptual experience, objects such that the claim to perceive them has the same unchallengeability as the claim 'It seems to me that . . . .' They must be intra-experiential objects, or objects of seeming, such that we can translate claims about how things seem to us into claims about the kind of objects of seeming that make up our experience. As Ayer puts it, we have 'to pass from "it seems to me that I perceive *x*" to "I perceive a seeming-*x*", with the implication that there is a seeming-*x* which I perceive'.[5]

This step has been challenged as being based on some rather laughable confusions. Ayer cites Gilbert Ryle's arguments in *The Concept of Mind*.[6] But it seems to me that Ayer's counter-arguments here are very cogent. In the name of what restriction of language should I rule out talking of how things seem to me in a language of seeming-objects? Is there something wrong with making a substantive out of what is normally expressed in a that-clause? Is it even abnormal to talk in this way? Can we not talk of our experiences? For instance, 'I had an extraordinary visual experience', or 'It was fantastic, my visual field was saturated with blue, and then suddenly, it got lighter . . .'

Equally inconclusive are Ryle's arguments in *Dilemmas*[7] which Ayer cites earlier in the same chapter[8], where Ryle points out that the verb 'to see', for instance, is an achievement verb, and 'does not signify any experience, i.e., something that I go through, am engaged in'.[9] That is as may be, but it surely in no way makes it illegitimate to talk about my visual experience, my visual field or the parts or constituents of that field.

So it appears that the two steps discussed above are legitimate. First, we can scale down our perceptual claims so as to get something of which we are certain, and take this right down to a claim about the nature of perceptual experience which avoids going beyond it. We do this with such statements as 'It seemed to me that . . .', 'It looked an awful lot like . . .', 'It had all the appearances of . . . .' Of course, these can be used also to make guarded claims about how things were; but they have a perfectly understandable use as restricted statements about experience alone. Secondly, it seems also that we can convert these statements into statements about certain objects. We can speak about the experiences which we often describe in 'It seems to me that . . .' statements in statements of ordinary subject–predicate form, where what occurs in the subject place are referring expressions designating our experiences or parts of them, as we can already see with 'my visual experience', or 'my visual field'.

So the way seems open to talking about sense data in a perfectly coherent way. All we need to do is to introduce the terms as expressions designating experiences in the stripped-down sense where statements about experience make no claim about how things stand in the world. We can say, 'My sense data are blue, rough', and so on.

But in fact things are not that simple. For in combining the above two steps we are in danger of sliding over a crucial issue. When we normally step back and restrict our claim in the name of greater assurance and certainty, such as the case of the witness above who describes more exactly what he saw, the stripped-down claim still deals with an object in the world, albeit more circumscribed ('I saw him take out his knife, wave it' and so forth). It deals with an object which is independent of our activity. The point of the scaling-down is to separate out what we are rock-bottom certain of from what should more strictly be considered as inferences or interpretations made on the basis of this firmer evidence. So I admit that I did not actually see the killing, but I did see him take out his knife, and so on. The inferences follow what we plausibly know about the relations between objects and events in the world.

But the case where we scale down our claim to simple statements of experience is not necessarily parallel. For it is not clear that the subject of the claim is an object independent of our activity, as it is in the ordinary case. True, we can translate our 'It seems to me that . . .' statements into ones about objects – for example, our experiences or visual or auditory fields. But this does not mean that these objects are, like those in the normal case, independent of our activity, as is the event above of his pulling the knife. Thus, although we might be induced to step further back from our first careful testimony – 'I saw him pull the knife' to 'It seemed to me that he pulled a knife', or 'I thought I saw a knife glinting in his hand' – and although in both cases we can be said to be restricting our claim, and we might even in both cases say that we were circumscribing more narrowly the object of our claim, it does not follow that in each case we step back to an object in the same sense: that is, one which is independent of our activity. Nor does it follow that the inference, if there is one here, is grounded on what we know about the relations of such independent objects or events.

In other words, though we can undoubtedly speak of our experiences, we may not be able to speak of them, as we do of objects in the world, as though they were independent of our activity. But, I should like to claim, it is essential to the notion of a sense datum that we be able to do so. For the epistemological point of the sense datum is that it give us rock-bottom certainty at the cost of stripping down our claim. But what does rock-bottom certainty mean in this context? It means that we have a description of experience which avoids any stepping beyond the bare content of experience to any claims about how things stand which could turn out to be mistaken; and, since any claim about how things stand in the world could turn out mistaken, any step by which we come to such a claim must be forgone.

But what we isolate as underlying our false perceptual claims when we examine them later are what we describe as inferences, or identifications, or interpretations, or the relating of something to others, or the placing of some object in the stream of experience. Experience-description statements to give us the kind of certainty we are looking for would have to describe an experience which was somehow shorn of all such activity of identification, interpretation, placing in experience, relating to other realities, and so on. The objects of this experience would have to be pure givens, independent of any activity of ours which might shape them in a certain way, by identifying them as something or other, seeing them under a certain description, linking them in certain ways, making certain features salient, and so on.

Sense data, in other words, must be thing-like objects, which are like objects in the world in being independent of our activity. They are there as the rock-bottom givens of experience, which are irrecusable just because we have added nothing to them ourselves which could be challenged or called into question.

Of course, in one sense they do not need to be seen as independent of our activity. For instance, we can recognise that I get certain sense data by turning my head in a certain direction, or putting myself in a certain surrounding. But this is just to invoke a certain causal link between some event in the world and my having a certain experience; part of the contingent antecedents of the experience include my activity; and the experience itself is an object which is independent of my activity, in the sense that it is not essentially constituted by it. I *could* have the experience of seeing this perspective if someone wheeled me there while I was in a coma and then woke me up. In a similar way, the objects in the world which I have called independent of my activity could be contingently so dependent – as, for instance, when I am reading the above paragraph on this page that I have just typed. The marks there were made by me. My activity figures in a story of their genesis; but they are for all that objects independent of my activity just as much as the knife that I saw in the accused's hand.

But I should like to argue that the sense datum is an incoherent or impossible notion because there is no experience which is independent of our activity – not just in this weak, historical sense, but also in a stronger sense, which I should now like to explore.

Our phenomenal field, or the world as it appears to us, which is what our sense-datum language is supposed to describe, is what I should like to call a patterned activity. I am introducing 'patterned activity' as a term of art for purposeful activity the end of which is not a product separable from the activity itself, but rather consists in the attainment, by our performance, of a certain criterion or form. When I execute a dance step, or do a perfect turn on the parallel bars, I am engaging in patterned activity in this sense. The achievement I am aiming at consists in the activity's taking a certain form, and not in any separable end product. The activity itself is intrinsic to the achievement.

Now, our phenomenal field can be called a patterned activity because we cannot have a phenomenal field which is not in some way shaped by some features' being objects of salient focus, while others are peripheral; by the objects' being at least in rudimentary fashion identified in a certain way, or by at least one identification's being salient; and by the field's being organised so that its parts stand in some kind of relation to each other, and also to what went before and is expected after. In other words, it is a condition of things' appearing to us, of there being a way the world seems to us, which is what our sense-datum terms are meant to describe, that our perceptual activity focus, select, fasten on certain features; that it in this way organises a field, the elements of which are also identified in a certain way (for instance, as trees and shrubs, rather than just as green and brown patches, or as typescripts and magazines, rather than just as undifferentiated reading matter on my desk).

There is no room here for a pure given, for an object which would be quite independent of our activity. We can take the simplest case, one of the most oft-quoted examples of a putative sense datum: a patch of red which is here in my visual field now. This was thought to be the potential object of the simplest, most rudimentary factual report or protocol statement, of the form 'red here now'. But the words 'here' and 'now' already reflect the subject's activity of selection and focus. The red is 'here', at this point in the field, which is thereby made central; it is 'now', at this point in the developing stream of events. And it is 'red' – that is, I am focusing on this patch not just as coloured, or perhaps as brightly coloured, or as having a visual texture not unlike my carpet at home, but as red. This is my identification of it.

Nor can we plead that 'red here now' is used only to record the experience, or to communicate it to others, and that, while I need such a word as 'here' to show another where something is, I do not need it to show myself: the red is just there. For the point is that the sentence 'red here now' corresponds to a certain organisation of the field – and a rather rare and odd one, we might add, which perhaps only a painter, a draughtsman, or a philosopher imbued with phenomenalism would adopt. And, indeed, the whole relationship between experience and report which phenomenalism assumes should be challenged. There is no such thing as a bare report of experience which simply records the presence of an independent object, because the specific kind of report sought always corresponds to a certain organisation of the field. When asked to describe my experience in terms of colour patches, I shall give a different report from when reporting the salient objects before me, or when asked to pick out the edible fruit, and so on. There is no reason to consider one of these organisations as more basic, more rock-bottom epistemologically, as though the others were all constructed from it.

Thus, in so far as we can characterise our perceptual experience, or the way things appear to us, it is not as a set of independent objects, but rather as a patterned activity, because this experience is not a detachable product of our activity of organisation; rather, our phenomenal field's being organised in a certain way is just our selecting, focusing, relating, identifying the things before us in the way we do.

But, of course, this does not mean that there is no given, that the activity is purely gratuitous. It would fail in another way to be a patterned activity if this were so. For a patterned activity is directed to a certain criterion of achievement, as I remarked above. And in the case of perception the criterion is veridicalness. Different organisations of the field correspond to different interests, voluntary or involuntary, conscious or unconscious; but there is a standing constraint on our organising activity, which is our sense of the real. This can be overridden by powerful unconscious motives; we can and do suffer delusions; but it imparts a direction to our perceiving activity which we can never eradicate.

When we open our eyes to take in some scene, we are led irresistibly to organisations of the field which give a perspicuous view of what is there. Of course, some features will be salient, some will be the focus of interest, but within this selective focus it is impossible to avoid a certain degree of perspicuity, a certain richness of articulation. Once I have come to discern that those objects in the distance are not all contours on one surface, but should be articulated in perspective, it becomes virtually impossible for me to recapture the 'flat' look they had before. And, indeed, the objects closer to me altogether resist being put in the flat-surface type of arrangement. Indeed, the ability to flip back and forth between two radically different perceptual interpretations belongs to very special cases – for instance, very sketchy drawings, such as the famous duck–rabbit drawing, or the cube which can be seen in two orientations – where the field is artificially impoverished. Within certain limits it is hard, and at certain stages next to impossible, not to see the world right.

Thus, our selection–identification–organisation of perception is directed not only by our interests and desires but also by our sense of what is real, by the demands of verdicalness. And this is what makes the sense-datum language impossible. For perception yields no basic, hard, rock-bottom data which are prior to all inference or interpretation. Rather it consists of fields which are always organised, always shaped by our selecting, identifying, articulating; fields which are organised partly by our sense of the real.

This sense is nourished, of course, not just by all our past experience, but also by the grasp of our immediate context, so that the organisation of my present field coheres with what preceded and with my anticipated future. We never encounter, nor can encounter, the pure datum, something given independently of any organisation based on previously existing presumptions concerning reality. Anything which could count as a datum, such as red here now, always stands in a matrix of motivated organisation and articulation, which is itself guided by a sense of how things stand.

But the whole point of the sense datum was that it was to be such a hard datum. The aim was to strip down the claim by giving a report which did not go farther than the experience strictly warranted, and that means to give an experience description free of all the interpretations and inferences and interrelatings which underlie our claims about objects in the world, and which we sometimes discover *ex post* to have been mistaken when we suffer from errors and illusions of perception. But there are in fact no percepts which are free of such inferences and interpretations, for there are none which are not organised at least partly by our sense of the real. When we err, we do indeed find that this sense has perhaps been seriously deficient, and we can sometimes retrace the deficiency, perhaps to an earlier defective grasp of the situation. But this trace never leads to a point zero of raw uninterpreted data, for nothing we could call a percept could be of that kind.

The sense-datum language was born from a fatal misapplication of our familiar procedure of scaling down claims to achieve greater certainty or reliability. Some things are more readily identifiable, either in general or in a particular context, and we can avoid error, or jumping to hasty conclusions, and can make claims for which we can vouch more confidently, by restricting ourselves to these more available identifications. So the witness above claimed to be sure that the accused took out his knife, surer anyway than that he actually did the murder. Or I might say, 'I'm not absolutely sure it was a Mercedes, but I know the back was curved', or 'I'm not sure it was his car, but I know it was a Mercedes.'

But in each case what we scale down to is a claim about an object or event in the world, one that is given independently of our activity (except perhaps in the weak historical sense above). Of course, our knowing about it, identifying it and being sure of it is not independent of our activity, but the event itself is. But it is a mistake to suppose that we can continue this process of scaling down the claim, buying more certainty with each further restriction, right across the boundary where we begin to talk no longer of objects in the world but of appearances.

We can indeed imagine a set of stages where each time greater certainty is bought at the expense of less amplitude of claim. Thus, in the murder trial referred to above, we could imagine the witness as being forced back from the claim that the accused took out a knife to the weaker claim that he saw something glint in his hand. This new claim defines a new rock-bottom: 'OK, maybe it wasn't a knife, but I saw something glint in his hand; it could have been a watch or a mirror . . . .' The business of building plausible inferences has to start from here and not from higher up, now that the witness has been forced to back down on his earlier account. We have gone farther down the ladder, as it were.

But are there further rungs down the same ladder where the witness talks about *appearances*? Supposing he backs down further and says, 'Well, it sure *looked* to me as though something was glinting in his hand.' Is this the retreat to a new rock-bottom, or is it rather a partial taking back, a partial undermining of the previous rock-bottom? Surely here all the witness is giving is an admission of uncertainty about even this. We have not gone a stage further down the same ladder, but started to put a foot off the ladder altogether, to the great joy of the defence attorney.

Of course, this point was often made in the debate about sense data: that the language of 'it appears', or 'it looks', was used not to introduce a new object, but, rather, to make tentative and guarded our claims about ordinary objects. But it is not my intention here to make an ordinary-language argument against sense data. Indeed, the proponent of sense data could reply by finding cases in which we might treat appearances as rock-bottom data. Supposing no one was sure, but a large number of people thought they saw something glinting, i.e. were willing to say, 'It seemed to me that something glinted in his hand' – would not this be strong evidence that there really *was* something in his hand, perhaps a knife?

The point about this case would be, of course, that the new rock-bottom datum would be the fact that things appeared so to so many people. This fact would be an independent object for the judge or the jury. But this does not mean that appearances are independent objects, in the sense of being given independently of the activity of the subjects to whom things appear. And that is why in saying, 'It seems to me that . . .', I am not describing a new rock-bottom datum for *me*, but, rather, am expressing my uncertainty.

But what is crucial here is not that in ordinary language we *do not* use 'It seems that . . .' expressions to describe a new, independently given object more rock-bottom than the smallest claim about the world: I want rather to claim that we *could not* so use it, for there is no such independent object. But the whole point of the sense-datum language is that it be used for a further scaling-down of our claim from the most unambitious report on the world, in order to buy still greater certainty, ultimately reaching perhaps the point of unchallengeable certainty where we have got down to the appearances which are purely given, shorn of all questionable inferences and interpretations. Sense-datum language would make sense only if our experience consisted of independent objects; if it were made up of thing-like entities such as the objects we see in the world, only somehow epistemologically privileged. But, since experience is not and cannot be like this, the language of sense data has no application. The sense datum is a concept without a possible use.

The attempt to apply a language of independent objects to the patterned activity of perception led naturally to some of the confusions and contradictions which have frequently been raised against sense data. Thus, sense data as independent objects ought to be describable in their own language, not one which is parasitic on the material-object language. But such a language seemed impossible to devise; it always eluded the defenders of the theory – and quite naturally, since perception as the patterned activity of grasping things in the world obviously could not be characterised independently of its purpose, of the achievement at which it aims. Again, sense data, it was noted, unlike objects, may be indeterminate: the sense-datum leopard in my field is many-spotted, but has no exact number of spots, unlike a real leopard.

But, it might be objected, in denying that we can speak of percepts as independent objects, are we not going too far? Are we not denying that there can be any account of perception in terms of such objects? But surely a physiological account, and certainly one on mechanist principles, would account for perception in terms of such objects and events – for instance, states of the retina, of the cortex, and so on. The answer to this is that we are not ruling out such a physiological account of perception (although no one can guarantee that one can succeed along mechanist lines). All we are saying is that our perceptual *experience* cannot be described as constituted by independent objects. But obviously it is always possible to claim that there are things going on underlying our perception which are not part of our *experience*.

But *this* defence is not open to a sense-datum theorist. For sense data are meant to be objects of immediate awareness. This language is supposed to characterise experience itself and nothing else.

This brings us to another underlying confusion of the sense-datum

theory. I have been talking above of the epistemological motivation
for the theory; but it also had its roots in the common-sense
reflections of a mechanistic psychology. How do we become aware
of the world? This question was interpreted to mean: how do
the things out there come to be mirrored here in my head? And
the answer to that seems to be, or at least include, some process
of my being affected, whereby things impress themselves on me,
my receptors or my mind, or perhaps one through the other. The
sense datum, in its line of development from Locke's 'idea' through
Hume's 'impression', owes a great deal to this background of general
psychological notions. It is the basic element of input, an impress
I receive from the outside world. My sense data are the way the
world affects me.

One of the basic confusions in empiricism from the beginning
lay in the belief that one could combine such an efficient causal
account of perception with a proper account of experience. And
this leads to incoherence. The pattern of light coming from the
objects around me does indeed make an impression on my retina.
There is a certain pattern of retinal stimulation which results from
it. But there is no such thing-like entity which is the immediate
object of experience. Sense-datum talk partly results from the impossible attempt to fit bits of an efficient causal account of perception
into a description of experience.[10]

If these arguments from the nature of experience go through,
the sense-datum theory ought to be buried for ever. But, as I
remarked above, I am not sanguine about this kind of philosophical
progress; and the more so in that this argument is not new. It
has, of course, been very strongly urged in the twentieth century,
notably by phenomenological writers. In particular, the introductory
part of Merleau-Ponty's *Phénoménologie de la perception*[11] is devoted
to an account of the phenomenal field which carries these consequences; and something of the same import can be gleaned from
Wittgenstein's discussions of 'seeing as' in the second part of the
Philosophical Investigations. But the argument in essence goes back
to Kant.

Kant saw that perception was possible only through the activity
of the subject, organising a field – an activity which he called
'synthesis' (which term perhaps showed the residual hold of the
earlier atomist prejudices of empiricism on Kant's theory). But
this synthesising activity was not gratuitous: it was concerned with
making judgements – that is, establishing relations which are objectively valid.[12] Without this discipline of objectivity, there would
be no unity of experience, and hence no unity of consciousness,
and hence nothing which we could call experience at all. Our

'perceptions would not then belong to any experience, consequently would be without an object, merely a blind play of representations, less even than a dream'.[13]

Let us leave aside Kant's particular view on how the demands of objectivity were laid on experience – namely, through *a priori* concepts which were imposed by our understanding. Kant nevertheless makes the fundamental point that experience must be an organised whole, shaped by the demands of objectivity; that anything other than this could not be understood as experience, i.e. as the subject's awareness of the world. What lacked this connectedness under the demands of objectivity would be 'less even than a dream'; it would lack even this degree of coherence. For there would be no sense at all of correct or incorrect, veridical or illusory, subjectively felt or objectively valid. With *no* notion at all of objectivity, should we even have a subject in a recognisable sense?

But in experience so organised, there would be no room for the sense datum, a hard datum prior to any inference or interpretation, which would by definition be as yet unconnected with any larger pattern laying claim to objective validity.

The citing of an argument nearly 200 years old which has had to be constantly recovered tells us something about the endlessness of philosophical debate (something we did not need telling). But Kant's argument also shows how the issue of sense data can be interesting and fruitful to explore even if they are no longer in fashion. For this refutation of sense data from the nature of experience opens up a number of avenues which are well worth exploring. In particular, it opens up the question of the activity of the subject which underlies our awareness of the world; and this in turn will enable us to pose questions about the nature of the subject, which have been too long neglected in contemporary English-language philosophy.

NOTES

1. A. J. Ayer, *The Problem of Knowledge* (London: Macmillan, 1956).
2. Cf. ibid., ch. 2.
3. Ibid., p. 105.
4. Ibid.
5. Ibid., p. 115.
6. Gilbert Ryle, *The Concept of Mind* (London: Hutchinson, 1949).
7. Gilbert Ryle, *Dilemmas* (Cambridge: Cambridge University Press, 1954) pp. 102–3.
8. Ayer, *Problem*, pp. 108–9.
9. Ryle, *Dilemmas*, p. 103.

10. It follows from this that sense-datum theorists cannot so easily be cleared of the charge that they conceive the mind 'as a merely passive receptor' as Professor Ayer implies. Cf. Ayer, *Problem*, p. 120.

11. M. Merleau-Ponty, *Phénoménologie de la perception* (Paris: Gallimard, 1945).

12. Kant, *Critique of Pure Reason*, B141–2.

13. Ibid., A112 (quoted from the Kemp Smith translation, London: Macmillan, 1929).

6 A Defence of Induction

J. L. MACKIE

I. INTRODUCTORY SURVEY

To many people, justifying induction seems rather like squaring the circle. It has so often been shown to be impossible that anyone who attempts it risks the suspicion of being mildly insane. Yet it seems evident that we do reason inductively, we accept and believe, perhaps with some reservations and caution, the conclusions of that reasoning, and we rely on them in practice. It would be nice if we could show that it is in some sense rational or reasonable to do so, that this is not merely an instinct that we cannot help following or a convention that we just happen to have adopted.

Sir Karl Popper's many forceful objections to what he calls inductivism do not dissolve this problem. We can concede that science is not much concerned with simple inductive generalisation or extrapolation from the observed to the unobserved; that science does not in general proceed by mere fact collecting – that we have to ask questions, frame hypotheses, put nature to the test; that there are no methods guaranteed to advance science significantly; and that good scientists do not, at the price of lack of content, prefer hypotheses that are highly probable, or merely try to confirm their hypotheses or to save them in the face of contrary evidence, but rather follow procedures that expose their hypotheses to a high risk of falsification. Again, we can concede that we should not aim at certainty, or even, perhaps, at established truth; and perhaps that we cannot find starting points or data which are themselves certain partly because they are theory-free. But none of these concessions affects the fact that we accept both common-sense and scientific generalisations about the causal behaviour of material things and rely upon them in practice. We do not accept them merely as worthy subjects for further testing: we act on the assumption that well tested generalisations are either true or near enough to being true to have true entailments for applications fairly similar to those for which they have been tested. It is the rationality of such beliefs, taken tentatively, and of the connected practical policies that is to be defended. We are not seeking a proof that bread will always nourish us. Of course we may become allergic to it, or if it is made from ergot-infected grain it may poison us; what we want is merely to justify a presumption that bread will not gratuitously start to poison us, without some cause that could in principle be discovered.

But the problem is wider than that of such causal generalisation or of the equivalent ascription of dispositional properties to things. Any grounds that Hume or anyone else has for denying the rationality of belief in empirical generalisations, particularly causal laws and quasi-causal statistical laws, apply equally to the belief that material objects will persist more or less as they are if not interfered with. This belief equally involves extrapolation beyond what either has been observed or can be validly deduced from observations. The inductive question is not merely whether bread will continue to nourish us, but also whether pieces of bread will continue, even for the next minute, to be bread. Or, if we take our ordinary terms for material objects to entail such persistence for a time if not interfered with, the question will be whether we are ever justified in applying these terms. Is this really bread, or merely something superficially like bread but too ephemeral to deserve that description? Also, the belief in an objective world goes along with the belief in such persistences and regularities of behaviour: if the latter belief is not rationally justifiable, neither is the former. Selective scepticism about induction, conjoined with unquestioning acceptance of the objective and continuous and extrapolable existence of material things, would be arbitrary. But of course this only widens the problem; it does not resolve it.

We should distinguish between all such extrapolations from observed to unobserved things or time-slices of things or processes or sequences of events – in particular from the past to the future – and inferences from what is more directly observed to a deeper explanation. The latter are of far more interest to science, the former being normally taken for granted. Of course, the two cannot in practice be separated. Even with the former there is the question of what to generalise or project, what to take as a causal or quasi-causal law; while deeper explanations are ordinarily extrapolated without hesitation. Also, both raise the inductive problem. We may reasonably be more tentative about explanatory theories than about causal generalisations connecting readily observed features, more willing to admit that they are likely in the end to be abandoned and replaced by better ones; but such theories are at least provisionally accepted and relied upon in practice, and there is a real question whether, and if so why, this is rational.

Also, I believe that ultimately similar answers can be given to both halves of the inductive problem. Nevertheless, the two halves can be distinguished: it would be one thing to justify the generalising, the especially temporal extrapolation, another to justify the preference for this or that deeper explanation. Nor would the latter carry the former with it, or make the former unnecessary. However good and reliable an explanation we had of why something had worked as it had to date, there would still be a question of whether and why we could expect it to go on so working and could believe that that explanation would still hold. In what follows I shall concentrate on the first half of the problem, that of justifying generalisation or extrapolation.

This is of course Hume's problem. But Sir Alfred Ayer, at several places in *Probability and Evidence*, reports and endorses Hume's argument that our belief in law-like connections between events can never be rationally justified, that we can never have good reason to accept an empirical generalisation, and he criticises attempts, such as that of Harrod to answer Hume, to solve the problem of induction by justifying at least some projective procedures. However, he refuses to see this as a reason for scepticism.[1] And elsewhere, in what is admittedly an *argumentum ad hominem* against Popper, he argues that there would be little point in testing hypotheses if they gained no credit from passing the test.[2] Like many others, Ayer is reluctant to give up the belief that inductive reasoning is reasonable, and yet he neither can find, nor will allow, any escape from Hume's proof that it is not. I shall try to show, however, that Hume's argument and some related ones are not as conclusive as they seem, so that a rational defence of inductive reasoning is not ruled out *a priori*; and then I shall offer the outline of such a defence.

II. CRITICISM OF SCEPTICAL ARGUMENTS

Hume argues that, if it were reason that guided our causal thinking, when we go from observed past sequences to unobserved future ones, it would be relying on the principle that 'the course of nature continues always uniformly the same'. If this principle itself is to be proved, it must be either by 'demonstrative arguments' or by 'probable reasonings'. But the former is impossible and the latter would be circular, because probability always rests on causal relations, and therefore on the very presumption of uniformity which we are trying to establish.[3] These alternatives, 'demonstration' and 'probability', mean for Hume not valid deduction and non-deductive support, but, rather, valid deduction from *a priori*, analytic truths and valid deduction from synthetic, empirical truths. Only on the assumption that the second alternative requires deductive validity is Hume justified in saying that the uniformity principle itself is needed here. For, suppose that we allow that there is such a thing as relational epistemic probability – that is, the logical-relation kind of probability proposed by Keynes and Carnap, or what is often misleadingly called subjective probability. Then, for all that Hume has said it might be that an observed constant conjunction of *A*s with *B*s somehow *probabilified* that this new *A* would be conjoined with a *B*, or that in some such way evidence non-deductively supported an inductive conclusion that went beyond it. Given this approach, there would be no need to rely on the principle of uniformity, and hence no vicious circularity. Hume's dilemma as he intended it does not exclude this possibility; it does not even consider it. Hume appears to consider and reject this possibility only if his 'probability' is misinterpreted as referring to a conceivable probabilification and his 'demonstration' correspondingly extended to cover all deductive arguments. But with this misinterpretation Hume's claim that 'probability' would have to appeal, circularly, to the uniformity principle would be false.

In reporting Hume's argument, Ayer considers the possibility that 'we can at least show [the principle of uniformity] to be probable'. But he says that any judgement of probability must have some foundation, which 'can lie only in our past experience. The only ground we can have for saying that it is even probable that the course of nature continues uniformly the same is that we have hitherto found this to be the case. But then we are arguing in a circle. . . .' He adds that

> the same objection would apply to any attempt to by-pass the general principle of uniformity of nature and argue that inferences from one matter of fact to another, although admittedly not demonstrative, can nevertheless be shown to be probable. Again, the judgement of probability must have some foundation. But this foundation can lie only in our past experience[4]

and then the circularity breaks out again.

The first part of this *resembles* Hume's argument; the second part (as he has conceded privately) is Ayer's own extension, not a paraphrase of anything in Hume. But both parts are plainly intended by Ayer to exclude any showing of induction to be 'probable' in some modern sense, not in the queer sense that Hume, as he tells us, took over from Locke and found 'ridiculous' even when he wrote section xi of Book i, part 3, of the *Treatise of*

Human Nature. But, if it is intended to exclude epistemic probabilification, the essential premiss, that probability must have a foundation
which can lie only in our past experience, does not hold. A frequency
or a propensity, say, would need to be empirically established,
but not a logical relation of non-deductive support. Ayer's argument
requires that anything like a logical relation of probabilification,
any principles of non-deductive support that were acceptable *a
priori*, should be excluded from the start.

Ayer could reply that he has a separate argument against the
logical relation theory of probability. Indeed, in *Probability and
Evidence* he refers to this argument, first published fifteen years
earlier, and says that he has not yet seen any effective rejoinder
to it. However, I think that effective rejoinders have since been
published.[5] The argument is essentially that the logical relation
theory cannot explain why we should prefer one to another of
the different degrees of probabilification that would, on this theory,
relate different pieces of evidence to the same conclusion, all holding
as logical truths. The rejoinder turns upon the distinction between
a simple epistemic probability and a relational one. We prefer
one logical relation to another only in that it is the probabilification
by all the relevant evidence that someone has that determines the
simple epistemic probability for him, the degree of belief that it
is rational for him to give to the conclusion. Ayer also asks why
it is sensible, sometimes, to look for more evidence rather than
to be content with the 'logical' degree of support by the evidence
you already have. The answer is that in general if you do so
you are more likely to be right in accepting or rejecting the conclusion, where this 'likely' represents another epistemic probability.
This argument of Ayer's, like a related one of Popper's,[6] shows
only that the logical relation theory does not cover the ground:
we have to recognise probabilities, even epistemic ones, which are
not purely relational, and of course we also have to recognise
various non-epistemic items, such as frequencies and perhaps propensities, that can also be called probabilities. But none of this
has any tendency to prove that there cannot be such logical or
quasi-logical relations, which might be acceptable *a priori*, of non-
deductive support. Yet it is such a proof that would be needed
to fill the holes in the argument that Ayer has constructed by
reinterpreting and extending Hume's dilemma.

Yet another argument can be developed from Hume's by reinter-
pretation. If we use 'induction' in a very broad sense, to cover
non-deductive reasoning as a whole, and ask whether it can be
rationally defended, it seems clear that induction cannot be justified
deductively; it cannot without circularity be justified inductively;

therefore it cannot be justified at all.

The cogency of any dilemma depends on the exhaustiveness of the alternatives. Here the alternative methods of justification are made exhaustive simply by defining 'inductively' so that it covers all rational procedures other than deduction. But then all that the argument shows is that this body of non-deductive procedures cannot be justified as a whole. Any justification must start somewhere, with something other than deduction. There is no way of rationally overcoming the scepticism or curing the doubts of someone who is systematically suspicious of all reasoning that is not deductively valid.

But this conclusion leaves open the possibility of justifying some procedures that are inductive in this very broad sense in terms of others. In particular, we may take 'induction' in a narrower but still fairly broad sense as including the two things that we distinguished earlier: generalisation or extrapolation, and inference to a deeper explanation. And then there are other kinds of reasoning which are neither deductive nor inductive in this sense. For example, there is that which yields judgements of epistemic probability about games of chance. I have a bag which I know to contain nine black balls and one white one, all equal in size, weight, and so on. The balls have been stirred around, and I now put my hand into the bag and take hold of one ball. I have no way of telling what colour it is, and no reason to expect one rather than another of the ten balls to have come to hand. In this mixed state of knowledge and ignorance I say that the ball I have is probably black: my information and lack of information together probabilify the judgement 'This ball is black', and, if something of importance turned upon my stating the colour correctly, the practically reasonable thing to say would be that it was black. And, if there had been ninety-nine, rather than nine, black balls to one white one, both the theoretical and the practical conclusion would have been more strongly supported. This kind of reasoning seems cogent. (Most people admit that, in the ninety-nine-to-one case, if their lives depended on a correct answer, they would say that the ball was black.) Yet it is not deductive. Nor is it inductive in the sense just defined. It makes no extrapolation from observed to unobserved cases, and no inference to a deeper explanation. You need never have played a game of this sort before and you need no theory about it. There is no appeal to Hume's uniformity principle or to any specifically causal judgements. (No doubt in setting up the example I have assumed that the balls have not changed colour, that the black ones have not all shrunk, and so on, since they were examined; but this extrapolation forms no part of the reasoning the example is intended to illustrate: from the premiss that there are now so many similar black and white balls in the bag and I have hold of one of them, along with the lack of any further relevant information, to a conclusion about the colour of this ball.) Now, it is at least conceivable that we should be able to justify what was defined above as inductive reasoning by showing it to be supported by some kind of application of the probabilistic reasoning illustrated here.

We have to take account, then, of three proposed dilemmas which seem to show that induction cannot be rationally defended. The first is Hume's own. Induction rests on the uniformity principle; this cannot be established by deduction from *a priori* truths; to deduce it from empirical truths we should need the principle itself as a premiss; so this principle, and hence the inductions which rest on it, cannot be (deductively) justified at all. The second is Ayer's. Induction cannot be conclusively justified; to show it to be probable, we should need a judgement of probability resting on past experience, and therefore an induction from that past experience to the present application, and this would be circular; therefore induction cannot be rationally supported at all. The third equates induction with non-deductive reasoning as a whole. Induction so defined cannot be deductively justified; it cannot without vicious circularity be inductively justified; therefore it cannot be rationally supported at all. But there is a suggestion that escapes all three dilemmas: the suggestion that induction in a sense which covers generalisation or extrapolation (especially temporal) and inference to deeper explanations may be rationally justified by showing that in each such inference the conclusion is probabilified by the premisses or evidence in accordance with the apparently cogent sort of reasoning illustrated by the example of balls in a bag. This suggestion escapes Hume's dilemma because it does not claim that the conclusion is reached by a sound deductive argument. It escapes Ayer's, because Ayer's begs the question against any such probabilification by assuming that any judgement of probability must rest on past experience. And it escapes the third because what this rules out is a justification, from no starting point, of non-deductive reasoning as a whole; it does not exclude the possibility of defending one variety of non-deductive reasoning by the application of principles on which we rely in non-deductive reasoning of another sort.

However, this proposal still seems to be threatened by Goodman's 'new riddle of induction'.[7] The suggested probabilification is of a logical or quasi-logical sort. It is not an empirical probability, such as a frequency or a propensity, but is supposed to rest on purely formal relations between the premisses and the conclusion to which they are alleged to give non-deductive support. In order to be acceptable *a priori*, it must have such a formal basis. But Goodman's use of such predicates as 'grue' shows that the temporal extrapolations we make cannot even be described in any purely syntactical way, since rival, unwanted extrapolations are syntactically on exactly the same footing. It seems to tell not merely against the traditional aim of justifying induction, but even against the more modest aim of describing systematically what we count as confirmation or as respectable inductive reasoning. 'Formal', however, may be more exacting than 'syntactical'. We can stick to the common-sense view that things which are green (especially if they are of the same shade of green) at different times resemble one another in a way that things called grue by Goodman's definition at different times may not. And then it is plausible to suppose that any formal principles of probabilification there may be will take account of the presence or absence of real resemblances rather than the merely syntactical forms which 'grue' can satisfy as well as 'green'. The new riddle, therefore, does not undermine our proposal.

III. OUTLINE OF A POSITIVE JUSTIFICATION

So far I have been defending the mere possibility of a justification of induction, replying to various arguments which seem to rule this out completely. To go further and actually sketch such a justification we must formulate some principles of probabilification. In the balls-in-a-bag example, we were relying on some version of the principle of indifference or insufficient reason – say, that an incomplete body of information (a mixture of knowledge and ignorance) equally probabilifies each of a set of exclusive possibilities to which that incomplete information is similarly related. This principle has, of course, often been criticised. Yet (as I have argued elsewhere) it is implicit in every transition from a frequency or a propensity, no less than from a classical set of alternatives, to a simple epistemic probability about a particular case.[8] Ayer argues, I think correctly, that Harrod in effect uses this principle, though he explicitly rejects it; and so does Ayer himself.[9] Much of the criticism it has incurred applies not to the principle itself as determining epistemic probabilities, but to plainly fallacious attempts to use it to determine frequencies or propensities. Another criticism is that it yields contradictory results where there is more than one plausible way of dividing a range of possibilities into exclusive alternatives. For example, when we ask what is the probability that a chord of a circle will be shorter than the side of the inscribed equilateral triangle, we can get the rival answers $\frac{1}{2}$, $\frac{1}{3}$ and $\frac{3}{4}$ by classifying possible chords in different ways; we seem unable to reach a determinate conclusion unless we think of the chords as being generated by some particular randomising mechanism which would have equal propensities to generate chords along some one scale.[10] Now, if we could apply the principle of indifference only where there was some such range of propensities, the principle would indeed be useless for our purpose, since it will always be an inductive conclusion that something has such and such generative propensities. But this criticism shows only that, where a range of possibilities does not divide unambiguously into similar alternatives, we must have recourse to the propensities of a generative mechanism; where the division is unambiguous, we can apply the principle directly.

However, whereas this principle immediately applies only to problems in direct probability, it is pretty clear that any justification of induction along the lines suggested will involve some inverse probability argument. We want to argue that, because some result which the falsity of a certain hypothesis would render improbable has been observed, it is now likely that that hypothesis is true. But, when we try to formulate the principle involved in such an argument, we naturally have recourse to Bayes's theorem, and this gives us a final probability for the hypothesis only as a product of its initial probability. We have

$$P(h, b \& e) = \frac{P(e, b \& h) \times P(h, b)}{P(e, b)}$$

where b is background knowledge, h is the hypothesis in question, and e the observed evidence. Adding e to b raises the probability of h in the same proportion as adding h to b raises the probability of e. I have argued elsewhere that this theorem holds for epistemic probabilities, that it tells us what degree of belief it is reasonable to give to h when what we know is the conjunction of b and e, on the assumption that the probabilities on the right-hand side also represent degrees of belief that are reasonable for us.[11] However, this formula leaves us with several problems. How are we to establish initial or antecedent probabilities – that is, probabilifications of h and e by b? If the initial probability of h either is or may be very low, even strongly favourable evidence – an e the probability of which is very markedly increased by adding h to b – may leave the final probability of h too low for this hypothesis to be reasonably accepted. And, if the initial probability of an unrestricted generalisation is always zero, its final probability will also remain zero, no matter how strong the evidence in its favour. We shall have to see to what extent these difficulties can be overcome.

It is a striking fact that we do not generalise with equal confidence all observed conjunctions of features and events. It is primarily causal sequences that we are prepared to generalise, and those analogous ones that we can call causal in an extended sense, such as the persistence, more or less unchanged, of material objects and the growth processes and metabolic processes of animals and plants. Where we do generalise, the coexistence of features not related as cause and effect, as in such stock examples as that all birds of the shape, size and so on that make them count as ravens are black, we suppose that there are underlying causal relations – that the raven shape and the black colour stem alike first from a certain genetic make-up, and more remotely from connected processes of natural selection, that blackness was somehow advantageous for birds with the life-style for which the raven features fitted them. A Humian might say that it is a trivial tautology that it is causal sequences and causally based coexistences that we are prepared to generalise, that it is just the fact that we are prepared to generalise certain sequences that makes them count as causal. But their causal or quasi-causal character is linked with other matters. There are the manipulative experiments that suggest various conditional statements: if I do this, that will happen; if I had not done that, this would not have happened; if I put this cup here, there will be a cup here a moment later; if I smash this cup, there will not be a cup here a moment later; and so on. Also, a causal process typically consists of a change in one thing following closely upon contact of another thing with it, or of a chain built up from such episodes, while our quasi-causal processes consist of successive states of the same substance, either just like one another or varying only gradually. Even where a cause and its effect are superficially separate and unlike one another, there is commonly some underlying causal mechanism the discovery of which reveals persistences and continuities of features from which the superficial discontinuities result. Causation is a matter of one time-slice of a thing or process producing the next – or, rather, the latter is the result of 'producing' the former in something like the sense in which a line is 'produced' in geometry: clusters of features project themselves into the future.' In Hume's terms, the assumption on which our inductive extrapolations and generalisations proceed is not merely that unobserved instances resemble observed ones, but that the *course* of nature – that is, the time-flow of events – continues uniformly the same. Or, if we speak of instances, we must ask, 'Instances of what?', and the answer will be 'Instances of laws of working' as I have tried to distinguish these elsewhere, or of what Mill tried to pick out by contrasting uniformities of succession with uniformities of coexistence.[12]

This suggests that Hume and Mill were not so wrong after all, that in the order of justification the primary induction is that which supports some principle of the uniformity of nature with respect to its ways of operating through time, and that particular generalisations and extrapolations are supported by the conjunction of this principle with specific experiments and observations. But the content of this principle can be more fully brought out. It says, first, that individual things and goings-on tend to persist as they have been; secondly, that a confluence of two (or more) goings-on tends to produce goings-on which partly continue each of the original ones; and, thirdly, that most detectable events flow in this sort of way from detectable neighbouring antecedents and likewise lead to detectable neighbouring sequels to which they are related by at least approximate generalisations. This third part includes something like the traditional formulation 'Every event has a cause', but it adds to it something like 'Every event has an effect.' It strengthens these by requiring that the antecedents and sequels should be neighbouring and detectable, but it also restricts the subject to detectable events and weakens the claims from 'Every' to 'Most'.

I have shown elsewhere how Mill's eliminative methods of induction can be tightened up and made more accurate by exhibiting each of their variants as combining a standard pattern of observations with an assumption which says that a certain kind of occurrence is related to some necessary and sufficient condition drawn from or built up out of a restricted range of possibly relevant factors.[13] We can apply this result here with modifications. The restricted range of factors, in any particular case, will be supplied by the qualifications 'neighbouring' and 'detectable'. The principle that most detectable events fit into a certain pattern will make it epistemically probable that events of a certain specific sort do so, if we have no special reason to suppose that they do not: this is just a rough direct probability argument. The fact that our principle speaks only of at least approximate generalisations adds a further respect in which the argument along the lines of an eliminative method has to be reduced from a deductively valid one to a probabilistic one. On the other hand, our principle is so framed as to allow the identification of (partial) effects as well as that of (partial) causes: we can simply invert the observation pattern for the method of difference, for example, as between antecedents and sequels, and by an exactly similar argument reach an (incomplete) generalisation about the effects to which a certain phenomenon leads. Also, the first and second parts of our principle will aid the process of elimination, telling by direct probability arguments against the causal character of sequences where no such continuities can be found. Altogether, then, it is plain that if we had such a principle we could, by conjoining it with suitable observations, probabilify just those sorts of causal and quasi-causal generalisations that we ordinarily accept and rely upon in practice – elliptical generalisations, with implied clauses about other things being equal, taken to hold only in certain rather vaguely specified fields or background conditions, and so on. But they would be generalisations, going beyond the observations on which they were based, and they would be epistemically probable – that is, supported in some degree by the mixture of knowledge and ignorance that we have, in accordance with the principles of epistemic probability illustrated by our balls-in-a-bag example. This support would make it reasonable for us to accept them provisionally and to rely on them, with something less than complete confidence, in practice.

The crucial question, then, is whether we can defend, by an inverse probability argument, the primary induction that supports the proposed principle of uniformity. Surely we can. We might consider first the simple pair of alternative metaphysical hypotheses, that there is a world which conforms throughout to our principle, and that the world as a whole is purely random, a fortuitous concourse not indeed of anything as solid and persistent and moderately well behaved as Epicurean atoms, but (to borrow a phrase from Ayer) of 'variations of scenery in a four-dimensional spatio-temporal continuum'.[14] Now, we have countless observations that conform to and illustrate our principle, the general pattern of which, therefore, is expectable on our first alternative hypothesis but improbable in the extreme on the second. If we had just these alternatives to choose between, it would be reasonable to prefer the former in the light of our observations, unless it was antecedently almost infinitely less probable than the second. As far as I can see, the only line of thought that would suggest that the hypothesis of uniformity is almost infinitely less probable than that of randomness is one which rests on what is in this context the question-begging assumption that things are really totally random, and that order could be achieved only by a fantastically improbable piece of luck. Since this assumption is question-begging, I see no good reason for assigning so low an initial probability to the uniformity hypothesis that the observations which tell so massively in its favour are unable to make it more acceptable than its rival.

However, it may be objected that to offer only these alternatives so oversimplifies the issue as to introduce fallacy. It is true that we could split our principle into its three parts, and consider various more modest hypotheses saying that the world conforms to some of these parts but not to them all. But it is obvious that for each part of our principle there is any amount of observed evidence which illustrates it, and which would be left unexplained by, and extremely improbable in relation to, any hypothesis which omitted that part. So there is no need to work tediously through such complications as these.

A complication which deserves to be taken more seriously is one introducing, as rivals to our alternatives of uniformity through-out the world and pure randomness, hypotheses of extensive but still limited order – that uniformity holds only over some range that is limited spatially or temporally or both, and then terminates or gradually fades out. But we can cope with these. First let us consider the indefinitely large set of hypotheses all of which assign the same spatio-temporal extent to uniformity, but locate it differ-ently – for example, that uniformity holds for this, that and the other stretch of time, where each stretch lasts a million years. It seems a legitimate application of the principle of indifference to assign equal antecedent epistemic probabilities to the various hypotheses of this set. Some of them, however, will have been ruled out by the already-observed spread of uniformity. Suppose that this covers, say, 100,000 years. Then, of the hypotheses not so ruled out, if the extent which is common to the hypotheses of the set (here a million years) is considerably greater than the observed spread of uniformity, relatively few will say that uniformity will terminate either at once or very soon – few of the surviving hypotheses of this set will locate the cut-off of uniformity either at or near the edge of its observed spread. So, taking the not-yet ruled-out hypotheses of the set as equally probable, we can conclude that, even if uniformity lasts only for this limited extent, it is not likely to end very soon. But, secondly, let us consider the set of sets of such hypotheses, comparing all million-year hypotheses with all 110,000-year ones, and so on. Clearly, the shorter the extent characteristic of each set of hypotheses, the smaller the proportion of the hypotheses of that set that will cover the observed spread of uniformity: this proportion falls dramatically when the characteristic extent is little greater than the observed spread. Conse-quently, by an inverse probability argument the observation of, say, a 100,000-year spread of uniformity raises the probability that *some* million-year hypothesis holds much more than it raises the probability that some 110,000-year one holds, and so on. The obser-vation of a certain spread of uniformity raises the probability that the extent of uniformity is considerably greater than that spread much more than it raises the probability that that extent is equal to or only a little greater than that spread. Now, we cannot, perhaps, use the principle of indifference to assign equal antecedent epistemic probabilities to the various hypotheses as to the extent of uniformity – 100,000 years, 110,000, a million, and so on – but we can appeal to a similar but weaker principle of tolerance to justify our not giving a zero antecedent probability to all hypotheses assigning more than a certain extent to uniformity.[15] So long as the greater-extent hypotheses are not ruled out by such an unfair initial assignment, they can come out more probable in the end, their probability being raised more by the observation of some considerable spread of uniformity. Assuming that the observed spread is 100,000 years, it is more likely that uniformity holds for some extent of more than 110,000 than that it holds for some extent less than this. And, as we have seen, once we have confirmed such a greater-extent hypothesis, we can go on by a direct probability argument to infer that uniformity is not likely to end very soon. We can still reach such a modest but mildly reassuring conclusion even if we bring into consideration hypotheses of extensive but limited order.

It may be objected that this argument must be fallacious, because it would prove too much. For it seems to show the following: even if there were a purely random distribution of uniformity, so that there was an even chance of its occurring or not occurring in any small region, and such persistences of uniformity as did occur were the product of pure chance, it would still be more probable than not that uniformity would continue significantly beyond the region over which it has been observed. But of course this cannot be right: the conclusion would contradict the assumption. However, the argument is not committed to generating this absurdity. The assumption of a purely random distribution would entail that greater-extent hypotheses were initially much less probable than smaller-extent ones: this assumption is equivalent to an assignment of initial probabilities so extreme, so adverse to greater-extent hypotheses, that the raising of probabilities by the inverse argument could not outweigh it. This is similar to the proposal which Carnap considers, but rejects, to give equal initial probabilities to all state descriptions. If we start with such an assumption, then indeed no amount of inductive evidence will enable us to advance. We shall in effect have ruled out from the start any possibility of inductive support. But it is enough to see that this is an extreme assumption; it is arbitrary to lay it down dogmatically *a priori* that the distribution of uniformity must be purely random. If, instead, we allow from the start that there is some better-than-zero probability of some not purely random pattern – as opposed to purely local appearances of order which really result from chance – then the inverse argument can work in the modest but reassuring way outlined above.

We can go thus far even if we treat the problem as one of generalisation or extrapolation alone, of determining the likely extent of a certain kind of uniformity among what are in themselves no more than variations of scenery in a four-dimensional continuum. But we can also take our principle as indicating a deeper explanation: the hypothesis that what is really there is not adequately captured by this talk of four-dimensional scenery, and that our ordinary way of thinking in terms of persisting things, and of what there is now producing what there will be, which makes the time dimension significantly different from any purely spatial one, approximates to some metaphysical truth.[16] On the four-dimensional scenery view, such uniformity as we have observed was antecedently highly improbable. As I have said elsewhere, it is remarkable that nearly all the four-dimensional worms we have encountered are temporal ones, occupying possibly causal lines, and hardly any are (purely) spatial ones, occupying what could be lines of simultaneity. On the hypothesis that all that is really there is four-dimensional scenery, the observed distribution of four-dimensional worms is a surprising coincidence; but on the rival hypothesis, which is hard to formulate but the point of which is that it finds some metaphysical truth in the thought of things as persisting through time and processes as projecting themselves in time, the general pattern of what we have observed is expectable. So, unless the latter hypothesis is antecedently far more improbable than the former, it will have been made the more probable by what we have observed. I can see no reason for saying that the latter hypothesis is antecedently less probable. An objection that might be raised is a phenomenalistic attack on its meaningfulness or intelligibility as an alternative to the four-dimensional scenery view; but I have argued elsewhere against the theory of meaning on which such an objection would have to rest.[17] The inference to the suggested metaphysical truth as a deeper explanation is, then, a good inverse probability argument, and this metaphysical truth, whatever its precise formulation should be, would make it more reasonable to accept the principle of uniformity which we need for the support of specific extrapolations and generalisations. It clearly entails the first and second parts of that principle. It does not entail the third part, and yet it suggests it in a way that I cannot make precise. If what was there at one time simply and exactly persisted into the succeeding time, there would be exact generalisations relating all detectable items

to detectable neighbouring antecedents and sequels. I should like
to have a weakened variant of this thesis, that if there is some
persistence and some projecting of processes it is likely that these
will be in accordance with at least approximate generalisations;
but I do not see clearly how to establish this. Even without this
thesis, however, the inverse probability argument for our suggested
metaphysical truth gives some further support to the extrapolation
of uniformity, which in any case can be defended in a modest
form by an inverse probability argument of its own. And, once
we have even a modest form of our uniformity principle, claiming
only that such uniformity is likely to hold for some considerable
time to come or generally over a spatio-temporal range significantly
greater than that in which it has been so far observed to hold,
we have the necessary assumption on which observations in the
style of the eliminative methods will support similarly modest inductive generalisations.

  That is, we can do the trick. The rational defence of inductive
extrapolation is not only left open as a mere possibility by the
rebuttal of the sceptical arguments which purport to show it to
be impossible: we can also see the main lines of an argument
by which it can be carried through. The materials used in this
argument are all extremely familiar – the support of causal generalisations by eliminative induction; a principle of the uniformity of
nature; inverse probability; and the principle of indifference – but
I have defended their use against the stock objections. My argument
resembles Harrod's in its emphasis on the probability of limited
extrapolations, but the method of supporting them is different,
making explicit use of the principle of indifference, which Harrod
tries to do without – though, as Ayer argues, it is implicit in
his procedure after all. My argument resembles Mill's in its two-stage
procedure, eliminative methods supporting specific causal generalisations and a separate argument in favour of the causal principle
which they have to assume; but, whereas Mill treats this separate
argument as a simple induction,[18] I rely here on inverse probability.
My central idea is that we must use inverse probability somewhere
to give epistemic probabilistic support to an ampliative or extrapolat-
ing induction, and that we must rely on the principle of indifference
(or some weakened variant of it, such as my principle of tolerance)
to supply the antecedent or initial probabilities on the right-hand
side of Bayes's theorem, but that these moves can be made more
legitimately in the case for an appropriate version of the uniformity
principle than in attempts to vindicate specific inductions, starting
from cold. In the order of justification, therefore, the primary
induction is that which supports a certain general view of the

world – either our uniformity principle or the metaphysical conception which would provide a deeper explanation of at least part of the pattern of phenomena which that principle describes.

There is a possible weaker claim than the one I am making. Someone who rejected the inverse probability argument for our uniformity principle could admit that such a principle may well be *true*, while denying that *we* can establish it or even show it to be probabilified by the information we have. If it happens to be true, there is a sense in which the eliminative inferences by which we support specific causal generalisations will in fact be rational, even if we cannot show them to be so. On this view, our correct causal beliefs would constitute knowledge in the sense that it was no accident that these beliefs were true, though they would not constitute what I have called authoritative knowledge.[19] It may be worth noting that there is this second line of defence to which we could, if necessary, fall back; but I would rather try to hold the forward position.

NOTES

1. A. J. Ayer, *Probability and Evidence* (London: Macmillan, 1972) esp. pp. 3–6, 63, 88 and 91–110.

2. In *The Philosophy of Karl Popper*, ed. P. A. Schilpp (La Salle, The Open Court Publishing Co, Ill., 1974) p. 686.

3. D. Hume, *A Treatise of Human Nature*, I. 3. vi. My interpretation follows that of D. C. Stove in *Probability and Hume's Inductive Scepticism* (Oxford, Oxford U.P., 1973) which criticises scepticism about induction on much the same grounds as I rely on in this part of this paper.

4. Ayer, *Probability and Evidence*, p. 5.

5. Ibid., p. 57, referring to A. J. Ayer, 'The Concept of Probability as a Logical Relation', in *Observation and Interpretation*, ed. Stephan Körner (Dover Press New York, 1957); repr. in A. J. Ayer, *The Concept of a Person and Other Essays* (London: Macmillan, 1963). For rejoinders, see R. G. Swinburne, *An Introduction to Confirmation Theory* (London, Methuen, 1973) pp. 27–8; and J. L. Mackie, *Truth, Probability, and Paradox* (Oxford: Clarendon Press, 1973) pp. 196–202.

6. Karl Popper, *The Logic of Scientific Discovery* (London, Hutchinson, 1972) pp. 407–9.

7. Nelson Goodman, *Fact, Fiction and Forecast* (Cambridge, Mass: Harvard, 1955) chs 3 and 4.

8. Mackie, *Truth, Probability, and Paradox*, pp. 161–2 and 197–204.

9. Ayer, *Probability and Evidence*, pp. 107 (Harrod) and 62–3 (Ayer's own use of an argument in which there is an implicit appeal to the Principle).

10. J. M. Keynes, *A Treatise on Probability* (London, Macmillan, 1921) pp. 47–8.

11. Mackie, *Truth, Probability, and Paradox*, pp. 214–23.

12. See J. L. Mackie, *The Cement of the Universe* (Oxford: Clarendon Press, 1974) pp. 208–28; J. S. Mill, *A System of Logic*, III. 5. ix and 22.

13. Mackie, *Cement of the Universe*, pp. 297–321.

14. Ayer, *Probability and Evidence*, pp. 10–11.

15. Cf. Mackie, *Truth, Probability, and Paradox*, pp. 229–30.

16. Cf. Mackie, *Cement of the Universe*, pp. 225–8.

17. J. L. Mackie, *Problems from Locke* (Oxford: Clarendon Press, 1975) pp. 56–60.

18. J. S. Mill, *A System of Logic*, III. 21. ii.

19. For the distinction between authoritative knowledge and knowledge in the sense of non-accidentally true belief, see Mackie, *Problems from Locke*, pp. 217–20. Ayer suggests a similarly weak justification of factual inferences in *Probability and Evidence*, pp. 86–7.

7 Ayer on Monism, Pluralism and Essence[1]

DAVID WIGGINS

I

I read *Language, Truth and Logic*, then in its tenth impression, in 1954, and very shortly afterwards *The Foundations of Empirical Knowledge*. At that time I was an undergraduate at Oxford reading Literai Humaniores; neither work was an assignment for a weekly essay, nor on a vacation book list. Nor had I been prepared by undergraduate friends in other colleges, whose tutors had apparently used the first of these books to introduce their pupils to philosophy, for the liberating – in my case astonishing – effect of A. J. Ayer's philosophical writings. It is perfectly true that *Language, Truth and Logic* and *The Foundations of Empirical Knowledge* did not equip me to please better my own kind but frighteningly irascible tutor in the subject, who was the last or second to last of the Oxford Hegelians. But what mattered was that Ayer restored to a student of philosophy the sense that, by deductive argument from premisses commending themselves simply to common sense, one with a mind can make some dent of his own on a philosophical problem. It was this as much as the doctrines of *Language, Truth and Logic* that made it the beacon it so quickly became for beginners hopelessly perplexed and baffled by the arcane criteria of interest and relevance which were so notable a feature both of the philosophy I was being taught and of the philosophy which was then replacing what I was trying to learn.

It happens sometimes that a particular tradition of philosophy enjoys a domination which is so long and so effortless that those who enlist in its school become afraid to think anything out for themselves. They fear to make some mistake long since exposed, or to overlook something which they imagine that the initiated have already established beyond question. Perhaps this was the state of Oxford philosophy in 1930. It is nothing like this now in Oxford, Cambridge or London – or anywhere probably – but it could be so again. And the tiro critic's fear of having overlooked something is not in itself the slightest bit irrational. (The possession of a formally valid argument is an incomplete protection, for the premisses may be false or equivocal. And, validity apart, much else can be wrong.) As a dominant philosophical world view becomes progressively less inadequate and contrives, in response to all the exigencies of self-defence and running repair, more and more flexible and detailed philosophical techniques of analysis and inter-pretation, the higher the probability that a member of the school really will be able to point to something overlooked by any new-comer who is disposed to be hostile or critical. It is by consolidation, after all, that secure, satisfying and responsible philosophies are constructed. But danger is inherent in this however necessary pro-cess. The further the construction gets from the original basis of everyday experience and conviction, the more likely it is that in the end a newcomer of Gilbert Ryle's discursive sanity, or A.J. Ayer's devastating and passionate intellectual simplicity, will be able to topple and destroy the whole thing – good with bad, scholar-ship with claptrap, insight with absurdity, all together.

If philosophers and schools of philosophy want protection from this hazard, then I should claim that, however else they see it, they have to see philosophy under the aspect of some special passion for the elementary – as a willingness (possessed by certain of the greatest metaphysicians) to take with a seriousness which is not of the everyday perfectly everyday things, accepting cheerfully that the unfolding and excogitation of what is implicit but objectively discoverable within our most commonplace practices of thought and feeling is work – requires indeed a tedious thoroughness which, will appear, to anyone reluctant to believe that most of the really important mistakes in human thinking are elementary mistakes, like nothing so much as the tic of an obsessional. If a school of philosophy aspires to renew itself, and be not engulfed in the dissatisfactions of each new generation, it must return often to the starting point, conceived not as one indubitable proposition, or some 'minimum' knowledge distilled from so much softer stuff, but as an inexplicit world-knowledge only incipiently articulate, but replete with the potentiality for being ever better elucidated and better understood (by philosophy but not only by philosophy).

Finally, none of this is much good without a feeling for the concretely particular, for detail, and for *theory* – or without the distaste, which the linguistic philosophy that Ayer mocked in the 1950s so conspicuously lacked, and which later scholasticism (to judge from the standard histories) so conspicuously lacked, for the gratuitous and the *ad hoc*.

II

I have no clear idea what Ayer will make of these claims about the nature of philosophy (except to ask to be reassured that space enough is left here for science), but they echo faintly a sentence from *Language, Truth and Logic* which I transcribed and then found myself beginning to embroider and alter. The sentence is to be found in chapter 8, unforgettably entitled 'Solutions of Outstanding Philosophical Disputes'. Section iii of this chapter, called 'Monism and Pluralism', dealing with certain matters untouched by the rest of the book, has always had for me a special fascination. It expounds and summarily dispatches a doctrine of monism which says that absolutely all the properties of a thing, including its relations to everything else, are constitutive of the essence of that thing. If the argument which Ayer used on that occasion is correct, then it tells equally against pluralism – at least, as Leibniz conceived and defended it. It does not tell against Leibniz's doctrine of the individual concept, which was one part of his pluralism;[2] but it does, if correct, tell against Leibnizian views of nature and essence, against theories which entail that there are necessary properties of individuals, and even against the modest variant of essentialism which I have been arguing about with Ayer ever since 1959. 1959 is the year in which to my surprise I encountered him. (I think I had previously supposed he was a purely notional or legendary creature.) Trusting that it is the best form of homage one can properly pay one's elders and betters to persist vexatiously in the attempt to persuade them of something, I shall pick up threads and resume the argument, in a heavily qualified defence of Leibniz (the mature Leibniz of *Nouveaux Essais*) against Ayer's criticisms of all doctrines of essence.

III

A good statement of the point which is agreed, and which the whole argument starts from, is to be found at p. 148 of the second edition of *Language, Truth and Logic* (London: Gollancz, 1946):

> What makes this false assumption superficially plausible [the assumption is the monistic doctrine cited in the last paragraph of section II above] is the the ambiguity of such sentences as 'If this thing had not got the properties which it has, it would not be what it is'. To assert this may be to assert merely that if a thing has a property, it cannot also lack it – that if, for example, my newspaper is on the table in front of me, it is

not the case that it is not on the table. And this is an analytic
proposition whose validity no one would dispute. But to allow
this is not to allow that all the properties which a thing has
are defining properties. To say that if my newspaper were not
on the table in front of me it would not be what it is, is false
if it is equivalent to saying that it is necessary for my newspaper
to be on the table in the sense in which it *is* necessary for
it to contain news. . . . It is only when '*A* has not *p*' is a self-contradictory proposition that *p* can be said to be a defining or internal
property of *A*.

Even with the omission marked, this is a self-sufficient statement.
I think it is perfectly right, and that disagreement can only arise
about the status and meaning of these contentions. For Ayer, they
are all to be explained in terms of what some seventeen years
later, W. V. Quine called the first grade of modal involvement.[3]
Ayer says,

In discussing this question, we have employed the factual terminology in which it is commonly presented, but this has not pre-
vented us from recognizing that it is linguistic in character. For we
have seen that to say that a property *p* is a defining property
of a thing *A* is equivalent to saying that the sentence which
is formed out of the symbol '*A*' as subject and the symbol
'*p*' as predicate expresses an analytic proposition. And it must
be added that the use of factual terminology is particularly inadvis-
able in this instance, because a predicate which serves to express
an analytic proposition when combined with one descriptive
phrase may serve to express a synthetic proposition when combined with another descriptive phrase which nevertheless refers
to the same object. Thus to have written *Hamlet* is an internal
property of the author of *Hamlet*, but not of the author of
Macbeth, nor yet of Shakespeare.

But of course these are all one and the same man, Ayer's argument
continues (and at this point, whether consciously or unconsciously,
many philosophers have followed in his footsteps,[4] though not
necessarily in the same cause, or in the name of convictions of
which Ayer would approve). So we get a contradiction if we suppose
that internal properties or relations are genuine properties or relations of *individuals*.[5]

And here or hereabouts the ways divide. I shall argue, against
what Ayer believed then and still believes,[6] that analyticity and
de dicto necessity are not all there is to necessity; and that, once

we recognise this, we can read the conclusion on which Ayer and I are agreed (that is, the conclusion quoted from p. 148 of *Language, Truth and Logic*) in what Ayer would then have called the material mode – which is to say that there do exist necessary properties of individuals (far fewer, no doubt, than some of the authors Ayer attacked in section iii of chapter 8 supposed).

Note first that, even for the case of 'the author of *Hamlet* is necessarily the author of *Hamlet*', analyticity is not a very good instrument of analysis. If 'the author of *Hamlet* is the author of *Hamlet*' be analysed in Russell's fashion, then what analyticity is predicated of is an existential proposition.

(a) $(\exists x) ((y) (AHy \equiv y = x) \ \& \ AHx)$

or some variant on this. But (a) is contingent. Probably the claim of necessity *de dicto* is simply false, then. (*Mutatis mutandis* there is the same difficulty when the sentence is treated by the Fregean analysis of definite descriptions). It can hardly then be necessary or analytic.

We get closer to Ayer's probable intentions if we predicate analyticity of the sentence

(b) $(x) (AHx \equiv AHx)$

and, for the case of Ayer's other sentence, if we predicate analyticity of

(c) $(x) (x = $ my newspaper $\supset x$ contains news).

But the problem is not quite at an end even now, because (c) analytically entails

(d) $(\exists z) (z = $ my newspaper)

and if (c) were analytic then anything (c) analytically entailed would itself be analytic. But (d) is not analytic.

One thing we might do is to retreat from the reference to this very newspaper and make do with the claim

(e)   It is analytic that $(x) (x$ is a newspaper $\supset x$ contains news).

But this leaves unexplained the apparent correctness of the claim, *about my newspaper in particular*:

(f)   My newspaper necessarily contains news.

And (f) is a claim which Ayer was disposed to allow as correct.[7]

I expect there are several courses which could be proposed at this point, including the simple sacrifice of (f). What I propose to do here is to save it by taking 'necessarily' as governing simply the predicate 'contains news', and in a fashion I shall argue to be exempt from all Ayer's objections to internal properties as such. The outcome will be an essentialism for the sober contentions of which I still hope to win Ayer's assent. It is a very extensional variety of essentialism. To the adherents of *possibilia*, possible worlds, and stronger essentialisms, which entail such conclusions as the conceptual indispensability to anything of its actual origin, the outcome may seem to be a doctrine of laughable timidity.

IV

I begin with an enumeration of the anything but extravagant premisses, principles and assumptions that will govern the derivation of essentialism to be attempted in later sections. I believe that it is only empiricism as empiricism misconceives itself, not nominalism or extensionalism, which could find anything here at which to cavil.

(1) For the first assumption I rely on a response of Arnauld against Leibniz's digest of his *Discours de métaphysique*:

I have no conception of these purely possible substances, that is to say the ones that God will never create. . . . one can conceive of possibilities in the natures which he has created. . . . But I am much mistaken if there is anyone who dares to say that he can conceive of a purely possible substance, for I am convinced in my own mind that although one talks so much of these purely possible substances, nonetheless one never conceives of any of them except according to the notion of those which God has created.[8]

(2) The second principle is the requirement that the argument should nowhere rely upon possible worlds.

(3) The third principle or assumption I shall make is given succinctly by Ayer: 'We can significantly ask what properties it is necessary for something to possess in order to be of such and such kind . . . the answer may be to some extent arbitrary, but at least some answer can be looked for. On the other hand, there is no such definition of an individual.'[9]

It is the consequence of this that, to make clear which thing a thing is, it is not enough (*pace* the friends of individual essence) to say, however lengthily, that it is *such* or *so and so*: we have to say that it is *this* or *that* such. This is perfectly obvious when we think of trying to determine one entity by mentioning short or simple predicates. But it is difficult to see any reason to believe that by making predicates ever longer and more and more complicated we shall be able to overcome the obvious non-sufficiency, or evident non-necessity, for identity with just x which infects all the relatively simple predicates true of x.

(4) The fourth assumption or principle can again be given in the words of alien sources. The first extract is from a letter from Arnauld to Leibniz, the second from a book by Ayer.

> I can think that I shall or shall not take a particular journey, while remaining very much assured that neither one nor the other will prevent my being myself. So I remain very much assured that neither one nor the other is included in the individual concept [essence] of myself.[10]

> But we have to maintain some anchorage in reality if our references are to be successful. . . . There appear to be no *general* rules for deciding what this anchorage may be. . . . One could imagine that the Pyramids were built at a different time, or perhaps even in a different country. If one anchors Dickens to other items in his biography one can conceive of his not having been a writer: if one identifies him by his writings one can perhaps conceive of his having lived in a different century. But could we consistently place him in the distant future, or in prehistoric times? . . . It is a rather arbitrary question in this sort of case.[11]

Appearances perhaps to the contrary, what Ayer is claiming here does not depend upon the theory of reference as such. Nor, even if Ayer expresses the point in a way which invites this charge, does it depend upon a confusion between a supposition about what may in fact be the case, the world being what it actually is, and what might, contrary to fact, have been the case, if the world had been different. Of course, one can counterfactually conceive at t of an individual x not having properties by which, for the very purpose of conceiving of its being otherwise, one at t identifies x in the actual world. But, if serious conceiving is to have anything to do with conceptual possibility (and if it is excluded that not anything can be just anything), then some restriction must be acknowledged. We cannot, for instance, conceive of anything's not being identical with the very individual it is, nor, therefore, of its having a different principle of individuation from its actual principle.

The point of agreement may be put as follows, then. Where a thinker A conceives of an individual x as φ (and by moving from 'refer' to 'conceive of' we only make Ayer's claim more secure), φ cannot assume just any value. There are restrictions on φ and they depend on which entity the entity x is. What we then have in (4) is not a reduction or elimination of necessity and possibility (that is not in any case our concern), but the following elucidation of necessity *de re*:

(i) x can be φ just in case it is possible to conceive of x that x is φ;
(ii) x must be φ just in case it is not possible to conceive of x that x is not φ;
(iii) the position of the boundary between what one can conceive of x and what one cannot conceive of x depends on x, may depend on which thing x *actually* is, and may sometimes depend on a matter of degree, or be somewhat arbitrary – in which case, it must be unsurprising that at least some of the properties which it is definitely impossible (i. e. well beyond the last point of possibility) to conceive of x as not having are rather *unspecific*. For they may be the negations of long conjunctions of properties, any subconjunction of which it may be possible to conceive of x as not satisfying.

(5) The triadic relation 'A conceives of x as being φ' or 'A conceives of x that x is φ' may be cleared of all extentionalist and nominalist suspicions by viewing its connection with 'A conceives that p' on the model of Quine's theory of the relation holding between *believing that* and *believing of*. The triadic relation is then between the thinker A, the entity x (however described), and an attribute $\hat{z}(\varphi z)$ or $(\lambda z)\varphi z$. Quine has shown how, at a certain price this attribute can be nominalistically reconstrued.[12] Similarly, 'x is such that it is possible to conceive of x that x is φ' represents a complex dyadic relation between x and the attribute $(\lambda z)\varphi z$.

(6) Ordinary intuitive grammar suggests that 'necessarily' and 'possibly' can either govern a complete sentence (as in the sentences which submit naturally to treatment within the first grade of modal involvement) or govern a simple or complex predicate, as in the

analysis I gave notice (end of section ΙΙ) that I wish to apply to Ayer's sentence (f).[13] If it is asked what is meant by the latter usage, which lies altogether outside Quine's enumeration of the three grades of modal involvement, then I reply first that this is something which the reader is already familiar with under the verbal forms 'x can be φ' and 'for x, it is possible to be φ'; second, that (4) above was already a partial elucidation of some such usage; third, that anyone who speaks English is already deeply committed to a set of locutions which resemble this one in lying outside Quine's enumeration. For, if we supplant *de re* 'possibly φ' and 'necessarily φ' by 'can (be) φ' and 'must (be) φ' ('cannot help but [be] φ'), we shall notice that, so far as logical form goes, they seem to have formal affinities with the *de re* predicates of ability, obligation, capacity or disposition, which English speakers who have heard nothing of possible worlds apply effortlessly to the actual things of the actual world when they say that A can do otherwise than he is doing, that D could not help but strike C, or that x, y and z are soluble or fragile or fusible; or when they say (in near relative locutions) that B owes C five pounds, or that B needs five pounds.[14] None of these claims has a natural *de dicto* modal translation.

(7) I represent with the sign *NEC* the undifferentiated *de re* 'must' or 'necessarily' which I presume to underlie as a genus the various species of *de re* concept. For the corresponding *de re* 'can' and 'possibly' I use the sign *POSS*. *NEC* and *POSS* are conceived here as working upon predicates abstracted in a manner now to be described.[15]

To form the expressions to which *NEC* and *POSS* are to apply we take any open sentence, say 'x is a man' or 'if x is a man then x has genetic make-up G' or 'x is identical with y' and bind the free variable or free variables in the open sentence with an abstraction operator λ. Thus

$$(\lambda x)[\text{Man } x], \ (\lambda x)[\text{Man } x \supset Gx], \ (\lambda x)(\lambda y)[x = y]$$

These abstracts may as well be read 'the property which any x has just in case x is a man', 'the property which any x has just in case if x is a man then x has genetic make-up G', 'the relation in which any x and y stand just in case x is y' respectively. (Nothing will hang on whether explanations are given in this second-level fashion or not.) We may now express the judgement that an entity or a sequence of entities falls in the extension of some property or relation so designated as follows:

Caesar has $(\lambda x)[\text{Man } x]$
Everything has the property $(\lambda x)[M(x) \supset G(x)]$
$\langle$Hesperus, Phosphorus$\rangle$ have $(\lambda x) (\lambda y)[x = y]$

or more handily and conventionally by simple juxtaposition thus:

$(\lambda x)[\text{Man } x]$, $\langle$Caesar$\rangle$
$(\forall z) ((\lambda x)[M(x) \supset G(x)]$, $\langle z \rangle)$
$(\lambda x) (\lambda y)[x = y]$, $\langle$the evening star, the morning star$\rangle$

Putting *NEC* or *POSS* to work on these abstracts, and leaving the subject term incontrovertibly outside the scope of the modality, we then have

$[NEC (\lambda x)[Mx]]$, $\langle$Caesar$\rangle$
$(\forall z)([NEC (\lambda x)[M(x) \supset G(x)]]$, $\langle z \rangle)$
$[NEC(\lambda x)(\lambda y)[x = y]]$, $\langle$the evening star, the morning star$\rangle$

The last says that the evening star and the morning star necessarily have that relation which any x and y have just in case they are identical.[16]

V

Taking Leibniz's law in the form

For all F such that F is a genuine property of x or y, $(x = y) \supset (Fx \equiv Fy)$

and making the assumption (against which no effective argument now remains) that *NEC* properties are genuine properties, we have the following proof of the complete coincidence of the necessary satisfaction and the actual satisfaction of the predicate of identity, an *NEC* counterpart of the quantified modal theorem:

$(x)(y)((x = y) \supset \Box (x = y))$

Consider any individuals H and P (Hesperus and Phosphorus, say) such that $H = P$. Then it follows by Leibniz's law that, for all F such that F is a genuine property of P or H,

$F(H) \equiv F(P)$

Now, the following is a truth about H:

$[NEC\ \lambda x\ \lambda y(x=y)],\ \langle H,\ H\rangle$

and, the scope of this *NEC* being confined to the abstract, there then exists the abstractable property

$(\lambda z)([NEC[\lambda x\ \lambda y(x=y)]],\ \langle z,\ H\rangle)$

But *H* itself has this property, and if *H* has this property then so does *P*. And then, eliminating from the statement that *P* has it the outer lambda (by the principle of lambda abstraction), we have

$[NEC[\lambda x\ \lambda y(x=y)]],\ \langle H,\ P\rangle$

But now, since nothing depended on the particular choice of *H* and *P* which were such that $H=P$, we have

$(x)(y)((x=y)\supset[NEC[\lambda x\ \lambda y(x=y)]],\ \langle x,\ y\rangle)$

This proof follows almost line for line a famous proof of the necessity of identity which was given by Ruth Barcan Marcus in 1947. It was received with incredulity by those committed to the mutual assimilation (much criticised in more recent times by Kripke and others) of the categories of *necessity* and *a priority*, and rejected on the grounds that the identity of evening and morning star was an *a posteriori* discovery. But, even if 'statement ascertainable *a priori* to be true' and 'necessarily true statement' coincided perfectly in their extensions, Miss Barcan's theorem could still stand in our version. For the conclusion is not put forward here as a necessarily true statement. It is put forward as a true statement of *de re* necessity.[17]

What the proof comes down to is this: Hesperus is necessarily Hesperus, so, if Phosphorus is Herperus, Phosphorus is necessarily Hesperus. The only conceivable point left to argue is whether there is a *de re* use of 'must' in English. But the onus is on the contingency theorist and the anti-essentialist at last. He has to dispel as illusion what seems to be fact – that in English there exist many such *de re* uses. It is also a matter of some importance that this proof is unobstructed even if we suspect that *NEC* ought to create an opaque context. All substitutions in the proof are on *manifestly* extensional positions. But the proof also does much to relax the stringency of that supposition. For even in a context governed by *NEC* we should certainly expect *NEC* identicals to be intersubstitutable. And we now know that all actual identicals are *NEC* identicals. So we have demonstrated what is simply taken for granted by those who prove Miss Barcan's theorem by reference to a fully fledged model-theoretic semantics providing *ab initio* for the identification of particular individuals across all the possible worlds where they occur, under no matter what description. In lieu of assertion (or of claiming that the only test there can be of theories of modality is a holistic comparison of finished theories) we can *explain* how variables of quantification standing outside *NEC* contexts can reach into them.

VI

As good a place as any in which to advance these matters and to demonstrate the mutual congeniality of essence and extension is an area in which extensionality reigns absolutely – namely, set-theory. Let us explicate the *de re* 'necessarily' by reference to the explanations which those friends of extensionality who are also set-theorists give of the identification and individuation of classes.

> . . . what sets attributes apart from classes is merely that whereas classes are identical when they have the same members, attributes may be distinct even though present in all and only the same things.[18]

> . . . we use the word 'set' in such a way that a set is completely determined when its members are given.[19]

Suppose that we try to apply these criteria, and that we are invited to conceive a thing α identified as the entity (whether class or attribute we do not yet know) to which there belong the items x and y and only these.[20] Then it seems that, if we are to envisage α, what we have to ask is whether α, the very thing α, could have dispensed with the particular items x and y . If it could – if α could lack x or could lack y – then α is not a class. That is the thought which is suggested both by Quine's distinction of classes and attributes, and by the usual justification of the axiom of extensionality in terms of membership's *determining* set-identity.

The idea which motivates this whole way of talking is that, whereas there is no criterial connection between actual extension and being this or that property (this contrast is important), or between an actual position in space–time and being this or that man, there is a criterial connection between membership and set-identity. But neither the test nor the thought which prompts it can even be stated within the first grade of modal involvement, or in terms which Ayer and Quine would regard as respectable.[21] Given that the tautologous

$$\sim\Diamond(\exists x)(\exists\alpha)(x\in\alpha \cdot x\notin\alpha),$$

distinguishes classes from nothing else, and given the supposed unintelligibility of the statement

$$\sim(\exists x)(\exists\alpha)(x\in\alpha \cdot \Diamond x\notin\alpha),$$

what is needed is to express somehow else the thought that, if α is a class containing x and y then α could not have lacked x. This is a *de re* modal assertion. The very weakest form of it is

$$(x)(y)(\alpha)\{\alpha = \{x, y\} \supset NEC[\lambda s\ \lambda r[s\in r]], [x, \alpha]\}$$

exemplifying the general principle:

$$(x)(\alpha)((x\in\alpha) \supset [NEC\ \lambda z\ \lambda w[z\in w]][x, \alpha])$$

Set-theorists who say that it is a peculiarity of sets to be determined by their members, or who distinguish sets from attributes in Quine's way, are surely saying *at least* this. On the assumption of transparency of *NEC*, they can be counted as saying

$$(x)(\alpha)(x\in\alpha \supset NEC(\lambda z)[x\in z], [\alpha])$$

It should occasion no surprise that, in order to delimit an area within which extensionality will reign, or intuitively to justify the axioms of extensionality for sets and exclude attributes from the intended interpretation of the variables which range over the entities of the theory in question, one has to trespass for a moment outside the delimited area and talk in a language of richer expressive resources.

VII

When set-theorists give in to the inclination to justify the extensionality principle in set-theory, and when they talk of membership as determining set identity, they are already indulging in a very modest and reasonable essentialism, which such formulae as these put into more explicitly modal words. I now submit that the pair set {Eiffel Tower, Crystal Palace} is essentially a set, and essentially a set with just these members, *because nothing could count as envisaging it in a way which implied that it was not a set or lacked these members.* For 'set' is the most fundamental identification of this entity and there is no more unrestrictive identification of what this thing is. And any identification sufficient to fix which particular set it is will, in virtue of the fundamental theoretical principles which articulate and explicate the notion of set (for example, the axiom of extensionality), exclude its having different members.

I should make it clear at this point that I am not claiming that it is impossible to envisage {Eiffel Tower, Crystal Palace} under any *other description* than 'pair set the sole members of which are Eiffel Tower and Crystal Palace'. One might conceive of it under the description 'the pair set the members of which are in Z's opinion the most remarkable works of nineteenth-century engineering in the capital cities London and Paris' or in indefinitely many different ways. But to show that this set might *lack* the Eiffel Tower as a member one must envisage it under a description which actually *excludes* the description 'pair set consisting of Eiffel Tower and Crystal Palace'. And then concerning *what* would one be envisaging that it might have lacked Eiffel Tower? (Cf. assumption 4 in section IV.)

It may seem for a moment that one can envisage anything of anything – even 'lacking Eiffel Tower' of {Eiffel Tower, Crystal Palace} – provided that the identification one starts off with is as vague as, say, 'entity mentioned or had in mind at t by F. Hausdorff'. But starting off with so vague a description of the thing thought of by Hausdorff should make it not easier but harder for the would-be envisager to be sure that he has, in the serious sense, conceived of or envisaged that entity under the description 'lacking the Eiffel Tower'. The possibility we are interested in should not be *augmented by ignorance*.[22] The same goes for the necessity and possibility Ayer was discussing in his own enunciation of principle (4). The conceiving must be with regard to a definite actual compliant of the identification, and what it is possible to envisage with regard to that depends on what the particular entity was – Dickens, the Pyramids, or whatever. But then, if the description, whatever it is, which the thing is envisaged as satisfying, must respect the identity link between the entity of the envisaging and the actual entity with respect to which the envisaging takes place, it seems it must not be incompatible with absolutely every description individuating the actual entity as 'this f' or 'that g' or whatever. Otherwise the envisager will surely have lost all grip on the subject of his speculations. This after all is the point agreed between Ayer and myself. (Cf. assumption 4.) Where we may possibly disagree is in my further contention that special importance attaches, in the context of such explanations of which thing is being envisaged, to *what* the thing is.[23] I do not mean that sayings-which necessarily require explicit announcement of a sortal predicate which specifies what the thing is – only that the explanation given must, however latently, *determine* some sortal specification, or lead to some set of sortal specifications, all of them (on pain of identity's becoming relative) determining some single principle of identity.[24] Whatever the strength of this a general doctrine – and I believe that its denial will involve the senseless fiction of characterless 'substratum', the relativity of '=', or the total rejection of any ontology of separate particulars – the argument about classes has displayed at its best this conception of the individuation of particulars. For the argument turned upon bringing α or {Eiffel Tower, Crystal Palace} under one of the fundamental concepts of some theory outside which the entity was not envisageable or individuable or identifiable at all.

VIII

A handy way of summing up the general requirement which results from conjoining (4) with the said conception of individuation is this: when a thinker genuinely conceives of x as φ there must be some sortal concept f which adequately answers the question 'What is x?' (i.e. commits to some persistence condition for x him who subsumes a concrete particular x under f) such that x can be identified as *this* or *that* f thing, and such that f and φ are coconceivable of x.[25]

The next step would be to apply this to (f) (section III above), and to the newspaper lying all those years ago on Ayer's table. But newspapers are artifacts, and as such they have nominal not real essence and are relatively devoid of interesting *de re* necessary properties (over and above the property 'is a newspaper').[26] It will prove to be more instructive to take concrete things in nature picked out under natural kind words, and consider the however hackneyed example of Julius Caesar.

It is possible to conceive of Caesar's having a different career. It is possible to conceive of this very man's not being consul in 69 BC, or his not conquering Gaul, or his not crossing the Rubicon, or even of his not in fact being male or not living through adolescence. What then is it impossible to envisage of Caesar? Ayer would say it becomes progressively harder to preserve the link with the actual Caesar and to anchor the 'this' if we try to envisage Caesar lacking certain longer disjunctions of his actual properties. If there is anything in this contention of Ayer's, then it seems likely that the 'this such' conception of individuation which I defend may make it possible to organise these longer disjunctions and to see order beneath apparent absence of system. But, whether this is so or not, there is something else which the paradigm of the preceding class argument will certainly make us expect to find it hard to envisage Caesar's not being. That is human.[27] For if anything here plays the part which we found the concept *class* to play in the earlier argument, then it is *man* which plays it. Or so it would appear. There is one doubt. Someone may allow that there must be some sortal predicate f such that, whatever else Caesar is envisaged as being, no genuine envisaging of Caesar excludes his being *this f*. But he may wonder whether there is a less specific sortal property than *man* which is capable of fixing the persistence conditions of this entity and answering the question 'What is Caesar?' Could not the generic property *animal* serve as the value of f? (See section XI.)

This is by no means the only obscurity or perplexity to be encountered in adapting the {Eiffel Tower, Crystal Palace} argument to the things to be encountered in nature. But before we prune back the doctrine it must be allowed to put on more leaf.

IX

Suppose that every natural thing x satisfies throughout its actual existence some sortal predicate f which has to be treated as invulnerable to all envisagings of states and histories alternative to its actual states and history; and suppose that f denominates a natural-kind concept which not only says what x is but also leads *a posteriori* to a passable criterion of identity and persistence for members of its extension. Then not only will such sortal concepts f be owed much or most of the honour accorded by Aristotle and Leibniz to the *infima species*[28] – provided only that they really do represent the least specific account of the character of their bearers which will suffice to articulate these very bearers from the rest of reality; it will also be possible to derive some surprising *a posteriori* consequences.

Suppose that *man* (and every other natural-kind term, whether species or genus) has its sense fixed by reference to some hypothesised generic constitution, which users of the term are committed to think of as exemplified under the actual physical laws of the actual world by the actual instances which they encounter and group together as men.[29] And suppose G is some feature (for instance, some genetic feature, in this case) which is scientifically or *a posteriori* definitive of that constitution. Now consider anything that is a man. He is necessarily, if a man, then *G*. It may be objected that the conditional governed by this 'necessarily' is no conceptual necessity, because it is contingent upon the laws of nature which actually obtain, and other laws might have obtained. But, if the concept of 'man' behaves in a manner consonant with the suggested mode of definition of 'man', then the existence of men is contingent on the very same thing. For it is on the same actual laws that the delimitation and significance of the said internal constitution depends.[30] Since *G* and *man* depend for their existence on the same thing, and it is by reference to *G* that (in the last analysis) anything counts as a man, it follows that a man is necessarily, if a man, then *G*. So, with this established, we can go on to the next step. In the last section we gave an argument to show that whatever is a man is necessarily a man. If that is right (see below, section XI), then anything that is a man is necessarily *G*.

It is sometimes complained that essences 'explain nothing'. But, if the foregoing argument is correct, then, apart from the least interesting (and least controversial) necessary properties (for instance, *identity with Caesar*, which is too special,[31] and *self-identity*, which is too general), they do have a function. In the first place, there are predicates which stand for essential properties of a thing and register the condition the satisfaction of which is a prerequisite of the very thing's being articulated at all from the rest of reality (that is the role of *f* in our foregoing discussion). These predicates are not in the business of explaining, because they are presupposed to there being anything to explain. But, in the second place, there are more interesting predicates, such as *G* above. These represent *a posteriori* or scientific accounts given by some (at the appropriate level) fundamental theory of the natural kind or articulative sort outside which *x* cannot be envisaged at all. It is to the satisfaction of this complex requirement that such properties as *G* owe both their focal place in the theory of individuation and their necessity.

We may add to the maxims of section IV a principle long since acknowledged in every interesting or thoughtful essentialism.

(8) The practical scientist does the business; but the philosopher keeps the books.[32]

I agree with those who deny that forms are to be used in seeking to explain specific and special causes.[33]

X

I hope that it is now clear that the essentialism which I have sought to defend from Ayer's argument in *Language, Truth and Logic* has it in common with Leibniz's to accord with the new maxim just given; but that it is not an essentialism of *individual* essences. Individuals *have* essences without which they would not 'be what they are', i.e. would not be; but (apart from unhelpful essential properties such as *necessarily identical with Caesar*) their essences are shared.

The requirement that essences should be unique (like almost any other attempt to say anything or deny anything by means of the idea, as absurd in theory as it is barbarous in expression, of *haecceitas*) is seriously contaminated with confusion (from which Leibniz cannot be acquitted). We get from the 'this' of 'this *f*' (where *f* is or determines some sortal specification) all the particularity which is required for anchorage to the actual entity when we conceive of it in various counterfactual ways. Whether or not Strawson has ever fully demonstrated the conceptual necessity of individuals to thought as we know it, I believe him to have conclusively demonstrated that, for thought which does recognise individuals, the functions of 'this' and 'such' are (regardless of any *limited* interchangeability in the functions they enjoy) mutually irreducible.[34] A *haecceitas* would be something which by attempting both could perform neither function. The non-particularised properties which pass the test of being invariant under all successful counterfactual speculations representing *de re* conceivings of Gaius Julius Caesar are those with negations not co-conceivable with *man* (or, more weakly, not co-conceivable with *animal* – see below, section XI), All such properties are multiply satisfiable. Our essentialism accomplishes what Locke first envisaged and then mismanaged with his doctrines of real and nominal essence.[35]

The claim that Caesar is necessarily a man, that he cannot not (or cannot help but) be a man, is founded, according to our elucidation of these matters, in Caesar's being such that it is impossible to envisage with respect to him his having any attribute or sortal property exclusive of his being a man. What kind of a 'must' is this?

Of course, the locutions 'can' and 'must' are normally put to other work. *De re* modal claims are usually based upon people's abilities or inabilities, capacities or incapacities as of some time and relative to the circumstances of that time, or upon their obligations or debts or compulsions of that time.[36] If a man must repay five pounds then the source of the necessity is perhaps a borrowing transaction and consequential state of indebtedness from which he has not been released. If a man cannot help but slide down a slope, then what necessitates his falling may be a trip, say, the gradient of the slope, and the man's lack of the strength he would need to regain control. This is more unalterable than a state of being obliged to pay money. But what I suggest is that we should see the *de re* necessity of essence as the limiting case of the other *de re* necessities with which their form appears to conjoin them. The essential necessity of a trait arises at that point of unalterability where the *very existence of the bearer is unqualifiedly conditional* upon the trait in question. Here, at this point, a property is fixed to its bearer by virtue of being inherent in the individuation of it, in the drawing of a spatio-temporal boundary around it. The closer the source of the attribute to the singling out of the thing itself – the more it is bound up with the whole mode of articulating reality to discover such an object in reality – the more exigent, obviously, is the necessity that, *if there is to exist any such thing as the bearer*, it should have the feature in question. The *de re* 'must' of the causally inflexible here passes over at a certain threshold into an inflexibility which is conceptual (though only loosely speaking logical). There is no reason why this should make the essentialistic *de re* attribute any less of a real attribute of the thing itself. If all this is right, then (subject to the caveat to be entered in the next section) being a man is an absolute individuative prerequisite for anything's being Caesar, in reality or in supposition. And, similarly, once it is Tully we conceive of or single out, and once it is Cicero (who is the same as Tully) whom we conceive of or single out, the things we have singled out must on pain of incoherence be the same. Thought is not, it is true, constrained here by anything like the definition of logical constants, which are the source of strict logical necessity, or by explicit stipulations, definitions or meaning postulates, nor by any form of words. For, as we have already emphasised, the meaning of 'Caesar' is not fixed or stipulated by a definition. Since names are not given their sense by being annexed to an enumeration of properties, nor defined at all, no *analytic* truths can be generated from the meanings of such expressions. But why should this result in looser constraints upon the conceivability of the thoughts the expression of which involves namable individuals? All that follows is that the constraints must be of somewhat different nature or provenance. The constraints are still constraints of meaning, even though, where reference is involved in the fixing of sense, this meaning itself is conferred in a significantly different way from the meaning of, for instance, 'bachelor'. The difference is just the difference which the attempt to discover a proper semantics would lead one to expect.

XI

I come now to the charge of overspecificity in the identification of 'man' as the highest individuative sortal for Caesar. It has been claimed that, if we go to the length of trying to conceive of Caesar's not being a man, then the speculation loses grip of its intended subject. Why should not the link with the actual Caesar be secured by the continued identifiability of the object of the speculation under the description 'this mammal' or even 'animal'?

Suppose first that this objection were correct, and that one or other of these very unspecific sortal specifications were a good enough sticking point. Even then there would be *de re* necessities to be discovered. 'Animal' excludes 'stone', 'insect', 'paddle steamer', 'number' (and 'mereological fusion of animal parts' too, in my judgement). The objector might say that the resulting essentialism lacked much of the interest of the position first stated. But our Leibnizian doctrine of natural kinds would still have a point at the level 'mammal' or 'animal': and, even at such a distance from the specific, there is still something to be made of scientific discoveries, generic and abstract though the property G of section IX would then have to be made.

The damage the objection can inflict, then, is limited. But the proper reply to the objection is that our constraints on envisaging, taken in conjunction with our existing theory of individuation, do seem to suffice to rule out 'this animal' as too weak a link between the envisaging and the actual man if, as this objector desires, it is to sustain an envisaging of Caesar as not a man.

Recall first the very weak disjunctive properties, complicated and very likely numerous, the denial of any of which Ayer allows to be sufficient to loosen the *de re* anchorage between the object and envisaging of the object. It is not very clear that, for all such disjunctions $\emptyset$, '$\emptyset$ and not a man' are consistent (conceivably cosatisfiable by anything) – in which case the *de re* requirement, as we have framed it, for conceiving *not being a man* of Caesar is already breached.

More conclusively, it may be recalled that the whole justification of our criterion for essential properties is the claim that there can be no envisaging a particular thing, this or that particular thing, as having a different principle of individuation (different existence and persistence conditions) from its actual principle. But, seen in this light, 'this animal' is by no means obviously a good enough identification of Caesar to sustain the envisaging of him as not a man. For 'that animal' is not itself *autonomously individuative*. The words 'this animal' certainly suffice to determine designations, and rough-and-ready identifications in ordinary contexts of what things are. This is because 'animal' can take on an individuative force from the context or some other sortal word which is ready to hand.[37] But the designation 'this animal' is supported in all sorts of different ways, and it determines no single principle of individuation. How, then, could it work in the context of the claim 'NN conceived of this particular animal's not being a man', if (as we have suggested in our account of the truth conditions of such claims and elucidation of the three-place relation 'conceives of') 'man' were not available to supplement 'animal' in the anchorage of the object conceived to conceiver and the property conceived by him of the object? In order that it be true that there was an envisaging of Caesar as being not a man, there must be available, to link the actuality of Caesar and the envisaging, an identification of Caesar both co-conceivable with 'not a man' and not less specific than the highest (least specific) individuative sortal which is possessed of an autonomous principle of individuation. I should call such a predicate an ultimate sortal predicate. In the case of natural things, such as Caesar, this ultimate predicate, however far it be above the level of *infima species*, must be conditioned by some sufficiently specific causal generalisation to provide decidable (or to the appropriate degree decidable) conditions of identity and persistence for members of its extension. (There are generalisations to which, whether or not he knows or wishes it, anyone who subsumes a thing under the concept is committed.) This requirement is breached unless there is a sortal term lower than 'animal' which is individuative and suffices to fix Caesar with Caesar's very principle of individuation. If someone can find such an ultimate sortal for Caesar which is higher than 'man'; then he may substitute it for 'man' throughout the argument.

At this point an element of the indeterminacy which Ayer predicted and which was anticipated at (4) of section IV above creeps in. But it is no part of essentialism to deny that in exploring the grounds of *de re* modal attributions we encounter vagueness, indeterminacy and questions of degree. Nor is this a new admission on the part of the essentialist.[38] (Distinguishing grounds and truth conditions, we are not even obliged by the admission to make room for degrees in applications of the *de re* essential 'must' itself, except in so far as vagueness is already present in the property which it governs.) Nor does a problem of vagueness, or the need to decide whether a certain threshold has been reached or not, entail that the choice to make a modal assertion, or not make it, is unprincipled or arbitrary, or a matter of no moment. Nor does it undermine any point and interest we have succeeded in attaching to these questions, or the complexity of what is involved in seeking to establish, well below the level of how things superficially appear to be, whether one can or cannot envisage some property $\emptyset$ of Caesar.

XII

It is certain that it will not conciliate every anti-essentialist to be assured of the extensionality of the position here defended, or of the sincerity of the essentialist's adherence to the book-keeping resolution (see IX). One kind of opponent will ignore all the declarations already made to the effect that the essentialist claim concerns not the world's need to contain Caesar, but only the kind of thing Caesar had to be if there was to be any such thing as Caesar; and he will persist in the accusation that what the essentialist is really trying to fabricate is some engine by which to invest with indispensability the particular conceptual scheme – and with necessary existence the creatures of the particular conceptual scheme – which from our limited, cosmically insignificant point of view, we bring to bear upon the world. This is the conceptual scheme, he will point out, which systematically delayed the progress of natural science beyond the jejune approximations of Aristotle.

I categorically assert on Leibniz's behalf, and on my own, that no such engine of reaction is being invented or fabricated here. Let our conceptual scheme and the associated ontology, which articulate the entities the essences of which (*exempli gratia*) have here been discussed, be as arbitrary and provincial as you please. Let there be no need whatever for the entities that scheme articulates ever to have been descried or picked out at all from reality. What does not follow from these admissions (which, if it were relevant, I should qualify) is that those very entities could have been just anything at all, or could have had just any principle of individuation or criterion of identity. The essentialist's chief concern is precisely with the falsity of this last suggestion, and with the real commitment in which anyone who picks out an entity must be involved by the conceptual scheme which articulates that entity. His concern is not with the necessity or superfluity, or the universality or parochialism, of that scheme.

In the idea the essentialist has here to combat – the notion that a given ontology is perfectly insensitive to all changes in conceptual ideology, or that two radically different theories or conceptions of the world can descry one and the same set of entities – lies the royal road to the two most absurd things in philosophy, the myth of 'substratum' and the myth of 'the given'. And is this not a perfectly mysterious idea? There is a range of basic sortal attributions which we apply to various everyday things – 'this is a horse', 'this is a tree', 'that is a man'. The anti-essentialist whom I am attacking[39] accepts these attributions in their unmodalised form, and then (one stage too late, in my opinion, for he has already consented to pick out that thing and to involve himself in the relevant theory) adduces as a reason to deprecate the suggestion that these things *had* to be a horse, a tree and a man the anthropocentric viewpoint which underlies and conditions the attributions. But of *what* could one be speaking here if one said that *it* might have been a prime number or a fire-shovel?

If it were right to say that there is no such thing as bad weather, only the wrong clothes, then I suppose it might follow that, in some weird sense, tempests were the creatures of our interests. But would that not make it harder, rather than easier, to deny of anything picked out as a tempest that it necessarily involves rough or dangerous weather conditions?

It is difficult to dismiss the suspicion that what the essentialist is up against is the idea that what a thing is is independent of what one can say about it. All further discussion of that I must now adjourn, leaving the last word with Ayer himself: 'we have seen that the world cannot be prised away from our manner of conceiving it'.[40]

NOTES

1. By kind agreement of both publishers, parts of sections IV to XI of this paper correspond in part to one stretch of Chapter 4 of the replacement for *Identity and Spatio-Temporal Continuity* (Oxford: Blackwell, 1967) to be published autumn 1978 under the title *Sameness and Substance* (Oxford: Blackwell and Mott).

2. 'Mea certa opinione nihil est in universitate creaturarum, quod ad perfectum suum conceptum non indigeat alterius cujuscumque rei in rerum universitate conceptu, cum unaquaeque res influat in aliam quancumque ita ut si ipsa sublata aut diversa esse fingeretur, omnia in mundo ob iis quae nunc sunt diversa sint futura' – Gerhardt, vol. II, p. 226.
This expression of pluralism is only equivalent to what Ayer calls monism in the presence of the very questionable identity *individual concept = individual essence*. See Ishiguro, *Leibniz's Philosophy of Logic and Language* (London: Duckworth, 1972). It is Leibniz's doctrine that every substance, in addition to determining a concept including each and all the properties of this individual, including the relational and extrinsic, is the very entity it is in virtue of a *subset* of these, the subset being a set of intrinsic denominations: 'Etiam quae loco differunt, oportet locum suum id est ambientia exprimere, atque adeo non tantum loco seu sola

extrinseca denominatione distingui, ut vulgo talia concipiunt' – Gerhardt, vol. II, p. 250. Here we get closer to what is distinctive of essentialism.

3. See W. V. Quine, 'Three Grades of Modal Involvement' (1953), repr. in *Ways of Paradox and Other Essays* (New York: Random House, 1966).

4. A nice example is at pp. 125ff. of Richard Cartwright's 'Identity and Substitutivity', in *Identity and Individuation*, ed. Milton K. Munitz (New York: New York University Press, 1971). Another is at p. 185 of Quine's *Ways of Paradox*.

5. Ayer makes the same point in 'Internal Relations', in *Proceedings of the Aristotelian Society*, Suppl. vol., 1935.

6. Cf. 'Identity and Reference', which Ayer contributed to *Language in Focus*, ed. A. Kasher (Dordrecht: Reidel, 1976) pp. 3–24.

7. Someone might try to get the effect of (f) by saying that his newspaper instantiates (e). But (e) itself is not a generalisation at all, if it is interpreted as involving only the first grade of modal involvement. He might say that his newspaper instantiates the generalisation (x) (x is a newspaper $\supset x$ contains news), and that this generalisation is itself analytic. Does this get the effect of (f)? The trouble is that everything instantiates this generalisation. Does anyone wish to conclude that, suitably interpreted, 'everything necessarily contains news' is true?

8. Arnauld to Leibniz, 13 May 1686, in Gerhardt, vol. II, pp. 31–2; trans, H. T. Mason *Leibniz–Arnauld Correspondence* (Manchester, 1956). Cf. W. V. Quine, 'On What There Is', in his *From a Logical Point of View* (Cambridge, Mass.: Harvard University Press, 1953).

9. A. J. Ayer, *The Central Questions of Philosophy* (London: Weidenfeld and Nicolson, 1973) p. 197.

10. Arnauld to Leibniz, Gerhardt, vol. II, p. 33; H. T. Mason.

11. Ayer, *Central Questions*, pp. 197–8. A mischievously selective quotation, it may be complained. The italics are mine, but sense and designation have been carefully preserved. For similar expressions, see Ayer's 'Names and Descriptions', in his *The Concept of a Person and other Essays* (London: Macmillan 1963).

12. See W. V. Quine, 'Quantifiers and Propositional Attitudes', *Journal of Philosophy*, LIII (1955); repr. in *Ways of Paradox*; pp. 183–94.

13. The truth predicate is defined for a language containing this predicate in David Wiggins, 'The *De Re* "Must"; A Note on the Logical Form of Essentialist Claims', and, for a richer language, C. A. B. Peacocke, 'Appendix to David Wiggins' ' "The *De Re* 'Must' " ', both in *Truth and Meaning: Essays in Semantics*, ed. Gareth Evans and John McDowell (Oxford: Clarendon Press, 1976).

For the idea of treating 'necessarily' as a predicate-modifier, see P. T. Geach, *Logic Matters* (Oxford: Blackwell, 1972) p. 174; R. Cartwright, 'Some Remarks on Essentialism', *Journal of Philosophy*, LXV (1968); and Wiggings, *Identity and Spatio-Temporal Continuity*, p. 42.

14. For a more extended attempt to describe the transition of other *de re* locutions into that limiting case which is the essentialist 'must', see D. Wiggins, 'Identity, Continuity and Essentialism', *Synthèse*, XXIII (1974). See also section X below. For Quine's practical (spoken or written) involvement in *de re* modality note this passage: 'Man will never know how many cars will have entered your city between now and midnight tonight. He will never know and never care. But he *could* know this number if he cared enough and had the foresight to make arrangements for keeping count of the cars. The serious question is whether there are things that man could never know, however foresighted he may be.' – W. V. Quine, 'The Limits of Knowledge', in *Ways of Paradox*, enlarged edition (New York: Random House, 1977) p. 59.

It may conciliate the positivist somewhat if it is pointed out that the experientially unexhausted potentiality I speak of is potentiality for what he could, in some loose sense, call behaviour. When we have a good lifelike account of the thoughts which sustain modal language, and freshly reasoned canons of ultimate intelligibility, the time will be ripe for a reappraisal of the significance of modal language. In the meanwhile I am engaged in the first of these two tasks (the account of the thoughts, that is).

15. The decision to signal these occurrences specially by this particular notation is quite without prejudice either for or against the appropriateness of $\Box$ and $\Diamond$ to this role. It is in no way excluded by the syntax or semantics of *NEC* and *POSS* that the pairs *NEC* and $\Box$, and *POSS* and $\Diamond$ will prove to be related very much as the theory of truth relates say predicate negation and sentence negation. (The latter is assimilated, as a special case, to the former in the standard Tarskian treatment. Frege evidently envisaged an opposite assimilation.) Our purpose is simply to circumnavigate this question and, with it, all those logical difficulties which have been raised against previous presentations of the essentialist viewpoint and which are irrelevant to the extensional essentialism I defend.

16. Thus the modal enrichment of the first-order logical framework is explained in the first instance not in terms of possible worlds, but rather in terms of the English vernacular which suffices for the introduction of any other fundamental notion. It is managed in such a way that the *de re* 'necessarily' starts life at least with credentials no worse than those of Quine's relational senses of saying and believing. Just as Ralph believes of the man in the brown hat (or of the man seen at the beach – it makes no difference, for they are identical) the attribute λx (x is a spy), or just as the man in the brown hat (alias the man at the beach) is believed by Ralph to have the attribute spyhood; so, in this *prima facie* innocuous sense of 'necessarily', Caesar is necessarily such that he has the attribute 'man'. (Or Caesar is such that it is necessary for him to have the attribute 'man'.) So we can say that '*NEC* (λx) [Mx], [Caesar]' is to '$\Box$ (Man (Caesar))' as the Quinean *relational* '(λx) [Man x] is universally believed of Caesar' ('It is universally believed of Caesar that he is a man') is to the *notional* 'It is universally believed that (Man (Caesar))'. Compare (5) above (in section IV).

17. In *Central Questions*, p. 197, Ayer writes, 'What of the proposition that the Morning Star is identical with the Evening Star and that both are identical with Venus? Surely it is a contingent fact that one and the same planet is to be found at the places in question in the morning and at night.' It is important that *this is not denied here*, as is very obvious when the sentence is written out in Russell's fashion and the *NEC* is applied only to the last conjunct, but as could also be made out with any other theory of names and descriptions.

18. W. V. Quine, *From a Logical Point of View* (Harvard U. P., Cambridge, Mass., 1953) p. 197. Cf. his *Word and Object* (MIT, Cambridge, Mass., 1960) p. 209. 'Classes are like attributes except for their identity conditions.'

19. Patrick Suppes, *Introduction to Logic* (Princeton, NJ: Van Nostrand, 1957).

20. Suppose we decided that α was not an attribute. We could then test whether α was a class or a mereological whole. We could ask whether x and y had parts; and, if they did, then, since we were told that x and y were all that *belonged* to α, we should have disproved that α was a mereological entity. Cf. p. 151 of Nelson Goodman's new 'A World of Individuals', in his *Problems and Projects* (Indianapolis: Bobbs-Merrill, 1972): 'while a class of individuals is uniquely a class of just those members, a whole made up of individuals may also be made up of quite other parts'.

21. Cartwright has put an essentially cognate point as follows: '$(x)(y)(z)(z \in x \leftrightarrow z \in y) \rightarrow x = y)$ . . . will be a theorem of any pure theory of classes but presumably

of no pure theory of attributes ... but it is a difference between theories, and I know of no coherent way in which it can be supposed to carry over to the objects dealt with in the theories. It does, of course, reflect a difference between the *concepts* class and attribute' – R. Cartwright, 'Class and Attribute', *Nous*, I (1967). See also R. Sharvey, 'Why a Class Can't Change Its Members', *Nous*, II (1968).

22. Cf. Arnauld's objection 'De Natura Mentis Humanae', against Descartes, *Oeuvres de Descartes*, ed. Adam and Tannery (in vol. VII), p. 201.

23. Cf. Aristotle, *Categories*, 2. b33 and 3. b19; and P. F. Strawson, *Individuals*, (London: Methuen, 1959) pp. 168–9.

24. If, using Ayer's principle (4), I succeed in finding more necessity *de re* than Ayer does, this will be almost entirely owing to the emphasis here placed on the role of the 'What is x?' question in picking out or identifying x. It may be important to the evaluation of my claims that I see the specification implicitly determined by a saying *which* as having a canonical form with two elements – both a sortal component ('What is x?' 'It is an f') and a deictic or particularising component ('Which f is an x?' 'It is this f'; or 'It is the f which is φ'). To put it again in Aristotle's way: every particular is a 'this such'. (Here, as elsewhere, I have written 'this f' to mean 'this member of the extension of the sortal concept f'.)

25. What could undermine this claim is a weaker requirement which arose equally naturally from a theory of particular identification, respected the absoluteness of identity, and which, as (4) requires, represented a substantial requirement on the *de re* relation of thinker, object, and attribute.

26. Cf. Wiggins, in *Synthèse*, XXIII (1974) 336.

27. Of course, the inconceivability of Julius Caesar's not being a man is not logical inconceivability. The point of calling a sentence a logical truth is that its denial can be shown by logic alone to involve contradiction. A logical truth is a truth forced upon us by the meanings of the logical constants. By this criterion not even 'all bachelors are unmarried' qualifies. Because logical necessity in the useful and strict sense is exigent, the species of a possibility which is its dual is hopelessly permissive. 'But it's logically possible that not-Q' is the principal weapon in some analytical or Humian philosopher's armoury. But it is a useless one – unless he means by 'it's logically possible' 'it's conceptually possible'. But that is usually the question at issue, and one may need to have thought into the *implications* of Q to decide that question. Logic alone (in the serious or strict sense) will not always suffice for that. Where available, definitions can help supply what is needed. But we have claimed that individuals such as Caesar have no explicit verbal definition. We are now exploring what in effect plays the constraining role in our thinking about the entity Caesar which definition plays in constraining our thought about bachelors.

28. Cf. Aristotle, *Metaphysics*, Z; Leibniz, *Nouveaux Essais*, III. 6. xxxvi and 3. vi.

29. This does not mean that anything whatever that we call a man is a man. It is because the possibility of mistake is recognised, and yet recognised in the absence of any definition of man, and because there is no prospect of such a definition, that the sentence in the text needs to allude to *that constitution by reference to which* mistakes are possible – namely, the constitution of men. That this is in large part unknown to speakers in no way prevents their recognising that correctness and incorrectness have to be adjudicated in the last analysis by reference to this property of the actual members of a collection which they delimit not necessarily without mistake, but, as it were, provisionally and by the use of

partly conjectural criteria. It is precisely because the said constitution is largely unknown to ordinary men that they recognise that their judgements of doubtful cases can only be provisional. (Cf. Locke, *Essay Concerning Human Understanding*, III. 6. xxvi; and Leibniz, *Nouveaux Essais*, xxvi, on monsters.) Leibniz describes this process in several places and connections. See especially his account of clear but indistinct knowledge (Gerhardt, vol. IV, p. 422): '*Clara* ergo cognitio est, cum habeo unde rem repraesentatam agnoscere possim eaque rursus est vel confusa vel distincta. *Confusa*, cum scilicet non possum notas ad rem aliis ab aliis discernendam sufficientes separatim enumerare, licet res illa tales notas atque requisita revera habeat in quae notio ejus resolvi posset.'

Compare the account in the *Nouveaux Essais* of how, for lack of definitional knowledge of natures, 'l'extérieur en tient bien, quoique nous reconnoissions qu'il ne suffit pas pour avoir une définition exacte, et que les définitions nominales mêmes dans ces rencontres ne sont que conjecturales: et j'ai dit déjà cy dessus comment quelquefois elles sont provisionelles seulement' (III.6.xiv). They are provisional pending a real causal definition (III.3.xviii).

Compare also *Nouveaux Essais*, III. 6. xiii: 'plus on approfondira la génération des espèces et plus on suivra dans les arrangemens les conditions qui y sont requises, plus on approchera de l'ordre naturel … [si nous] connoissions asses les choses peutestre y trouverions nous des attributs fixes pour chaque espèce, communs à tous ses individus', and the remarkable account of how this idea can be worked out in the category of gold: 'le nom de l'or par exemple signifie non pas seulement ce que celuy, qui le prononce, connoist; par exemple: un jaune très pesant, mais encor ce qu'il ne connoist pas, et qu'un autre en peut connoistre, c'est à dire un corps doué d'une constitution interne dont decoule la couleur et la pesanteur, et dont naissent d'autres propriétés, qu'il avoue estre mieux connues des experts' (III. 11. xxv). 'C'est comme si l'on disait qu'un certain corps fusible, jaune et très pesant, qu'on appelle or, a une nature, qui luy donne encore la qualité d'estre fort doux au marteau et a pouvoir estre rendu extrêmement mince' (III. 10. xvii).

Ayer has resisted modern expositions of what is substantially the same theory, which has been rediscovered in our own times by Putnam and Kripke. But I cannot forbear to quote an independent rediscovery, which Leibniz would surely have enjoyed: 'When God said "Goose" [to Adam] He must have meant the specific pattern which was within the egg and which, as Watson and Crick discovered, was "too pretty not to be true", namely: a particular, specific molecular structure, in which genetic directions to form the life of a goose were written in the form of a beautiful double helix' – Stefan Themerson, *The Artifacts of Mind and Body* (London: Gaberbocchus, 1973).

30. See here, and in connection with the matters of the previous note, chapter 4 of Hide Ishiguro, *Leibniz's Philosophy of Logic and Language*, to which I am in several places here indebted. See her forthcoming paper 'The Primitiveness of the Concept of a Person', in a collection to be edited by Z. van Straaten in honour of P. F. Strawson.

31. Cf. A. J. Ayer 'The Identity of Indescernibles', in *Philosophical Essays* (London: Macmillan, 1954) esp. p. 30, on these artificially particularised properties.

32. Goodman, *Problems and Projects*, p. 168.

33. Leibniz, 'Specimen Dynamicum', in Gerhardt, *Leibnizens Mathematischen Schriften*, vol. VI, p. 235. Cf. *Discourse of Metaphysics*, ch. 10 (Gerhardt, *Philosophischen Schriften*, (vol. IV): 'I agree that consideration of these forms is of no service in the detail of natural philosophy, and must not be used for explaining phenomena in particular. And it was in this that our scholastics failed, and the

Physicians of past times following their example, believing that they could account for the properties of bodies by mentioning forms and qualities without going to the pains of examining the manner of operation; as if one were willing to content oneself with saying that a clock has the horodictic quality resulting from its form, without considering in what all this consists. . . . But this failure and misuse of forms must not make us reject something knowledge of which is so necessary in Metaphysics' – trans. Lucas and Grint.

34. I believe that this, plus the requirement that in any speculation not absolutely every way of saying of *which* particular *f* it is be removed, fully explains the apparent necessity of the long disjunctive properties which first engaged Ayer's interest in this problem.

35. Locke had a real insight into these matters, and a perception clearer than Leibniz's of the importance of the question whether a given predicate is such that the onus is on the would-be satisfier to conform to an already determinate specification (the case, one might say, of nominal definition *par excellence*, and the case, underestimated by Leibniz, where nominal essence, such as the essence of an artifact, is at its best), or whether the predicate is such that the onus is on the concept of that kind of thing, and so on the sense of the word standing for it, to match the nature of the things lying in an extension which has been established already as the extension of the term. (I here use the term 'onus of match' too loosely for it to contrast in exactly the manner which J. L. Austin originally intended, in 'How to Talk', *Proceedings of the Aristotelian Society*, LIII (1952–3), with 'direction of fit'. See also M. J. Woods, 'Substance and Quality', unpublished B. Phil. thesis, Oxford, 1958.) Locke saw well the importance of this contrast, and noticed that, so far as our practice goes, we use natural–kind predicates in a manner conformable to the second of the two ways. He saw that in real life we start with a class of objects which, provided only that they are not unluckily chosen, *represent* some extension, the onus being on the sense of the predicate to conform to how the objects are. But it is that feature of practice and the idea of real essence which Locke finds so objectionable, recognises explicitly, and explicitly disapproves. He counts the practice an abuse of words. See Mackie's 'Locke's Anticipation of Kripke', in *Analysis*, June 1974: and Locke, *Essay*, III. 10. xviii–xx. Perhaps Locke lost sight of his own insight principally because he was victim of confusion or lack of imagination about how the sense of a putative real-essence word, standing for the particular constitution of the insensible parts of the thing from which the sensible qualities flowed, could be learned in experience. For lack of anything like Leibniz's account of how natural-kind words have their sense – which, once he has grasped the point of it, a sane empiricist should welcome as consistent with both empiricism and science – Locke was tempted to supplant the real essence of a natural thing by what he called the nominal essence. (Cf. Leibniz' criticisms at *Nouveaux Essais*, III. 6. xvii and 3. xv.)

36. Even after we separate off the irrelevant epistemic senses, there are all sorts of hard questions of ambiguity here, and there are constant temptations to confuse differences in the grounds for modal attributions with differences in their meaning. It is not necessary to settle here the question of whether we have here an array of distinct senses disposed around a focal idea, or a univocal idea which can conjoin with different parameters to yield a variety of different kinds of semantic output.

37. Or because it does not matter very much to know more than roughly what the thing in question is. 'What's under that blanket?' 'It's an animal – I should sit on the other blanket if I were you.' In the context it is probably perfectly obvious that it is not a leopard, say, or a gila-monster under the blanket. This

is ordinary indoor life. (One can sit next to the blanket, for instance.) It does not matter whether it is a cat or a dog or even a nanny-goat under the blanket. It does not matter *exactly* what is under the blanket.

It is important to remember that, here and throughout, the individuative principle for a particular, *x*, and the condition of *x*'s existence and persistence is not something special to the particular *x* with its particular life history, but something general which, according to the theory of individuation that I should defend, is required to determine the *point at issue* in matters of *x*'s existence and survival, and the point at issue in matters of the existence or survival of all other things in the highest genuinely individuative kind to which *x* belongs.

At *Nouveaux Essais*, III. 3. vi, Leibniz represents Locke as saying, 'les mots deviennent généraux lorsqu'ils sont signes d'idées générales, et les idées deviennent générales lorsque par abstraction on en sépare le temps le lieu, ou telle autre circonstance, qui peut les déterminer à telle ou telle existence particulière'. In his objection to this doctrine Leibniz exploits the distinction which I am pressing here. The principles we have to use in keeping individuals under continuous observation can yield genus terms. There is abstraction from species to genus. (Cf. Ishiguro, *Leibniz's Philosophy*.) But there is no abstraction from individuals to species. The principle we use in observing and tracing a particular does not come with a species concept which we get by *abstraction* from individuals. That would be impossible, for, inasmuch as we have a species concept for an individual, the possession of this concept and the ability to pick out the thing under it cannot be *separated*. For general terms, however, which *presuppose* individuation, there is no such difficulty. 'Je ne disconviens point de cet usage des abstractions, mais c'est plutôt en montant des espèces aux genres que des individus aux espèces. Car (quelque paradoxe que cela paraisse) il est impossible à nous d'avoir la connaissance des individus et de trouver le moyen de determiner exactement l'individualité d'aucune chose, à moins que de la garder elle même.'

38. Leibniz made it willingly: 'Les passages d'espèce en espèce peuvent être insensibles, et pour les discerner ce seroit quelque fois à peu près comme on ne scauroit decider combien il faut laisser de poils à un homme pour qu'il ne soit point chauve. Cette indétermination seroit vraye quand même nois connoistroins parfaitement l'interieur des creatures dont il s'agit. Mais je ne vois point qu'elle puisse empecher les choses d'avoir des essences réelles independamment de l'entendement, et nous de les connoistre: il est vray que les noms et les bornes des espèces seroiyent quelque fois comme les noms des mesures et des poids, où il faut choisir pour avoir des bornes fixes' (III. 6. xxvii; cf. III. 5. ix); 'il est vray qu'on peut disputer les plus basses espèces, logiquement prises, qui se varient par des accidens dans une meme espèce physique ou tribu de generation; mais on n'a point besoin de les déterminer; on peut même les varier à l'infini comme il se voit dans la grande variété des oranges, limons et citrons [cf. III. 6. viii]. Lorsqu' on ne veut parler que de l'extérieur ... il y a de latitude; et disputer si une différence est spécifique ou non, c'est disputer du nom; et dans ce sens il y a une si grande différence entre les chiens qu'on peut fort bien dire que les dogues d'Angleterre et les chiens de Boulognes sont de différentes espèces. Cependant il n'est pas impossible qu'ils soyent d'une même ou semblable race eloignée ... on peut même croire aussi sans choquer la raison, qu'ils ayent en commun une nature intérieure, constante, specifique, qui ne soit plus sous-divisée ainsi, ou qui ne se trouve point icy en plusieurs autres telles natures et par consequent ne soit plus variée que par des accidents; quoy qu'il n'y ait rien aussi qui nous fasse juger que cela doit estre necessairement ainsi dans tout ce que nous appellons la plus basse espèce (*speciem infinam*). ... Ainsi dans les différentes sortes de chiens, en parlant des apparences,

on peut distinguer les espèces, et parlant de l'essence intérieure on peut balancer' (III. 6. xxxvi).

39. Russell was an opponent of essentialism, but these paragraphs are not directed at his position. For he pursued the logic of his position (and the logic of my paragraphs here) to the point of rejecting the ontology which is presupposed to saying 'this is a man'. See Wiggins 'The *De Re* "Must" ', in *Truth and Meaning*, ed. Evans and McDowell.

40. Ayer, *Central Questions*, p. 235.

8 In *Self*-Defence[1]

JOHN FOSTER

I

It is not just good fortune – not even the kind of good fortune that comes by natural selection or divine grace – that the functional role of our mental states, both (motivationally) in the production of behaviour and (cognitively) in the processing of sensory stimulation, is, by and large, appropriate to their psychological character. We cannot envisage someone in whom, throughout his life-history, role and character systematically conflict, someone whose behaviour is seldom or never rationally appropriate to the attitudes that cause it and whose sensory intake is seldom or never evidentially appropriate to the beliefs it causes. Why not? If, as many physicalists would like, we construed psychological character *as* functional role, this question would answer itself. But the answer would not do justice to our concept of mind. It would oblige us, counter to our intuitions, to ascribe mental states to any purely physical system which embodied the right functions.

The correct explanation is found in two related points. First, while psychological character and functional role are, as such, logically independent, the presumption that they agree is the indispensable basis of our ascription of mental states to others. We observe goal-directed behaviour and construe it as the product of an inner aim that provides a reason for its performance. We observe discriminatory behaviour and construe it as the product of inner judgements that discriminate the sensory cues. As far as possible, we ascribe to others those mental states which permit us to construe their behaviour as rational and informed, and thereby we adopt criteria for ascription which seek to match psychological character to functional role. Nor could we reasonably do otherwise. Unless we ascribe mental states on the basis of *these* criteria, we have no right to ascribe them at all. For it is only when governed by *these* criteria that our ascriptions provide any explanation for, or confer any intelligibility on, what we can observe. Secondly, the general agreement between psychological character and functional role is necessary for the existence of that sort of entity – the *person* – to whom both mental and bodily states are ascribable. We cannot envisage someone in whom role and character systematically conflict, not because character as such sets a logical constraint on role, but because such systematic conflict precludes the existence of the kind of subject in whom it is supposed to take place. We cannot envisage someone whose behaviour typically misrepresents his attitudes and whose beliefs typically misrepresent his sensory intake, since it is only because things are arranged, psychophysically, so as to ensure a general appropriateness, that we can properly speak of the subject of consciousness as possessing a body and, through that body, having sensory and muscular extensions.

These two points are, as I said, related. In fact they are complementary aspects of a single point. For, on the one hand, our reason for having that concept of a person of which the appropriateness of role to character is an essential ingredient is that it is such appropriateness that we are obliged to presume in any well grounded ascriptive practice. On the other hand, construing behaviour as rational and informed involves attributing it to an agent who has both a body and a mind. Thus, to locate the need for appropriateness both in the concept of a person and in the basis of our ascriptive practice is, in effect, to locate it in the same place. The point of the concept is to permit the practice, and the aim of the practice is to apply the concept.

These considerations are, I think, in keeping with much recent work in the philosophy of mind. But I want to use them to refurbish a doctrine which most current philosophers regard as discredited. The doctrine has two counterbalancing parts. On the one hand, it claims that the concept of a person, a subject of both mental and physical attributes, is to be analysed in terms of the special way in which two logically separable components, a body and a mind, combine. On the other hand, it insists that the person himself, though qualifying for personhood only in virtue of this combining of body and mind, is essentially mental and only contingently corporeal. According to the first claim, mental and physical states are ascribable to a common subject in virtue of the way in which a separable body and mind are linked together. According to the second, this common subject, while essentially the subject of mental states, is the subject of physical states only through his contingent attachment to a particular body. Put together, these claims amount to what we may call the *dualistic doctrine of the person*. My proposal is that we should accept this doctrine in the following form: a subject of consciousness constitutes a person, a subject of both mental and physical attributes, if and only if there is a body with which his mind causally combines in such a way as to ensure the general appropriateness of functional role to psychological character, and thereby to ensure the general adequacy, in respect of that subject, of our criteria of third-person mental ascription; and the person himself, the subject of consciousness, is, as Descartes conceived him, a simple mental continuant, a pure ego, not requiring a body for his existence, but possessing that body with which his mind thus causally combines.

What I hope to do in the remaining sections is, while not to prove this doctrine, at least to render it intelligible and plausible. Even here my aims are limited. For I shall take for granted the dualistic distinction between mental and physical states. I shall assume that mental and physical states are numerically distinct, and that psychological facts are not reducible to, or supervenient upon, physical facts. These assumptions gain credibility from the fact that a plausible theory can (I hope) be constructed on their basis. But my paper is designed chiefly for those, such as Sir Alfred Ayer, who already accept them.

II

It was Professor Strawson who, in a celebrated essay, first laid such emphasis on our conception of a person as the subject of both mental and physical attributes: 'What I mean by the concept of a person is the concept of a type of entity such that *both* predicates ascribing states of consciousness *and* predicates ascribing corporeal characteristics, a physical situation &c. are equally applicable to a single individual of that type.'[2] Moreover, as I do, though in a quite different way, he took this concept to enshrine the adequacy of our criteria of third-person mental ascription. But Strawson laid emphasis on this concept not to support, but to refute, a dualistic analysis. His main contention was that the concept of a person is logically primitive and not capable of analysis at all. He hoped thereby to avoid the traditional problems of body and mind.

The core of Strawson's argument can be put as follows.[3] (1) One's capacity to ascribe mental states to oneself logically depends on one's possession of a procedure for ascribing similar states to other subjects of the same type as oneself. (2) An essential part of this procedure is the capacity to identify, in appropriate circumstances, other subjects. But (3) other subjects cannot be identified *only* as mental subjects, only as possessors of mental states, as minds or pure egos. For (4) there is no way of identifying another subject only as a mental subject except by identifying him as that which inhabits a particular body. And (5) such identification would have to proceed by analogy from one's own case. One would have to rely on some such identifying description as 'the subject that stands to that body in the same special relation as *I* stand in to this one' or 'the subject of those experiences which stand in the same unique causal relation to body *N* as *my* experiences stand in to body *M*'. But (6) this would require a prior method of self-identification and self-ascription, which is precluded by (1). Hence, from (3), (7) other subjects must be identified as the possessors of both mental and physical states, i.e. identified as *persons*. Hence (8), the concept of a person is logically prior to the concept of a mental subject – logically prior to the concept of a mind and the concept of a pure ego. Hence (9), the concept of a person cannot be analysed in terms of how a body and a mind, or a body and an ego, combine. But (10) – and here Strawson relies on a subsidiary argument – if the concept of a person cannot be analysed thus, it cannot be analysed at all. Hence (11), the concept of a person is logically primitive.

If this argument succeeds, the dualistic doctrine of the person is wrong in both parts: the concept of a person cannot be analysed in terms of the combining of a body and a mind; nor is a person himself only contingently corporeal. In fact, however, the argument fails at a number of points. It begins, inauspiciously, with a false premiss. Although we have a procedure for other-ascription, and one which is well grounded, the possession of such a procedure is not, as Strawson claims in (1) a logical requirement or precondition of self-ascription. The most that self-ascription logically requires is the capacity to conceive of the existence of other subjects of the same type as oneself and with similar mental states. And it is possible that someone should conceive of the existence of other subjects without knowing how to identify them and, therefore, without having a procedure for other-ascription. The falsity of (1) robs (5) of its sting. But (5) too is, in any case, false. There is no reason why the subject–body relation should not be specified in purely general terms, without reference to oneself; nor, indeed, is there any reason why our grounds for employing this relation, in the identification of other subjects, should be supplied by an argument from analogy. The correct account has already been indicated in section I: a subject inhabits a body in virtue of that causal combining of body and mind which ensures general appropriateness of functional role to psychological character, and our grounds for taking a body to be thus inhabited are that we thereby provide the most plausible explanation of its behaviour. Without

(1) and (5), Strawson's argument collapses, since he can no longer establish (3) and hence cannot establish (7). But, even if we allowed (7), it is not clear how (8) can be inferred from it. Strawson's idea seems to be that priority in order of identification entails priority in order of analysis, that, if things of type F can only be identified by identifying things of type G, the concept of G is logically prior to, and cannot be analysed in terms of, the concept of F. But I cannot see why this should be so. At the very least, Strawson needs to provide some argument here. Finally, (10), though in my view true, is not established by Strawson's subsidiary argument; but I shall defer discussion of this point until section III.

Not only does Strawson's argument fail, but in addition its conclusion, as he concedes, leaves us with a problem: how can we explain our possession of the concept of a person – the concept of something to which both mental and physical attributes are ascribable – if we cannot analyse it in terms of how a body and a mind combine? How is the primitive concept of a person possible? He thinks that we can find the 'beginnings of an answer' by focusing on those person predicates, such as 'going for a walk' and 'coiling a rope', which signify some kind of action.[4] What is crucial about these predicates is not just that what they signify has both a physical component (a characteristic pattern of bodily movement) and a mental component (an intention), but that these components do not seem to stand in the sharp contrast which makes co-ascription problematic. The bodily movement is one which the agent can know about, as he knows about his mental states, without observation or inference, and the intention is one which we ascribe to the agent not as a distinctive experience, but as an interpretation of the movement. In other words, we discern in action a point where the co-ascription of mental and physical attributes has, or seems to have, a natural intelligibility. Strawson thinks that, by taking this point as central, we can go on to explain, by their connections with predicates of action, the co-ascription of mental and physical predicates that are sharply contrasted. As he puts it, 'the class of P-predicates that I have moved into the centre of the picture are not unconnectedly there, detached from others irrelevant to them. On the contrary, they are inextricably bound up with the others, interwoven with them. The topic of the mind does not divide into unconnected subjects.'[5]

Strawson's picture is a pleasing one, but I cannot see in it even the 'beginnings of an answer'. For I do not see how to avoid, even in the case of action, the sharp contrast between mental and physical states. It is true that the intentional element in action is not a distinctive experience and true that its ascription is a

way of interpreting the bodily movement. But it would be dis-
ingenuous to ignore the distinctively mentalistic character of the
interpretation. To construe a movement as intentional is not simply
to construe it as part of a goal-directed physical process, as we
might construe the movements of a homing missile or a mechanical
rat. It is to construe it as rationally motivated, as under the control
of propositional attitudes possessed by a conscious subject and
functioning appropriately to their psychological character. But now
the contrast between the mental and physical components is as
sharp as ever. And how are we to explain their ascription to a
common subject unless by the dualistic doctrine of the person?
How are we to explain the concept of an agent, except in terms
of that interlocking of a mind and a body which secures the rational
appropriateness of the states of that mind to their causal control
over the movements of that body?

III

Well, there is an alternative and one which is, in a sense, dualistic.
I have in mind a theory which analyses the concept of a person
in terms of the causal combining of a body and *mental items*,
but denies its analysis in terms of the combining of a body and
a *mind*. It holds that mental items are states of the same mind
solely in virtue of being states of the same person, and that a
mental item, though non-physical, is a state of a person solely
in virtue of being causally attached, in an appropriate way, to
a certain body, the body by which that person is identified. Strawson
dubbed this the 'no-ownership' or 'no-subject' theory, on the
grounds that causal attachment to a body does not constitute the
'logically non-transferable kind of possession' required for genuine
ownership by a subject.[6] His point is that, if an experience is
genuinely owned by a subject, it is logically impossible for that
same experience to have been similarly owned by a different subject,
but that, if an experience is merely causally owned by a body,
it is logically possible for that same experience to have been similarly
owned by a different body. This second claim can be disputed,
and it would be fairer to describe the theory as one of 'body-owner-
ship' rather than 'no-ownership'. But I shall continue to refer to
it in Strawson's way. Whatever its correct title, the no-ownership
theory falls between Strawson's position and mine. By claiming
that it is solely in virtue of being states of the same person that
mental items are states of the same mind, it concedes to Strawson
the logical priority of the concept of a person to the concept
of a mind: there can be no minds other than embodied minds

and no subjects other than corporeal subjects. And here it contrasts with the views of orthodox dualists, who construe the unity of the mind in purely mental terms – both with the Cartesian, who grounds it on the identity of a mental continuant, and with the Humian, who grounds it on inter-experiential relations.[7] Where the theory differs from Strawson is in denying that the concept of a person is primitive. It claims that this concept can be analysed in terms of how discrete mental items, without the benefit of prior unification, are causally attached to a body. In short, it accepts Strawson's propositions (8) and (9), but rejects his (10) and (11).

As I mentioned in section II, Strawson has a subsidiary argument to establish (10), and it is his objection to the no-ownership theory which forms this argument. The objection is that the theory does not permit a non-circular way of causally assigning the right experiences to the right bodies. For how, he asks, does the theorist say *which* experiences are attached to a particular body? Only, it seems, by identifying them as those of a particular person, and then he is either going round in a circle or illicitly using a concept of ownership which his own theory excludes. Ayer, in an excellent critique of Strawson's whole position, exposed the flaw in this argument.[8] Strawson has been misled by the false picture of a heap of experiences which have first to be identified and then causally assigned to their bodies. The truth is that, at least in the case of third-person ascription, assignment precedes identification. Following our ordinary ascriptive criteria, we begin by saying not *which* experiences, but *what sorts* of experience are causally attached to a given body; we then go on to identify the particulars, of these sorts, as the ones thus attached. Thus the no-ownership theorist is not trapped in a circle, since he rightly rejects the supposition on which Strawson's question was based, the supposition that causal assignment requires prior identification. The cause of Strawson's error is easily discerned. He starts with the (arguably false) assumption – the assumption which gave the theory its title – that the identity of an experience is independent of its causal relations, that an experience which is causally attached to one body could have been attached to another. From this it is a short, though invalid, step to the conclusion that experiences can be identified without reference to their causal relations, that we can say *which* experience without saying to which body it is attached. As Strawson sees it, the picture of the heap of experiences is implicit in the no-ownership character of the theory he attacks.

Having disposed of Strawson's objection, Ayer goes on to present and, with some misgivings, to defend his own version of the no-ownership theory. But before considering it, I want to examine whether the charge of circularity can be sustained in another way. This examination forms something of a digression from my main theme. But the issue is an important one, and the result, though negative, contributes to the positive account of subject identity that I advance in section v.

The starting point is a question of concern to any form of dualism. Can a dualist, of whatever persuasion, give a coherent account of the psychophysical causal relations which he supposes to obtain? If we assume, in the tradition of Hume and Mill, that causal relations between particulars are wholly explicable by nomological relations between types – I shall call this the nomological assumption – then causal relations between mental and physical particulars, conceived dualistically, become problematic.[9] With time as the only dimension which the mental and physical items share, the problem is to find psychophysical laws which sustain the right causal pairings when either item has a simultaneous duplicate. Thus, suppose Smith and Jones simultaneously have mental states M_1 and M_2, of exactly the same psychological character ψ, as a causal result of, respectively, brain states B_1 and B_2, half a second earlier, of exactly the same physiological character φ. Given the nomological assumption, we must explain the causal dependence of M_1 on B_1 and of M_2 on B_2 by psychophysical law. But we cannot do so by a law such as L_1, 'Every φ state is half a second earlier than some ψ state', which specifies only a *temporal* relation between antecedent and consequent states, since this provides no basis for causally pairing B_1 with M_1 rather than with M_2, or for pairing B_2 with M_2 rather than with M_1. What we want is a law which links each φ state with a unique ψ state and each ψ state with a unique φ state. But how can there be such a law if time is the only dimension in which both φ and ψ states are located?

The obvious suggestion is to link the mental and physical states by the relation of embodiment, for it is by this relation that we identify a mind location relative to a body and a space location relative to a mind. In short, we envisage a law such as L_2, 'For each person P, every φ state of P is half a second earlier than some ψ state of P', which locates the physical cause and the mental effect in the same person and, thereby, pairs B_1 with (uniquely) M_1 and B_2 with (uniquely) M_2. But, given a dualistic analysis of persons, this is only to shelve the problem, not to solve it. For we still have to give an account of the psychophysical causal relations on which the existence of a person – the embodiment of a mind or of a group of mental items – is logically grounded. Thus, what do we say if each of Smith's mental states has a simultaneous duplicate (not necessarily duplicates all drawn from

Jones)? Laws such as L_1, which link the mental and physical states only temporally, would fail to explain any of the causal pairings on which Smith's personhood depends, while laws such as L_2, which specify the mental and physical states as copersonal, beg the question. It seems that, if we retain both dualism and the nomological assumption, the envisaged systematic duplication entails, absurdly, that Smith is not a person at all – that he is, depending on how we look at it, either a non-embodied mind or an uninhabited body.

In an earlier article I argued that, in the face of this objection, we could and should retain both dualism and the nomological assumption by envisaging psychophysical laws restricted to a designated body and a designated mind.[10] In the Smith and Jones case, for example, we could secure the right causal pairings by a separate law for each person: 'Every φ state of S_1 is half a second earlier than some ψ state of S_2,' and 'Every φ state of J_1 is half a second earlier than some ψ state of J_2', where S_1 and S_2 designate Smith's body and Smith's mind and J_1 and J_2 designate Jones's body and Jones's mind. With their irreducible reference to particulars, such restricted laws perhaps run counter to the spirit of the nomological assumption. But nothing else comes anywhere near meeting it at all, and when I wrote that article I was convinced on general empiricist grounds that we required this assumption, or something very like it, to make sense of causation at all. One clear consequence was that the no-ownership theory, which construes the unity of the mind in terms of causal attachment to a body, must be rejected. For, in the face of simultaneous duplication, the laws we need to secure such causal attachment presuppose that the boundaries of each mind have already been drawn. It would be blatantly circular to fix these boundaries by causal attachment and then explain the attachment by laws which refer to minds.

However, I now think that what my argument really shows is that the nomological assumption is false. This becomes clear if we reconstruct the essentials of the Smith and Jones case in the purely physical realm. Suppose that, for a certain kind of metal, it is a law of nature that, when a spherical lump of it reaches a specified temperature, a flash occurs half a second later somewhere (unspecified) in the region of points no further from the centre of the sphere than twice its diameter. Suppose further that there is no stronger law which fixes the position of the flash more precisely — that, at the moment when the critical temperature is reached, all positions within the specified region are equiprobable. Now imagine that two spheres, a few inches apart, simultaneously reach the critical temperature and there occur, half a second later, two flashes of the same intensity, each flash falling within the specified region for each sphere. The envisaged law gives no basis for causally pairing each sphere with a unique flash and each flash with a unique sphere. Indeed, since the law is all we have to go on, the correct pairings are undecidable. But the undecidability is not, in this case, grounds for anti-realism. We can certainly envisage that there *are* correct pairings – indeed, have good reason to hold that there are. But this involves rejecting the nomological assumption. For here we are envisaging causal relations which are not fully explicable by laws.[11]

This conclusion robs my former argument of its crucial premiss. Our pairing of B_1 with M_1 and B_2 with M_2 does not oblige us to find laws which explain it, since we should not assume that causal pairings are always nomologically explicable. In this respect the case of Smith and Jones is analogous to the two spheres. But there is also an important difference. We cannot represent the former case, as we represented the latter, as one of causal undecidability. For we cannot even individuate M_1 and M_2 except by their causal attachment to their respective bodies. Knowledge of psychophysical laws could, conceivably, supplement our ordinary ascriptive criteria in deciding what *sorts* of mental state are attached to a given body. But, at least in third-person perspective, the correct pairings of states and bodies is never at issue, since it is only through the pairings that the states are, *qua* particulars, identified.

What then of the no-ownership theory, now that we have cleared it of both Strawson's and my charge of circularity? The theory holds that mental items are states of the same mind solely in virtue of being states of the same person and that a person's ownership of such states 'consists', as Ayer puts it, 'in their standing in a special causal relation to the body by which he is identified'.[12] Ayer goes on to specify this relation as that of direct causal dependence on some internal bodily state. The notion of identifying a person by a body is open to different interpretations. Ayer's own interpretation is, if I read him aright, unduly austere, taking no account of the sort of considerations I advanced in section I. His position seems to be that any human body on which mental items directly depend serves to identify a person, of whom all items thus dependent are states. This is clearly wrong. The mere notion of a class of mental items dependent on a certain body, with no further constraint on their functional role, yields no notion of a subject – the person – to whom both the items and the body can be ascribed. A more promising version would be that a body serves to identify a person if, and only if, for some substantial period, a sufficient number of the mental items dependent on it are the sorts of item ascribable by our ordinary criteria, and that a person then has as states all items dependent on the body by which he is thus identified.

However it is formulated, the no-ownership theory excludes the logical possibility of disembodied subjects. Ayer welcomes this on verificationist grounds, pointing out that such subjects could not be identified. What Ayer fails to notice is that the theory excludes disembodied subjects only at the cost of admitting the much stranger possibility of subjectless experience. For, if mental states are not, as the theorist concedes, bodily states, and if their ownership by a subject consists in their causal dependence on a certain body, then, even though it may be (*de dicto*) necessary that mental *states* have subjects and (*de re*) essential to any mental state that it is a mental state, it must be logically possible for there to be mental items that are intrinsically just like mental states but which, having no bodily attachment, lack subjects – thoughts, pains and desires that are no one's. Only the no-ownership theorist is in quite this predicament. The Strawsonian can accept that mental states are causally attached to the body of the person who owns them, but, by keeping the concept of a person primitive, can regard ownership as an indispensable attribute of the sorts of item thus attached. The orthodox dualist can accept the possibility of mental items with no bodily attachment, but, construing the unity of the mind in purely mental terms, can ascribe such items to a mental subject. The physicalist accepts that ownership by a subject is a relation to a body, but, taking this relation to be 'is a state of', excludes the possibility of a mental item that is unowned. But the no-ownership theorist rejects all these positions. He denies that mental items are bodily states, denies that there can be minds without bodies, and denies that the concept of a person is primitive. The combination of denials entails the possibility of subjectless experience. Here at least, if rather uncomfortably, the theory proves itself worthy of the title Strawson accorded it.

This consequence is clearly counter-intuitive – so counter-intuitive that we could accept it only as a last resort. At least, then, we must ask ourselves whether there is a better theory. Ayer himself came to think that there was, and I shall give a brief account of his new position in due course. But before that I want to examine the possibilities in more general terms and in a broader historical perspective, giving prominence to orthodox dualists, who seek to analyse the unity of the mind in purely mental terms.

IV

Orthodox dualists, who reject the no-ownership theory and hold the mind to be logically independent of the body, are not unanimous in their conception of the mind nor in their conception of the mental subject to whom its states are attributed. Traditionally, there are two main doctrines. The one, advanced by Descartes, holds the subject to be a simple, unextended continuant, a thinking substance, and grounds the unity of the mind on the identity of that continuant.[13] The other, advanced by Hume, grounds the unity of the mind on relations between its constituents and construes the subject as the collection of mental items thus related.[14] The Humian could put his doctrine in more conciliatory terms. Instead of construing the subject as a collection, he could construe it as a continuant 'logically constructed' from the collected items. He could, that is, retain the Cartesian language of the persisting self, but claim its reducibility, at all points, to the canonical language of unifying relations. But such conciliation does nothing to lessen the philosophical contrast between the two positions, the one putting all the weight on the concept of a continuing subject, the other putting all the weight on interexperiential relations.

On the face of it, neither doctrine is acceptable. Against the Humian there is the familiar point, already made against the no-ownership theorist, that the mental items the interrelations of which supposedly define the unity of the mind can only be conceived in the first place as states of a subject. We can, it seems, only make sense of a thought, perception or belief as the state of something which thinks, perceives or believes, and this intelligibility seems to evaporate if the *something* is equated with, or dissolved into, a collection of discrete items. The Humian might claim that this is a conceptual illusion sustained by dispensable features of our mental language. But the point goes deeper than that. Contrary to Hume's celebrated pretensions to self-effacement ('I never can catch *myself* at any time without a perception, and never can observe anything but the perception'[15]), it is reflected in the nature of our introspective awareness. Such awareness (despite its tendentious title) is not, as Hume supposed, a kind of inner observation of mental objects, objects first detected and then, in virtue of their detection, self-ascribed. Rather, it is knowing, without observation or inference, that one is in a certain state, and knowing this simply because one is in that state. Hume would have done better to say, in the spirit of Descartes: 'I never can catch a perception without *myself*.' On the other hand, against the Cartesian there is the equally familiar objection that the concept of a continuing subject, construed realistically, appears to be unintelligible. If we are to make sense of it, we must make sense of subject identity – provide an account both of *individuality*, the differentiation of simultaneous phases of distinct subjects, and of *persistence*, the continuity between successive phases of the same subject. But, with time as the only dimension in which subjects are essentially located, we cannot render this account, as we can render it for physical continuants, in terms of the differences and continuities among occupied positions. We cannot say that simultaneous phases of distinct subjects occupy distinct mental positions or that successive phases of the same subject occupy the same mental position, since there are no mental positions other than those which the identities of subjects create. It seems, then, that to make sense of individuality and persistence, we are forced back on unifying relations between mental items, relations which hold between items that are states of the same subject and fail to hold between items that are states of distinct subjects. But this is just what the Cartesian cannot allow if he grounds the unity of the mind wholly on the identity of the subject.

If this account of the matter is correct, the deficiency in each of the doctrines we have considered consists in its exclusion of any insights in the other. Descartes does justice to our intuitive notion of the subjectivity of experience, but, by making his subject do all the work of unifying the mind, deprives himself of an account of its identity. Hume's unifying relations may serve to explain identity, but the identity of something – a collection or logical construct – which fails to meet our intuitive requirements. A reasonable strategy, therefore, would be to look for some middle way, a balanced theory which gives due weight to the Cartesian subject and due weight to the Humian relations.

One philosopher who tries to strike a balance, and who falls both historically and philosophically between Descartes and Hume, is Locke. Locke, like Descartes, held that mental items are states of, inhere in, a mental substance. But, unlike Descartes, he refused to equate this substance with the mental subject, the self, and, indeed, regarded the identity of the substance as logically independent of the identity of the self.[16] He held that two momentary slices of mental substance are slices of the same self (same mental subject) just in case, in a special sense, they share the same consciousness and that the sharing of consciousness, in this sense, is a relation which can both hold between slices of distinct substances and fail to hold between slices of the same substance. In this way Locke combined a Cartesian acceptance of mental substance with a Humian view of subject identity. In effect, he construed

the subject as the fusion of those substance slices (whether or
not they are consubstantial) the mental states of which stand to
each other in the appropriate unifying relations. Unfortunately,
this theory, while a compromise between Descartes and Hume,
combines the deficiencies of each. On the one hand, if mental
substance is, as the dualist assumes, immaterial, we are still looking
for an account of its identity.[17] On the other hand, if this substance
is not to be equated with the subject, it cannot satisfy our conception
of mental items as states of something in the relevant sense –
the sense in which a thought, perception or belief is a state of
that which thinks, perceives or believes. Indeed, Locke's theory
not only retains these deficiencies, but also, in a dualistic framework,
appears to be incoherent. For, on the face of it, there is no sense
to the notion of an immaterial substance of which mental items
are the states unless we equate that substance with the subject
to whom they are ascribable in the ordinary sense, and this would
force us to take the identity of the substance to be the same
as the identity of the subject. Ironically, Locke unwittingly acknowledged this incoherence by retaining Descartes's term 'thinking substance' and by talking of 'the spirit which thinks in me'.

But there is a better and more obvious way of striking a balance
between Descartes and Hume – namely, to construe the subject
as a simple and genuine mental continuant, but explain its identity
in terms of unifying relations between its states – to provide a
Humian analysis of unity adequate to sustain a Cartesian conception
of the self. In such a theory the concept of a subject and the
unifying relations are mutually supporting: the relations are conceived as applying to a domain of subjective states; the subject
is conceived as the locus of states thus related. But there need
be no circularity, provided the relations are explicable without
appeal to the identity of the subject. It is a theory of this kind
that I shall try to provide.

Obviously, in the provision of such a theory, the Cartesian goal
sets special constraints on the character of the Humian analysis.
In particular, if the persisting self is to be construed realistically,
the analysis must yield a conception of its identity which is both
unitary and determinate, one which attributes the same form of
subject persistence to all subject phases and ensures definite, though
not necessarily discoverable, answers to all identity questions. These
are not constraints on the Humian: indeed, it is characteristic
of Humian theories that they fail to reveal, in the unity of the
mind, the simplicity and exactness required for a Cartesian interpretation. There is, however, one crucial respect in which the project
I envisage increases our flexibility. The Humian, by rejecting a

realistic construal of the persisting subject, is obliged to analyse
the unity of the mind *exclusively* in terms of unifying relations.
But for my project the only obligation is to analyse in such terms
those aspects of unity that explain the identity of the subject,
and it may be possible to discharge *that* obligation while leaving
a residue of mental items the unity of which is grounded on the
very identity thus explained. In other words, the analysis of unity
may divide into *pre-* and *post-*Cartesian stages. In the former stage,
we give a Humian analysis for some restricted range of mental
states, but adequate to secure subject identity; in the latter, we
net the residue by the single clause that mental states belong to
the same mind if, and only if, they are states of the same subject.
This, in fact, is the course I shall follow. Initially restricting myself
to the domain of sense experience, I shall explain the identity
of a subject in terms of actual and potential sensible continuity
among items in that domain. Items outside that domain are then
assigned to minds in accordance with their assignment to subjects.

However, I use the term 'sense experience' in a specially broad
sense, to cover not only experiences acquired through the operation
of the sense organs, but also hallucinations, bodily sensations and
mental imagings – to cover, in fact, all experiences which consist
in the awareness of a sensible object. What it does not cover
are propositional attitudes (beliefs, desires, hopes and so on) and
propositional acts (judgements, thoughts, decisions, and so forth).
I shall assume it to be a necessary truth that all subjects have
the capacity for sense experience in this broad sense.[18]

V

To understand the nature of sensible continuity we must begin
by distinguishing, within sense experience, between phenomenal
objects and presentational acts. A phenomenal object (phenomenon)
is a repeatable and intersubjective universal, a sensible quality pattern which can be presented to different subjects and at different
times. A presentational act (presentation) is a private and unrepeat-
able particular, a unique subject's momentary awareness of a quality
pattern. For present purposes, the most important aspect of this
distinction is its application to the *temporality* of sense experience:
in distinguishing phenomena and presentations, we must also distinguish phenomenal time relations, which structure the presented
pattern, and presentational time relations, which order the presentations themselves. Thus, within auditory experience, we must distinguish a phenomenal succession of sounds (for instance, C #-before-
G), which forms a structured phenomenal pattern, from a mental

succession of sound presentations (for example, the hearing of C#
before the hearing of G), which forms a sequence of mental particulars. Sensible continuity is the product of the special way in which
phenomenal and presentational time interlock.

At first sight the relationship between phenomenal and presentational time seems to resist coherent description. Suppose I observe
a moving object – for instance, the flight of a red ball. The fact
that I directly see the movement, directly see the successive occu-
pancy of adjacent positions, shows that each of my total presentations, except perhaps the first and the last, is of some temporal
pattern, and that the patterns of successive presentations qualitatively overlap. For example, if R is the relevant round red patch
and P_1, P_2, P_3, ... , P_n the series of spatial positions, relative
to the background pattern, that it successively occupies, we can
envisage, as the initial phase of my experience, a presentation of
$[R$ at $P_1]$-before-$[R$ at $P_2]$ followed by a presentation of $[R$ at
$P_2]$-before-$[R$ at $P_3]$, each presentation being of a temporal pattern
and both patterns sharing the non-temporal component $[R$ at $P_2]$.
But there is a fact which seems to undermine this characterisation.
If the temporal patterns of successive total presentations overlap,
we seem forced to say that their common component is twice
presented, first as the object of one presentation and then as the
object of another. If I successively see $[R$ at $P_1]$-before-$[R$ at $P_2]$
and $[R$ at $P_2]$-before-$[R$ at $P_3]$, then surely I must have two presentations of $[R$ at $P_2]$. Granted that phenomena are universals, this
consequence is logically unobjectionable, but the fact is that it
is not true to the character of my experience. Although I directly
see the ball successively occupy adjacent positions, so long as the
ball keeps moving I only once see it at any given position.

The resolution of this paradox is the key to sensible continuity.
The point is that where the temporal patterns presented by successive total presentations overlap in quality, in that some last portion
of the first is the same as some first portion of the second, the
two total presentations overlap in a corresponding way, in that
the component presentations which in their respective totals present
this common sub-pattern are themselves numerically identical. In
other words, a presentation of a temporal pattern is itself temporally
extended, and it overlaps its predecessor and successor in, so to
speak, presentational substance to the extent that its pattern overlaps
theirs in phenomenal content. It is this double overlap which provides the sensible continuity of sense experience and unifies presentations into a stream of awareness. And it is in the unity of a
stream that we primarily discern the identity of a subject.

Presentations in the same stream of awareness are states of the same subject – are, as I shall put it, *consubjective*. This important truth – call it *C* – we knew already. But the analysis of sensible continuity yields a definition of *stream* whereby we can derive *C* from first principles, and this derivation provides our primary insight into the nature of subject identity. Thus we can define a *stream* as any complete temporal series of total presentations the successive members of which overlap, where a *total* presentation is one which is not a part of any other. To derive *C* we need two self-evident principles. The one, which may be called the principle of presentational unity (PU), states that presentations which are parts of the same presentation are consubjective, it being understood that every presentation is a part, though not a *proper* part, of itself. The other, which may be called the principle of temporal equivalence (TE), states that consubjectivity is a qualified equivalence relation: reflexive, symmetric and, as I shall put it, *temporally* transitive. In claiming consubjectivity to be *temporally* transitive I mean that, if x, y and z are presentations such that x is consubjective with and no later than y, and y is consubjective with and no later than z, then x is consubjective with and no later than z. I avoid making the stronger, though not implausible, claim that it is transitive *simpliciter* so as to avoid automatically excluding the case, recognised by some philosophers, in which subjects split and fuse. For in such a case (if it is possible) two concurrent subject phases that are not themselves consubjective are alike consubjective with the subject phase from which they divide or into which they merge. PU and TE yield *C* as follows: if two presentations overlap, we know from PU that each is consubjective with the presentation that is a part of both, and hence, by TE, that each is consubjective with the other; thence it follows, by TE, that members of the same stream are consubjective; and thence it follows, by PU and TE, that constituents (i. e. parts of members) of the same stream are consubjective. Thus *C*.

What light, then, does this derivation shed on the nature of subject identity? It shows, in effect that the unity of a stream is no more nor less than the projection through time of the unity of a presentation and that the subject's persistence through a stream is no more nor less than the projection through time of his individuality at a moment. At any moment in the stream the subject is individuated by the boundaries of his presentational awareness, presentations being simultaneously consubjective if, and only if, they are simultaneous parts of the same presentation. Through the stream he persists in the overlapping of his successive total presentations, the same awareness being preserved, as it were, through a constant contraction and expansion at its temporal edges. Thus, within a

stream the identity of a subject consists, in effect, in the unity
of a common awareness, an awareness first delineated by the boundaries of a presentation and then transported beyond these boundaries by sensible continuity. And thus far we have, in line with
my Cartesian goal, a unitary and determinate conception of subject
identity, attributing to all phases of a stream that form of subject
persistence prescribed by consubjectivity within a presentation.[19]

However, our account of subject identity is not yet complete.
Presentations in the same stream are states of the same subject,
but a subject is not, typically, confined to a single stream. Many
streams, separated by periods of presentational unconsciousness,
may themselves be consubjective. In what, then, does their consubjectivity consist? How can we explain the subject's persistence
between them? Addressing himself to much the same question,
Ayer, in an ingenious reconstruction of the ideas of William James,
sought the answer in links of memory and bodily continuity.[20]
Let us say that two streams are *recollectively linked* if, and only
if, they stand as first and last members (not in a *temporal* sense)
of an ordered set of streams the successive members of which
are recollectively adjacent, where two streams are *recollectively
adjacent* if, and only if, an apparent memory of a presentation
in the one consciously accompanies a presentation in the other.
Let us further say that two streams are *corporeally linked* if, and
only if, each contains a bodily sensation and all the bodily sensations
of both are located in the same body. Ayer's theory is immensely
complicated, involving an elaborate system of rules for deciding
'deviant' cases. But its central tenet is that in the standard case
consubjective streams are rendered consubjective by being both
recollectively and corporeally linked.[21]

Ayer's aspirations are, of course, entirely Humian, and to those
who share them the account he gave may appear to be on the
right lines. Apparent memory and bodily continuity are clearly
relevant to deciding questions of subject identity: other things being
equal, we expect consubjective streams to be those that are recollectively and corporeally linked. But such an account will not sustain
a realistic, Cartesian construal of the subject, for it does not yield
a homogeneous form of subject persistence. What it yields are
two forms, one within streams and one between streams, which
cannot be represented as species of the same genus except, trivially,
by defining the genus as their disjunction. To a Humian a disjunctive
analysis may be acceptable so long as it agrees with our ordinary
judgements of subject identity. But it is not acceptable to a Cartesian.
For it is only by discovering a homogeneous form of persistence,
both within and between streams, that we are entitled to take

seriously the notion of there being something that persists throughout. What I need is an analysis which extends to sets of streams
the kind of unity found within a single stream, an analysis which
represents the subject's persistence, even through periods of unconsciousness, as, in a sense, the preservation of a common awareness.

On the face of it this sets an impossible goal. For, if awareness
ceases, how can there be a sense in which it is preserved? But
we can get what we want by putting the right interpretation on
one crucial fact, that consubjective streams have what non-consubjective streams lack: the potential for being phases of a single
stream. To keep things initially simple, I shall provisionally assume
(an assumption stronger than TE) that consubjectivity is an equivalence relation (reflexive, symmetric and transitive), thus excluding
cases of fission and fusion. Suppose, then, we have two streams,
S_1 and S_2, the last presentation in S_1 being, say, five minutes
earlier than the first in S_2. If S_1 and S_2 are consubjective, then,
had S_1 continued for a further five minutes, with S_2 occurring
just as it did, S_1 and S_2 would have formed phases of a single
stream. Conversely, if S_1 and S_2 are not consubjective, then no
continuation of S_1 would have made them phases of a single stream.
So, whatever our definition of consubjectivity, it must agree with
these counterfactuals: it must confer on consubjective streams and
exclude from non-consubjective streams the potential for joining
when the earlier stream is sufficiently extended.

The problem is to get this condition to yield something non-trivial.
For, on the face of it, the potential for joining is logically grounded
on the continuity of the subject: on the face of it, two streams
are potentially unistreamal in virtue of being essentially consubjective and therefore, by *de re* necessity, logically guaranteed to meet
if sufficiently extended. But there is an alternative, and an attractive
one, namely to take the potential as resting on certain natural
laws – laws statable without recourse to the concept of a subject,
though constitutive of his capacity for interstreamal persistence. Thus
let us say: (a) that a relation R is *non-transferable* if, and only
if, R-related presentations are *essentially* R-related and non-R-
related presentations are essentially non-R-related;[22] (b) that R
is a *persistence relation* (or a persistence relation for a certain
class of subjects) if, and only if, R is a two-place non-transferable
equivalence relation, not involving the concept of a subject, and
it is a law of nature (or a law of nature for that class of subjects)
both that presentations in the same stream are R-related and that
simultaneous R-related presentations are in the same stream; and
(c) that two streams are *persistence-linked* if, and only if, their
constituents are persistence-related, i.e. there is a persistence relation

in which the presentations in the one stand to those in the other. I then propose as the required definition: two streams are consubjective if, and only if, they are persistence-linked. This meets the prescribed condition. For, granted there is a persistence relation, two streams are potentially unistreamal if, and only if, they are persistence-linked. Moreover, it meets the condition without triviality, since persistence linkage is not grounded on subject identity.

The meeting of the condition is best demonstrated by a not implausible example. Let us suppose, at least for the class of embodied subjects, that every presentation is directly causally dependent on a brain, that brains are not capable of fission or fusion, and that we have as natural laws (1) that presentations in the same stream are dependent on the same brain, and (2) that simultaneous presentations dependent on the same brain are in the same stream. If we take it, as I think we should, that the identity of a presentation is tied to the identity of the brain on which it causally depends, the relation of being dependent on the same brain (cocerebral dependence) is non-transferable. Moreover, granted the rejection of the nomological assumption and the argument which I once advanced on its basis, cocerebral dependence does not involve the concept of a subject.[23] Consequently, given the laws (1) and (2), cocerebral dependence qualifies as a persistence relation, at least for the class of embodied subjects. Accordingly, to show that the condition is met, we must show that two streams are potentially unistreamal if, and only if, their presentations depend on the same brain. This we can do as follows: Let S_1 and S_2 be streams and B_1 and B_2 be brains such that S_1's presentations depend on B_1, S_2's presentations depend on B_2, and the last presentation in S_1 is earlier than the first in S_2. Assume first that $B_1 = B_2$ and, holding S_2 constant, envisage the extension of S_1 to the time when S_2 begins. Since cocerebral dependence is non-transferable, (1) ensures that the first presentation in S_2 and the last in the extended S_1 are simultaneously dependent on the same brain, whence (2) ensures that S_2 and the extended S_1 form a single stream. Assume, conversely, that $B_1 \neq B_2$ and, holding S_2 constant, envisage the same extension of S_1. Since cocerebral dependence is non-transferable, (1) ensures that S_2 and the extended S_1 do not form a single stream. Hence, given our original supposition, two streams are potentially unistreamal if, and only if, their presentations depend on the same brain.

This, I must emphasise, is only an example. For, while, on my account, it is a necessary truth that consubjective streams are persistence-linked, there is no one relation of which it is a necessary truth that they are linked in that way. Persistence-relatedness is not defined as cocerebral dependence, though cocerebral dependence may be, contingently, what secures it. A logically possible alternative would be a persistence relation of a purely mental kind, such as some specific relation of phenomenal resemblance or causal connection, though I cannot think of any empirically plausible example.[24]

My definition of consubjectivity between streams, combined with the earlier established *C*, yields the conclusion that presentations are consubjective if, and only if, they are constituents of either the same stream or streams which are persistence-linked. Does this conclusion provide the unitary conception of subject identity required for a Cartesian construal? Well, one could argue like this: 'Since persistence-linked streams are potentially unistreamal, the subject's persistence between streams is, in effect, a subliminal version of his persistence through a stream – sensible continuity sustained, as it were, below the threshold of actuality by the factors that are nomically correlated with its actualisation. Subject persistence remains, in essence, the preservation of a common awareness, an awareness initially demarcated by the boundaries of a total presentation, then extended through successive overlaps, and finally stretched across periods of unconsciousness by a law-based potential.' But we can do better than this. It is surely a necessary truth that any subject has the *genuine* capacity to persist for a period without sense experience – a capacity, that is, which could be actualised without alterations to natural law. Consequently, on my account, it must be a necessary truth that, if there are subjects, there is a persistence relation, and therefore a necessary truth that presentations in the same stream are persistence-related. This means that we can assert the simpler conclusion that two presentations are consubjective if, and only if, they are persistence-related, and this conclusion provides a strictly unitary conception of subject identity in which the so-called subliminal version applies at all phases of subject persistence. What it provides is given by the principle that momentary subject slices of the same subject if, and only if, their actual (or potential) presentational states are (or would be) persistence-related. The persistence of a subject is the persistence of a capacity, sustained by natural law, for persistence-related sense experience.

We have reached this conclusion on the basis of the assumption that consubjectivity is an equivalence relation. If this assumption is dropped, in favour of the weaker TE, we can no longer maintain that, if two streams are consubjective, a sufficient extension of the earlier is guaranteed to join the later. For, if the subject divides during the interval, there are alternative subjective routes which the hypothetical extension could take. But, even if we revert to TE, our conclusion stands, provided we correspondingly adjust the definition of 'persistence relation'. All that is required is that we attribute to a persistence relation the formal properties we attribute to consubjectivity – strict equivalence under the assumption, temporally qualified equivalence under TE. Thus, if we adopt TE, cocerebral dependence still qualifies as a persistence relation provided laws (1) and (2) hold, although, being merely temporally transitive, it permits the case of brains', like subjects', splitting and fusing. That is to say, if two, contemporaneous brain phases B_1 and B_2 are either continuations or precursors of a single brain phase B, and P_1, P_2 and P are presentations respectively dependent on B_1, B_2 and B, P_1 and P_2 are not persistence-related and therefore not consubjective, though both are persistence-related to and therefore consubjective with P.

Whether consubjectivity is an equivalence relation is an important question, though not one I have space to discuss here. Clearly, if we recognise the possibility of subjects' splitting and fusing, we must speak not of two subjects' being identical with the same subject, but of two subjects' sharing the same subject phase, i. e. having, for a certain period, numerically the same mental states. It is not clear that such a notion is intelligible, but, if it is, my account is flexible enough to allow it.

VI

Let me try to bring the various strands of my argument together. In sections I to III, I defended the thesis that the concept of a person is to be analysed, dualistically, in terms of how a body and a mind causally combine. I maintained, in particular, that the combining of a body and a mind yields a person – a subject of both mental and bodily attributes – if, and only if, it ensures the general appropriateness of functional role to psychological character, thereby ensuring the general adequacy, in respect of that body and mind, of our criteria of third person mental ascription. Defending this thesis involved rejecting both (II) Strawson's claim that the concept of a person is primitive and (III) the no-ownership theory, which analyses the unity of the mind in terms of its causal embodiment. This left me with an obligation to analyse the unity in some other way, and in sections IV and V I tried to discharge it by defending a realistic, Cartesian conception of the mental subject backed by a quasi-Humian analysis of its identity. I argued, in particular, that the identity of a subject consists, in effect, in the preservation of a common awareness, a preservation secured by the persistence-relatedness of its presentational states, whereby states thus related have the law-based potential for being constituents of the same stream. As for non-presentational states, I hold that they are states of the same mind simply in virtue of being states of the same subject. Put together, the dualistic analysis of personhood and the Cartesian conception of the subject yield Cartesian dualism: a person is a persisting mental subject who qualifies for personhood in virtue of the contingent embodiment of his mind, and the conditions of personal identity are simply the conditions of subject identity restricted to the domain of subjects who thus qualify. And this is just the doctrine, the dualistic doctrine of the person, which in section I I set out to defend.

In one respect my version of this doctrine is not as radically dualistic as Descartes's. Descartes held subjects to be non-physical substances, capable, both logically and nomologically, of existing without the existence of the physical world. My own conclusions are somewhat weaker. Certainly I have to recognise the possibility of subjects who are self-sufficient in Descartes's way. But I am not committed to saying that *all* subjects are of that sort, nor, in particular, that *we* are. This is because the form of the persistence relation, which secures identity, is not settled *a priori*. If in our case the relation turns out to be cocerebral dependence, then, though capable of disembodiment (for example, through a severing of the neural connections between brain and body), our existence is dependent on the existence of our brains and on those laws, (1) and (2), whereby the same brain sustains the same awareness.

This modification to strict Cartesianism reflects, of course, my substantial concession to Hume. Like Descartes, I construe the subject, and hence the person, as a genuine continuant; but, like Hume, I have sought to analyse its identity in terms of unifying relations between its states. In my view, it is only thus that we can form a conception of the subject that is both intuitive and intelligible, only thus that we can do justice to our*selves*.

NOTES

1. I am grateful to Mr H. M. Robinson for his helpful comments on an earlier draft.
2. P. F. Strawson, *Individuals* (London: Methuen, 1959) pp. 101–2.
3. What follows is my attempt to summarise Strawson's chapter 3, section iv.
4. Strawson, *Individuals*, p. 111.
5. Ibid., p. 112. By '*P*-predicate' Strawson means a predicate applicable to persons, and only applicable to subjects of consciousness.
6. This dubbing and Strawson's discussion of the theory are in chapter 3, section iii.

7. That is, the *pure* Cartesian and the *pure* Humian. In sections ɪᴠ and ᴠ I provide a theory which has both Cartesian and Humian aspects.

8. A. J. Ayer, *The Concept of a Person* (London: Macmillan, 1963) pp. 116–18.

9. By 'conceived dualistically' I mean, in particular, that mental and physical states are numerically distinct.

10. John Foster, 'Psycho-physical Causal Relations' in *American Philosophical Quarterly*, ᴠ, no. 1 (1968).

11. In support of this conclusion, Dr R. M. Sainsbury suggests the following refinement to my example: we suppose that the intensity of a flash is proportional to the size of its sphere, so that it is only with two spheres of the same size that the overlapping of specified regions may prevent the decidability of causal pairings.

12. Foster, in *American Philosophical Quarterly*, ᴠ, no. 1, p. 116.

13. See esp. Descartes, *Discourse on the Method*, ɪᴠ, and Meditation, ᴠɪ.

14. See Hume, *A Treatise of Human Nature*, ɪ. 4. vi.

15. Ibid., ed. L. A. Selby-Bigge, p. 252.

16. See Locke, *An Essay Concerning Human Understanding*, ɪɪ. 27.

17. To be fair to him, Locke did not rule out the possibility that mental substance is material.

18. If space permitted, I should give a detailed defence of this assumption along the following lines. Any subject must either have the capacity for sense experience or the capacity to form propositional attitudes. But the capacity to form propositional attitudes requires the possession of concepts, and the possession of concepts requires the capacity to form mental images (this is not to equate concepts with images). The forming of mental images is a species of sense experience in the relevant sense. Hence, any subjects must have the capacity for sense experience in this sense.

19. This seems to be close to Locke's claim that subject slices are consubjective if, and only if, they share the same consciousness. But Locke construed identity of consciousness primarily in terms of memory.

20. A. J. Ayer, *The Origins of Pragmatism* (London: Macmillan, 1968) pp. 263–88. The theory supersedes his earlier no-ownership theory.

21. First, the division of the topic into consubjectivity within streams and consubjectivity between streams, and the resulting terminology of recollective and corporeal links are mine and not Ayer's. I have tried to re-express Ayer's position, or the gist of it, so as to bring out its relevance to my own approach.

Secondly, notice that, while Ayer continues to regard bodily continuity as a factor in subject persistence, the attachment of experience to bodies is now specified not (as in the previous theory) causally, but phenomenologically. This is because he came to accept my former argument based on the nomological assumption.

22. Strictly speaking, a weaker definition of non-transferability would suffice for my purposes, namely: R is non-transferable if, and only if, K is the class of all presentations; then (a) if P_1 and P_2 are R-related presentations, there could not be circumstances in which all the members of K occurred and P_1 and P_2 were not R-related, and (b) if P_1 and P_2 are non-R-related presentations, there could not be circumstances in which all the members of K occurred and P_1 and P_2 were R-related.

23. Hence my remark in section ɪɪɪ that the result of my 'digression' into psychophysical causal relations contributes to my account of subject identity. The result permits us to envisage cocerebral dependence as contingently securing, though not as defining, a subject's persistence between streams.

24. Incidentally, those who expect to survive their physical death are not obliged to take the persistence relation to be purely mental. They could take it to be the disjunction of two relations: a cerebral relation applying exclusively in this life; a mental relation applying exclusively in the life to come. Such disjunctiveness would not undermine the homogeneity of subject persistence. For persistence is defined by persistence-relatedness, not by the persistence relation.

9 Memory, Experiential Memory, and Personal Identity

RICHARD WOLLHEIM

I

In a number of passages to be found across his writings, Ayer has turned his attention to a claim which consistently found favour within that philosophical tradition to which he has always, and justly, seen himself as standing in natural succession. The tradition is, of course, that of classical British empiricism, and the claim is the claim that memory (or some particular type of memory) provides an adequate criterion of personal identity.

In *The Foundations of Empirical Knowledge*[1] Ayer seemed to accept the claim, at least so far as the inner aspect of personal identity is concerned; but in his later writings, while continuing to look upon it sympathetically, he rejects it. He rejects it on, in effect, three separate counts. Memory fails to provide us with a sufficient condition of personal identity. Memory fails to provide us with a necessary condition of personal identity. And the claim made on its behalf involves circularity.

Evidently, for Ayer the charge of circularity is the least serious of the three, and at two places at least he suggests that the circularity might be avoided with a more careful formulation of the claim. The circularity arises for him because, if the claim has it either that a man's remembering a certain experience suffices to make it his own or that his remembering it is necessary for the experience to be his, this overlooks the fact that in remembering the experience the man already 'claims' it (the phrase used in *The Problem of Knowledge*), 'acknowledges' it (the phrase used in *The Origins of Pragmatism*), or 'thinks' of it (the phrase used in *The Concept of a Person*), as his own.[2] But nowhere does Ayer expand on the force of the 'already', nor does he distinguish between the harmless connotation of this term to indicate what memory implies and the vicious connotation to indicate what memory, or even putative memory, presupposes. And all this suggests that for him the charge is not one that he would wish to see pressed.

To show that memory is not a sufficient condition of personal identity is for Ayer a comparatively straightforward matter.[3]

The crucial consideration is that there is no self-contradiction involved in supposing that a man should remember an experience everything else about which would lead us to think of it as not his own, or indeed as someone else's. Ayer allows that, if at some moment it looked as though such a possibility was about to realise itself, then we might try to block it by legislating that the man could not really remember the experience (though he seemed to) or that the experience was really his (though it seemed not to be), and in our efforts be motivated solely by the desire to preserve the truth that no one can remember experiences other than his own. Furthermore, Ayer is sufficiently susceptible to conventionalism to suppose that such attempts on our part could succeed. But their success would be arbitrary. So, when we have taken full account of all the concessions to conventionalism that Ayer might wish to make, it remains his view that, at any rate from any non-arbitrary point of view, the existence of memories of experiences other than one's own is a logical possibility. Paths of the appropriate type of memory could – and, if I introduce this terminology to summarise Ayer's position, I shall return to it in advancing views of my own – not merely run along persons, but also run across them. And, if they did, they would not, of course, suffice to produce biographies.

That memory is not a necessary condition of personal identity elicits from Ayer a more elaborate argument.[4]

The initial consideration is that there will be many many cases where we have pairs of experiences everything else about which would lead us to think of them as experiences of one and the same person, yet which are not related by the memory relation. They are not so related because either the later of the two experiences is not a memory at all or it is a memory of something other than the earlier experience. Now, an obvious way of dealing with such counter-examples is to extend the memory relation so that it may hold between experiences indirectly as well as directly. So two experiences are directly related by the memory relation if one is a memory of the other, and they are indirectly related by the memory relation if they both belong to a series of experiences each of which is directly related by it to some other experience in the series. We introduce, in other words, the ancestral of the memory relation and now construct memory series by reference to it. But this way of dealing with counter-examples is open to the objection that it still requires that every experience of a person is either a memory of some earlier experience of that person or the object of some later memory of his. And, when this requirement is spelt out in full, what is objectionable to it becomes more evident. All experiences must enter biographies either through being memories or through being remembered – such is the thesis. So, let us first consider those experiences which enter biographies through being remembered: the full requirement upon them is not just that they are remembered but that they are remembered totally – for otherwise that part of any experience that is not remembered falls outside the biography. Secondly, let us consider those experiences which enter biographies through being memories: the full requirement upon them is that they are numerous enough to include not only memories of all those experiences of the person which are not themselves memories, but also memories of all those experiences of his which are memories but are not memories of other experiences of his. And, to satisfy this requirement, there will have to be both multiple memories, i.e. memories of more than one experience, and reiterated memories, i.e. memories of memories, and in both cases well beyond the bounds of plausibility.

At this stage it is usual to try to save the claim by further relaxing the conditions upon memory series; and this is done by, first, introducing the notion of one experience's accompanying another, and, then, allowing that memory series may deviate through accompanying experiences, so that, if a particular experience belongs to a certain memory series, so does any experience that accompanies it and so do all experiences that are either directly or indirectly related by the memory relation to this accompanying experience.

But to this manoeuvre there are two objections to be made, and Ayer is found making both of them. In the first place, whatever the manoeuvre saves, it is not the original claim, or at any rate the claim in its original character. If memory series are allowed to be constructed in this new or relaxed way, and memory series are equated with biographies, there is no longer cause to think of memory as a necessary condition of personal identity. For it is no longer the case that any two experiences in one and the same memory series must be related by the memory relation, even indirectly: even, that is, by the ancestral of the memory relation. Of course, they may be related by the memory relation, but they may be related solely by the new relation of accompaniment, which is certainly a different relation. And here the second objection takes over. For, if we ask what this relation of accompaniment is, the only satisfactory answer seems to be that it is the relation that holds between any two contemporary experiences just when they are parts of the total experience of one person at one time. In other words, accompaniment is the synchronic version of that very relation which in its diachronic version has given rise to the problem thus far considered: that of personal identity. And it is quite unwarranted for someone, at any rate for an empiricist, who sets himself to solve the problem of personal identity over time, to find the problem of personal identity at a time quite unproblematic.

II

This last sentence was framed advisedly. For, if Ayer's arguments against the claim favoured by the empiricists are, as I am convinced that they are, sound – if, that is to say, they effectively dispute both the sufficiency and the necessity claimed by memory in respect of personal identity, for I think that Ayer would be content for us to leave the charge of circularity to one side – it is important to see that these arguments are sound against the claim *in so far as it is considered in the form favoured by the empiricist*. But it will be a theme of this essay that, in so far as the claim is considered in this form, it is not only open to serious objection but also deprived of its natural appeal. Brought into conformity with the epistemological assumptions of classical empiricism, the claim loses the support of those natural intuitions from which it initially springs.

This may suggest that this essay will be negative in character. In a way this is so. I shall not prove, or even attempt to prove, that, if the claim is considered in some other form, memory can indeed provide an adequate criterion of personal identity. I have not the space in which to do so, nor am I certain of the materials that are required for the purpose, nor, as I see it, is the thesis straightforwardly true. However, I shall try to assemble in this essay some indications about the proper contribution of memory to personal identity, and I shall include a rather sketchy assessment of how far this goes.

But, first, what is the specific form in which the empiricists considered the claim of memory to provide an adequate criterion of personal identity?

The form in which the empiricists favoured the claim is, of course, very closely connected with what it was about the claim that led them – though not, I should argue, those philosophers guided to the claim by natural intuition – to look upon it with favour, and this was that it appeared to promise economies of just the kind to which they were philosophically drawn. If personal identity could be accounted for in terms of memory, then there were obvious metaphysical economies that could be effected. There would be no need to postulate either an underlying thinking or spiritual substance in which the person's identity might be held to inhere or some elusive property which would present-tensedly belong to the person for the term of his existence and which would sustain identity over time. But, the empiricists saw, there was no reason why the economies should stop here. Memory's claim to account for personal identity could permit one to take an even more parsimonious view of the matter, in that, with the claim appropriately framed, one could dispense even with persons themselves as original or primary phenomena. For, if the memory relation were conceived of as a relation between experiences, persons could be introduced only at a later stage, just when experiences, or enough of them, were found to be positively related. And to the objection that experiences themselves are always the experiences of persons little weight was felt to attach – unless, of course, the objection meant that experiences presuppose persons for their intelligibility. But, if this was the charge, then the onus of proof was placed squarely on the side of the objector. Interpreted otherwise, the objection came (so the empiricists maintained) to no more than the factual claim that it is always into sizable bundles that the memory relation ties experiences.

Now, it is an easy step from the specific hopes that the empiricists entertained of memory if its claim to be criterial of personal identity could be established to the form in which they considered this claim. Using a distinction given circulation in this context by Bernard Williams,[5] we may say that memory was looked to by the empiricists to furnish not a principle of identity but a principle of individuation. Ultimately, of course, memory would be employed to answer questions of the form 'Are a and b the same person?' But not initially. Initially memory is employed to answer questions of the form 'Are x and y experiences of the same person?' And what underlies this strategy is the conviction that, having asked enough questions of the second kind, we shall then be able, out of the answers we have got to them, to answer questions of the first kind. Confronted with the question 'Are a and b the same person?', we have, seemingly, to change the subject and ask, 'Are the experiences associated with a and the experiences associated with b experiences of the same person?' But in doing so we may rest sure in the conviction that, once we have answered this question, we have answered the question with which we were confronted. It is because this is so, and because the answer to the question of whether the experiences associated with a and the experiences associated with *b* are indeed experiences of the same person depends solely on whether the two sets of experiences are positively related by the memory relation, that memory provides an adequate criterion of personal identity.

To some this particular employment of memory in the resolution of questions of personal identity may seem self-evidently correct. They may, that is to say, find it by no means self-evident that questions of personal identity should be resolved by the application of a principle of individuation, or (the same thing) that identity of person should be established on the basis of certain relations holding between experiences. Yet I have in mind their finding self-evident the following: that, *if* memory is to be crucial in the resolution of questions of personal identity, *then* such questions must be resolved by the application of a principle of individuation. How else, they would argue, could memory determine identity of person other than by supplying some appropriate relation between experiences on the basis of which such identity is established? In talking of memory's claim to be criterial of personal identity I have talked of the specific form in which this claim was favoured by the empiricists, and thereby I have talked as though there were several distinct forms that such a claim could take. But – such a person as I have in mind might argue – this is just not so: there is only one form, which the empiricists favoured, and they favoured it because (rightly or wrongly) they favoured the claim.

Such an argument is ill founded. There is no warrant for holding that, if one thinks that memory is criterial of personal identity, one is committed to the parsimony of empiricist epistemology: that is to say, that one should start off with experiences, and then construct persons and their identity out of the relations holding between such experiences. The best way to argue for this is, I suspect, to go over to the offensive. So I shall try to identify two aspects of memory, both of which are essential to it, both of which must figure in any full or even adequate account of the contribution of memory to personal identity, and neither of which is comprehensible if we take as original or primary only experiences and their interrelations, and not persons.

These two aspects of memory are, first, that memory is rooted in or expresses a capacity; and, secondly, that memory has a specific causation.

III

That the contribution of memory to personal identity is only incompletely before us until we introduce the notion of memory as a capacity is something that has been, at any rate in a general way, anticipated in the preceding discussion. More specifically, the need for this notion, or a notion close to it, is implicit in the criticism that memory as the empiricist conceives of it – that is, uniquely as a relation holding between experiences – does not provide a necessary condition of personal identity. For any such criticism really amounts to this: if the empiricist is neither to allow certain experiences that we should otherwise think of as belonging to a certain person to slip out of that person's biography – in which case memory could not be said non-arbitrarily to provide a *necessary* condition of personal identity – nor to supplement the memory relation with some other, non-mnemic relation, such as that of accompaniment (in which case it could no longer be said to be *memory* that provided a necessary condition of personal identity), then he has to make a deeply implausible assumption. That assumption is that every experience that is an experience of a person either is a memory of some earlier experience of that person to whom it belongs or is later remembered by him; and that this is a necessary truth about persons. The introduction by the empiricist of the memory relation as holding not only directly but also indirectly between experiences does nothing to alter this. The quest, therefore, must be for some third way in which an experience can enter a biography and which belongs to the category of memory. And the most obvious candidate for this is that an experience should be capable of being remembered by the person to whose biography it belongs.

Now, it is important to see that the 'can be remembered by . . .' that occurs here is not simply – as some philosophers have argued that it must be if the claim is to be true[6] – a rewrite of 'belongs to the biography of . . .'. On the contrary, it makes a definite reference to a capacity that persons have and whose scope is highly germane to their identity. It is important to see this for two reasons. In the first place, if it were simply a rewrite, a charge of either vacuousness or circularity would be in place. And, secondly, since it is not a rewrite, it allows us to see that, in introducing memory as a capacity into the account of personal identity, we have abandoned the parsimonious view of the matter that is characteristic of the empiricist approach. Once memory as a capacity is introduced, we must introduce persons. Without persons, with only experiences and the relations between experiences, we should have nowhere to house such a disposition; which is why the empiricist, so long as he is faithful to his original project, has no truck with this aspect of memory.

However, if the notion of memory as a capacity requires the notion of persons, it is also, I should maintain, required by the notion of memory itself. In other words, no fully coherent notion of memory can be extracted exclusively from memory experiences. There are, of course, cases where memories assail us: they are 'alien guests'[7] in our consciousness. But, apart from the question of whether memory could consist only in memories of this sort, there is the prior question of whether even memories of this sort can be understood without introducing memory as a capacity. For it would seem to be an essential feature of such memories, on the basis of which they function as memories – as, that is, messengers from the past – that, taking our cue from what they tell us, we can then go on to ask of ourselves what happened next, or what we felt about it, or why it was. And this clearly involves the capacity I have in mind.

Whether, once memory as a capacity has been introduced, memory can indeed make good its claim to be a necessary condition of personal identity is somewhat beyond the range of this essay, but it is worth considering what would need to be, and what would not need to be, established before the claim was made good. On any reasonable understanding of the matter, it would not have to be established that, at any given moment in his life, a person had the capacity to remember all the previous experiences that were constructed on the basis of the memory relation's holding indirectly; one could relax the requirement so that it was now satisfied if, or certain experiences could be said to be his only if, at any given moment in his life he had the capacity to remember certain previous experiences that he had had at a time when he had the capacity to remember just those experiences. And, if it is now objected that this is not only to introduce an analogue to the indirect memory relation, but also to reintroduce the unwarranted relation of accompaniment, it is important to see why this objection now fails. It fails because we are now no longer within the epistemological assumptions of empiricism. When we were within those assumptions, which insist that persons are constructions out of relations between experiences, it was evidently unwarranted to take as primitive relations between experiences that require persons for their identification. But, now we are outside those assumptions, and feel free to introduce persons straight off, there seems to me nothing at all objectionable in predicating of one and the same person synchronically an experience *and* a disposition – and to do this even though we are still uncertain about the criteria of identity for persons diachronically.

However, it is another matter how freely we do wish to distribute dispositions along the biography of a person, and whether too liberal a distribution of them, while preserving the letter of the claim that memory is a necessary condition of personal identity, might not offend against the spirit. On that I shall have nothing further to say, save by implication.

IV

It would lend the discussion a desirable neatness if it could next be shown that the need to introduce the causal history of memory if the contribution of memory is to be fully before us is implicit in the criticism that memory as the empiricist conceives of it fails to provide a sufficient condition of personal identity. In point of fact I believe this to be true, but the neatness that it appears to offer the discussion is largely illusory and that is because the point is not something that can be simply shown. Accordingly I shall disregard it and pass on to the substantive issue. I shall consider the question 'How does the introduction of the causal history of memory bear upon the contribution of memory to personal identity?'

V

There is, however, a preliminary issue to be resolved: that of what type of memory we are talking of. For there are varieties of memory, and to make the claim, with some of these types of memory in mind, that memory is criterial of personal identity can only be ridiculous.[8]

The point is familiar, and it was probably Locke's desire to identify the type of memory correctly that led him to equivocate between 'memory' and 'consciousness' as the adequate criterion of identity. I shall call the relevant type of memory 'experiential memory', and wish to suggest straight away two differential features that serve to distinguish it from other types of memory. If I experientially remember an action, then, in the first place, I remember that action from the inside, and, secondly, if the action that I remember is, say, an action that I did *and* I report this memory – which is, of course, something that I may, alternatively that I may not, do – I characteristically report it by saying, 'I remember doing such-and-such' or 'I remember my doing such-and-such', rather than 'I remember that I did such-and-such', which is more appropriate to an external type of memory.

I shall later have something to say in amplification of the first feature. For the moment I shall rest content with pointing out that to accept this as a differential feature of experiential memory means that the claim of experiential memory to be recognised as a separate type of memory rests – not exclusively, but distinctively – upon its phenomenology. As to the second feature, attention should be drawn to the fact that my statement of it has been so framed as not to preclude definitionally someone's experientially remembering a doing or a suffering of someone else's. For, if, say, I were to experientially remember an action that you did, or an action that X did, then it would be altogether consistent with what I have said that such a memory would be characteristically reported by my saying either 'I remember doing such-and-such', or 'I remember your, or X's, doing such-and-such.' There is no point in trying to decide which of these two kinds of locution is the more appropriate or whether there is not a third kind that would be apter. For, since such memories evidently do not occur, it is barely surprising that no form of words has been assigned the task of reporting them. However, the important thing to see is that, as I have characterised experiential memory, there is no reason why a form of words should not be assigned the task, were the task to present itself – that is, were such memories to occur. And this is important. For, if it ultimately turns out that necessarily someone can experientially remember only a doing or a suffering of his own – and, of course, it must turn out so if experiential memory is a sufficient condition of personal identity – it is crucial that this sufficiency is not achieved trivially or by fiat.

These two features of experiential memory indicate a powerful and instructive analogy between it and another psychological phenomenon which I have considered elsewhere and in some detail. This is the phenomenon that I have called 'centrally imagining'.[9] Experiential memory and centrally imagining may be fruitfully made use of so that each throws light on the other. In the course of this essay I shall draw upon the parallel.

In *The Problem of Knowledge*[10] Ayer gives some attention to the varieties of memory. However, he does not recognise experiential memory as a separate type of memory. Since this is clearly no mere oversight on his part, we may ask why. The answer lies, I suggest, in Ayer's overall view of what memory is, which in turn determines how memory should be classified or the various types of memory distinguished. This overall view of memory is not peculiar to Ayer, and, since, in my opinion, it is as much of an obstacle to perceiving the proper contribution of memory to personal identity as the classical empiricists' assumptions about how the issue of personal identity is to be resolved, the view is worth considering in its own right.

If we put to one side habit – memory (as it is often called) or

remembering – how, which, it is generally conceded, has little or
nothing to do with the issue under discussion, then the overall
view of memory to which Ayer subscribes has in effect two aspects.
These two aspects are clearly related. In the first place, memory
is intimately associated with the way in which we sort out different
claims to knowledge according to the kind of justification that
they presume. Indeed, on this view, memory is primarily to be
understood as a category that we employ in such an undertaking.
Secondly, memory is, and just as decisively, dissociated from mental
states in general and from specific mental states in particular. On
a given occasion memory – or, to spell it out, a claim to know
something or other based on a particular kind of evidence – may
be accompanied by some mental state or other. But, according
to this view, there need not be such a concomitant state, and,
if there is, no inference is justified to the kind of state to which
it belongs. In other words, the concomitance is always contingent,
and furthermore it occurs on the level of token rather than of
type. It is a consequence of this that no insight is to be gained
into the nature of memory from any investigation into its phenomenology. And the two aspects of this overall view of memory,
one of which we may think of as positive and the other as negative,
are related within it thus: if memory is primarily a category under
which we sort out claims to knowledge, then memory cannot include
a reference to mental states either in general or in particular. This
is because, as we have seen, claims to knowledge are sorted out
according to the way in which they are or might be justified,
and a concomitant mental state never provides any justification
of a claim to knowledge – except, that is, in the limiting case
where the claim to knowledge is just a claim to know about a
concomitant mental state. However, when I report, 'I remember
. . .', my claim is never a claim relating to my present mental
state: it is a claim relating to some state of the world between
which and my present mental state there is no evidential link.
Therefore there cannot be anything except a contingent connection
between the claim that I make to know something or other, which
is memory, and my mental states either specifically or even generally.
For Ayer this point is clinched by the fact that, when we set
out to rebut (or for that matter to confirm) someone else's memory
claim, it is no part of our undertaking to inquire into the state
of mind he was in when he made the claim.

Now, this overall view of memory bears upon Ayer's non-recogni-
tion of experiential memory as a separate type of memory in the
following way. The right of experiential memory to be recognised as
a separate type of memory rests – not exclusively, but distinctively –

upon its particular phenomenology. If phenomenology is held to be irrelevant to memory, it must be held to be irrelevant to the classification of memory. And so the separate status of experiential memory lapses.

VI

If experiential memory is the type of memory relevant to the claim that memory is criterial of personal identity, and if I am right in suggesting that this claim cannot be properly assessed until we take account of the causal history of memory, then it looks as though the next step is to ask, 'What is the specific causal history of experiential memory?'

Once again, though, there is a preliminary issue to be resolved. For, if the point is really to be made that the contribution of memory to personal identity is not fully before us until we have paid attention to the causation of memory, then clearly it needs to be established that memory, or the relevant type of memory, is essentially causal. Appeal to the causal history of memory in general, or of experiential memory in particular, cannot lend support to the claim that memory is criterial of personal identity, if these histories are held to be only contingently related to their outcomes.

Interestingly enough, in *The Problem of Knowledge*[11] Ayer discusses just the very kind of case that seems to me to establish that memory – both generally and in its varieties – is essentially causal, and I want to consider how this is done.

But, first, an observation on Ayer's own position. For I said 'interestingly enough' in order to make the point that, though Ayer discusses these cases, he himself holds that memory is not essentially causal. He does not, of course, wish to deny that memory, like presumably any other empirical phenomenon, is a causal phenomenon, but its causation is, according to him, inessential to it. And what leads Ayer to this position is what we have already seen leading him to be indifferent to the status of experiential memory as a separate type of memory, only this time it is the positive, not the negative, aspect of his overall view of memory that is operative. For, in holding that memory is primarily a category that we use when we sort out claims to knowledge in respect of their justification, Ayer has in mind the kind of justification that the claimant himself is, or would be, in a position to offer. Now, a man who claims to remember something or other is most unlikely to have access to the causal history of his belief, and, accordingly, the causal history of the belief is not something that he could offer in justification of it. But, if this is so, it cannot be required that, before a certain claim to knowledge is, or is categorised as, a memory claim, what the man claims as knowledge should have a certain history. For related though different reasons, memory can no more include a reference to causation than it can to phenomenology.

If Ayer's overall view of memory protects him from thinking that memory is essentially causal, the kind of case that, to my mind, conclusively establishes the thesis runs as follows. A man has knowledge of a certain event, and this is agreed to on all hands. Furthermore he is – in virtue of his biography, that is – in a position to remember the event: the event is, let us suppose, an action that he himself performed, though many years ago. However, he has, and knows that he has, often had the action retold to him by others. Accordingly, when he lays claim to knowledge of the event, he is uncertain whether this is, as of now, an instance of memory or whether it is an instance of hearsay. And he wishes to resolve the uncertainty.

Such a case is not only a possibility, but also an actuality, and, I suspect, not a particularly uncommon actuality. At the very beginning of his autobiography Goethe expresses just such uncertainty over the earliest event in his life known to him,[12] and for this reason I shall call any such case a 'Goethe case'. What is the situation of a man in a Goethe case, and what does he wish to resolve?

The man is not uncertain about the truth of what he claims to know. That he did what he says he did is *ex hypothesi* beyond all doubt. Nor is he uncertain whether he has reasons for claiming to know it. For he has, clearly, a superfluity of reasons, and that once again is beyond all doubt. Surely what he is uncertain about is which of these reasons is here and now active.[13] Is his claim to know of the action made because he did it or because he has been told of it? – that surely is what he is uncertain about. Now, if this is so, and if the 'because' here is a causal because – and here at least it seems right to ask what else it could be[14] – then it would appear that whether a claim to knowledge is an instance of memory does indeed depend on the causal history of the belief; from which it follows that the causal history of memory is essential to it, or that memory is indeed essentially causal.

One further aspect of any Goethe case, implicit in the account I have given, needs to be made explicit, if the moral I have thus far drawn is to be secure. I have spoken of a man in such a situation as uncertain whether 'as of now' he remembers the event or knows of it in some other way, and I have suggested that what lies behind this uncertainty is the question which of two

reasons he has is 'here and now' active. And by these phrases
I wanted to bring out the fact that in a Goethe case the epistemic
situation of the person involved is inherently unstable. Whether
he remembers the event or knows of it in some other way is
open to change, perhaps to sudden or unpredictable change. Ayer
recognises this fact when he says that, suppose the man's knowledge
is initially an instance of hearsay, nevertheless the event might
suddenly 'come back to him'[15] and then indeed he would find
himself remembering it; but Ayer does not draw from this the
conclusion that I should. For surely, in a situation thus described,
there could be no reason to correlate the epistemic switch with,
say, the man's sudden acquisition of new reasons, and the only
available explanation is that a change occurs in the relative causal
efficacies of the two reasons. Now, if as the man switches from
memory to hearsay, or hearsay to memory, what happens to him
is that at one moment one reason causes him to know of the
event, at the next moment the other – this is just what we should
expect if memory is essentially causal.

To the account I have offered of what goes on in a Goethe
case an objection might be raised which I shall take next, not
least because it is just the kind of objection that, from what I
have said, might be thought likely to come from Ayer. It is this:
if it is true that a man who is uncertain whether he remembers
a certain event or knows of it only by hearsay is indeed uncertain
about the causation of his knowledge, then it would seem to follow
that a man who is free of such uncertainty and is (let us suppose)
just certain that his knowledge is an instance of memory, must
have, somehow or other, ascertained for himself its causal history.
But it is extremely dubious (the objection would continue) that
any man who is, say, certain that he remembers a certain event
has ascertained for himself the causal history of his knowledge,
not least because it is totally problematic how he would set about
doing this. Therefore the essential connection, proposed in my
account of the Goethe case, between the man's epistemic situation
and its causation cannot hold.

But what is wrong with this objection is that the consequence
it seeks to derive from my account just does not follow. Certainly,
if the man does indeed remember the event, then his knowledge
has the appropriate causation; and if he knows this and also knows
that he remembers the event, then he is in a position to know the
causation of his knowledge. But it does not follow from any of
this that the man must have ascertained for himself its causation –
where this is taken to mean that he has conducted a historical
inquiry into its causation – before he could be certain that his

knowledge is an instance of memory. For another possibility, and surely one that is far likelier, is that the man's certainty that his knowledge is an instance of memory is just another effect of its causation. What makes it memory also makes him certain that it is memory: though this is not to exclude the possibility that a man, in thinking that he remembers something, is wrong, for he does not. (A philosophy of mind that excluded this last possibility could scarcely claim realism amongst its virtues.)

However, it is now necessary to correct and elaborate upon – that is, to introduce one correction and one elaboration into – the account thus far offered of a Goethe case. It is necessary to do this first in the interests of philosophical accuracy, and, secondly, if from a consideration of such cases we are to learn all that they have to teach us.

The correction is to the way in which the epistemic situation of the man involved in such a case has been described. For he has been described as if poised somewhere between memory and some form of knowledge (I have used the term 'hearsay') which is quite distinct from memory. But this is not correct. The man is uncertain whether he knows of some event because he was there or because he has since been told of it. But, if it turns out that he knows of it because he has since been told of it, that too is memory. For to have been told some fact and not to have forgotten it is to remember it – though it is not, of course, to recall it – and what in my account of the Goethe case I referred to loosely as 'memory' now needs to be recognised as the particular type of memory that it is, i. e. recollection. A corrected account of the epistemic situation of a man in a Goethe case would be that he is poised between the type of memory called recollection and another type of memory, which I shall call 'retention'.

(At this stage it might be objected that to present the man's situation in this way is to follow usage slavishly, to the point of altogether trivialising the concept of memory. For, if we accept the equation of having been told something and not forgotten it with memory, are there going to be any cases of factual knowledge that are not subsumable under memory? To this question, presumably posed rhetorically, the answer is yes. The following are clearly recalcitrant cases: where someone was not told of what he now claims to know, but worked it out for himself; where someone was told of what he now claims to know, but did not believe it at the time, and had to convince himself of its truth; where someone was told of what he now claims to know, believed it straightaway, but this was within the immediate or practical present. None of these seem to me to be instances of memory.)

Once Goethe cases are thus redescribed, it should be clear that they show more than that memory itself is essentially causal. For, if we now consider the epistemic situation of a man in such a case, we can see that, for at least two types of memory – that is, recollection and retention – differences between types of memory are essentially (essentially though not, of course, exclusively) differences in kind of causal history. Accordingly, if these two types of memory are characteristic, Goethe cases may be taken to show that, as well as memory itself, types of memory are essentially causal, where this means not just that they must have a causation but that they must have the particular kind of causation that they have.

So the question arises, 'Are recollection and retention in this respect characteristic?', or, more specifically, 'May we extrapolate from them to experiential memory?' – for that, of course, is the other type of memory with which we are, at the moment, specifically concerned – and may we say that all these types are essentially causal?

It is in order to answer this question that I now propose to elaborate upon the account given of the Goethe case. The elaboration consists, in effect, in the introduction of experiential memory into the case, but it is important to see how it is introduced. There could be objections to introducing experiential memory as one of the types of memory between which the man in a Goethe case is poised: in other words, to describing his epistemic situation as one in which he is uncertain whether he recalls or merely retains *or* experientially remembers the event in question. Whether these objections are valid or not – and I believe that ultimately they are not, but I shall return to them later – I shall go along with them at the moment to the extent of introducing experiential memory at a later point in the case, where they do not apply. So I shall suppose that the man is, as before, initially uncertain whether he recalls or merely retains the event; he resolves which it is; and then the event may come back to him and come back in such a way that he finds himself experientially remembering the event. Of course, in order to make this supposition we must further suppose, as we did with recollection, that the man's biography has put him in a position to have a memory of this particular type. (Note that what this requirement is, either in the case of experiential memory or in that of recollection, is something about which I have as yet said nothing.) Once this further supposition is made, there seems no difficulty at all in supposing that what I have called the instability of his epistemic situation should be thus increased, so that the situation is now unstable between three types of memory.

If, however, this elaboration upon the Goethe case is accepted, how are we to account for this new possibility? And surely the answer is that we should account for it in precisely the same way as that in which we accounted for the instability in the man's epistemic situation when the possibilities open to him were not, as they now are, three in number, but only two. So, if the man suddenly finds himself experientially remembering an event which up till then he had remembered in some other way, we should explain this switch by invoking a change in the relative causal efficacies of the reasons related to the different types of memory.

If this is right, then it looks as though we may generalise our findings about retention and recollection, and conclude that, at any rate for three types of memory, and they are the only relevant types, differences between types of memory are essentially, if not exclusively, differences in kind of causal history, and thus the types of memory themselves are essentially, if not exclusively, causal.

VII

But is this right? For, if the general principle of my argument – that is, that new cases should be explained in the same way as old and like cases – seems altogether acceptable, there is very real uncertainty about how to apply it in the present case. For, if we are to say confidently of the man who, thanks to his biography, now retains a certain event, now recalls it, now experientially remembers it, that at these different times he is under the causal influence of different reasons, we need to have some idea, however vague, of what these different reasons might be. In the case of retention and recollection there is little difficulty in seeing what these reasons must be, and this is why there has been little difficulty in seeing how it is that the man with a suitable biography might now retain the event, now recall it. But in the case of experiential memory there is very real difficulty in seeing what the reason might be. More specifically, there is very real difficulty in discriminating between the reason that might be causally effective for it and the reason that is causally effective for recollection, and there is a corresponding difficulty in seeing how it is that a man even with a suitable biography might now recall the event, now experientially remember it.

But this invites the retort that the difficulty arises so acutely only because of the way in which I have insisted that the argument should unfold. In the interest of making a point I have allowed the issue of whether different types of memory are essentially causal – that is, of whether they essentially have the kinds of causal history that they have – to get so far ahead of the issue of what kinds of causal history the different types of memory actually have. So I should now turn to this second issue if the essentially causal character of (at least) experiential memory is to be saved.

In order to regiment the different kinds of causal history of the different types of memory I propose to introduce the notion of an 'acquisition condition' – more properly perhaps, 'acquisition or reacquisition condition'.[16] For any possible memory there must be an acquisition condition and, for that memory to be actual, or to occur, that acquisition condition must be satisfied. As a first approximation – and this is a phrase that will recur to designate this proposal – I shall say that the acquisition condition for a memory is satisfied by a cognitive state that meets the two following requirements. In the first place, it is either that state of a person in which he first came to know of whatever is remembered or a state in which he would have come to know of it if he had not already had knowledge of it; or, to put it another way, it is one out of a disjunction of states of a person, which includes (a) the state in which he originally came to know of whatever is remembered, and (b) all those later states of his which provided him with a second chance of coming to know of it. Secondly, the cognitive state is causally responsible at the time in question for the rememberer's having that memory, or for that occurrence of the memory.

If these requirements seem tortuous, it is worth pointing out that they have been framed as they have in order to accommodate two possibilities for which room must be made. The first possibility is the logical possibility that histories of memory may run across persons – which is simply a generalisation of the constraint that my ability experientially to remember something that someone else did or suffered must not be ruled out definitionally. To permit this first possibility, the requirements do not ask that the cognitive state that satisfies the acquisition condition for a memory should belong to the rememberer's biography. All they ask is that the rememberer's biography should be such that this state can, at the appropriate point, i. e. around the time of the memory, have a causal influence over it in that it causes a memory to enter it. The second possibility, which, as Goethe cases show, is no mere logical possibility, is that one and the same memory should at different times, on different occurrences, have a different causation. To permit this second possibility the requirements do not ask that for any memory there should for all time be one and only one cognitive state that may satisfy the acquisition condition. On the contrary, the first requirement specifies a range of states any one of which may satisfy the acquisition condition, and, if the second requirement goes on (as it does) to select just one state out of this range, and say that just it satisfies the acquisition condition, it does só only for a given time or for a given occurrence of the memory. At another time, or on another occurrence of the memory, another state may be selected to satisfy the acquisition condition and thus cause the memory to occur.

We may now make use of this notion of the acquisition condition to articulate the thesis that different types of memory essentially differ in their causal history thus: at any given time, a memory instantiates one type of memory rather than another depending upon the cognitive state that currently satisfies the acquisition condition for that memory – more specifically, depending upon the way in which that state is related to whatever is remembered.

And now everything hangs on the last phrase. What do I mean by talking of 'the way in which a cognitive state is related to whatever is remembered'? To explain what I mean by this phrase, I cannot do better than give examples of its use. So what I shall do is to go through the different types of memory, and indicate for each the particular way in which the cognitive state that satisfies the acquisition condition is related to whatever is remembered. Throughout, for the sake of convenience, I shall assume that what is remembered is an action. So, if the memory now instantiates retention, the cognitive state that currently satisfies the acquisition condition must be one that is related to the action *as an instance of coming to know of it at second hand*: it may be, for example, the hearing of it, or the reading about it. If, however, the memory now instantiates recollection the cognitive state that currently satisfies the acquisition condition must be one that is related to the action *as an instance of coming to know of it at first hand*: it may be, for example, the hearing it, or the seeing it. And, if the memory now instantiates experiential memory, then the cognitive state that currently satisfies the acquisition condition must be one that is related to the action *as an instance of coming to know of it from the inside*; and of this the only examples that I can think to give are the performance of it, or the suffering of it, knowingly.

Of course, in trying to clarify the problematic phrases by giving examples of its use I have in effect given answers to the question before us, 'What are the causal histories proper to the different types of memory?', and therefore it is appropriate to ask whether these duly regimented accounts do anything to allay the difficulty experienced a short while back. I refer to the difficulty involved in trying to square the case of the man whose biography has placed him in a position now to recall a certain event, now experientially to remember it, with the general thesis that types of memory differ essentially, though not exclusively, in causal history. For I entertained the hope that, once we had the relevant kinds of causal history before us, the difficulty might disappear. On the present showing, does it?

Not only is the answer no, but in addition the causal histories as we have them only make the difficulty look worse. For what do they ask of us? They ask that we should think of the man who now recalls a certain event, now experientially remembers it, as at one moment under the causal influence of a cognitive state in which the event came (or could have come) to be known of at first hand and at the next under the influence of a cognitive state in which the event came to be known of from the inside. They do not, as we have seen, further ask that we should think of both these cognitive states – or indeed either of them – as belonging to the man's biography. Nevertheless, common sense surely demands that, at the lowest, this should remain a possibility. To say that a man's biography has enabled him both to recall and experientially to remember a certain event cannot be incompatible with thinking that the cognitive states that satisfy the acquisition conditions for these two types of memory were actually part of that biography. But here is the difficulty. The difficulty is that of thinking of one and the same biography as containing two cognitive states each related in the required way to one and the same event. We have already seen that, if the case of the man whose biography has enabled him now to recall a certain event, now experientially to remember it, is problematic, the case of the man whose biography has enabled him now to retain a certain event, now to recall it, is unproblematic, and let us now make use of this comparison to bring out the difficulty in the former case. For what makes the latter case unproblematic is that there is no difficulty at all in seeing how one and the same biography could contain a cognitive state in which a certain event came (or could have come) to be known of at second hand and a cognitive state in which the same event came to be known of at first hand. The difference between the two cases, from the present point of view, comes down to this: whereas in the unproblematic case the two required states could occur at different times, so both may be accommodated in one biography, in the problematic case there is only one time for either to occur – that is, simultaneous with the event – and so one squeezes the other out.

But where does this leave us? Does this mean that, unless we deny the surely indubitable truth that a man may now recall a certain event, now experientially remember it – or, certainly no better, concede this only in the case where the causal history of at least one of these memories runs across from another to him – we must reject the general thesis that types of memory differ, essentially if not exclusively, in kind of causal history?

My answer would be no. I think that the thesis is true, and the difficulty encountered with in applying it comes from taking too restricted a view of how the causal history of the different types of memory is to be written. This view is one that I have taken first implicitly, then explicitly. The view is that the relevant causal histories must originate in a cognitive state, and I took it explicitly in the first approximation that I proposed to an answer to how the acquisition condition for the different kinds of memory is to be satisfied. The view is too restricted precisely because in the case of experiential memory it is not the case that the satisfier of the acquisition condition is a cognitive state – if this is taken to mean a purely cognitive state.

Before developing this point, which is crucial, I want to try and show just how much of what I have said so far about experiential memory should have prepared us for it.

VIII

In the course of this essay I have expressed the thesis that different types of memory have essentially the kind of causal history that they have as types of memory differ *essentially if not exclusively* in causal history. Now, in using the italicised phrase I intended reference to a point that I made in introducing experiential memory as a type of memory – and, for that matter, cited in explanation of Ayer's failure to afford it recognition as a type of memory. The point is that experiential memory has a distinctive phenomenology, or that experiential memory differs from other types of memory in phenomenology. And since, whatever is ultimately the case, a difference in phenomenology is a different difference from a difference in causal history, it cannot be that types of memory differ exclusively in causal history.

It is to this different difference between types of memory, or, more particularly, between experiential memory and other types of memory, that I now turn. What are its implications for my argument?

Let me begin by pointing to the influence that I have already allowed this different difference, or the distinctive phenomenology of experiential memory, to have upon my argument – or, more accurately, upon the presentation of my argument. For it will be recalled that, when I elaborated on the Goethe case by introducing experiential memory, I avoided introducing it at what might have seemed the obvious point: that is, by supposing that a man in such a case is invariably uncertain whether he is retaining some event or recalling it *or* experientially remembering it. Instead I introduced it at a later point in the case, and I did so out of deference to certain objections which I said at the time that I did not accept. The objections I had in mind were objections which, starting from the fact that experiential memory has a distinctive phenomenology, conclude from this fact that therefore a man – at any rate, one in his right mind – could not be uncertain whether he was experientially remembering some event or whether he was remembering it in some other way or whether, indeed, he was in some quite other mental state. Why I do not accept these objections is that I cannot accept an assumption that they make: that is, that phenomenological differences are somehow self-evident or self-intimating. On the contrary, I should think that there are situations where a man could be uncertain or even mistaken about the phenomenology of his current mental state. Furthermore, that a particular mental state has a distinctive phenomenology is not incompatible with the reproduction of this very same phenomenology by a suitable combination of mental states, which thereby mimic the original state.

I shall, in fact, return to this last point later on. Meanwhile, I have brought up this erroneous view of the implications of the difference in phenomenology between experiential memory and other types of memory only so as to clear the way for the correct view. What are, then, the implications of this difference for my argument?

My initial observation would be as follows. It is quite correct to say, as I said just now, that a difference in phenomenology is a different difference from a difference in causal history. Nevertheless, it is reasonable to think that a difference in phenomenology will go along with a difference in causation, where the different causal history suffices to explain the different phenomenology. Accordingly, if there is an overall difference in phenomenology between experiential memory and other types of memory, this should go along with an overall difference in causation between experiential memory and the other types of memory. This is so because the difference in causal history is required to explain the phenomenological difference.

However, in order to make use of this observation, we need to know something about the differences in phenomenology that are to be explained, and my next observations will concern what is indeed distinctive about the phenomenology of experiential memory.

In introducing experiential memory I said that one differential feature of it is that, if I experientially remember some event, I remember it from the inside, and the time has now come for the amplification of this feature that I promised at the time. (In amplifying this feature, as indeed in other things that I find to say about experiential memory, I am heavily influenced by the analogy, already indicated, between experiential memory and the mental phenomenon that I have called 'centrally imagining'. Since this analogy must necessarily remain implicit, the reader may choose to match what I say here about experiential memory against what I have said elsewhere about centrally imagining.)

If I remember an event from the inside, there are two distinct though related characteristics of my memory. Let us assume that the event I thus remember is an action that I did or suffered. The first characteristic is that, in so far as I remember what I did or suffered, I *shall tend to* remember, both systematically and liberally, what I thought and what I felt in the doing or the suffering of it. By 'systematically' I mean something like 'as and when they – that is, the thoughts and feelings at issue – occurred in the history of the action'. And by 'liberally' I mean 'quite a lot'. The second characteristic of remembering an event from the inside is that, as I remember what I thought or what I felt at the time, I *shall tend to* rethink or refeel those very thoughts and feelings. There will be a tendency for the state or condition that those thoughts and feelings constitute to set itself up afresh in the mind, and this tendency I shall call 'the affective tendency' of experiential memory, and the state or condition that results when this tendency actualises itself I shall call 'the affective tone' of experiential memory.

I shall not attempt to lay down the general conditions under which the affective tendency of experiential memory does indeed actualise itself and experiential memory thus acquire an affective tone, but it must surely be a good approximation to psychological truth to suppose that this tendency will vary positively with the affective strength or significance of the event remembered. But the more important point to make, for the purpose to hand, is that in this respect it is with experiential memory as it is with centrally imagining: that is, that when, for whatever reason, an affective tone does adhere to the mental phenomenon, then that tone is part of, and not just an accompaniment to, the phenomenon. This is important because, in so far as it shows what is distinctive to the phenomenology of experiential memory, it also shows how the causal history that we assign to experiential memory must differ in an overall way from the causal histories we assign to other types of memory. It must be a causal history that can explain the affective tendency in experiential memory. Conversely, any causal history written for experiential memory that ignores – as did, for instance, that which I proposed a while back – the fact that experiential memory has, in principle at any rate, this affective aspect is doomed to insufficiency.

Let me, therefore, without further ado, propose a new causal history for experiential memory, cast in the same form as that which it supersedes, thus: when a memory of an action currently instantiates experiential memory, the state that now satisfies the acquisition condition must be one that is related to the action *both as an instance of coming to know of it from the inside and as an instance of experiencing it from the inside* – in other words, a state in which the action modified at one and the same time the cognitive store and the affective store of the person whose state it was.

And now, to bring the causal history of recollection into line with this new history for experiential memory, the former needs to be rewritten thus: when a memory of an action currently instantiates recollection, the acquisition condition is now satisfied by a cognitive state that is related to that action *either as an instance of coming to know of it at first hand or as an instance of coming to know of it from the inside.* This rewriting is necessary, for it is only when it has been done that we can fully account for the case of the man who is in a position both to recall and experientially to remember an action and in point of fact merely recalls it. For such a man is currently under the influence of and only of the cognitive impact of the remembered event – though he is also in a position, biographically that is, to experience the influence of the affective impact of the event. It is specifically to be observed that with this rewriting we have a way of distinguishing this case from the distinct (and, of course, far more likely) case of the man who experientially remembers an event and yet the affective tone of his memory is unconscious.

IX

It is now time to return to the claim that memory is criterial of personal identity. Given that the type of memory that is relevant to this claim is experiential memory; given, further, that experiential memory has essentially the causal history that it has; and given, finally, that the causal history of experiential memory conforms to my new proposal – how does the claim now fare? Is there increased support for the view that, if I in the relevant way remember an action, then necessarily that action was something that I either did or suffered? Or is there the same possibility that paths of memory – that is, paths of experiential memory – may run across, and not simply along, persons?

Some way back I said that Ayer's overall view of memory is as much as anything else – as much, that is, as the empiricists' overall view of personal identity – an obstruction in the way of seeing the full contribution of memory to personal identity. Part of what I had in mind has now emerged. For Ayer's overall view of memory is of something that is through and through cognitive. Memory is for him essentially the capacity to have beliefs of a certain kind – so that the crucial concession to wring from epistemology is an account of those conditions under which such beliefs rise to the condition of knowledge. This view of memory (which, incidentally, is not peculiar to Ayer but is shared by most of those philosophers who, whatever their other disagreements, agree in disputing the connection between memory and personal identity[17]) I have argued to be inadequate at least for one type of memory – and that, in the present context, the all-important type. For experiential memory has, in addition to its cognitive aspect, an affective aspect. To show that the purely cognitive view of memory is indeed obstructive to seeing the truth about personal identity, I must now establish that, not only has experiential memory an affective aspect, but in addition its claim to sufficiency as far as personal identity is concerned is considerably enhanced by it. Can this be established?

But, first, a preliminary note on the argument: on the face of it, or at any rate on the face of everything that I have said thus far, there would seem to be three distinct ways in which it might be shown that it is impossible to have experiential memories of experiences or actions other than those of one's own. An argument might start from the way in which an experiential memory must be reported; it might start from the phenomenology that experiential memory must have; or it might start from the causal history that experiential memory must have – must have, that is, given its phenomenology. It will already be clear that my own argument will be of the third kind, but the other two possibilities are worth briefly reviewing.

Over the years philosophers who have addressed themselves to this problem have had a weakness for arguments of the first kind. I have already, I hope, said enough to show why I think that any such argument must be either trivial or inconclusive. Trivial, if it insists that experiential memories must be reported by sentences of the form 'I remember my *f*-ing': and inconclusive if it tries to allow any leeway to the seemingly plausible view that how experiential memories must be reported must be to some extent, at any rate, influenced by what they can be of. But what of arguments of the second kind?

My own surmise is that it should be possible to mount a successful argument of this kind. But I must also concede that I have no clear idea how this would be constructed. So the only observation that I have to make, and it is an important one, is this: that we cannot just *assume* that, if we had memories deriving from the experiences and actions of others in just the same way as our experiential memories currently derive from our experiences and actions, and we knew this, and we correspondingly adjusted our way of reporting them, then we should have experiential memories of the experiences and action of others. We cannot just assume that there would not be a further phenomenological obstacle, which might be insurmountable. Elsewhere I have maintained that we can centrally imagine others' as well as our experiencing or doing something or other, and the assumption that I am now challenging might be expressed by saying that, other things being equal, the phenomenology of centrally imagining is fully available for experiential memory. I think that we should look upon this assumption with guarded suspicion, though I freely admit that the only reason I shall offer for doing so lies concealed in what I shall later say about the function of experiential memory.

So I return to my own argument: an argument of the third kind. According to my latest proposal, histories of experiential memory are twists of two strands. One strand transmits the cognitive influence of the event remembered; the other strand transmits the affective influence of that event. In both cases the influence is causal. Now, since the strand that transmits the affective influence of the event accounts for what is distinctive to the phenomenology of experiential memory, it would look as though a question crucial to ask from my point of view is 'Can the affective influence of an event be exerted across persons?'

I suggest that, in trying to answer this question, we should pass a certain self-denying resolution. And that is that, though we may continue to imagine psychological facts to be quite other than as they are, we should not take the same liberties with general psychological laws or processes. For, if we do, we run the grave risk of finding ourselves not so much speculating about the imaginary as stipulating for the magical, and there can no more be a philosophy than there is a science of the magical.

So let us begin by asking how, as things stand, an event may exert an affective influence over a person, and then see whether these ways either are compatible with, alternatively can secure, the exercise of such an influence across persons. I can straightway identify two ways in which an event does exert affective influence.

In the first place, an event can exert an affective influence over a person through that person's performing or suffering it. This is self-evident; and I shall spend no more time on it here and now than is necessary to make the equally self-evident point that this is certainly compatible with, indeed is presupposed by, the exercise of affective influence across persons, though just as certainly it could not secure the exercise of such an influence.

Secondly, an event can exert an affective influence over a person through that person's experientially remembering it. That an experiential memory can have an affective influence over a person comes about because of the affective tone that it, the memory, tends to have. Through this tone the memory can exert an affective influence over him like the original event. And, since, as we have seen, the tone derives from the original event, then in exerting an affective influence over the rememberer, the memory not only exerts an affective influence like the original event, but also exerts the affective influence of the original event.

But this account of how it is that an event can exert an affective influence through experiential memory would also seem to make it pretty clear that experiential memory could not initiate the exercise of such an influence across persons. It could presumably facilitate the onward transmission of such an influence along a person, once that influence had crossed over to him, but it could not be, for any person, an original way in which the influence was exerted over him. And this is so because, if experiential memory relies for its affective influence over a person upon its affective tone, the affective tone itself attests to an affective influence already exerted over the person by the event. Accordingly, if, as is *ex hypothesi* the case, the person has not been affectively influenced by the event in the first way, is there some further original way, some third way, in which this influence might have made itself felt? If there were, then, of course, experiential memory could reinforce that influence.

I contend that there is not. The crucial consideration here to my mind is that the affective influence of an event upon a person is invariably mediated by his beliefs, desires, and feelings: it is, in other words, mediated by that affective store which it also modifies. To do full justice to this consideration, one could talk not just of the affective influence of the event, but also of the affective influence either of the impact of the event or of the event as lived through. But this would be pedantic. Now, this consideration bears on the possibility of 'a third way' thus. For a variety of obvious reasons, of which the fact that events have affective influence over persons is only the most currently obvious, a person's affective store changes over time. It has different temporal states. If this is so, and if an event's affective influence is mediated by a person's affective store, we might ask, 'For any given event, is there any particular temporal state of the person's affective store that must mediate its original affective influence upon him?' And to this question it seems to me that there is no uncertain answer: the affective store of a person that mediates the original affective influence of an event upon him must be *that at the time of the event*, or what I shall call 'the contemporaneous affective store'. Yet precisely what any third way must require us to believe is that an event could have over a person an affective influence that was at once original and also mediated by a state of the person's affective store later than that at the time of the event.

In support of the thesis that any original affective influence of an event upon a person must be exerted through his contemporaneous affective store, I can appeal only to self-evidence and to the following general consideration: that for any apparent counter-example or any case where it might be claimed that an event was exerting an affective influence upon a person through his later affective store – for I should rule out as incomprehensible a similar claim in respect of his earlier affective store – there is always available some more accurate redescription, which provides the base for a better explanation.

In the present context two broadly identified kinds of case will have to stand in for such others as there may be. In the first kind of case, a certain event putatively exerts an affective influence over a person. The person is undoubtedly affectively influenced, but the influence is not that of the supposed event but that of some later event directed upon it. Normal and quite unproblematic cases are those where the actually influential event consists in being told about, or in reading of, the putatively influential event. Super-ficially problematic cases arise when the actually influential event is related to the putatively influential event as an instance of imagina-tively reconstructing it or of recalling it. That this redescription is in order, however, can be seen from the way in which, at later times, we should judge whether the affective influence is still active over the person. We should do so by matching his affective store at any such later time against what we should expect it to be, given not the original event but the event directed upon it. Now, if this kind of case is to be thus redescribed, it presents not even a *prima facie* counter-example to my thesis. For in any such case the affective influence of the actually influential event upon the person is indeed exerted through his contemporary affective store –

that is, through his affective store as at the time of *it*. The second kind of case I have in mind is where what is actually influential – affectively, that is – is not an event at all, but is rather some enduring condition of the world: most likely, a condition initiated by the event that is putatively influential. Such a case could be one which we are originally led to describe as that where a man is affectively influenced by his father's death. '. . . could be' I say, for this description is significantly ambiguous. The affective influence exerted over the man may indeed be that of an event: it may be that of his father's dying hours, which he – we are further to assume – has lived through. But at least as likely a situation is one where the influence is that of his father's absence from the world, which is not an event but a condition, a condition initiated by an event, and it will be appreciated that the description before us equally fits this situation. Now, in such a case too we have not even a potential counter-example to our thesis and that is because with something like a condition there is no question of the person's contemporary affective store through which its affective influence is exerted – for, we might ask, contemporary with what?

At this stage it might be objected that I have been not only perfunctory with, but also unfair to, the requirements of a third way. For, after all, a third way is a way in which an event exercises over a person an affective influence that is original as far as he is concerned or from his point of view, but is also derivative; and it is a highly significant fact (the objection continues) that the influence is derivative from an original affective influence exerted by the same event over another person, for this earlier affective influence was certainly exerted – or we have no reason to doubt this – through that person's contemporary affective store. Does not this further fact, which is obviously vital if the third way is to do what is asked of it – namely, to secure transmission of affective influence across persons – considerably diminish the plausibility of my thesis?

I do not see that it does. The complexity to which this objection points is certainly there in the supposition of a third way. A third way looks not only to the future – it secures the exercise of an affective influence over some future rememberer '– but also to the past – for it derives from an affective influence exercised over the past experiencer. And heavy emphasis placed on how it is that the supposed third way does look to the past could, I suppose, have this consequence: it could diminish, in the mind of anyone who concentrated on it, the intelligibility of the whole supposition. But I do not see how it could diminish any requirement that

a third way must satisfy before it can be thought of as looking
to the future. After all, until the affective influence of the event
is supposedly transmitted to the future rememberer, *he* has been,
we are to assume, quite untouched by that event. If we, then,
lay down requirements that must be satisfied if the affective influence
of the event is to pass to him, surely these requirements could
not be affected by consideration of any requirements that had
to be satisfied for the past experiencer to undergo the affective
influence of the event – so long, that is, as the past experiencer
and the future rememberer are required to be different persons, a
requirement which is, we must remind ourselves, central to the
whole supposition.

If there is no third way, then it looks as though paths of experiential memory could not run across persons. Does that, then, leave
the claim that memory is criterial of personal identity vindicated?
I have not held out hope that this claim could be vindicated.
And certainly before anything like this could be said on its behalf,
there is another possibility that needs to be considered. I shall
turn to this possibility in the section after next.

X

I now turn to an objection. The objection is to the causal history
that I have written for experiential memory, and the ground of
the objection would be that this history is more specific than is
required by that which it is intended to explain. Furthermore,
it is this unwanted specificity, it and nothing else, that makes
it look a necessary truth that a person could not experientially
remember something unless it was something that he himself had
done or suffered.

The objection concedes that any adequate causal history of experiential memory must account for two things: the cognitive aspect
and the affective aspect of experiential memory. The objection
further concedes that the cognitive aspect has to be accounted
for by tracing it back causally to the event itself – or, more accurately, to the impact of the event. However, it is not necessary,
according to the objection, to account for the affective aspect by
similarly tracing it back to the remembered event or its impact.
What has to be accounted for, in effect, is what might be called
the rememberer's affective adequacy – that is to say, the adequacy
of his current affective store to provide the experiential memory
with the affective tone that it tends to have – and, though the
remembered event may well have contributed to this, there is no
a priori reason why it should have. The causal antecedents of

the rememberer's current affective store may very well be varied: they could be just as varied as his experience of life.

At this stage the objector might invoke against me the analogy that I have had implicitly in mind in so much of what I have found to say about experiential memory: the analogy, that is, between it and centrally imagining. For what I have done, he could very well point out, is to make use of the analogy when it was a matter of proposing a phenomenology for experiential memory, but then to abandon the analogy when it came to proposing a causation for experiential memory. With both phenomena there is, according to me, an affective tendency, and of just the same general character. For, if I centrally imagine someone's doing something or other, I shall not only tend, systematically and liberally, to imagine his thinking and feeling what he would have thought and felt in the doing of it, but also tend to think and feel those very things themselves. But I have never claimed that such affective tone as attaches to centrally imagining must be causally owing to whatever is imagined. Indeed, for very obvious reasons, how could I have? If the person is affectively adequate to his imaginative project, then he owes this to his general experience of life. Now, the objector continues, why should not the same be recognised as true of the person who engages not in centrally imagining but in experiential memory, and is affectively adequate to that? If the causal history of experiential memory must obviously deviate from that of centrally imagining in so far as it has to account for its cognitive aspect, why should not the two coincide in accounting for the affective aspects of the phenomena?

Let me start my reply to this objection just where it, or my exposition of it, leaves off : that is, with the attempt to assimilate – or, rather, partially assimilate – the causation of experiential memory to that of centrally imagining. For, in trying to carry this through, our objector has made things easier for himself, if unwittingly, by overlooking a further, or third, mental phenomenon distinct from both experiential memory and centrally imagining, though occupying a place between them. The phenomenon is, as this indicates, a complex phenomenon, and it is instantiated when someone who is in a position experientially to remember a certain action merely recalls that action, and then proceeds centrally to imagine himself doing the action. All the thoughts and feelings that he ascribes to himself in imagination faithfully reconstruct the original event. I shall introduce a name for this phenomenon and, since it bears a general resemblance (but perhaps no more than that) to a mental phenomenon that Freud discussed under this name, I shall call it 'screen memory'.[18]

Now, once our objector has had his attention drawn to screen memory, he is bound, I should suggest, to concede two points. In the first place, screen memory *is* a distinct phenomenon from experiential memory. If he resisted this concession, then one way of extracting it from him would be to point out one use to which screen memory might be put. Someone might engage in screen memory of an action so as to get himself experientially to remember it: in the course of the screen memory, the action might come back to him – would be the hope – in such a way that he would then find himself experientially remembering it. The second concession that our objector would have to make is that the causation that he has proposed for experiential memory seems precisely that required by screen memory. He has written a causal history for one mental phenomenon, only to find it pre-empted by another and distinct mental phenomenon.

This is not, I am aware, a decisive retort to the objection. There seem to be at least two possibilities that are perfectly compatible both with what the objection urges and with what my retort to it insists upon. For it could be that, within the broad characterisation that we have been considering, the causal histories of screen memory and experiential memory do coincide, but that a finer characterisation of these histories would bring out the divergences between them. Or it could be that experiential memory and screen memory altogether agree in their causation, however finely that is characterised, and that they differ elsewhere.

If, then, it is to be shown that the causal history proposed by our objector for experiential memory is wrong, if, more particularly, it is to be shown that this causal history is wrong in so far as it tries to account for the affective aspect of such memory, there are, as far as I can see, two ways in which this might be attempted. There are two different lines along which the argument might run.

But before I develop this I want to reformulate the issue. My aim is to bring it more vividly before us. For, if what our objector claims about experiential memory and its causal history were true, then it could be said that, in experientially remembering an event, as indeed in centrally imagining an event, we recruit our affects to the mental phenomenon. However, if my account of the matter is right, a more accurate or perspicuous way of putting the matter would be to say that, when we experientially remember an event, our affects accrue to the mental phenomenon. Let us then make use of this reformulation and ask what are the two ways along which we might try to show that we do not recruit our affects into the service of experiential memory, but that, on the contrary, they accrue.

First, there is the way of phenomenology. It may be that the phenomenology of experiential memory, examined in a pure-enough culture, will oblige us to recognise that affects accrue to the memory.

I am, however, doubtful that any argument based on phenomenology will take us far enough. Since I introduced experiential memory through its phenomenology, such an observation may seem in need of explanation. My point would be that it is one thing to indicate certain rather general phenomenological limits within which a certain mental phenomenon is to be found – and to do so in the reasoned hope that these indications will reverberate with the reader's own intuitions; but it is altogether another and far more dubious thing to try to discriminate one phenomenon from another that in many respects mimics it by appealing to phenomenological minutiae that manifest themselves on the margin between the two phenomena – and, moreover, to do this in the foreknowledge that there is likely to be little coincidence of intuition between oneself and the reader now turned adversary.

In point of fact, I suspect that in many cases where appeals to phenomenology do work to achieve agreement there is a special but neglected reason why this should be so. And it is because we start off with a shared sense of what these mental phenomena are there to do. We perceive clearly what their phenomenology is, we get others to participate in these perceptions, and this is all because there is agreement between us on the functions of the mental phenomena themselves. At least in our philosophising about them, phenomenology follows function. (Indeed, I should suggest that one of the principal tasks of the philosophy of mind, which goes almost totally by default, is to exhibit, over as wide a range of mental phenomena as is feasible, how function is served by phenomenology.[19])

And this leads directly on to the second way in which our objector's proposed causation for experiential memory might be challenged. This is the way of function. Is there, then, some function of memory that obliges us to think that affects accrue to, rather than are recruited into the service of, experiential memory; for otherwise experiential memory could not discharge this function?

I suggest that there is; and this suggestion, which will have to remain largely unargued for, is in effect the most substantial thesis that this essay contains. The suggestion is *that the function of memory is to place us under the influence of the past.*

As it stands, the thesis is stated generally and crudely: generally, in that it is stated for all types of memory, and it is a reasonable supposition, to which I shall shortly return, that this function will be discharged in different ways by different types of memory; and, crudely, in that it provokes an immediate objection. For are there not many other mental phenomena that place us, and of which it may as plausibly be said that it is their function to place us, under the influence of the past? For instance, emotion, or imagination. When we experience an emotion, what we feel derives from the past; when we imagine something or other, what we imagine, or at least the elements of what we imagine, derive from the past. How then does memory differ functionally from these other mental phenomena? The objection incorporates a misunderstanding of the function of memory, and the best way to meet it is to refine upon the original statement of that function. So, the function of memory is to place us under the influence of the past, in that it places us under the influence of a particular piece of the past; and this is not true of emotion or the imagination. If they place us under the influence of the past, they place us under the influence of the past generally.

If this is accepted, the next question that arises is 'Which piece of the past?' Given a particular memory, what determines which particular piece of the past it is under the influence of which we are thereby placed? And the obvious answer to this question might seem to be 'That which is remembered.' But reflection will show that this is not the right answer. Indeed, over a range of cases the answer is evidently wrong, and, over those cases where it appears to be right, the appearance can be traced to confusion, if understandable confusion. An alternative answer which is, I think, right is, 'That which currently satisfies the acquisition condition for the memory.'

That the obvious answer is wrong emerges evidently in the case of retention. For, if it is true of retention too that it serves to place us under the influence of a piece of the past – and it is only if it is true, I should contend, that the otherwise puzzling classification of retention as a type of memory, enshrined in ordinary speech, is justified – then a fatal objection to the obvious answer is that what is remembered in retention need not be a piece of the past at all; for we may have been told and have not forgotten – which is what it is to retain – that something is the case, either timelessly or present-tensedly, or that something will be the case. By contrast, and in support of the alternative answer, the acquisition condition for retention is invariably satisfied by a piece of the past. In the case both of recollection and of experiential memory, it is, of course, true that what is remembered is a piece of the past, but what makes it plausible to think that it is this piece of the past under the influence of which these two types of memory place us is the very close connection that invariably holds between what is remembered and what satisfies the acquisition condition for any such particular memory. The connection is particularly close in the case of experiential memory. Indeed, with experiential memory we do not have, properly, a distinction of event between what is remembered and what satisfies the acquisition condition. We have, rather, two aspects of the same event, in that the latter is the inner core, or the heart, of the former. For this reason there is no real harm in thinking that, in the case of experiential memory, we are brought under the influence of what is remembered, and harm arises only when we seek to generalise this thought to other types of memory.

In the light of these last remarks, it is now possible to offer those more particular statements of the function of memory to which I referred just now: statements, that is, showing how the function of memory is differently discharged by the different types of memory. More specifically, I suggest that the function of recollection and of experiential memory might be stated thus: *the function of recollection is to place us under the influence of some piece of the past as this was perceived; the function of experiential memory is to place us under the influence of some piece of the past as this was experienced.*

It would be tempting now to reformulate the last statement as 'The function of experiential memory is to place us under the influence of some piece of the past as this was experienced by us, or, of some piece of our experienced past' – tempting, but altogether premature. Nothing as yet warrants such a reformulation. Nevertheless, even on the present formulation, even with the function of experiential memory stated as it is, there seems good reason to think that we do not recruit affect into the service of experiential memory or (the same thing) that the affective side of experiential memory must also be traced back causally to the event remembered. For consider two types of retro-cognitive experience, both endowed with affective tone: one type is both cognitively and affectively owing to the event remembered; the other is only cognitively owing to the event remembered. Surely there can be little doubt but that the former type of experience is better adapted to bring its owner under the influence of the event at issue than is the latter type of experience. Indeed, it might be said that it is only the former type of experience that is, as a type of experience, calculated to exert this influence. Experiences of the latter type may do so, fortuitously, when their owner's affective store is adequate to the task, but there is no earnest or assurance of success.

It is important to see that the superior functional adaptation of the first type of experience, which is equivalent to experiential memory as I have characterised it, over the second type of experience, which is closely related to screen memory as I have characterised it, has nothing to do with such things as the superior force of experience over imagination. On the contrary, everything that I have to say is perfectly compatible with imagination's having sometimes, or indeed often, greater efficacy than experience, which is precisely what I believe to be actually the case. Fantasy can exert more influence over our lives than memory, but the relevant question is, 'What influence?' And, if we are talking of the influence of a particular piece of the past, then memory must be more efficacious than fantasy.

If initial reflection upon the function of experiential memory seems to oblige us to think that affect accrues to, and is not recruited into the service of, experiential memory, more sustained reflection upon this function – upon the function and upon how it is discharged – can only reinforce the obligation. For as yet the function is by no means fully before us.

Long before Freud it was observed that, if memory serves to bring us under the influence of the past, it can also serve to liberate us from that influence when it becomes undue or excessive. As Freud himself might have put the matter, to poets and thinkers this had long been a known fact, but it was left to him to see that this fact received scientific recognition: he retrieved it for science. And he retrieved it for science because of his crucial insight, which is highly relevant to the present inquiry, that memory not merely serves these two functions, but does so in virtue of one and the same aspect of itself. How can this be?

Here I can offer only a highly abbreviated account of a very complex matter, but my hope is that the following summary will, when suitably expanded and refined, achieve explanatory adequacy.

The influence of the past – that is, of some particular piece of the past – can become excessive (let us begin here) in a range of cases. At one end of the range is the case where we have a falsified perception of the present, in that we assimilate it to some particular piece of the past, and then react to it accordingly. At the other end of the range is the case where we revert from the present to the past, and simply live in that particular piece of the past which we have revived. In all such cases there are two tasks to be accomplished if the influence of the past is to be overcome, and the two tasks turn out to be more closely connected than may at first seem to be the case. In the first place, we need to recognise the difference between the past and the present, and to appreciate the futility of trying to understand and deal with

the present uniquely through the past. Secondly, we have to understand what it is about the particular piece of the past that binds
us to it. Now, if the Freudian insight is that memory has a central
role to play in the accomplishment of these tasks, what is it about
memory that fits it to do so? How is it that, in Freud's terminology,
'recollection' can be the solvent of 'repetition'?

The most general answer to this question is that memory allows
us an opportunity to 'relive' some particular piece of the past.
Reliving the past allows us to recognise how we failed to deal
with it at the time in a way that we did not acknowledge, and
this recognition in turn can rid us of the need to go on indefinitely,
appositely or inappositely, re-enacting the unacknowledged failure.
In other words, the efficacy of memory depends on the fact that
it is a necessary part of what can, in favoured circumstances, be
a sufficient condition of our 'working through', and, thereby, unlearning, some particular piece of the past.

But what are the favoured circumstances for 'working through'?
In the first place, the memory must have an affective aspect as well
as a cognitive aspect. Mere recollection – in my terminology –
will not do. But will it do if the affective aspect of the memory
simply matches the affective aspect of the pathogenic event – or
must it be the case that, if the past is to be relived, the affective
aspect of the memory must be causally owing to that event? I
maintain that it must, and that this is a second circumstance favourable to working through; for, if the affective tone of the memory
were not causally owing to the event remembered, if it were merely
recruited into the service of the memory, how could any exploration
of it do anything to weaken the influence of that very event?
A screen memory of an event might certainly give us insight into
that event. We might on the basis of such a memory recognise
how inappropriately we had reacted to the situation. But there
is no reason why all this should have therapeutic, as opposed
to educational, value, or why it should constitute an unlearning
of some particular piece of the past. In order to do that we surely
have to be in the presence of something causally owing to the
relevant piece of the past; and then we may be able to break
the causal chain. If, then, it is true that experiential memory can
alleviate, as well as reinforce, the influence of the past, and that
this too is achieved largely through its affective tone, we have
another reason for thinking that experiential memory has the kind
of causal history that I have ascribed to it, and so ultimately
another reason for thinking that experiential memory cannot run
across persons.

The relevance of the function of memory to the claim that memory

is criterial of personal identity is not yet exhausted. I shall return to
the issue in the next section when I consider a further challenge to
that claim. Before I do so, however, there is another, and ultimately
more important, point that I should like to make. Undoubtedly,
reflection upon the function of memory does something, which
will be variously assessed, to raise the degree to which the claim
is confirmed; but where such reflection is really effective is in
raising the intuitive appeal of the claim. To put the matter very
generally, until its function is introduced, memory appears basically
as a backward-looking phenomenon, more or less isolated from
the rest of the personality. At t_2 I become aware of something
that happened at t_1. Introduce this function, and memory becomes
also a forward-looking phenomenon, which, in its onward roll, invariably spreads itself over the whole of mental life. Whatever happened
at t_1 returns to affect me at t_2 and from then onwards. And
I have every sympathy with those philosophers who have found
in memory as a purely backward-looking phenomenon too meagre
and, above all, too arbitrary a basis on which to rest the identity
of a human life.[20] On the first view of memory, we are presented
with the image of a man who, situated at a certain point, looks
back over life, and finds that everything that he surveys – where
this is to be understood as 'every experience that he surveys' –
is his. But it is hard not to sympathise with, say, Bishop Butler's
intuition that, even if this is true, we still need to know why
it is true. If everything that he surveys is his, we seem to need
a better reason why it is his than the mere fact that he surveys
it; for his surveying it surely cannot make it his. And a better
reason is just what the second view of memory appears to offer.
For it is through looking out over life – something, moreover,
to which we are chronically committed – that we develop into
the persons that we become. And if it seems strange that looking
out over life should have such a deep effect upon us, we must
reflect that we respond not only to the colours and the contours
of the scene but also to the feelings and emotions that these familiar
objects arouse within us. A partial explanation, then, of why
it is that what we survey in memory is ours is not the absurd
one, rightly ridiculed by Reid, that surveying it makes it ours,
but the profounder one, that surveying it makes us its.

This is expressed gnomically. But I should like to revert to the
point, already reconsidered, that it is Ayer's overall view of memory
that most effectively prevents him from doing full justice to the
claim that memory is criterial of personal identity. The point can
now be restated. For it is only when a purely cognitive view of
memory has been abandoned that the view of memory as a forward-

looking phenomenon can come into its own; and it is only when it does that the claim ceases to seem a purely fortuitous hypothesis in philosophy, that may or may not pay off, and comes to look like a truly explanatory account of human identity. At the core of the account is this insight: *if experiential memory is criterial of personal identity, it is so just because it is also creative of personal identity*. In experiential memory the past affects us in such a way that we become creatures with a past: creatures, that is, tied to the past in the way peculiar to persons.

XI

One challenge to the claim that memory is criterial of personal identity comes, as we have seen, from taking seriously imaginary situations in which – or so it is alleged – paths of experiential memory run across persons. There is, however, another challenge to the claim, and this comes from taking seriously a different set of imaginary situations. These are situations in which – once again allegedly – paths of experiential memory bifurcate. These situations are now usually referred to as cases of fission,[21] and, before I turn to consider the challenge that they present, a useful preliminary would be to consider the broad differences between the two kinds of imaginary situation.

In the first kind of imaginary situation, which I have been so far considering, there is a background condition which gives no cause for doubt. This is multiplicity of person. Multiplicity of person is introduced *ex hypothesi*, and there is nothing either in the hypothesis itself or in the way in which it is introduced to arouse suspicion. Given this background condition, a further supposition is then introduced. This is the supposition that paths of experiential memory run from one person to another. Superficially this supposition is compatible with the background condition – indeed, it presupposes it – and the supposition in itself is unobjectionable. But the conjunction of background condition and supposition is incompatible with the claim that memory – that is, experiential memory – is criterial of personal identity. However, under investigation, or so I have been suggesting, things turn out to be otherwise than as they superficially seem. The supposition is not compatible with the background condition, and the only sense in which the supposition is unobjectionable is the excessively weak one that it is not self-contradictory.

In the second kind of imaginary situation, to which I now turn, there are certain clear differences. For there is no single background condition that is beyond suspicion. Instead, there are two suppositions about the feasibility of which it is not hard to experience at any rate initial doubt. One supposition is that a given path of experiential memory can branch. The other supposition is that two different persons can experientially remember performing or suffering some action which in point of fact only one person actually performed or suffered. However, the superficial structure of the case is the same in both kinds of situation. For here too the second supposition is compatible with the first supposition – indeed, this time, it not merely presupposes it, but also is explained by it – and the conjunction of the two suppositions is evidently incompatible with the claim that memory (that is, experiential memory) is criterial of personal identity.

Thus far the challenge presented by the second kind of situation may seem less formidable than that presented by the first kind of situation, in that what is hypothesised in the fission situation initially – and not just ultimately – invites suspicion. However, what is crucial to the second challenge is the effort to convert what looks like its weakness into strength. For, in order to allay suspicion, in order to give the two dubious suppositions – the splitting of the memory path, the diversity in person of the rememberer – feasibility, there is introduced into the fission situation a further element, to which no explicit reference is made in the telling of the first kind of imaginary situation. This further element is the body. The body is introduced to make the two suppositions feasible, and what needs to be appreciated is that the introduction of the body not only serves to make both suppositions feasible, but does so simultaneously or to the same degree. And this in turn serves to confirm their mutual compatibility.

Let us briefly consider how this is done. A memory path, we are told, branches. But, it may be countered, the only evidence that there could be in support of this supposition supports another supposition equally well: that is, that after some moment a (let us say) event that had been experientially remembered by one person now seems to be – seems to be but is not – experientially remembered by two persons. It is to block this alternative supposition – which would, of course, constitute no challenge whatsoever to the claim that experiential memory is criterial of personal identity – and to ensure the proper continuity between the earlier and the later memories that each of the branching memory paths is then invested with as much of the circumambient flesh, nerve, tissue in which the original track of the memory path ran as the neuro-physiologist may require and the other branch can spare. Then the deficit is made up, let us suppose, synthetically, or from waste material. But, if the branching memory paths are thus embodied, it follows that, when along either branch an experiential memory is entertained, this is not just a memory belonging to a person, but a memory belonging to one or other of two different persons. In other words, concentration upon, or elaboration of, what physically occurs at the moment of fission, or how the body is implicated in the occurrence, has for the theorist of fission a dual bonus. For it shows at a single stroke how before the moment of fission there was one and only one track from which two branching memory paths diverge, and how after the moment of fission there are two distinct persons along whom these branching memory paths run.

It should also be clear from this consideration of the second kind of imaginary situation how the challenge that it presents is to be met if it can be. It must be shown that the introduction of the body into the situation does not in fact achieve what the theorist of fission hopes for from it, and there are two possible tactics by means of which this might be attempted. The first would be to show that, even with the body in, the two suppositions integral to the situation are not compatible. More specifically, one might try to show that branching of memory paths, in so far as this is compatible with the continued existence of the person as a person (and this is a very real cause for reservation), requires identity of person between the two rememberers. The second tactic would be to show that, once again even with the body in, the first supposition fails the requirement of feasibility. In other words, it remains impossible that paths of experiential memory should divide.

I shall limit myself to suggesting – suggesting rather than implementing – a strategy for meeting the challenge arising from the second kind of imaginary situation, and this strategy consists in a distinctive combination of the two tactics I have just indicated. The combination comes about through the exploitation of a feature in the imaginary situation which has thus far escaped attention, but which takes on a new significance in the light of the function assigned to memory in the last section.

The first step is to show that the two suppositions on which the imaginary situation relies are not compatible.

And here a preliminary observation is necessary. To some it may seem that the hypothesis of identity of person between the two rememberers is just not open to us. For, they would maintain, the hypothesis is self-contradictory.[22] Now what is certainly true is this: that, given the way in which the fission situation has been hypothesised, any description of the two rememberers is going to be such that pre-theoretically we should think of them, first of all, as persons, and, secondly, as different persons. But 'pre-theore-tically' here is the crucial word. For the possibility that, when theory is forthcoming, we shall be obliged to revise the second of these two thoughts – or even, for that matter, the first – cannot be eliminated *a priori*. If we were required to revise the second of these thoughts, while yet retaining intact the first, we should have made a conceptual discovery. We should have discovered that the concept of person is a concept that can be applied not only to entities whose spatio-temporal configuration is that of a capital I but also to things whose spatio-temporal configuration is that of a capital Y. And to suppose that such a discovery could be made is not (whatever else it may be) self-contradictory.

But what else is it? Is there any reason to think that such a supposition does not violate the bounds of possibility?

Having disposed of the question of the self-contradictory, I now want to introduce that aspect of the fission situation which seems to me to have been wrongly ignored. I have in mind the age of the person when fission occurs, or, more accurately perhaps, the point in his life-span – 'more accurately', I say, because, though what is of primary significance is the length of time between birth and the moment of fission, secondary significance (at any rate, on this present tactic) attaches to the length of time still to run between the moment of fission and death.

How does concentration upon this factor do anything to dispute the compatibility of the two suppositions on which fission relies? And my suggestion is that, if the person is sufficiently old – where what is crucial is if he has enough of his life behind him – there is good reason to doubt that fission will produce multiplicity of person. For there will be such a substantial shared past under the influence of which experiential memory places the two remem-berers that they will not present the required externality to one another. Let us consider the situation that is justifiably thought to weigh heavily in favour of the thesis that in the two rememberers we do indeed have two persons: namely, that when they communicate they communicate interpersonally.[23] But do they? For it is certainly true that in such a situation speech comes now out of one mouth, now out of another; now one pair of ears receives the words that are listened to, now another. But all this belongs to the pre-theoreti-cal description, and what theory has to take account of is the way in which each rememberer has such access to the inner life of the other, is so attuned to his thoughts, beliefs and feelings, that, when they communicate, more is understood than is uttered and this understanding is direct or immediate. The last condition is important, if notoriously difficult to spell out; for, it could be objected, there are clear cases of interpersonal communication where the hearer hears what the sayer left unsaid, and sometimes does so in advance of anything said. But in such cases the under-standing is mediated or inferential. Indeed, one of the best ways of grasping just what is wrong in thinking of the outcomes of late fission as cases where interpersonal communication occurs would be to contrast them with cases where two people who have lived in each other's company from birth for just as many years as the person was old at the moment of fission communicate and do so interpersonally. (The all-important thing is that, having once decided that it is not self-contradictory to suppose that the two rememberers are – that is, are constitutively, or form, as we might say – one and the same person, we should not then go on and stipulate as the only evidence favouring this supposition something to suppose which is indeed self-contradictory.) Part of the difference between the two cases is that, even if in the second case the two people understand each other 'perfectly', they lack the certainty of it which is a feature of the first case. What gives the certainty is, of course, the common causation, and, once this is grasped, it can be seen that the case for thinking that the two rememberers are one and the same person is not, as has been claimed,[24] exhausted by the fact that they instantiate the same personality, and hence that, in the foregoing argument, person is equated with personality type. The most that could be claimed is that person is equated with personality type plus specific causation.

The argument for saying that in cases of late fission the two suppositions central to the hypothesised situation are not compatible is not yet complete. For, if one way of establishing this is to argue that late fission preserves identity of person and does so necessarily, another would be to establish that, where late fission does not do this, it necessarily destroys personhood. The difficulty, with the discussion on the present level of generality, is to point out convincingly under which conditions the argument ought to go one way and under which conditions it ought to go the other. But I shall leave the issue upon the observation that it seems highly likely that there will be some considerations that point the second way, towards extinction of person, in addition to those considerations which point the first way, towards identity of person, as the outcome of late fission.

So much then for the first tactic for meeting the challenge. Now, to the second tactic: that is, disputing the feasibility of one of the two suppositions on which the imaginary situation depends, or showing that it is impossible that paths of experiential memory should branch. Once again I suggest that we introduce the notion of the age at which fission occurs. And my new suggestion is that, if fission occurs sufficiently early on, there is good reason to doubt that it produces branching of paths of experiential memory.

The crucial consideration here is not, as one may be ready to think, that in cases of early fission the shared past is very small. For that by itself would have only the consequence that there are no more than a few paths of memory that branch on early fission. But my suggestion is more radical, and is to the effect that none do. To make my point I should like first to introduce a distinction between branches *of* a memory path and branches *off* a memory path, and then to formulate the point by claiming that early fission does not give rise to branches of a memory path – it produces only branches off a memory path.

To make the distinction acceptable it is required to say something on a topic that ordinarily – that is, in a world that, like ours, does not contain fission – is totally unproblematic. I refer to the identity of a memory path. Now, superficially it may seem – and, furthermore, may seem consistent with what I have said – that the identity of a memory path is given by its causal origin. It is in its causal origin that we find what it is in virtue of which a memory path remains self-identical over time; or different memories belong to the same memory path because they have the same point of causal departure. But this is only superficial. At least in the case of a path of experiential memory the proper conclusion is that causation is necessary but not sufficient for the identity of a memory path; and, furthermore, this is implicit in what I have said about the affective influence of an event (or its impact) upon a person, where this is, as we have seen, one of the things transmitted along the path of an experiential memory. To show that this conclusion is required by my whole argument as well as to try to exhibit its truth, let me go over the relevant considerations again.

The affective influence of an event upon a person is in part the result of the original impact of that event upon him. The impact, when it takes place, is mediated by his contemporary beliefs, feelings and sensations. But in part the affective influence of an event – that is, the continuing affective influence of the event – is owing to the reinforcement of the original impact by later experiential memory of the event. This reinforcement by experiential memory is in effect the impact on the person of the affective tone of the experiential memory, where this in turn derives from the original impact of the event. However – and here we approach the vital consideration – the impact of the experiential memory too is mediated by the person's contemporary beliefs, feelings, and sensations: that is, the beliefs, feelings, and sensations contemporary with the memory. And the upshot of this is that, with the passage of time after the moment of fission, the branching paths of experiential memory that result from fission will increasingly diverge, despite their common causal origin. They will do so for two different though closely related reasons. To see these reasons at work, let us suppose that, after an adequate interval of time since fission, an experiential memory of an event that occurred before fission is entertained by one of the two potential rememberers. Then the first reason for the ever-increasing divergence of paths is that the beliefs, desires and feelings of the rememberer, by which the impact of the memory is mediated, will differ qualitatively from those of the other potential rememberer. The difference in experience of life between the two since fission may be assumed adequate to account for this. The second reason is that the affective tone that accrues to the memory – and the impact of which is just what the beliefs, desires, and feelings I have been talking of will mediate – will differ qualitatively from that which would have accrued to it had the other entertained the memory. And this is so because, on each previous occasion when the rememberer's affective store from which the affective tone comes was reinforced by an experiential memory, the impact of the memory was mediated by his current beliefs, desires and feelings, which, as we have just seen, become increasingly peculiar to him.

Now, it is important to see that, though both these reasons evidently reflect the fact that, if fission occurs sufficiently early, there is much time that is likely to pass for the person or persons surviving fission, they basically reflect the fact that little time has passed for the person before fission. But that, as I pointed out, must not be taken simply to mean that there is a quantitatively small shared past. It means rather that fission occurred at a tender age, and it is because it occurred at a tender age that the affective store is that much weaker or that much the less resistant or more permeable to later experiential memory (let alone later experience).

Now, if the branching paths of experiential memory are likely to diverge in this way and for these reasons, I shall reckon them to be branches off, rather than branches of, the same memory path.

And now I can imagine a protest. For, it may be said, despite my claim that all this is compatible with, indeed is implicit in, what I have said about the transmission of the affective influence of an event through experiential memory, it remains a fact that, in my account of experiential memory, I gave no indication that the affective tone of a memory could, let alone would, thus diverge from the affective tone of the original event (or its impact). Indeed, did I not say that in experiential memory the thoughts and feelings entertained in the course of the original event tend 'to set themselves up afresh in the mind'? I did; but I did not have in mind that the experiential memory should literally reproduce the original event with *trompe l'oeil* effect, or that in experiential memory we should relive the past to the point of hallucinatory fidelity. Such experiences, of course, can occur, when the past is embalmed in the memory and then brought out into the present incorrupt, but they verge on the pathological. Normally memory works both for the survival and for the erosion of the past – and none of this causes any theoretical difficulty, so long, that is, as paths of experiential memory run along one person. But introduce fission, and branching paths of experiential memory with the same causal origin but subject to differential erosion – differential, because erosion is determined conjointly by the event remembered and the affective store of the rememberer – and the question must arise, 'When is erosion incompatible with identity of memory path across branching paths?' When, as I have put it, is a branching path a branch off, as opposed to a branch of, an original memory path? To this question the most likely answer would seem to be this: when what it is like for one rememberer experientially to remember an event ceases to match what it is like for the other rememberer experientially to remember it.[25] And the second tactic for disputing the relevance of cases of fission to the claim that memory is criterial of personal identity can now be seen as aiming to establish just this: that, given early fission, such a match cannot be anticipated.

Now, let us suppose that each of the two tactics can be successfully carried out – does this mean that the overall strategy is assured of success? If the first tactic succeeds, what is established is this: if fission is sufficiently late, it does not produce two different persons along whom branches of the same memory path might run. If the second tactic succeeds, what is established is this: if fission is sufficiently early, there are not different branches of the same memory path which could then run along the two persons who result. But whether the combined success of the two tactics amounts to the overall success of the strategy – something which, it will be recalled, I never promised – depends, of course, on whether there is any interval of time between the age that is sufficiently early for fission not to result in splitting of memory paths and the age that is sufficiently late for fission not to produce diversity of person, provided also that fission occurring within this interval does not accomplish that other ever-present possibility: destruction of personhood. So, is there such an interval? This, the one remaining and now decisive question is, I need hardly say, something that only psychological theory can answer. That result I welcome.

XII

My last remark reveals that the argument of this essay has been developed in conformity with a thesis, now familiar in philosophy through work carried out by Saul Kripke[26] and Hilary Putnam,[27] to the effect that the semantics of natural-kind terms cannot in the long run be properly understood independently of good theory; for good theory, when it is ultimately forthcoming, will serve at once to fix the precise reference of any such word and to reveal its full sense. However, the argument of this essay does not derive from that thesis. It derives from another thesis, at once more particular and more powerful, which addresses itself specifically to psychological words including the concept of the person. If we may leave aside the abstruse question of whether these words are rightly reckoned natural-kind terms, their semantics too is dependent on good theory. But not just in the long run. For, if in the long run the application of these words is justified by reference to theory, in the short run theory controls their application. And this is so because, though psychological theory has, of course, to be made explicit through the usual procedures of scientific theory, implicitly it is – at any rate, in its more general reaches – employed from the very beginning in the inevitable human tasks of self-understanding and the understanding of others.[28] In other words, I have assumed for the course of this essay – though with what precise consequences for the argument and at what precise points I could not always say – that knowledge of good psychological theory is, in some prevailingly weak sense of that term, innate.

XIII

It was an invaluable intuition on the part of classical empiricism that, whatever else personal identity resides in, it does not reside in a continuing unchanging substance. This intuition was brilliantly enunciated by Hume,[29] and Ayer in various writings on the subject has pleaded the case with great clarity and persuasiveness.[30] It may very well be that psychological considerations weighed most heavily with Hume and metaphysical considerations with Ayer, but this is an issue where the two kinds of consideration come intriguingly together. Though in what I have speculated about personal identity I have departed considerably from the epistemological assumptions of these two philosophers, what I have said is just another attempt, from another direction, by another method, to do justice to the truth with which their names are, and will continue to be, rightly associated.[31]

NOTES

1. A. J. Ayer, *The Foundations of Empirical Knowledge* (London: Macmillan, 1940) pp. 142–4

2. A. J. Ayer: *The Problem of Knowledge* (London: Penguin, 1956) pp. 222–3; *The Origins of Pragmatism* (London: Macmillan, 1968) p. 297; *The Concept of a Person* (London: Macmillan, 1963) pp. 114–15.

3. Ayer: *Problem*, pp. 160–3 and 219–21; and *The Central Questions of Philosophy* (London: Weidenfeld and Nicolson, 1973) pp. 115–16.

4. Ayer, *Problem*, pp. 221–2.

5. Bernard Williams, 'Personal Identity and Individuation', *Proceedings of the Aristotelian Society*, LVII (1956–7) 229–52; repr. in his *Problems of the Self* (Cambridge: Cambridge University Press, 1973).

6. For example, Anthony Flew, 'Locke and the Problem of Personal Identity', *Philosophy*, XXVI (1951) 53–68.

7. Sigmund Freud, 'A Difficulty in the Path of Psycho-analysis', in his *Complete Psychological Works*, ed. James Strachey (London, Hogarth Press) vol. XVII, p. 141.

8. For example, Flew, in *Philosophy*, XXVI.

9. Richard Wollheim: 'Imagination and Identification', in his *On Art and the Mind* (London, 1973) pp. 54–83; and 'Identification and Imagination: the Inner Structure of a Psychic Mechanism', in *Freud: A Collection of Critical Essays*, ed. R. Wollheim (Anchor Books, New York, 1974) pp. 172–95.

10. Ayer, *Problem*, pp. 149–65.

11. Ibid., pp. 163–4.

12. J. W. von Goethe, *Wahrheit und Dichtung*. I am indebted to Elizabeth Anscombe for having first drawn my attention to the philosophical interest of this passage, in a paper read many years ago at University College, London. This paper in a much revised form has been printed as her 'Memory "Experience" and Causation' in *Contemporary British Philosophy*, 4th ser., ed. H. D. Lewis (London: Allen and Unwin, 1976).

13. In saying this I am using 'reason' in what might be called a substantive sense: to refer, that is, to the event or condition that the man cites in giving his reason, or what might be called the subject matter of the reason. Thus, my case is unaffected by certain arguments that would have it that, as ontologically inappropriate to that task, reasons cannot be causes.

14. The point is best made in C. B. Martin and Max Deutscher, 'Remembering', *Philosophical Review*, LXXV (1966) 161–96: an article to which I am evidently much indebted.

15. Ayer, *Problem*, p. 163.

16. The notion of an acquisition condition as used in this essay is clearly related to that of the 'previous awareness condition' as used in Sidney Shoemaker, 'Persons and their Past', *American Philosophical Quarterly*, VII (1970) 269–85. But there are important differences. In the first place, Shoemaker is open-minded whether the previous awareness condition and the memory are or are not causally related. He considers, successively, both possibilities. Secondly, and more importantly, Shoemaker insists that for all types of memory – not that he classifies them exactly as I do, but that is barely relevant – there is a 'correspondence' between the

234 Perception and Identity

memory and the previous awareness condition. I can make something of such a correspondence in the case of experiential memory, but I cannot project it over all types of memory. Now, at the same time, Shoemaker rightly to my mind resists the temptation to assimilate all types of memory to experiential memory: so that, for instance, if I (seemingly) recollect that you caught a train I (really) experientially remember my seeing you catch the train or, if I (seemingly) retain that Alexander the Great burnt Persepolis, I (really) experientially remember my reading that Alexander the Great burnt Persepolis. But, without this unwanted assimilation, the notion of correspondence seems gratuitous.

17. For example, Derek Parfit, 'Personal Identity', *Philosophical Review*, LXXX (1971) 3–27; repr. in *Personal Identity*, ed. John Perry (Berkeley and Los Angeles, Cal., 1975).

18. Sigmund Freud, 'Screen Memories', in his *Works*, vol. III, pp. 303–22.

19. Cf. N. J. Block and J. A. Fodor, 'What Psychological States are Not', *Philosophical Review*, LXXXI (1972) 159–81.

20. Cf. David Wiggins, 'Locke, Butler and the Stream of Consciousness: and Men as a Natural Kind', *Philosophy*, LI (1976) 131–58; repr. in a revised form in *The Identities of Persons*, ed. Amélie Oksenberg Rorty (Berkeley and Los Angeles, Cal., 1976).

21. Cases of fission are discussed in, for example, Sidney Shoemaker, *Self-Knowledge and Self-Identity* (Ithaca, NY: Cornell University Press, 1963); David Wiggins, *Identity and Spatio-Temporal Continuity* (Oxford: Blackwell, 1967); Roderick Chisholm and Sidney Shoemaker, 'The Loose and Popular and the Strict and Philosophical Senses of Identity', in *Perception and Personal Identity*, ed. Norman S. Care and Robert H. Grimm (Cleveland, Ohio, 1969); Parfit, in *Philosophical Review*, LXXX; John Perry, 'Can the Self Divide?', *Journal of Philosophy*, LXIX (1972) 463–88; Williams, *Problems of the Self, passim*; and several of the contributions to *The Identities of Persons*, ed. Rorty.

22. Cf. A. N. Prior, 'Opposite Number', *Review of Metaphysics*, II (1957) 196–201, and 'Time Existence and Identity', *Proceedings of the Aristotelian Society*, LXVI (1965–6) 183–92.

23. Wiggins, in *Philosophy*, LI, and *The Identities of Persons*, ed. Rorty. In this article Wiggins presents an argument different from any I use (though complementary) against the genuine possibility of what is entertained in fission or fusion thought experiments.

24. Williams, in *Proceedings of the Aristotelian Society*, LVII.

25. I am here exploiting a phrase used to good effect in Thomas Nagel, 'What Is It Like To Be a Bat?', *Philosophical Review*, LXXXIII (1974) 435–50.

26. For example, Saul Kripke, 'Identity and Necessity', in *Identity and Individuation*, ed. Milton K. Munitz (New York: New York University Press, 1971).

27. For example, Hilary Putnam, 'Is Semantics Possible?', in *Languages, Belief and Metaphysics*, ed. H. Kiefer and M. Munitz (State University of N.Y. Press, Albany, NY, 1970); repr. in his *Mind, Language and Reality* (Cambridge: Cambridge University Press, 1975).

28. Cf. Richard Wollheim, 'The Mind and the Mind's Image of Itself', *International Journal of Psycho-Analysis*, L (1969) 209–20; repr. in his *On Art and the Mind*.

29. Hume, *A Treatise of Human Nature*, I. 4. vi. Cf. David Pears, 'Hume's Account of Personal Identity', in *David Hume: A Symposium*, ed. D. Pears (Macmillan, London, 1963); repr. in his *Questions in the Philosophy of Mind* (London: Duckworth, 1975).

30. Ayer, *Problem*, pp. 199–212.

31. In the preparation of this paper I have incurred a debt of gratitude to Jane Howarth, Hide Ishiguro, Michael Slote, Jerry Valberg, John Watling, and David Wiggins for their extremely valuable comments and criticism.

10 I Do Not Exist

PETER UNGER

It seems utterly obvious that the question 'Do I exist?' may be correctly answered only in the affirmative; of course the answer must be 'Yes.' Descartes, it may be said, made this idea the keystone of his philosophy, he found it so compelling. Hume, however, in his characteristically sceptical style, at least at times questioned the propriety of an affirmative reply. My teacher, Professor Sir Alfred Jules Ayer, to whom this essay is dedicated, customarily expressed himself in a conditional manner, which I find quite congenial:

> The sentence 'I exist', in this usage, may be allowed to express a statement which like other statements is capable of being either true or false. It differs, however, from most other statements in that if it is false it can not actually be made. Consequently, no one who uses these words intelligently and correctly can use them to make a statement which he knows to be false. If he succeeds in making the statement, it must be true.[1]

Of course Ayer is right in pointing to the absurdity of a person's trying to deny his own existence. Prepared to pay this price, in this brief essay I mean to deny my own putative existence, a position which I take to be even more radical than Hume's. This is owing not to a desire to be more perverse than any of my predecessors, but, rather, to certain arguments which have occurred to me, and which seem quite far from any of their thoughts. As may be expected of a student of Ayer's, and as I have indicated, I appreciate the utterly paradoxical position into which these arguments lead me. But I venture to suppose that this does not reflect badly on my reasonings in any relevant regard. Rather, it may show their great scope, thus highlighting obscure defects in prevalent conceptions. With this understanding, I mean to present herein the main lines of reasoning against my own existence.

I offer my arguments as a challenge to any others that there may be, so that they may dissuade me from the path of extreme nihilism that reason appears to require. Accordingly, I shall present my ideas as forcefully as possible, not to indicate any enormous confidence on my part, but rather to provoke others to reply most promptly and effectively. For my own part, I can find nothing importantly wrong with the uncomfortable thoughts I shall thus boldly put forth. The more I reflect upon them, the more I become convinced of their essential truth or justice, for any errors I ever find are superficial mistakes, requiring at most only minor changes in formulation. As a consequence, there appears to be growing within me an inclination to expend much effort toward developing the required nihilism in great detail, no matter how painfully laborious the attempt may be. Perhaps this growth had best be stopped, but then only by an appropriate rational argument.

To compound my dilemma, I notice that, in general outline, the same view lately has been conjectured by another writer, Samuel Wheeler, or so it appears. In a pioneering paper, 'Reference and Vagueness', Wheeler conjectured that there may not be any people; I should suppose he meant to include himself.[2] While he does not offer a positive argument for the nihilistic surmise, he does disarm prevalent ideas which would point the other way. Appearing to find a similar current in another, but no adequate compelling force in the opposite direction, the situation encourages my thoughts to move, however slowly and painfully, toward their properly destructive denial. Perhaps a response to my challenge may save me from the ultimately fruitless labours I seem required to undertake.

The challenging position is this: I do not exist and neither do you. The scientific perspective, especially as developed over the last few centuries, compels this result. Now, there is nothing especially unfortunate in this as regards the human condition. For, as regards almost everything which is commonly alleged to exist, it may be argued, in like manner, that it in fact does not. There are, then, no tables or chairs, nor rocks or stones or ordinary stars. Neither are there any plants or animals. No finite persons or conscious beings exist, including myself Peter Unger: I do not exist. So much for this challenging position. To the main arguments for it, rather briefly presented, I now turn.

I. THE SORITES OF DECOMPOSITION

Tables, as well as chairs, have often been believed to be paradigms of existing things or entities, but I shall argue that they do not exist at all. They are, if you will, only fictions, though nothing whatever depends on my use of such a term of convenience. My argument will be in the form of an indirect proof, wherein I reduce to absurdity the supposition of their existence.

According to our modern scientific view, if there are any tables, then each of them is constituted of, or is composed of, or comprises, or consists of, or whatever, many atoms, and still more 'elementary particles', but only a finite number of each. Now, nothing here depends on the expression 'is constituted of', or on any similar expression. Baldly put, the point is this: where and when there are no atoms present, there and then there is no table. This idea is not crucial to the argument; a 'less scientific' analogue will work as well, so far as the purer logical features go. But it is good to have nature appparently so co-operative.

Now, at the same time, according to our common-sense view of the matter, which for something like a *table* is, of course, all but definitive, one atom, or only a few, removed, or added, quite innocuously, will not make a relevant difference. If you have a table at the start, then, after an atom has been gently ticked off the edge somewhere, there will still be a table present. These simple ideas, when brought into combination, leave nothing for reason but to conclude that there really are no tables. It takes no great acumen to see this, as the reasoning is utterly simple, and most just and suitable to the subject before us.

For, if there is a table there, then it has only a finite number of atoms – say, a billion billion; it does not matter. The net removal of one, then, leaves us with a supposed table of a billion billion minus one atoms; after two are removed, the supposed table has a billion billion minus two; and so on. After a billion billion atoms have been removed, we have a table consisting of no atoms at all. In this simple fashion, I suggest, we have reduced to an absurdity the supposition that the table in question exists, or ever did exist. As this argument may be most readily generalised, we may conclude that there really are no such things as tables.

To advance discussion, it may be helpful if I give the argument just presented something like a formal shape or presentation. We begin with a supposition of existence:

(1)   There exists at least one table.

But, from our scientific perspective, we may add this second premiss:

(2)   For anything there may be, if it is a table, then it consists of many atoms, but only a finite number.

From these two premises, we may deduce that there is at least one table which consists of many atoms, but a finite number of them. The crux and bite of my argument, however, may be supposed to come with a third and final premiss:

(3)   For anything there may be, if it is a table (which consists of many atoms, but a finite number), then the net removal of one atom, or only a few, in a way which is most innocuous and favourable, will not mean the difference as to whether there is a table in the situation.

These three premisses, I take it, are inconsistent. The assessment of this inconsistency, I submit, leads one to reject, and to deny, the first premiss, whatever one may subsequently think of the remaining two propositions.

Discounting minor matters of formulation, I doubt that many would deny our second premiss. Many more, I imagine, are liable to deny our third and final proposition. It has, I must admit, been stated in a way which leaves matters less than completely clear and evident. Accordingly, I shall try to provide some clarificatory interpretation, to the extent that this seems merited even in a very brief treatment.

I have said that an atom is to be removed in a way which is most innocuous and favourable. What do I mean by such a way? First, I mean for the removal to be *net*, of course, and in the fullest way. The process which removes an atom does not put something else in its place, or in anywhere else; nor does such a thing happen in any other way. And, what is removed is randomly cast aside, so to speak. Secondly, I mean for the net removal to take place with as little disruptive effect as possible on what remains, especially as regards the question, if it really has any substance, as to whether or not any table remains. In other words, we might say, it is most unlikely that an atom will ever be blasted out of a central position; rather, one will be gently dislodged from an outside spot. Additionally, we are to conceive of the most favourable, or least disruptive, conditions, as regards temperature, pressure, electricity, magnetism, and so on. Further, if an occasion arises where, vary conditions as we may, a single atom cannot be removed without substantial relevant disruption, then we remove as few as possible, balanced against a disruptive effect. Finally, I close this interpretation with a remark on the alleged matter of whether an entity may be *as much as possible*, or be *as well off toward being*, a table. I am supposing this matter to have substance, of course, but only on way toward exposing its absurdity. This is an indirect argument.

Thus clarified, perhaps we may profitably divide what our premiss is saying under two heads. First, it makes a 'causal' claim: there is no relevant breaking point where, no matter what is done to be gentle and to retain things, the whole business, or a substantial portion thereof, collapses, or turns into an apparent donkey, or disappears, or whatever. Rather, things are relevantly quite gradual. To deny this, I believe, is to cast aside science, and even common sense as well. And, secondly, our premiss claims that, in this rather gradual way of things, the difference made by the small removals encountered, by one atom, more or less, is never nearly so much as the difference, merely alleged as it may be, between a table's being there and not being there. To deny this premiss, then, is as much as to affirm that there comes a place where, by taking away an atom or so, presumably *any one or few of millions* still, one makes a table cease to exist. And this, I suggest, is as much as to expect a miracle.

Now, as it is stated, of course, our final premiss points to conditions, and a way, that are quite ideal. That is no fault. It may make one think, however, that the whole argument has an 'airy-fairy' character, and is quite unrealistic. But conditions close enough to those which are most favourable do occur almost all the time. And, very small bits, if not nearly so small as an atom, can be removed in stepwise fashion, for an argument to similar effect. Whatever 'airy-fairy' features are there, then, cannot be basic to the argument.

Within fine points of formulation, our third premiss thus fairly compels belief. As a move to escape our just but uncomfortable conclusion, it remains only to deny the reasoning employed. In this vein, some may object that 'the logic' I have used is what is at fault. If some 'alternative logic' is chosen, they may respond, instead of the system of rules and formulae I have employed, the integrity of our tables may be secured. But I do not believe that good reasoning can ever be captured or frozen into any such system, or that the matter is really one of choosing one or another optional pieces of logical apparatus, like so many hammers or wrenches. There is not, I suggest, here a question of this logic or that one. Without my now being less than sceptical, it is a question of whether my reasoning has been sound, and has been just and appropriate to the topic before us. Now, if I have been in error in my reasoning, or unjust to my subject matter, then such an error or injustice should be made manifest. But, excepting small points of formulation, and with a proper sceptical hesitancy, I doubt that this will be done. Of course, I am no mathematician.

But, I think that a fair appraisal of the matter by those more mathematically inclined will find them to view things in much the way that I here recommend.

In a somewhat deeper vein, perhaps, it should be re-emphasised that my argument is not dependent upon the existence of atoms, at least not in any fundamental way. Perhaps there are no atoms, and in 'removing an atom' what really happens is something involving, say, an underlying plenum, which is the only existing (physical) reality. If so, then perhaps the argument presented is acceptable only provisionally; perhaps it operates only on a superficial level. But, whatever changes or profundities may be compellingly envisioned, I hardly think that the reinstatement of tables is among them.

As a related, already anticipated point, while the gradual nature of things is needed for my argument, no deep theories about material reality are important. While it is nice to have ready-made units there to remove – molecules, atoms and particles – the slightest contrivance will work about as well. Thus, from an alleged table, one may remove a tiny chip or splinter, until not a single one remains.

In the manner of G. E. Moore, some will object to my argument along the following lines. First, they will claim to be *more certain* of the existence of tables than of *anything* which I am bringing to bear against such alleged existence. And, then, they will say, with apparent caution and modesty, that, while they are *not sure which* of the things I advance is in error, there *must be at least one* weak link, or fault, in my reasoning. Now, it well may be that this Moorian reply is often, or even usually, a proper answer to a philosophical attack on common sense. But, is it *always* proper, appropriate or correct? Is common sense *always* to be believed, while philosophy, along with science, is *always* to yield? I cannot believe that this is so, and that *no exceptions* can be made to this popular Moorian doctrine. What of the *present case*, then: may not *that* be just such an exception? We have seen, I suggest, that to deny my argument amounts to supposing a miracle: the gentle, innocuous removal of a single atom, or only a few, *which is not even perceptible to the unaided senses*, takes us from a situation where a table is present to one where there is no table at all. Indeed, the removal of *any one*, or *any few*, of *millions* of removable atoms or groups, will be enough to work the trick. This is, after all, where the issue does lie. Can common sense be so powerful as to sustain such a miraculous supposition as this? I do not think so.

In contrast to its employment with tables and chairs, our argument does not seem nearly so compelling, if at all, against *physical objects*. Intuitively, we have the idea that if we consider a biggish physical object, consisting of many atoms, as we take one away and then another, and so on, what we have left is always a physical object, so long as any object at all remains. The last atom, particle or whatever, it may be supposed, is as well off toward being a physical object as is the biggish thing at the start.

Let us be a bit particular as regards the differences between our sorites against tables, or any other ordinary things, and a similar attempt against physical objects. In the first place, we cannot say, in parallel with (2), that, for anything there may be, if it is a physical object, then it consists of many atoms but only a finite number. For an atom itself is a physical object and it does not consist of atoms, let alone many of them. Nor will matters improve if we look for a finer component than atoms, for what we find may also be regarded, I suppose, as a physical object if it is any proper component at all. Nor can a parallel with (3) be accepted readily. Unlike with a table, if you have a physical object and remove an atom, you may have left no physical object at all. For that atom, now removed, may have been the only physical object there to be removed. Now, none of this is to suppose that physical objects do exist. But, as the present argument does not compellingly disprove their existence, they appear to be a somewhat extraordinary thing, whether truly existent or only alleged for all that.

All in all, it may be said, I hope, that the argument I have employed is a rather *simple* piece of reasoning. I call this sort of argument the *sorites of decomposition*. A parallel argument, going the other way, suggests itself, *the sorites of accumulation*, as well as variations upon, and combinations of, both of these forms of reasoning. In particular, counterfactual variations should be of interest to many contemporary writers.

We employed our argument against tables, which, if they exist at all, have certain more or less special features. They are in some sense functional things; they are typically man-made; and so on. But none of this, it will be easily recognised, has anything to do with the matter at hand. Our argument may be employed equally well to deny the existence of such alleged things as sticks and stones, mountains and lakes, planets, (ordinary) stars and galaxies, ships and carriages, pieces of hair and of money, bodies of horses and of generals, and so on, and so forth. Such things as are not susceptible to decomposition withstand this form of argument: certain sub-atomic particles may provide an example. More importantly, decomposible things which are in a relevant way 'defined with precision' escape the present reasonings. Accordingly, I shall not now deny the existence of most molecules, even some 'quite large' ones, nor, perhaps, even certain crystal structures. However, something such as a blue 1968 Chevrolet four-door sedan, while according to most accounts not something vaguely described, will fall prey to our sorites. While much of physics and chemistry thus *might* remain relatively unscathed, biological entities, above the molecular level, appear to be nothing but fictions. I deny, then, not only the bodies of animals, including human beings, but also their organs, such as livers, hearts and brains, their tissues, and even individual cells, such as neurons.

Similar decomposition arguments make it clear, as well, that many alleged substances in fact do not exist at all. Unlike water and gold, which may be real, but which do not come in drops or hunks, juice and brass are only fictions. Also among the sorts of stuff that do not exist are, I should think, air and earth, meat and flesh, wood and rock, cloth and paper, and so on.

None of the things so far placed in the range of our reasonings, however, is of nearly so great an interest, I imagine, as we ourselves. Accordingly, I now turn to begin a new section, devoted to this topic, wherein I explicitly reason to deny, not without paradox, but perhaps with success, the very thing that Descartes would have me consider *certain*: my own present existence.

II. A DISPROOF OF MY OWN EXISTENCE

The developing scientific perspective, especially owing to gains in biology and chemistry over the last few centuries, renders it exceedingly likely, at least, that no finite people or beings exist. In particular, and more conservatively, this perspective indicates that I myself do not exist; that I never have and never shall.

To achieve this paradoxical result, I shall again employ the sorites of decomposition. Now, the 'normal growth of the human being from conception' also provides, I believe, a sound sorites of accumulation. That sorites is naturally instanced, we might say, even though, with cellular growth not being clearly arithmetic, a unit of increment may have to be contrived: what happens during the first second; what happens during the next; and so on. But, the very artificiality of a gradual decomposition may better jar the mind. Thus, it may increase the chances for acceptance of the uncomfortable conclusion. Now, the most compelling decompositions are not yet attainable. We cannot remove, for example, one cell at a time, while keeping the remainder alive and functioning impressively. While it is not strictly relevant, I should think that this ability is not too far off for us, perhaps no more than a few centuries. In any case, if and when it can be done, I hope that it will not be. What is most relevant is that nature allow for the decompositions herein to be imagined.

As I have indicated, the unit of decrement which I shall choose is the cell. It is instructive for us now to argue at this level. As a cell consists of millions of atoms, a sorites of decomposition based on the atom can show that cells do not exist. Thus, the success of an argument against myself, or even my body, based on the cell, makes it quite clear that, in our argument against tables, the reliance on atoms was far from fundamental.

To mirror our previous argument, against tables, I now display the following three premises:

(1)   I exist.

(2)   If I exist, then I consist of many cells, but a finite number.

(3)   If I exist (and consist of many cells, but a finite number), then the net removal of one cell, or only a few, in a way which is most innocuous and favourable, will not mean the difference as to whether I exist.

As before, these three propositions form an inconsistent set. They have it that I am still there with no cells at all, even while my existence depends on cells. To escape this inconsistency realistically, we must suppose this. Even under conditions most favourable to me, the removal of a single cell, or only a few, *any* one or few of those in the situation, will mean the difference between my existence and no me at all. But, if I do exist, can my existence really be that tenuous? I think not. Therefore, I do not exist.

A bit more informally, the idea is this. One cell, more or less, will not mean the difference between my being there and not. So, take one away, and I am still there. Take another away; again, no problem. But after a while there are no cells at all. Indeed, as they have been replaced by nothing, in the relevant structures, it is unclear what will be there: perhaps, some salty water. Supposedly, I am still there. But given anything like the developed perspective of science, this is really quite absurd. Thus, the supposition of my existence has been reduced to an absurdity.

As before, it is important to discuss our third and final premiss. Because of the previous parallel discussion, various points may now be safely passed over. But a few new things arise in the present context which, even in a brief essay, are worthy of some consideration.

In the first place, it should be noted that, in the previous reasoning, about tables, we did not become involved in matters of identity, or persistence. There, I argued that *no* table, the same or any other, survived the decremental changes, and so *no* table existed in the first place. In contrast, the present argument does involve identity and, except for its counterfactual form, even persistence through time: I myself must survive. No new problems of importance are, I suggest, thus introduced for us. Indeed, we may abandon questions of identity entirely, and construct a general argument, upon the alleged existence of finite persons or beings, to parallel more completely our argument about tables. To play it safe with respect to such various forms as there may be of 'extra-terrestrial beings', we should then make our unit the atom, or even the particle, instead of the cell. It was to honour Descartes, so to say, and to pack the punch of particularity, that I focused the argument on myself, quite directly, thus becoming involved with identity. But that involvement is not essential.

In the second place, it will be maintained, I suppose, that my argument about tables did not involve considerations of life, or of consciousness. Let us grant this point. But how might such involvements as are now upon us serve to promote my own existence, or that of any finite being? I think there is no realistic way. Let us try to interpret our third premiss quite graphically, now, to clarify its import. On its most relevant interpretation, I suggest, life and consciousness, as well as the 'capacity' for them, will be present for as long as anyone might need to appreciate our argument's point. For it is supposed, in our third premiss, that the 'way' in which a cell is removed is one which is most innocuous and favourable – that is, with respect to me, or to my own identity. How might that happen?

At the present level of reasoning, the following scenario, I suggest, is more or less appropriate. At a certain stage in the decremental process, not very far along, it seems clear, life-support systems will be brought in to keep me going as well as possible. I shall be placed *in vitro*; nourishing fluids will be pumped into me; electrical stimulation will be provided, but not in such a way that any apparatus 'does my experiencing or thinking for me'; and so on. Cell after cell is pulled away. The remaining ones are kept alive, and kept functioning 'at the highest level of achievement of which they are capable'. The added apparatus has not, in the case here described, replaced the removed cells as part of me. In this present case, an electric wire will only be a means of support, much as a cardiac pacemaker serves even now. While *other cases* may be construed as involving the replacement of natural parts by synthetic ones, this present one is not correctly understood in such terms. Sticking to what might here most plausibly be considered myself, then, at a certain point we are down to a brain in a vat and, then, half a brain. So far, so good; but then we get down to a third of a brain, then a sixteenth. Still later, there are only fifty-three neurons in living combination. Where at the end, there is but one living nerve cell, and then it too is gone. Where will I disappear from the scene? Realistically, now, will the removal of a single cell ever, under such favourable conditions, mean my disappearance from reality? While that may be a 'logical possibility', it does not compel belief. The conclusion of our argument, in contrast, is quite compelling: I do not disappear at any time, because I was never around in the first place.

We may agree that at one time it may have been a very compelling thought that there were souls, or individual essences, one for each person. Many people even now believe in such things, and in minds, a life force, if not entelechies, ghosts, spirits, and so on. Many of these believers, I imagine, think that a person is not only real, but an immaterial, indivisible entity. Thus, I expect, they lay the ground for a hope in survival of bodily death, and perhaps even immortality. At the time of Descartes, for example, it may be that all of these suppositions fairly demanded or compelled credence. But they do not sit well, I suggest, with our developed scientific perspective. For that reason, I believe, they offer no compelling alternative now to the bleak conclusions drawn herein.

My sorites of decomposition, against my own existence, has, to be sure, required some speculative effort. But such speculation as there may be is, I submit, far from wild. Further, it does jar the mind, and lets us look anew at the process of cellular development. We may reason justly, then, about the embryo growing from a fertilised egg, and we may conclude again, less speculatively, that, just like you, I do not exist. Against this more 'natural' argument, some would object, I suppose, that I myself was once nothing but a fertilised egg. Now, while I admire attempts to be consistent, I think that, in the present case, the attempt has little to recommend it, and is in any case erroneous. If someone persists in such a thought, however, I should bid him consider whether even a sperm, or an egg, was any existing entity, much less a fertilised egg. Accumulation and decomposition arguments, it seems, may also be used to refute the supposed existence of any of them.

III. THE SUBSTANCE OF THE ARGUMENT AND THE IRRELEVANCE OF LOGICAL INVENTIONS

The main thrust of this argument is, in light of our scientific perspective, the same in my own case and in those of a table, a stone and, for that matter, even of a yo-yo. Let us reconsider the matter, then, with respect to alleged yo-yos, for they give us an example which is refreshingly light and calmly unemotional. Again the main issues seem to turn on a suitable third premiss:

> For anything there may be, if it is a yo-yo (which consists of many atoms, but a finite number), then the net removal of one atom, or only a few, in a way which is most innocuous and favorable, will not mean the difference as to whether there is a yo-yo in the situation.

Now, how could such a premiss as this be false, and untrue, and inaccurate and unacceptable? Apart from minor matters of formulation, there are, it seems clear, only two ways in which things might go wrong for it.

First, and more on 'the side of things in the world', it might be that nature protected yo-yos, or at least one of them, by giving it a place of its own in the world, set apart from other things, an essence if you please. But how might anything like this actually obtain? The matter is, I think, very important, so, even if we repeat some of our previous words, let us try to outline the possibilities. First, yo-yos would be protected if, either at the start or at some later point, we just could not take out any atoms from them. Or, being realistic, and supposing that that way is not available, they might still be saved if new atoms were to rush in whenever crucial old ones were extracted. Or if that is out, as it surely appears to be, it might be that at some point, even under the most favourable conditions for relevant gradualness, a spontaneous explosion should take place, a yo-yo's previous existence thus being preserved by such sudden destruction. Or, failing that, which does seem more in line with any actual experience of the world, a god on high, or a suitable natural law, might turn an endangered dwindling yo-yo into a sousaphone, perhaps upon the removal of the four million and twelfth atom, so that our concepts themselves would never have to be tested on its behalf. And so on; and so forth. There are, then, many logical possibilities for nature to conspire, as it were, so that things would fit our term 'yo-yo'. But we are confident that none of them actually obtain. To think otherwise, I should say, is to expect a miracle: if you will, a *miracle of metaphysical illusion*.

With the world being so unfavourable for them, as it surely seems to be, the only chance for yo-yos lies on 'the side of our terms and concepts'. But what can be expected here? At the very least, we need the concept of a yo-yo to be atomically precise. Certain concepts of molecules seem to be thus precise: when you snip a hydrogen atom off the end somewhere, and do not replace it, you no longer have in the situation a molecule of that original kind. But is the concept of a yo-yo relevantly like that? I think we ask too much of ourselves if we expect ourselves to be working here in such a precise manner. Accordingly, to suppose this much for ourselves and 'yo-yo' is to expect another miracle, perhaps a *miracle of conceptual comprehension*. On either hand, then, yo-yos require a miracle; for any who do not believe in miracles, there is no rational belief in yo-yos.

Our reasonings turn up for us an implicit contradiction in our beliefs. To strive to be reasonable we must give up one at least. To deny a suitable second premiss is to have yo-yos floating around with no atoms at all, nor any matter in the situation, and that is yet more miraculous than the two apparent wonders we have just considered. The only path to consistency, then, which is even remotely reasonable or realistic is to deny existence for alleged yo-yos, for we have just covered the whole story as to what wonders a commitment to them means. If this is appreciated we may see the irrelevance of remarks about clear cases, paradigms, family resemblances, and other soothing remedies, lately influential but now happily well on the wane. Perhaps more importantly, in these more technical times, we may also thus see the emptiness in the suggestion, currently favoured by certain philosophers, that we escape the argument by assigning to relevant sentences truth values other than truth and falsity.[3] For, whatever these values may be, they do not reduce one bit the miracles that yo-yos require; at most they occasion only a mildly different description of them.

Let us suppose we have before us a yo-yo. As atoms are removed one at a time, without replacement, we keep considering singular propositions each to the effect that at the appropriate new time a yo-yo is before us. We begin, as in any *reductio*, by assigning truth. As things progress, at some particular point, atomically counted, we are for the first time no longer to assign truth! Instead, when some peripheral atom is gently removed, and there would appear to be at least virtually no significant difference in what is before us, we are for the first time to depart from our initial kind of assignment, and to assign *some other* value. Perhaps the new value will not be falsity; it may be indefiniteness, or some numerical value just a shade less than unity, say 0.999, or some other newly invented candidate. But whatever else it is, there will be just as much of a miracle for us to expect. For, given that we have no miracle of metaphysical illusion to help us – that is, the world is indeed relevantly gradual – it will take a miraculous sensitivity on the part of 'yo-yo' to generate the difference, however we should choose to label such a wonderful discrimination. So sensitive is our concept of a yo-yo that, as a single atom goes away at the periphery, truth or unity or whatever is suddenly left behind! To expect that is, I submit, still to expect a miracle of conceptual comprehension. Hence, any new values, as well as the logical inventiveness they may occasion, are utterly irrelevant to the issues here.

Nor will it help matters to invoke a distinction between propositions and sentences, which may express or fail to express relevant propositions. Let us focus on the sentence 'There is a yo-yo before us now.' We may begin as before, with a putative paradigm yo-yo, and may then judge that our sentence expresses a proposition which is true. We then take off peripheral atoms, one at a time, and ask whether the sentence does something else, for the first time, with the removal of each single one. The supposition that with a single atom something else is for the first time done appears quite incredible, as well it should; it is but another form of our miracle of conceptual comprehension. But if this miracle may not be expected, then, if the sentence is not to express a truth with no atoms before us, we must conclude that our sentence never expresses a truth.[4]

Concerning the question of our putative yo-yos, then, it appears that only two responses are relevant: a belief in the miraculous or else an acceptance of nihilism. And the same choice, I submit, is there with alleged tables, and stones, and even my very own self. No matter how it is looked at, there is not much of a choice here. Habit and emotion appear on one side, while reason seems to be on quite the other.

IV. THE SCOPE OF THESE PROBLEMS

The argument I have employed derives, of course, from 'the paradox of the heap', an ancient problem devised by Eubulides, the great Megarian thinker. In way of reconstruction, we might say that Eubulides showed that there were and are no heaps. First, we may suppose the existence of heaps. Secondly, we note that, if any heap exists, it consists of various other entities – of grains of sand, or of beans, for example. Finally, we note that, if one bean is removed without replacement, and this is done most favourably and innocuously, what remains will be a heap. Thus, given anything like our view of reality, heaps, which many suppose to be ordinary existing things, are only fictions: there are no heaps.

I shall not here bother to detail the differences and similarities between Eubulides's original argument and my own variations upon it. So far as the compelling force goes, though, suffice it to say that our modern scientific perspective means that there is little difference between a heap and almost anything else, so to say, including myself. As far as repercussions or consequences are concerned, however, my own arguments are of course enormously more effective than the original version. While this is rather obvious, the details may be worth some presentation.

First, virtually all of our common-sense beliefs are untrue, and even as to nothing. Moreover, most of our learned studies are similarly unfortunate, at least in anything like their present formulations. Samuel Wheeler begins to put the point in a manner which is conjectural, and perhaps somewhat ironic: 'If there is no objective difference between possible persons and possible non-persons, much of what we believe about morality, psychology, etc., is in trouble.'[5] We may say, now, that the matter is not very conjectural, and that all of moral reasoning, as well as psychological understanding, looks to be in deep trouble indeed. This holds as well, of course, for the other studies concerning man. History, law and medicine are all a tissue of fictions, as are economics, linguistics and politics. Various related areas of philosophy, such as epistemology, the philosophy of language and the philosophy of mind, can contain nothing sound and true. Unless mathematics is clearly severed from connections with human beings, it too must fall prey to our sorites. Various other studies look to fare poorly. Biology, for example, is a tissue of nonentities and untruth, except as it becomes biochemistry perhaps, or something much of that sort. Astronomy too, except as it becomes astrophysics, or something similar, looks to be about anything but our universe.

Under a second head, we may notice that, while they may in some respects involve language importantly, our sorites arguments undermine all natural languages, while the argument of Eubulides hardly begins to do anything here. In the first place, as there are no human beings, there is no human language or thought. Waiving that basic point, and supposing the opposite, we shall notice that our existing expressions, at least by and large, fail to make any contact with whatever is there. For example, the proper names so far given do not refer to anything real. We may confirm this by a sorites argument directly involving such famous nonentities as Cicero, Descartes, Venus, Everest, and so on. Should someone name an individual atom 'Adam', things might be different on this score. The personal pronouns, we have seen, fare little better. Except for atoms, and so on, none of our referential devices look to be of much distinction.

But then, too, the picture looks bleak for the question of whether atoms exist, and so for any other things. For we cannot, in good faith, long waive the point that there is no human language or thought, nor even any human or other finite beings. And from such a standpoint even simple arithmetic looks to be beyond comprehension, there being none of us to grasp any realities or truth which might be there. Finally, the existence of any sorites arguments themselves cannot be relevantly affirmed, there being not a one of us ever to consider any such piece of reasoning. The chain of nihilistic propositions appears to come full circle.

This undeniable absurdity is, I suggest, no blameworthy fault of our Eubulidean reasonings. On the contrary, by such means, our sorites arguments allow us to perceive the truly thoroughgoing inconsistencies in our available language and thought. Continuing to speak in the paradoxical manner they expose, we might say this. For anything like truth's sake, these arguments counsel us to begin a radical reconstruction of our means of thought and expression. No available earthly means, which is sufficiently rich for many of our purposes, fares any better than does English. I have been disclosing no peculiar subtleties of our language which may be absent in Chinese, or in ancient Greek. But what steps should we take to make things better?

With something like a heap, and sticking to Eubulides's original level of argument, moderately good steps can be taken quickly and easily. For, if there are no heaps, we can define the word 'hoap', for example, so that a hoap may consist, minimally, of two items: for example, beans or grains of sand, touching each other. But, if there are no tables, trees or cats, what are we supposed to define; and, even very roughly, what is to be the definition of it? If I do not exist, then what does exist in which, so to speak, I should have an appropriate and rather intense interest? If you do not exist, as is here argued, what does exist over there which must not be inappropriately interfered with, or harmed? I am truly in darkness on these momentous matters, with no light at all to guide me.

These problems are, I believe, of the first importance for any who value philosophy and the traditional quest after truth. But I am far from sanguine that my challenge, from which they flow, will be met with an attempt to reply which is properly serious, let alone rationally effective. For it is easiest to shun the most pervasive difficulties in philosophy, to leave it to others, in times long to come, to explain their solutions. It is easiest to presume we know in advance, without knowing the details, which way the answer *must* go, letting the social acceptance of others serve as our assurance and even foundation, rather than anything like the light of one's own reason. But I am hopeful that one or two thoughtful souls may break the common easy pattern. Perhaps they will allow me to avoid the labours, apparently painful and fruitless, involved in developing an adequate philosophy of nihilism, which it now appears is the only adequate philosophy there can be. Or perhaps, on the contrary, they will provide me with further reason for thinking that this challenge is too powerful to be met adequately, and that there is no rational hope at all for the thought that anyone might be real. That might not be cheerful, but at least it would be something. Either way, I doubt that Eubulides ever had it so good.[6]

NOTES

1. A. J. Ayer, *The Problem of Knowledge* (London: Macmillan, 1956) p.50.
2. Samuel C. Wheeler III, 'Reference and Vagueness', *Synthèse*, xxx (1967) no. 3–4 367–79.
3. A recent example of a philosopher who would treat of vagueness by means of exotic truth values is David H. Sanford in his 'Borderline Logic', *American Philosophical Quarterly*, xii, (1975) no. 1, 29–39. Sanford provides references to other writers of a similar persuasion.
4. On these matters, I am indebted to discussion with David Sanford.
5. Wheeler, in *Synthese*, xxx, no. 3–4, 371.
6. I have been helped in writing this paper by discussion with various people; Ralph Silverman and Samuel Wheeler deserve special thanks.
   For a discussion of related matters, I refer the reader to my paper, 'There are No Ordinary Things'. Forthcoming in *Synthese*. For a detailed analysis of sorites arguments, see my 'Why There are No People', forthcoming in *Midwest Studies in Philosophy*, vol. iv: *Studies in Metaphysics*. And, for a discussion of relations between the nihilistic approach of this present paper and the sceptical approach in epistemology, see my 'Skepticism and Nihilism', forthcoming in *Nous*.

11 Another Time, Another Place, Another Person

BERNARD WILLIAMS

In *Language, Truth and Logic* Ayer proceeded on the basis that a sentence uttered by A on a given occasion, if it was to have empirical meaning, had to make a statement which was verifiable by A on that occasion, and this led to the well known reduction of statements about the past to statements about present evidence, and of third-personal statements about the mental to statements about observable behaviour.

Later[1] he moved to the position of saying that there is no class of statements which are statements about the past or about other minds, just as there is no class of statements which are statements about elsewhere. One and the same statement is made by one who speaks of a given event from a future, a present or a past perspective. An utterance using token-reflexive devices can be seen as doing two things at once: 'by combining a description of the event in question with a reference to the temporal position of the speaker, the use of tenses brings together two pieces of information which are logically distinct'.[2] This doctrine he employed to reject the reductionist views of *Language, Truth and Logic*: 'propositions about the past are not about the present or future: they are about the past', he rather misleadingly put it at one point,[3] meaning by that not the denial of what he had just asserted, but that such propositions are about the events they seem to be about, and not about some other and later events.

The theory starts, then, with *token sentences* (type sentences used on a given occasion by a given speaker), and uses, in effect, the notion of a *convergent* set of such sentences – where a set of token sentences is convergent if[4] all its members have, with regard to reference secured by token-reflexive devices, the same reference, and otherwise are synonymous. (A convergent set of token sentences can be regarded as having as members more than actually uttered sentences: we can identify type sentences, occasions and speakers, such that token sentences determined by these items can be conceived and assigned to a set, though not actually uttered – and no doubt type sentence and occasion alone may serve to locate a merely possible speaker as well.) The members of what I am calling a convergent set of token sentences are said by Ayer to have the same factual content[5] and to convey the same information (apart from the information about the speaker's perspective),[6] and he is prepared to say that in a way they have the same meaning,[7] though this is subject to the obvious reservation that there is an everyday application of 'meaning' under which members of a convergent set can have different meanings, as '*S*(. . . I . . .)' would naturally be said to have a different meaning from '*S*(. . . he . . .)' even when the first is said by *A* and the second is said by someone of *A*.

As we have seen, Ayer is disposed to see each member of the convergent set as both offering a common-core statement or proposition – in the simplest case, asserting it – and as revealing at the same time the perspective from which the proposition is, in each case, offered. In fact, he goes beyond this[8] in supposing, further, that it must be possible to represent the core proposition in its own right, so to speak, in the form of what I shall call a *neutral sentence*. Since a neutral sentence presents the proposition to which token-reflexive devices express particular approaches, it is itself free from all token-reflexive devices. With respect to time, the neutral sentence is what Quine calls an eternal sentence, a sentence which cannot change its truth value. Hence, on Ayer's theory, there lies behind the apparatus of token-reflexive speech a representation of the world *sub specie aeternitatis*, a representation of it as seen from no point of view (time, place, person) rather than any other; and the neutral sentences form this representation.

It is important to stress the point that this goes beyond the mere requirements of statement identity. We could understand the idea of a convergent set, and assign token sentences to such sets, without supposing that there could be a neutral sentence which represented their common eternal, impersonal, and so on, content. A consequence of this stronger view is that, if there is a sense in which all the members of a convergent set have the same meaning, then the neutral sentence at their core gives the meaning which they all have – a claim which seems less inviting than the claim, merely, that there is a sense in which they all have the same meaning. If we stick to their having the same 'factual content', however, it seems more acceptable to say that the members of the convergent set, and the core neutral sentence, share the same factual content: for one thing, there seems room for the idea that theoretical material might occur in characterising the factual content of both the neutral sentence and the everyday token-reflexive sentences which constitute the convergent set. (The question of theoretical material in the neutral sentence is one I shall touch on later.)

Ayer seems, in fact, to have made a further demand on the neutral sentence: that its non-logical vocabulary should consist only of descriptions, and should eliminate not only the token-reflexive expressions which it is required *ex hypothesi* to eliminate, but also all proper names. It may be, indeed, that Ayer has regarded this not as a further demand, but as following from the identity of factual content. He expresses a related idea in terms of the notion of descriptive adequacy: 'since what can be described in a language depends only on what predicates it contains, replacing indicators by predicates can never impoverish a language descriptively'.[9] The general doctrine, and any reasons there may be for it, need not concern us here; but there is a particular application of it, with regard to persons, which we shall encounter a little later.

There is one further point to be made about this apparatus, concerning the interpretation of token reflexives. I am taking 'token-reflexive' fairly broadly, in a sense in which 'now' is token-reflexive just because it is a rule of its meaning that, if you are to know what time is in question on an occasion of its utterance, you have to know when it is uttered. Ayer takes the token-reflexivity of 'now' in the strict sense that the token-reflexive reference is to be explained in terms of the token utterance, so that 'now' is actually explicated as 'at the same time as this utterance', and 'past', consequently, comes out as meaning 'earlier than this utterance'. But (even leaving aside Prior's well known difficulty of the content, on this account, of 'Thank God that's over') it is very doubtful that as an explication this will possibly do. Surely it is only in virtue of having already grasped 'now' that you can be led to the very special, variable application of 'this utterance' which is needed for this account. But this is a side issue in relation to the construction of convergent sets as such; it is a separate issue which token-reflexive expressions, and how many, are primitive.

We may now turn to the question of the verification of the neutral sentence. Let a given neutral sentence S state the occurrence of an event E_{jk} as occurring at place P_j at time T_k. It is assumed that there is an optimal verification point (OVP) for S. It is further assumed that this point is the space–time position (P_j, T_k). We shall accept the first assumption, leaving the possibility open, however, that the OVP for given S need not be unique. The second assumption, however, raises doubts. It is common ground, of course, that P_j and T_k will not be independently optimal: thus the time of verification T_k may be the best time only if one is at P_j, and the place of verification P_j the best place only if one is there at T_k. But, apart from that, relative to what order of assumptions is the combination (P_j, T_k) optimal for the verification of S – that is to say, the observation (if S is true) of E_{jk}? It may be said that it is a necessary truth that (P_j, T_k) is the origin of information about the event E_{jk}, and that in principle information must decay between (P_j, T_k) and any other at least moderately distant point. But this raises the question of what level of principle gives this result, and relative to what methods of verification or observation the 'information' – as genuinely knowledge-giving information – may be thought to decay. It might be thought that it was relative to some deep laws of nature that information decayed away from the origin; but then equally it could be relative to no less deep laws of nature that the event point was, for instance, not a possible point of observation at all, such as that which cosmologists call the first few seconds of the universe. Certainly this is not a question which can just be disposed of with a distinction between 'in practice' and 'in principle', like the old difficulty for phenomenalism about the hypothetical observer in whose presence Crippen would not have murdered his wife.[10]

It is hard to see in fact how the notion of an OVP (for a given kind of event, and hence – surely – for a given kind of observation) can be freed from empirical, or at any rate non-logical, considerations. But, if that is right, then some part of the traditional sceptical problem which has worried Ayer seems to evaporate. One thing that worries the sceptic, as Ayer represents him, is that, short of full-blown verification, grounds for merely probable or reasonable belief in the event cannot be found at all. But if the notion of full-blown verification implies the notion of an OVP, and the notion of an OVP, or rather the use of that notion in any given concrete kind of case, involves the kind of consideration just mentioned, that set of considerations might equally be expected to yield the idea of points other than the OVP from which observations might be gained – giving less than full-blown verification but leading to reasonable belief. The understanding, which is needed to set up the problem, that certain positions are disadvantaged relative to the OVP, could yield an understanding of why and how they are disadvantaged – and that is something which can give a backing to probable belief.

The treatment of scepticism is not my concern; but the present point has a wider application. It leads, in fact, to one paradox of positivism. For positivism, meaning has to be given in terms of verification, and meaning has to be prior to fact. Verification, moreover, has to be explicated, especially for positivism, in terms of observation. But what we understand about observation and its relations to different kinds of event is not totally prior to fact. We are left with unclear empirical assumptions in the concept of verification.

It is not easy to judge the extent of the purely necessary dimensions of the notion of an OVP. Relative to the propositions that causes precede effects and that all information is an effect, it is necessary that the present time does not contain the OVP for a sentence about an event which lies in the future. It is rather less obvious, relative to those assumptions, that the same is true with respect to all sentences about events which lie in the past. Other problems arise about what is happening elsewhere. It is not clear, moreover, to what extent the absolutely pure conception of verification is entitled to those assumptions themselves.

We shall leave these points, however, and consider what follows when we have identified some non-optimal verification points for a given event – allowing that, for many kinds of event, at least, being in the past or elsewhere relative to a given observer puts it away from the OVP for that observer. Ayer has worried a good deal about the conditions under which such an event could nevertheless be said to be verifiable by me, if I am that observer – where 'verifiable by me' means 'might in principle have been verified by me'. Thus, what is now happening elsewhere from where I am cannot, as things are, be (optimally) verified by me, since if I am at P_j at T_k, then necessarily I am not at $P_{j'}(j' \neq j)$ at T_k, nor is there anything I can now do to bring it about that I am there at just that time. But this is only a relative necessity. It is not necessary that I am at P_j at T_k, and in particular I might have been at $P_{j'}$ at T_k. This satisfies the demand for verifiability in principle by me.

A different application of what at first looks like the same thing occurs with the past. If E_i occurred at T_i (T_i earlier than T_k) then there is nothing I can do at T_k to bring it about that at T_k or later I optimally verify E_i. But I might have optimally verified it. It is even conceivable, perhaps, that I might have existed much earlier than I actually exist, so that it is conceivable that I might have verified events which occurred long before my actual birth-date.[11] This last idea involves of course a contrary-to-fact possibility, as did the issue of the verifiability in principle of what is elsewhere. But it is notable that, in the case of the past of my own lifetime, the possibility of having verified the event directly is not necessarily contrary to fact. Perhaps I actually did observe the event in question.

This consideration raises a problem about this whole set of procedures. Do these questions about what I can conceive as verifiable by me involve in any way my knowledge? The point, mentioned by Ayer, that there is an increasing difficulty in my conceiving my displacement to more remote times may imply that the thought experiment is to be regarded as one for me, and bounded by my knowledge of my own lifetime and circumstances. But relative to that perspective, no question about the verifiability in principle by me of my own remembered past seems to arise – I just did verify the propositions in question. I conceive myself in terms to which memory has already been given, before I embark on thought experiments about what may or may not be verifiable by me.

If, on the other hand, the question of verifiability by me can be considered from a purely neutral point of view, as an instance of verifiability by X, then it is quite unclear why conceivable verifiability by *me* is an issue at all, and not just a misplaced hangover from earlier views in the context of the 'neutral sentences' theory. Regarded from the outside, from the neutral point of view, it is of no interest at all for these problems whether an individual who actually exists at T_k, me, could in principle be extended or displaced temporally backwards to a time T_i earlier than T_k, so as to encounter an event E_i conceived from the neutral point of view as occurring then. If the neutral point of view is comprehensible to us at all, then the very most that could count from that point of view, surely, is that someone could directly verify E_i at T_i, and the whole issue of whether that person might conceivably have been me totally falls out of the question.

An ambivalence related to this is displayed in some of Ayer's arguments about other minds. Here he thinks that we have at least the same relative impossibility as with space: if I am the person with characteristics C, and you are the person with contrary characteristics C', then necessarily I am not you. Indeed, in a sense, under all circumstances I am necessarily not you, since 'I' and 'you' are deployed only by and with regard to persons characterised severally by such characteristics. However, it seems not to follow that I could not have had C': 'so long as I do not limit the possibilities by forming a picture of myself with which anything that I imagine has to be reconciled, I can conceive of having any consistent set of characteristics that you please. All that is required is that the possession of the characteristics be something that is in itself empirically verifiable.'[12] Earlier Ayer had thought that there might be some limits to what was conceivable in this

direction, some properties being taken as constitutive of oneself;
but this limit could be lightly lifted, since the question of what
was constitutive of oneself was itself conventional, arbitrary, and
to be decided on the spot.[13]

I shall not discuss the issue of how the notion of an OVP
applies at all to the question of psychological states, nor whether
Ayer is right in using the familiar model that one who is in pain
is in the best position for verifying that he is in pain. Using that
model, Ayer conceives verifiability in principle by me as the possibility that I might conceivably have satisfied the descriptions C′
which actually characterise you, and in those circumstances would
or would not have found myself (so to speak) in pain. Now it
is extremely unclear that Ayer has the right at all on his views
of token reflexives and the descriptive eliminability of indicator
words to describe this situation as that of *my* satisfying C′ – any
more than the conceivable situation of my being at P_j rather than,
as I am, at P_j would be a situation of P_j being here. Rather,
under Ayer's assumptions, the situation emerges as that of your
existing and my not doing so. At the very least, it cannot make
the slightest difference which way the situation is described, on
those assumptions: the 'factual content' will be the same, there
will be no 'descriptive difference'. Then verifiability by me finally
drops out: verifiability is the most that can be left.

This is just a special application of what has already been emerg-
ing: that there is a very poor fit between, on the one hand, the
matter of verification by me, which in the form of *conceivable*
verification by me, continued to preoccupy Ayer, and on the other
hand, the *sub specie aeternitatis* view of the world, with its descriptive
content embodied in neutral sentences. This is a second paradox
of positivism. The empiricist element pulls back to the egocentric
predicament, while the respect for the physicist's world-view leads
to the eternal or neutral conception of the world. Ayer sees the
neutral-sentences model as the correct model for science and equally
as a representation of the world as it is in itself, as opposed to
the various perspectives we have on it. This honours the commit-
ments of positivism as *wissenschaftliche Weltauffassung*. But the
role of verifiability by me, even of conceivable verifiability by me,
in relation to this model is incurably anomalous. In grasping the
neutral model, I already have the idea of a world of events, some
of which, from my particular location inside it, I may conceivably
verify or have verified, others not.

The issue, then, can at most be verifiability *by someone*. But
difficult questions remain about what force can be given even to
that in the context of the neutral-sentences view and, more generally,

in the context of a philosophy which tries to represent adequately a scientific view of the world. These difficulties present themselves differently depending on what motivation is assumed for the demand for verifiability. I believe that some version of them will always emerge under any verificationist assumptions; but I shall confine myself here to a kind of difficulty which arises specifically from the sort of interest Ayer has had in verifiability.

For Ayer, the motivation towards verificationism lay in the epistemological concerns of empiricism: verification was seen in terms of observation, and observation in terms of perception, and it was this consideration that underlay the approach to meaning. Even after the demands of the strongest reductive verificationism had been relaxed, the meaning of empirical sentences was to be controlled by what they could mean for us in terms of our experience. But, from the perspective of the neutral model, the question must arise of the respects in which our experience may itself be misleading or partial.

At a particular level, the neutral-sentences model admits this fact: any person's actual situation will be remote from the OVP for various events. Moreover, the model, or rather the philosophical explanations that go with it, even provide one quite pervasive sense in which our experience is misleading: it is metaphysically misleading, since it naturally presents the world to us as being other than as it is correctly displayed in the neutral-sentences model. But these considerations do not take us far enough. In the neutral-sentences model, all disadvantages of an observation point tend to be assimilated to the disadvantages of location: if one is not at the OVP, one is *elsewhere*. This emerges in the problems about temporal displacement we have already considered. It applies, in a way, to the problem of other minds: the observer is pictured, even if obscurely, as not being at the site of the psychological action. Earlier, I suggested that there was an empirical element in the notion of an OVP at all, and that question arises even when the idea of a better or worse observation point is considered, in this way, solely in terms of displacement. But it is far more so when the inquiry is extended, as it should be, beyond the displacement picture to the matter of the general quality or character of our perceptual experience. It is then a question not just of being at the right place at the right time, but of what happens to one when one is.

Scientific understanding can be expected to yield a critique of experience in the light of theory, and certain general aspects of our experience will be seen from that to be strongly influenced by our make-up. This goes importantly beyond the particular disad-

vantages of particular locations. The neutral-sentences model tries
to view all events from the outside, from no particular point of
view, but it will remain crucially flawed if it does not address
itself to the question of the terms in which the events which form
the contents of the model are to be characterised; how theoretical
the characterisation of them should be; how far it must abstract
from peculiarities of the human perception of the world. The objective of giving a representation of the world which is not a representation from here or from any other particular perspective will not
have been achieved, even after abstraction from time and place,
if the terms in which the representation is given are peculiarly
our perceptual terms – or, peculiarly, anyone else's. That would
be only another perspectival distortion. The aim of overcoming
that distortion could not in principle be achieved by verificationist
empiricism, and this provides a reason why (even when verifiability
by me is no longer the issue) its relation to the neutral-sentences
model must be incoherent.

Verificationism of this kind must be incoherent in relation not
just to the neutral-sentences model, but to any view which seeks
to offer what may be called an 'absolute' representation of the
world, in the sense (ambitious enough, but less ambitious than
some other senses that have been given to the expression) of a
representation of the world as it is, as opposed to how it peculiarly
appears to any group in virtue of that group's peculiarities.[14] Some
will doubt that any such absolute picture of the world can be
achieved, and in particular that it can be achieved by scientific
inquiry. But those who have hoped for a philosophy centred on
the scientific world-view have not doubted this, but have rather
based their philosophy on a hopeful vision of a scientific picture
of the world just because they thought, and with reason, that
such a picture was the only thing that could achieve an absolute
representation of things. It has been thought, and certainly thought
by positivists, that the positivist attachment to verifiability was
connected with its objective of being a philosophy of the scientific
world-view. But, if the present line of argument is right, the verificationist bias of positivism constituted, on the contrary, a basic obstacle to its being such a philosophy.

NOTES

1. Principally in 'Statements about the Past' and 'One's Knowledge of Other
Minds', both repr. in A. J. Ayer, *Philosophical Essays* (London: Macmillan, 1954);
and in A. J. Ayer, *The Problem of Knowledge* (London: Macmillan, 1956; Harmondsworth: Penguin, 1956). Because of the kind of points I want to discuss, I have

concentrated on Ayer's work of this period, ten to twenty years after *Language, Truth and Logic*, 1st edn (London: Gollancz, 1936). There is no suggestion that these were Ayer's final views on these subjects.

2. Ayer, *Problem*, Penguin edn, p. 180.

3. Ayer, 'One's Knowledge', in *Philosophical Essays*, p. 201.

4. Only a sufficient condition is offered; there is no need here to involve ourselves in the general problems of statement identity, in particular with regard to reference secured by expressions other than token reflexives.

5. Ayer, 'Statements', in *Philosophical Essays*, p. 186; cf. Ayer, *Problems*, pp. 179, 180.

6. Ayer, 'Statements', in *Philosophical Essays*, p. 187.

7. Ibid., p. 186; cf. Ayer, *Problem*, Penguin edn, pp. 180–1.

8. That there is a further step here is brought about by Michael Dummett in his *Frege: Philosophy of Language* (London: Duckworth, 1973).

9. A. J. Ayer, 'Individuals', repr. in *Philosophical Essays*, p. 21. The 'since' presumably introduces an inference, but I confess I find it hard to find an inference here which is not either question-begging or invalid.

10. A. J. Ayer, 'Phenomenalism', repr. in *Philosophical Essays*, pp. 151–2.

11. For example, Ayer, *Problem*, Penguin edn, p. 178.

12. Ibid., p. 249.

13. Ayer, 'One's Knowledge', in *Philosophical Essays*, pp. 211–12. '. . . whether it is conceivable that I should satisfy some description which I actually do not . . . will depend on what properties I choose, for the occasion, to regard as constitutive of myself . . . it is contradictory only if one chooses to make it so.

14. I have tried to say some more about this conception, its history and its present situation, in *Descartes: The Project of Pure Enquiry* (Harmondsworth: Penguin, 1978).

12 Ayer on Metaphysics

STEPHAN KÖRNER

At the beginning of the Introduction to the second edition of his important and influential *Language, Truth and Logic*, Ayer admits that the questions with which it deals are not in all respects so simple as it makes them appear. At the same time he reiterates his conviction that the point of view which it expresses is substantially correct. This attitude – not uncommon among philosophers whose first book is not their last – has in particular inspired the development of Ayer's views on metaphysics, which are the main topic of the present essay. Its aim is to argue that not only his early rejection of metaphysics as meaningless but also the later modification of his original view are open to serious objections; and to sketch an alternative account of the structure and function of metaphysics.

The essay thus falls into two sections, of which the first discusses the positivist thesis that metaphysics is meaningless (subsection 1); the thesis that metaphysical propositions are, or are dependent on, linguistic rules (2); and, lastly, the thesis that metaphysical systems are 'secondary', explanatory systems (3). Section II contains a brief characterisation of cognitive (as opposed to practical) metaphysical principles (subsection 1) and a discussion of their function as criteria of intelligibility, and the acceptability of explanations (2). It ends by showing that this account of metaphysics occupies a middle position between anti-metaphysical positivism and absolute metaphysics and has in this respect some affinity with the spirit of Ayer's later metaphysical views (3).

I

(1) *On the thesis that metaphysics is meaningless.* In any discussion of the nature of metaphysics, it is advisable to have before one's mind some suitable examples of 'metaphysical sentences', i.e. sentences which appear to express genuine propositions and (and yet) belong to metaphysics. The following selection of sentences seems

fair, since each of them has been regarded by some contemporary philosophers and at least one great philosopher of the past as expressing a metaphysical proposition.

(a) The principle of continuity to the effect that *natura non facit saltus*, especially in the version that all laws of nature are expressible by continuous functions. (Accepted by Leibniz and Kant, rejected by Bohr and some contemporary philosophers of science.)
(b) The principle that there are actually infinite sets – for example the set $\{1, 2, 3, \ldots\}$ of all integers. (Accepted by Plato and Gödel, rejected by Kant and some contemporary philosophers of mathematics.)
(c) The principle of excluded middle. (Accepted by Aristotle, rejected by Kant and by some contemporary philosophers of logic.[1])
(d) The thesis that there is a God, as conceived by, for example, Thomas Aquinas.

It seems further advisable to distinguish in a preliminary manner between those genuine or alleged metaphysical propositions which are 'immanent' – more precisely, immanent in common-sense empirical discourse, science, mathematics or logic – and those which are transcendent, i.e. not immanent. A genuine or alleged metaphysical proposition is immanent in one of these fields of inquiry if, although it is accepted in it, it cannot be established by it. The Newtonian physicist, who accepts the principle of continuity, the Cantorian set-theorist, who accepts the principle of infinity, and the classical logician, who accepts the principle of excluded middle (or a proposition with which it is deductively equivalent), cannot establish these principles as they establish the theorems of Newtonian physics, of Cantorian set-theory or of classical logic.

The original anti-metaphysical thesis of Ayer and other logical positivists follows from a statement to which many, if not all, metaphysicians would assent and a definition of significant or meaningful propositions. Ayer states that metaphysical sentences express neither tautologies nor empirical hypotheses and he defines a sentence as being meaningful or significant if, and only if, it expresses either a tautology or an empirical hypothesis. The conclusion implied by the fairly uncontroversial statement and the definition reads, in Ayer's words, 'And as tautologies and empirical hypotheses form the entire class of significant propositions, we are justified in concluding that all metaphysical assertions are nonsense.'[2]

There is no need to recall at length the cogent, but by now

rather hackneyed, arguments which forced Ayer, Carnap and other logical positivists to modify their position. It became, in particular, soon obvious that on any of the usual interpretations of its key terms – namely, 'tautology' and 'empirical hypothesis' – the original anti-metaphysical thesis is itself neither a tautology nor an empirical hypothesis, and hence, if one accepts the definition, meaningless.

Confronted with this *reductio ad absurdum*, the logical positivists could and did adopt one of two different strategies or some combination of them. The first consists in attempts at redefining all or some of the key terms of their original argument – 'tautology', 'empirical hypothesis', 'significant sentence' – in such a manner that, while in the newly stipulated sense the thesis becomes meaningful, as many metaphysical sentences as possible remain meaningless. The second strategy consists in undertaking a fresh examination of the structure of metaphysical principles and of their function in the thinking of scientists, mathematicians and logicians, as well as in common-sense thinking and in protecting this examination from the influence of those metaphysicians who claim that their metaphysics is the absolute truth and of those positivists who claim that all metaphysics is nonsense. Ayer's strategy has been a combination of attempts at conservative redefinition with attempts at independent re-examination, with a growing emphasis on the latter.

The change of emphasis seems to have been partly owing to the growing influence of pragmatism on the logical positivists, especially of the pragmatist theory of meaning according to which differences in meaning manifest themselves as differences in practice. It is in any case clear that at least some metaphysical propositions – for example, those given here as examples of immanent metaphysical propositions, make such a difference. The physicist who accepts and the physicist who rejects that all laws of nature are expressible by continuous functions will search for, and construct, different physical theories. Similar remarks apply to the mathematician who accepts and the mathematician who rejects actual infinities as well as to the logician who accepts and the logician who rejects the law of excluded middle. That the acceptance or rejection of transcendent metaphysical sentences – for example, that God exists – also makes a difference to practice does not disturb the logical positivists. For, while they acknowledge that the pursuit of science, mathematics and logic, to which immanent metaphysics is relevant, results in true or false propositions, they consider the activities to which the sentences of transcendent metaphysics are relevant – among which they would include the writing of religious poetry, the composition of religious music and the persecution of religious

dissenters – as having no similarly direct connection with the search
for truth.

(2) *On the thesis that* a priori *propositions, including the meaningful
propositions of metaphysics, are linguistic rules or dependent on the
acceptance of such rules.* The most conservative defence against
the *reductio ad absurdum* of the original anti-metaphysical thesis
consisted in interpreting metaphysical propositions as *a priori* propositions and to characterise *a priori* propositions as linguistic rules.
The weakness of this view is most obvious if one considers its
simplest version – namely, that all *a priori* propositions are stipulative definitions permitting the interchangeability of a defined expression, such as 'male parent', with a defining expression, such as
'father', in all linguistic contexts. For, even if we identify the stipulative definition, such as of 'father', with an *a priori* proposition,
such as that 'Being a father' is logically equivalent with 'Being
a male parent', the stipulative definition is useful only if the defined
and, hence, the defining expression is applicable. More precisely,
what makes the stipulation that 'father' and 'male parent' be interchangeable, useful, and, say, the stipulation that 'squircle' and
'square circle' be interchangeable, useless – except in paedagogic
contexts such as providing counter-examples to the proper function
of metaphysics – is that only the former and not the latter has
an extra-linguistic application. To consider stipulative definitions
and other linguistic rules only syntactically, i. e. as rules governing
the use of linguistic expressions independently of their extra-linguistic application and not also semantically, i. e. as applying to extra-
linguistic structures, was characteristic of those logical positivists
who understood logic after the fashion of Carnap's *Logical Syntax
of Language.*

Ayer very briefly accepted the view that *a priori* propositions
are linguistic rules in the sense that 'they do not describe how
words are actually used, but merely prescribe how words are to
be used'.[3] In place of this account which he abandoned because,
as he put it, *a priori* propositions 'can properly be said to be
true, which linguistic rules cannot', and are 'necessary, whereas
linguistic rules are arbitrary', he puts another account, according
to which *a priori* propositions are necessary 'only because the relevant linguistic rules are presupposed'. The new account is illustrated
by two examples, of which the first is here quoted in full:

Thus it is a contingent, empirical fact that the word 'earlier'
is used in English to mean earlier, and it is an arbitrary, though
convenient, rule of language that words that stand for temporal

relations are to be used transitively; but given this rule, the proposition that A is earlier than B and B is earlier than C, A is earlier than C becomes a necessary truth.

The other example concerns the *a priori* proposition '$q \cdot \supset \cdot p \supset q$' of *Principia Mathematica*, which according to Ayer is necessarily true because 'it is a contingent, empirical fact that the sign "$\supset$" should have been given the meaning that it has' and because 'the rules which govern the use of this sign are conventions which are neither true nor false'.[4]

Yet the new account is also unsatisfactory in that it does not even enable one to distinguish between contingent propositions and the necessary propositions of logic. What Ayer says about his examples of *a priori* propositions applies equally to other true propositions as expressed in some language. It is, for example, a contingent fact that the words 'Some', 'Englishmen', 'are', 'philosophers' (that the symbols 'p', '$\supset$', 'q') are used in English (in the language of *Principia Mathematica*) to mean what they do mean, and it is an arbitrary, though convenient conjunction of rules that the words (symbols) are to be used as prescribed by it. Yet clearly 'Some Englishmen are philosophers' ('$p \supset q$') is not *a priori*.

Like the attempt to derive the necessity of *a priori* propositions from stipulative definitions, the new account confuses a syntactical relation between accepted linguistic rules and linguistic expressions with a semantic relation between linguistic expressions and extra-linguistic entities. More precisely, it is necessary – and, moreover, logically necessary – that, if a conjunction of linguistic rules r governs the use of the symbols used in a sentence f, and if a person S as a matter of contingent fact accepts r, then S's uttering (or writing down) f is correct with respect to r. Yet this syntactical correctness of sentences within which one may further distinguish between a sentence's being well-formed and its being in addition a formal (syntactical) theorem, does not *in general* imply anything about the truth of the sentence with respect to an extra-linguistic structure or about its validity, i. e. truth with respect to all extra-linguistic structures of a certain kind. Only in very special cases does (the syntactic property of) being a formal theorem imply (the semantic property of) being valid.

Turning from logically necessary, *a priori* propositions to metaphysical *a priori* propositions – such as the examples of the principle of continuity, which is accepted by some metaphysicians and philosophers of science, and of the negation of this principle, which is accepted by others – the new account seems even more obscure. It is in particular not clear in which sense a person who accepts and a person who rejects the principle accept different linguistic rules for the use of the words (symbols) occurring in the linguistic formulation of the principle and its negation.

That the *a priori* character of meaningful metaphysical propositions cannot be derived from the acceptance of linguistic rules does not preclude the possibility of deriving it from rules of which, at least, some are not linguistic – a possibility explored to some extent by Peirce, who in turn acknowledged his indebtedness to Kant's philosophy, especially the *Transcendental Dialectics*. In his *The Central Questions of Philosophy*, published in 1973, Ayer adopts such an approach and characterises it as follows.[5] First, a metaphysical theory is not a 'primary system', i. e. a system which contains only 'purely factual propositions' describing what is 'actually observable', but a 'secondary system' which 'goes beyond the primary, in that it legislates for possible as well as actual cases and can also contain terms which are not directly related to anything observable'. Secondly, we are, Ayer thinks, 'entitled to require of any metaphysical theory that it should function as a secondary system, at least to the extent of having some explanatory value'. In assuming that a metaphysical theory may be meaningful, that it may contain *a priori* concepts ('terms not related directly to anything observable') and that it may have explanatory power, Ayer is no longer fighting a rearguard action for logical positivism but attacking one of its central positions.

(3) *On the thesis that metaphysical theories are secondary systems.* In order to examine Ayer's latest (1973) account of metaphysics, one has to distinguish between the 'legislation' by which any secondary system – whether metaphysical, scientific or of some other kind – goes beyond the primary, and the legislation which is specific to metaphysical systems. While the primary system contains only factual propositions, and while a secondary system is, as Ayer, following Peirce, puts it, 'concerned ... with the arrangement of facts',[6] the primary system is nevertheless not just descriptive of the observable. It involves some arrangement of what is observed and is thus itself already a theory albeit one that contains no *a priori* concepts and no propositions about possible, as opposed to actual, cases. Within the limits imposed by these two overriding constraints a primary system is characterised by the following features. Its factual propositions consist in applying observable properties to physical objects and can be cast in a form 'in which they serve to state that such and such observable properties are located at such and such particular places and at such and such particular times'. It can contain numbers, which in so far as they record

actual measurement 'will always be rational and finite' and can contain the logical connectives of truth-functional, classical logic.[7]

What principally distinguishes a primary from a secondary system and endows the latter with its explanatory power are propositions by the assertion of which we not only associate actual events of one kind with events of another kind 'which are believed in fact to stand in constant relations to them', but also to 'project this generalization over unknown and fictitious instances'.[8] The propositions by which this projection from the actual into the possible is achieved are therefore not truth-functional conditionals. In the case of such a 'subjunctive' conditional – say, the assertion that, if *p* were the case, then *q* would be the case – we may even know that *p* is false, so that the 'conditional is thus frankly an excursion into fiction', though 'a fiction with a moral'. For its 'point is to draw attention to the facts in the background which favour the truth of "*q*" on the supposition of "*p*" and to the generalizations which combine with those facts to link the two propositions'.[9]

Ayer's distinction between a primary and a secondary system seems to be either mistaken or in need of radical reformulation. As it stands, it implies that even a primary system comprises *a priori* concepts and that even a primary system allows for the formulation of propositions about possible cases. Since according to Ayer some of the factual propositions attribute observable properties to physical objects or to spatio-temporal regions in public or intersubjective space or time, the assertion of these propositions involves the application of *a priori* concepts. More precisely, 'being a physical object' (or 'being a spatio-temporal region' as conceived by Ayer) logically implies 'being objectively given'. And this concept of objectivity, as well as the weaker concept of being intersubjectively given or the still weaker concept of being perceivable by myself and somebody else, is *a priori*. For, while a person who perceives something may, under certain circumstances, be regarded as perceiving his own perceiving of it, he cannot be regarded as perceiving another's perceiving. In other words, in order to make the transition from something only subjectively perceived to something which is intersubjectively given, one must apply an *a priori* concept of intersubjectivity. This was clear to Kant, who, however, wrongly insisted that the transformation of subjective perception into objective experience required the application of his – and no other – Categories.

Just as both primary *and* secondary systems involve *a priori* concepts, so both allow for the formulation of propositions about possible cases. This follows from what Ayer says about the logical terms admissible in a primary system. For, by admitting the logical connectives of truth-functional logic into the primary system, one *ipso facto* admits the whole of the lower predicate logic, as restricted to finite domains of objects. (For any finite domain, universal and existential quantifications are respectively merely abbreviative devices for the expression of conjunctions and alternations.) And this logic does enable us to express a variety of propositions about possible cases. Thus, the logical necessity of a proposition, say f, can be defined as its logical validity in this logic, i. e. $/—f$. Logical possibility then can be defined as $\sim/—\sim f$. One can similarly define various kinds of 'material' necessity and possibility, i.e. logical necessity and possibility with respect to some conjunction of propositions – say, N by $f \wedge (N/—f)$ and by $f \vee \sim(N/—\sim f)$. The restricted predicate logic (and its metatheory) is rich enough for the expression of subjunctive conditionals – for instance, conditionals of form $f/—g$. In order to decide whether the conditionals which Ayer has in mind can be expressed in the restricted or, for that matter, the unrestricted predicate logic, more would have to be known about them than he tells us.

Although there is no doubt that Ayer regards metaphysical systems as a species of secondary systems, his distinction between this and other species is less clear. As a consequence, his account does not imply any clear view of the relation between metaphysics and science. He does suggest that some metaphysical systems differ from science only in having a much lower degree of explanatory power – a suggestion which reminds one of the early positivist doctrine that metaphysics is a primitive anticipation of science, by which it should by now be superseded. And he also suggests that some metaphysical systems contain presuppositions of science. Yet his account of metaphysical systems as secondary systems contains no reasons for regarding the difference between them and scientific systems as a difference in kind rather than of degree.

Connected with this uncertainty about the difference between metaphysical systems and scientific ones and about the relevance of the former to the latter, are further uncertainties some of which will be indicated by the following questions. First, what is the nature of the 'arrangement' by which a primary system is enlarged into a secondary metaphysical or scientific system? Is it the same in both cases and is it, in particular, in either case achieved by the introduction of subjunctive conditions. Secondly, to what extent is a secondary system regulative ('legislating'), i. e. a system of rules which are fulfilled by some arrangements and violated by others, and to what extent is a secondary system assertive, i. e. a system of propositions about what is and what is not the case?

Thirdly, to what extent is science or metaphysics like grammar or anthropology in making merely explicit what is implicitly accepted, be it as a rule or as a belief? Fourthly, what is the analysis of the (genuine or spurious) *a priori* necessity of some metaphysical propositions? While this problem was central to Ayer's earlier accounts of metaphysics, he seems in his latest account to have lost sight of it.

Of the many more or less relevant replies to the criticism that Ayer's distinctions between primary and secondary systems and between metaphysical and other secondary systems are unnecessarily and avoidably imprecise, one reply would be particularly pertinent. It consists in countering the criticism by arguing that Ayer's distinctions are necessarily and unavoidably imprecise and that any attempt at greater precision could achieve it only at the price of becoming unrealistic. That this is not so can only be shown by giving, or at least outlining, an alternative account of metaphysics and by comparing it with Ayer's.

II

(1) *On the cognitive supremacy of cognitive metaphysical principles and on their constituent* a priori *concepts.* The critical part of this essay was mainly concerned with Ayer's various accounts of the apparent or real necessity of metaphysical propositions and with his most recent analysis of metaphysical principles as constituting a secondary system by which – with the help of adding possible to actual cases and *a priori* concepts to observable attributes – the factual propositions of a primary system are arranged and thus explained. It is therefore proper that the proposed outline of an alternative analysis of metaphysics should concentrate on these issues. For this reason certain other aspects of metaphysics will have to be neglected, especially the relation between cognitive and practical principles.[10]

The system of a person's beliefs and, hence, of the propositions believed by him, exhibits a variety of structural relations the analysis of which is relevant to a proper understanding of the nature and role of metaphysical principles. Among them are on the one hand the relation between dominated and dominating propositions, and on the other hand the relation between interpreted and interpretative concepts. The analysis of domination helps one to understand the kind of necessity and of other modalities which are characteristic of certain beliefs, including metaphysical ones. The analysis of interpretation helps one to understand the nature of *a priori* concepts, especially of those *a priori* concepts which occur as constituents of cognitive principles.

The relation between dominating and dominated beliefs becomes manifest when one considers situations in which a belief of one kind, say a religious belief, is recognised as inconsistent with a belief of another kind, say a scientific belief, and in which the superiority of one kind over the other make one drop one of the beliefs and retain the other. More precisely, a consistent class of propositions, say α, dominates for a thinker a class of propositions, say β, if and only if, in any case in which he recognises an inconsistency between an internally consistent member of α and an internally consistent member of β, he rejects the latter. An internally consistent class of propositions α is a class of cognitively supreme propositions if, and only if, α cannot be decomposed into two classes, α_1 and α_2, of which one dominates the other, and α dominates the class of all propositions (believed by the thinker) which are not members of α. Examples of cognitively supreme propositions are the principle of continuity for Leibniz and Kant, as well as the other principles mentioned at the beginning of this essay, for the thinkers holding them.

When earlier on Ayer's distinction between a primary and a secondary system was criticised as being too vague, it was pointed out that already the primary system contains *a priori* concepts, since any transition from a proposition about a merely subjectively given entity to a proposition about an intersubjectively given entity involves the application of the *a priori* concept of being intersubjective. This transition is an example of the passage from the application of an interpreted concept to the application of a concept by which it is interpreted. It shows that two concepts (for example, 'being a subjectively given chair-like appearance' and 'being a chair') may be co-ostensive, i. e. not differ in their perceptually accessible content, and yet differ in their full content.

Consider now any two co-ostensive concepts F and G. We shall say that F is an interpretation of G if, and only if, the applicability of F to an observable phenomenon logically implies, *but is not logically implied by*, the applicability of G to it. If there is a concept A such that the applicability of F to an observable phenomenon logically implies, and is logically implied by, the applicability to it of F *and* A, then A expresses a non-observable attribute of the phenomenon (is an *a priori* concept) and is nevertheless applicable to it. Because A expresses the non-perceptual difference between two co-ostensive concepts of which one interprets the other, I shall call it 'an interpretative *a priori* concept'. If (as in our example) the application of A to a perceptual phenomenon in addition logically implies that the phenomenon is objective (or at least intersubjective) *A* will be called an 'objective *a priori* concept'. Kant's Categories – causality, substance and the rest – are clear examples of objective *a priori* concepts.

Obviously not all *a priori* concepts are objective or even interpretative. Among the non-interpretative, or, as I shall say, ideal, *a priori* concepts, we may distinguish in particular transcendent *a priori* concepts, which, while not applying to any observable phenomenon, apply – or are claimed to apply – to reality as a whole, and fictitious *a priori* concepts, which are not transcendent and do not apply to any observable phenomenon. Fictitious, ideal concepts may be useful as idealisations of concepts which are applicable to observable phenomena.

The traditional tasks of the metaphysician are to exhibit on the one hand *the* necessary and most general features of human experience, and on the other the relation, if any, of this experience to a transcendent reality. Here we are mainly concerned with the former task. It is to show how all human thought takes place within a *unique* categorial framework – in particular, by means of distinguishing between particulars and attributes and by a categorisation of the particulars into *summa genera* with which are associated principles determining the constitution and individuation of their members. The preceding definitions of cognitive supremacy and of objective and of transcendent *a priori* concepts allow us to replace the absolutist claims of some metaphysicians, which were rightly attacked by the logical positivists, by weaker claims which they wrongly ignored. Thus, the obscure notion of metaphysical necessity can be replaced by the notion of cognitive supremacy, and the obscure assumption of a unique categorial framework and, hence, of a unique system of indispensable *a priori* concepts by the admission of alternative categorial frameworks and systems of *a priori* concepts. One must, moreover, admit at least the logical possibility of a person's forgoing the use of all *a priori* concepts in his thinking – provided that one remembers that this person would, because of the *a priori* nature of the concept of intersubjectivity, have to be a solipsist. By addressing myself to others, I am, however, disregarding this possibility.

(2) *On metaphysical principles as criteria of intelligibility and some related questions.* It is now fairly easily shown that, and how, metaphysical principles function as standards of intelligibility. Let us consider a person's cognitively supreme principles which determine his categorial framework and which (unless he is a solipsist) contain at least some objective *a priori* concepts among their constituents. If we assume that *M* is an internally consistent conjunction

of such 'framework principles', from which all the others logically follow (say by classical predicate logic), then not only M but also f will be cognitively supreme and in this sense metaphysically necessary. We may, as indicated earlier (subsection 3), define the metaphysical necessity with respect to M by

(a) $\quad \square_M f \overset{=}{_D} f \wedge (M/\!\!-\!\!f)$

and the metaphysical possibility or coherence with respect to M by

(b) $\quad \Diamond_M f \overset{=}{_D} f \vee \sim(M/\!\!-\!\!\sim f)$

This notion of coherence with respect to M is sometimes – and as far as non-philosophers are concerned, excusably – mistaken for an absolute notion, although the intellectual history of mankind contains many examples of radical change in the framework principles accepted by different groups of people at different times.

Unlike, for example, some cognitively supreme religious dogmas, these principles contain objective *a priori* concepts, the application of which is involved in the interpretation of observable phenomena as intersubjective. Moreover, for a person who thinks in the framework determined by these principles of categorisation, constitution and individuation, the interpretation extends to *all* observable phenomena, and hence to both common sense and scientific thinking. It is in fact one kind of what Peirce and, following him, Ayer call the 'arrangement' of facts, as opposed to its description.

From the comprehensive arrangement of all observable phenomena through interpretation within a person's categorial framework by means of its objective *a priori* concepts, we must distinguish specialist arrangements of some observable phenomena through idealisation by some scientific theory and its ideal concepts. The idealisation, which can here only be roughly indicated, consists in the systematic replacement of concepts which are applicable to observable phenomena by ideal concepts which are not so applicable but which within the context and for the purpose of the theory can be identified with, or treated *as if* they were identical with, applicable concepts. The idealisation is determined by the logico-mathematical system in which the theory is embedded, as well as by various modifications of the conceptual net of the applicable concepts – modifications depending on the one hand on observable features of the investigated region of experience which can be safely neglected and on the other on fictitious attributes which can be usefully introduced as characteristic of it.[11]

Making use of a scientific theory (for instance, classical mechanics) thus involves three sets of concepts: namely, (i) a common-sense set, i. e. a set of concepts applicable to observed phenomena (for instance, 'being a physical object'); (ii) an ideal set, i. e. a set of ideal concepts (such as 'being a constellation of extensionless particles'); and (iii) a linking set, i. e. a set of concepts the application of which is the assertion of the qualified identifiability of a concept belonging to the common-sense set with a concept belonging to the ideal set (for example, 'being a material object and identifiable under . . . conditions with a constellation of extensionless particles'). In so far as metaphysics embraces cognitively supreme framework principles, it is thus *not* a rudimentary form of science, but provides standards of coherence (intelligibility, rationality, explanation) for science, because scientific thinking in its use of common-sense and linking concepts – that is to say, of intersubjective concepts – is subject to the scientist's framework principles.

A person's framework principles constitute at least part of his 'immanent metaphysics'; for they are necessary in the sense of being cognitively supreme and they are presupposed in all his thinking – common-sense, scientific or other – about intersubjective phenomena. Our conception of immanent metaphysics differs from that of Kant and other metaphysicians by admitting a plurality of categorial frameworks. But it does admit, as they do, the possibility of a transcendent metaphysics embracing speculative propositions about a reality which transcends subjective experience and its interpretation by means of objective *a priori* concepts. Indeed, the acknowledgment of a plurality of categorial frameworks acts as an additional spur to speculations about their relation to each other and to a reality beyond their reach.

Metaphysical principles, in particular those which determine a categorial framework, are indicative propositions. ('Whatever exists falls into one of the following *summa genera*, and has the following constitutive and individuating attributes: . . .'). But to every indicative proposition there corresponds a rule to conduct oneself *as if* it were true. Indeed, even rules which do not directly correspond to indicatives, such as heuristic rules, which require one to behave *as if* some propositions which may be false were in fact true, are indirectly based on the assumption that some indicative propositions are true. Both immanent and transcendent metaphysics leave room for such regulative guidance. It is the metaphysician's task to formulate indicative metaphysical principles, and regulative principles which – directly or indirectly – are based on them. It is the lot of common sense and scientific thinking to take place within some categorial framework i. e. to have an immanent metaphysics. The problem of the correspondence between implicit and explicit metaphysical systems is analogous to that of the correspondence between grammars which are implicit in natural languages and explicit grammars of natural or artificial languages.

(3) *Between the positivist rejection of all metaphysics and the claims of absolutist metaphysicians.* If we now look back at the examples of genuine or spurious metaphysical propositions set down at the beginning of the first part of this discussion, the following remarks about them are appropriate. Our first example – namely, the principle of continuity – is typical of immanent metaphysical principles as characterised in the constructive part of the discussion. The principle is for some thinkers cognitively supreme and constitutive of all intersubjectively observable phenomena. Again, it is a historical fact that, even among thinkers who belong to the same intellectual community, some may accept and some reject the principle. This opposition, moreover, does not exclude rational argument between the opponents, as is, for example, shown by the correspondence between Einstein and Born.[12]

Similar remarks apply to the second example – namely, the principle of actual mathematical infinity – if, for example, all observable phenomena arc regarded as instantiating numbers (as being a unity or a certain plurality) or as 'participating' in numbers in the Platonic or some other way. The principle of actual mathematical infinity is a particularly instructive example of a principle which, though accepted, may or may not have metaphysical status, as conferred by cognitive supremacy within the system of a thinker's beliefs. Thus, it does not possess metaphysical status according to Hilbert and other formalist philosophers of mathematics, who regard the concept of actual infinity as a fictitious concept belonging to the ideal concepts of a special theory.

The third example, i.e. the principle of excluded middle, is covered by the preceding account of metaphysics if, as I am prepared to argue, the classical logic of which it is a principle admits of alternatives. In this case its acceptance or rejection has some consequences for the world of observable phenomena, since, for example, its rejection makes room for the possibility of open futures of a kind which is excluded by its acceptance. The fourth example is a clear case of transcendent metaphysics, the relation of which to immanent metaphysics could only be very roughly indicated.

The general account of metaphysics which the examples were meant to illustrate is incompatible both with Ayer's early positivist rejection of metaphysics as nonsense, and with his later view according to which metaphysics is a 'secondary system'. His later view has nevertheless some affinity with the analysis proposed in the second part of this essay, since Ayer now admits that metaphysical beliefs may have some explanatory function and implies that, like scientific beliefs, they are not exempt from change.

It is clear from the preceding discussion that I disagree with Ayer's accounts of metaphysics. However, like most members of my philosophical generation, I found them stimulating and important and am glad to have been given the opportunity of honouring him by a contribution to this *Festschrift*.

NOTES

1. Kant's rejection is implicit in his rejection of apagogic proofs in transcendental arguments. See *Critique of Pure Reason*, B817.

2. A. J. Ayer, *Language, Truth and Logic*, 2nd edn (London: Gollancz, 1946) p. 41.

3. See A. J. Ayer, 'Truth by Convention', *Analysis*, IV (Dec 1936) 17ff.

4. Ayer, *Language, Truth and Logic*, 2nd edn, p. 17.

5. A. J. Ayer, *The Central Questions of Philosophy* (London: Weidenfeld and Nicolson, 1973) p. 33.

6. Ibid.

7. Ibid., pp. 142–3.

8. Ibid., p. 155.

9. Ibid., p. 152.

10. For an inquiry into this relation, see Stephan Körner, *Experience and Conduct* (Cambridge, Cambridge U.P., 1976) esp. ch. 16.

11. For details see S. Körner, *Experience and Theory* (London: Routledge and Kegan Paul, 1966).

12. See *Albert Einstein–Hedwig und Max Born – Briefwechsel 1916–1955* (Munich, 1969). For a comparison of arguments about metaphysical principles with scientific and mathematical arguments see, for example, Körner, *Experience and Conduct*, pp. 226ff.

13 Replies

A. J. AYER

I am very grateful to Mr Graham Macdonald for conceiving the plan of this volume and for the trouble which he has taken to put it into effect, and I am pleased and honoured by the interest which his chosen contributors have displayed in my work. Nearly all of them have been in regular contact with me for many years and I have surely learned more from their writings and conversation than they can have learned from mine. It will be seen that they differ quite widely in opinion not only from me but also among themselves, but we are in sufficient sympathy to make discussion profitable. Unfortunately I have not enough space to reply to each essay in detail or even to attempt in a more general fashion to cover all the interesting points that they raise. Instead I shall take advantage of the fact that the essays mainly concentrate upon a limited number of philosophical themes, with which I have indeed been principally concerned, and I shall make a fresh effort to elaborate these themes in the light of the foregoing discussions of them. The topics to which I shall devote myself are severally those of perception, induction, essentialism, personal identity, and verification in company with metaphysics.

I. PERCEPTION

(1) Professor Strawson is right in saying that the problem of perception has always occupied a central place in my philosophical thinking and also that the movement of my thought about it over the course of forty years has been from the phenomenalism of *Language, Truth and Logic* to what I describe in *The Central Questions of Philosophy* as a sophisticated form of realism. Strawson allows that my latest theory is subtle enough to deserve to be called sophisticated, though he has doubts and reservations about the form which its sophistication takes. Mr Dummett fastens onto the terms in which I describe the theory, but gives to each of them a technical sense of his own which turns them into what

he considers to be a misdescription of it. He proposes to say that realism, with respect to a given class of statements, consists in the view that the principle of bivalence applies to every member of the class. He speaks of such realism as sophisticated when it is combined with the view that the class of statements in question is reducible to some other class, and naïve when it is not. The thesis of reductionism, as he expresses it, is that 'a statement of the given class cannot be true unless some statement, or perhaps set of statements, of some other class, which I shall call the *reductive* class, is true'. It is to be remarked that this does not imply the stronger thesis, which has perhaps more commonly gone by the name of reductionism, that every statement of the given class is translatable into a statement, or a set of statements, of the reductive class.

On the basis of these definitions Dummett doubts whether I am a realist in this context, since I do not commit myself to saying that every statement about a physical object is determinately either true or false, and maintains that, if I did so commit myself, my realism would still be naïve and not sophisticated, since I no longer hold that statements about physical objects are capable of reduction, even in his relatively weak sense of the term. I think that he is justified on both counts so long as he confines his class of statements about physical objects to those that state that physical objects of such and such sorts exist, without implying that they are perceived. On the other hand, when it comes to statements which do imply that some physical object is perceived, then I am a reductionist, in Dummett's sense, since I hold that no such statement can be true unless it is true that the percipient is experiencing what, following my critics, I shall continue to call a sense datum, though I now prefer to follow C. I. Lewis and Nelson Goodman in using the term 'quale' in this context and in speaking, like Russell, of 'percepts' when the qualia are particularised. I shall return to the question of reductionism later on.

Dummett argues in favour of his terminology that it brings out a distinction – namely, that between realism and reductionism in his senses of these terms – which 'the traditional manner of using the philosophical term "realism" blurs'. I think, however, that he underrates the extent to which his usage breaks with tradition and overlooks the cost which this incurs. For instance, it is customary in this context to contrast realism with idealism, but a Berkeleian idealist must count for Dummett as a sophisticated realist, so long as he believes that every statement ascribing an idea to God or to a human mind has a determinate truth value. And what of a position such as Professor Armstrong's? No doubt he is a realist, in Dummett's sense, as well as his own, though he does not say so in this essay. But is his realism naïve or sophisticated? It would seem that, like mine, it is naïve with respect to statements which state that physical objects exist, without implying that they are perceived, but sophisticated with respect to statements which bear this implication. At least, this is how one might interpret his admissions that, 'when it is true that somebody sees an apple, then they see it *in virtue of* seeing very much less than an apple', that Russell and I have been right in claiming that 'ordinary judgements of perception such as "This is a table" entail an inference' and that 'It is reasonable to think that the *non-inferential* component of the perception, or the judgement based on the perception, is far less than "This is a table"'. It is not, however, entirely clear that Dummett would regard the thesis that the truth of statements about objects of a given sort depends on the truth of statements about parts of the objects as genuinely reductive.

One point which is clear is that, when Armstrong argues in favour of what he terms direct realism, he wants to show cause for rejecting the representative theory of perception. And how does this theory fare in Dummett's terminology? Once again we have to distinguish between statements which state that some physical object exists, without implying that it is perceived, and statements which imply that it is perceived. In either case there is no reason why a holder of a representative theory should not be a realist: nothing in his theory need commit him to believing that any statement about a physical object lacks a determinate truth value. The difference arises only when it comes to the question whether his realism is sophisticated or naïve. In respect of the first class of statements, it is presumably naïve, since he allows physical objects to exist unperceived, and differs from the phenomenalist in that he does not regard their unperceived existence as depending on the truth of hypothetical propositions about sense data. With regard to the second class, he appears to be sophisticated, since he holds that no physical object can be perceived unless something of the order of a sense datum is experienced. But, suppose that he holds, perhaps on the ground of the vagueness of observational terms, that some of the relevant sense-datum statements have no determinate truth value? In that case he seems to slip through Dummett's net, unless we still count him as a reductionist on the grounds of his holding that for it to be true that someone is perceiving a physical object it must at least be true that he is experiencing a sense datum of some sort or other, even though there is no way of saying, with determinate truth, of what sort it is. But now we may begin to wonder whether a terminology which facilitates

our making at least one useful distinction in the expression of
our views about the nature of physical objects is equally well adapted
to the discussion of theories of perception. If we conclude that
it is not, we can still recognise the fact that the two topics are
closely connected.

(2) I do not see how anyone could avoid being a reductionist,
with regard to perceptual statements, in the very weak sense of
allowing that no physical object can be perceived without the occurrence of some sense experience, and that the converse does not
hold. When I say that the converse does not hold, what I have
in mind is not just that people may truly be said to perceive
things other than physical objects, such as shadows or images
or the sky, but rather that, whereas their claims to perceive physical
objects may depart from the truth in various ways, ranging from
misdescription of the object's properties through misidentification
of it to complete hallucination, the same judgements, made on
the basis of the same sense experiences, could have been true if
certain other factors had obtained. It seems clear also that this
much must be conceded by those who hold, as most of my critics
seem to do, that perceiving physical objects consists at least partly
in their causing us to have perceptual experiences; for surely from
the fact that a sense experience has such and such a content it
cannot logically follow that it has this or that or the other cause.

I have been used to summarising these points by saying that
our everyday perceptual judgements 'go beyond' the sensory experiences which give rise to them, and from this I have drawn the
conclusion that it should be possible to distinguish the contents
of these experiences from the projections to which they lead, and
to formulate statements which are, as I have put it, 'tailored' to
those contents. These are the statements which, following my critics,
I am here calling sense-datum statements. I once held that not
only every perceptual statement, but also every statement about
a physical object, was reducible to a set of sense-datum statements,
in the strong sense of being translatable into them, but this thesis,
which is not held by any of my critics, with the possible exception
of Mr John Foster, is one that I have long since given up. I
shall not here recapitulate the course of reasoning, starting in 1947
with my essay 'Phenomenalism'[1] and culminating in my book *The
Central Questions of Philosophy*,[2] that has led me to do so. Dummett
thinks that, while I do not accept a reductive thesis with respect
to physical-object statements, even in the weak form in which
he defines it, my arguments do not rule it out. The fault here
is probably mine in that I have failed to make it clear that my

objection to such a thesis would not be merely that the statements about percepts, which would make up what he calls the reductive class, would have to take the form of subjunctive conditionals. I do not think that, in the case of every statement about a physical object to which I assign a truth value, it would always be possible to formulate a set of subjunctive conditionals about percepts which would be such that, unless they held good, the physical object statement in question could not be true.

The position which I do hold is most fairly set out by Strawson, though he raises some serious objections to my formulation of it which I shall presently try to answer. Almost the only point of importance which he overlooks is that I do not introduce sense data as objects in the world, and *a fortiori* not as private objects. Initially I assign them no ontological status at all. I treat the question of what there is as one that arises only in terms of a theory for which sense data provide no more than an epistemological basis. I have tried first in my book *The Origins of Pragmatism*[3] and again in *The Central Questions of Philosophy* to show how sensory patterns are concretised into what I there call percepts, and how percepts are standardised and transmuted, by postulation, into what Strawson approves of my calling 'visuo-tactual con-tinuants'. The theory which thus emerges, being realistic, in what Dummett calls the traditional manner of using this term, is, as I put it, 'cut loose from its moorings'. The elements on which it is epistemologically based are interpreted back into it and, so far from being treated as the only or even most fundamental things that there are, diminish into states of the percipient for which the objects which have developed out of them are held to be causally responsible. It was this process that I principally had in mind when I called my realism 'sophisticated'.

I hope this makes it clear that Armstrong is quite mistaken in attributing to me a representative theory according to which sense data are inserted between the physical world and the perci-pient's mind in such a way as to be the effects of the physical objects which he perceives and in turn the causes of his perceptions. I entirely agree that in this role they would be superfluous. In fact my position is much closer to one that he ascribes to Professor Sellars and himself regards as a possible answer to the question, which clearly puzzles him, of where secondary qualities are to be located. My allowing that percepts can figure in the theory which they have served to found as ways in which the observer is affected might well be viewed as a method of realising his 'possibi-lity that those qualities should be associated . . . with the perceptions themselves'. This is clearly preferable, in my opinion, to the view

which he seems to have Dummett's support in favouring, that
the problem can simply be disposed of by identifying colour with
light-waves, felt heat with mean kinetic energy and so forth, or
to the suggestion that colour and the rest are unanalysable properties, in fact possessed by nothing, the words for which are probably
due to disappear from our vocabulary.

Another point on which I agree with Armstrong, and disagree
with Strawson and Dummett, is that it is at least problematic
whether what Armstrong, again following Sellars, calls the 'manifest
image' of the world is reconcilable with the scientific image. Armstrong, indeed, goes further to the extent of maintaining that there
is no plausible way in which they can be reconciled. On the other
hand, I agree this time with Strawson, against Armstrong and
possibly also against Dummett, that it is by no means obvious
that the manifest image has to be sacrificed. Once more this is
a question to which I shall return later on.

(3) In mentioning the possibility that 'secondary qualities do not
exist', by which he appears to mean not that there is anything
amiss with these qualities as such, but only that nothing actually
has them, Armstrong quotes Berkeley's phrase 'a false imaginary
glare'. This phrase could have been more aptly applied by Dummett
to what he calls simple observational qualities. He does not offer
any examples of such qualities, since he thinks that there could
not be any, but he allows that many adjectives, such as 'red'
and 'sweet', are habitually used as if they stood for them, and
what he maintains is that this use of such adjectives is incoherent.

For the sake of simplicity, let us confine ourselves to the case
of colours. According to Dummett, colours would be simple observational qualities if they satisfied the following two requirements:
first, that one could frequently judge, with high probability, what
colour an object was, merely by looking at it, and, secondly, that
such a judgement could be overridden, if at all, only by an appeal
to other judgements, perhaps made under different conditions, or
by a different observer, which were themselves based merely on
looking at the object in question. From these requirements Dummett
believes it to follow that, if two objects are indiscernible in colour,
in the sense that, by merely looking at them under the same circumstances, one can never perceive any difference in colour between
them, they are of the same colour. But, in view of the fact that
indiscernibility in colour is not a transitive relation, this result
can lead to contradiction. It suffices, what is in fact known to
be the case, that there can be three objects, A, B, C, such that
A and C are different and discernible in colour, while B is indiscern-

ible from either. For then we have to draw the inconsistent conclusion that *B* is of the same colour as *A* and of the same colour as *C*. If colours form a continuum such that any three neighbouring instances stand in the same relation as has just been ascribed to *A*, *B*, and *C*, we arrive at the startling consequence that all objects are of the same colour, which is not only false but also can lead to incoherence, since the colour in question can be that of any instance with which we choose to begin. The same argument applies to sounds or tastes or any other candidates for being observational qualities, so long as the relation of indiscernibility between their instances is not transitive.

Dummett does not draw the conclusion that colours and sounds are just 'a false imaginary glare'. He merely infers that there are other criteria besides those of looking and listening, for deciding what colours things have or what sounds they make. He does, however, entertain the hypothesis that this does not apply to taste; that, as he puts it, 'the only characterisation of what it is for something to be sweet, for example, the only characterisation we could ever attain, would be that it tastes sweet to human beings, bears and the like'. I find this curious, since it seems to imply that 'taste' may after all stand for a kind of simple observational quality. Yet surely he does not believe that nothing can have any taste. Perhaps he could escape this consequence by appealing to simple observable relations, against which he can find no decisive logical argument, though he does not seem very confident of their existence. Then he could make it a condition for *A* and *B* to taste the same, not just that they be indiscernible in taste, but that there be no third object *C* which is discernible in taste from one of them but not from the other. This is the procedure that Nelson Goodman adopts to define exact sameness of colour in constructing his language of appearance. It has, however, the drawback that, while it allows us to discover that two objects which appear to be of exactly the same colour are in fact not so, by coming across some third object which is discernible from one of them in colour but not from the other, the requirement that there be no such third object is so strong that we can never be sure that it is satisfied. Consequently, the answer to the question whether two objects exactly match one another in colour must always remain uncertain, and, if the ascription of colour to an object depends on its exactly matching certain other objects in colour, it will be equally uncertain, on this basis, what colour any object really is. Neither will it help to substitute rough for exact matching; for the relation of roughly matching is also intransitive.

No wonder Dummett writes of our stepping into a morass. The question I now want to consider is whether sense data are extricable from it. Dummett himself does not explicitly refer to sense data, but he does speak of observational predicates as standing for 'a propensity to present a range of appearances under a variety of conditions', giving 'yellow' as one of his examples. And, if, as he must surely intend, a word such as 'yellow' is to have some proper application, in this usage, there must be a coherent sense attached to saying that an appearance which falls within the range is being presented. But is there any significant difference between saying that such and such an appearance is being presented to someone and saying that he is experiencing such and such a sense datum?

It might be suggested that there was, on the ground that sense data are supposed really to possess the properties which the corresponding physical objects merely look to possess, and that, whereas it is not possible that anything should really possess a property which cannot be coherently ascribed to it, there need be no contradiction implied in saying that something looks to possess it. However, this suggestion, if there were anything in it, would be of no help in the present case, since the only reason advanced for saying that colours cannot be simple observational qualities is that we run into contradiction if we ascribe colours to objects purely on the basis of the way they look; and the only ground that there can be for this conclusion is that our reports of the colours that objects look to be are themselves incoherent.

But must this really be so? The whole argument rests on the assumption that, if I cannot discern any difference in colour between *A* and *B*, I am bound in consistency to judge that they look to me to be of the same colour. But what is to count here as discerning a difference? No doubt if *A* and *B* are presented to me in isolation from other objects I must judge that their colour looks the same. But, suppose that they are presented to me in conjunction with *C*, which *B* looks to me to match in colour but *A* does not. Why should I not say, just for this reason, that *A* and *B* do not look to me to be of the same colour under this condition? They would still look the same if *C* were removed from the field of vision, but that is irrelevant. The very fact that the relation of looking the same in colour, when objects are taken in pairs, is known not to be transitive can count as a reason against making the question whether objects are discernible in colour depend on our taking them exclusively in pairs.

This is not quite to treat colour as a complex observational quality, as Dummett defines the term. I am not saying that judgements of colour can be made solely on the basis of perceptual comparison. The first condition laid down for simple observational qualities – that one can frequently judge with high probability what quality, in this case what colour, an object has – can still be taken to be satisfied.

It must, indeed, be satisfied if we are to attribute colour predicates, or for that matter any others, to sense data. For the mark of a sense datum is its being, so to speak, transparently honest. The contents of one's visual fields at different moments are what they are, and the function of the corresponding sense-datum statements is simply to monitor them, without implying anything further either about them or about anything else. One is therefore required to do no more than simply decide what character they have.

This does not, however, entirely dispose of the problem. I once held, and Mr Pears has again convinced me, that not even a sense-datum statement can be purely ostensive. It is true that in describing a portion of my present visual field as yellow I am not asserting that anything else exists. Nevertheless, as Pears correctly remarks, my statement would not be informative, even to myself, unless I were using the word 'yellow' in accordance with a meaning rule, and the question can still be raised whether any such meaning rule can be consistently followed. Evidently the rule must depend on actual or possible comparisons, so the question is whether its application must be inconsistent. I think that it need not be. Let us return to our old example, but now take *A*, *B* and *C* to be sense data, and assume that the difference between *A* and *C* is such that, being concerned with shades of colour, I apply different colour predicates to them. Then, if *B* is presented with *A* alone I may apply the same colour predicate to it as to *A*. If *B*, or another sense datum, *B'*, which is equivalent to *B*, in the sense that I should judge them to be of the same colour in all contexts, is presented with *C* alone, I may apply the same colour predicate to it as to *C*. If *A*, *B* and *C*, or their equivalents, are presented together, I may apply a different predicate to *B* from that which I apply to either *A* or *C*. There is no inconsistency here, since there is no reason why two sense data which are equivalent in the sense defined should not each satisfy different colour predicates in different visual contexts. But what if *B* is presented alone? In that case the rule allows us to follow whichever of the three options we choose. This makes it flexible but not incoherent, since it does not commit us to conjoining them in any given case.

(4) I agree with Pears that 'sense-datum statements form a loosely knit group', and I am content with his characterisation of them

as including 'statements about the location, intensity and qualities of bodily sensations, and a large variety of statements based on the use of an outward-facing sense but non-committal about the existence of the external object'. Agreeing with him also that the meaning of such statements needs to be fixed independently of the character of the sense data to which they refer, if they are not to be purely ostensive and so fail to qualify as statements at all, I have tried to show that it can be fixed coherently, with the result that these statements are capable of truth. If they are capable of truth they are capable of falsehood. There is, however, a problem about the way in which they can come to be false. Obviously I can tell lies about my sensations, and obviously I can misdescribe them – for example, through a slip of the tongue. The question is whether I can also be honestly mistaken about them. Can my beliefs about the way things currently look and feel to me be factually false?

The view that they cannot be has often been expressed by saying that sense-datum statements are incorrigible. This is an unfortunate usage, not only because it seems to imply the false empirical proposition that no sense-datum statement is ever subsequently withdrawn or revised, but also because it begs the question whether one's willingness subsequently to accept a factual correction of a sense-datum statement is either a necessary or a sufficient condition of one's having been mistaken. It might be sufficient if the correction fell within the specious present, though the point is arguable; clearly, it is not so otherwise, for one's memory might be at fault. It would not be necessary if Pears is right in saying that mistakes of this kind could go undetected: there is, however, the problem of deciding on the criterion for one's having made a mistake. In any event, it is better to follow his example in drawing at least a provisional distinction between the question of whether sense-datum statements are incorrigible and the question whether one's beliefs in such statements are infallible, so long as they relate only to the contents of one's present sense experiences, and in treating the second question as the one principally at issue.

If the claim to infallibility could be sustained, it would mark an obvious difference between sense-datum statements and statements, including those that I have been calling perceptual statements, which imply the existence of physical objects. For this reason, perhaps, some philosophers, such as Price,[4] have taken the lack or any possible doubt about its character on the part of the person to whom it is presented as a defining property of a sense datum, thereby allowing their critics to take their rejection of this property as a proof that the very idea of there being sense data is a misconception. But this is surely a mistake. It should, indeed, be part of the characterisation of a sense-datum statement that one cannot be mistaken about its truth in one of the principal ways in which one can be mistaken about the truth of a perceptual statement. Since it is intended that sense-datum statements should carry no implications about anything other than the contents of the experiences which they are used to monitor, they cannot come to grief, as I once put it, by issuing drafts on the facts which are subsequently dishonoured. It does not, however, follow from this, nor is it necessary to claim, that one cannot be mistaken about them in any way at all, still less that one cannot be in any doubt about their truth.

Even so, the question of infallibility remains open. I think that there have been two main motives for claiming it. One of them is the quest for certainty. It has been thought that our empirical knowledge must have a firm basis, that this basis must lie in our experiences, and that it would not be firm enough if our characterisations of our experiences were liable to error. But, while the first two of these propositions are acceptable, the third is not. What is important is that the perceptual judgements which are based on our experiences should most frequently be true, and this would be unlikely to be the case if the experiences in question were at all commonly misidentified. Clearly this provides no warrant for treating our characterisations of them as infallible.

The second motive has more to recommend it. One is inclined to ask what sense can be given to such statements as 'I believe that I have a bad headache, but I may be mistaken' or 'Possibly I am wrong in thinking that the leaves on this tree look green to me; it may be that they look some other colour', unless my doubts are merely about my choice of words. If English were not my native language, I might well think it possible that I was using the words 'green' and 'headache' wrongly. Yet, as Pears quotes Russell as saying, what I believed would be true, though my words were ill chosen. Is there room in such cases for any error of fact? If, as I have said, in making a sense-datum statement which one intends to be true, one is merely applying a meaning rule, it would seem to follow that the only way in which one can go wrong is through misapplying the rule. And why should this count as anything more than a verbal error?

The beginning of an answer is that, even in the case of sense data, the mastery of a meaning rule does not necessarily exclude all uncertainty about its application. The examples which Pears gives, taken mostly from Austin's work but in one instance from my own, make this sufficiently clear. But to allow that one may be uncertain is still not, as Pears acknowledges, to allow that one can be factually mistaken. If we draw the line where he proposes between verbal and factual mistakes, the question can become empirical so long as we have a criterion for distinguishing between the actual character of one's sense experience and the character one believes it to have. Pears does not supply such a criterion, but presumably he would argue that there might be a variety of circumstantial evidence. In his example of a series of increasingly difficult questions put to a subject about the way various substances tasted to him, the ground for deciding that the subject's answers were factually erroneous might be physiological; or it might be that his answers were at variance with those given by other persons or by the subject himself on other occasions, when there was no reason to suppose that there was anything on the present occasion to make any relevant difference to the character of his sensations.

If circumstantial evidence can override the subject's own beliefs in cases of this kind, I seem to have been wrong in saying that the subject, even if not infallible in such cases, must still be the final authority. In an example such as Pears's, there is no obvious reason even to make it a condition for the circumstantial evidence to predominate that the subject acknowledges its superiority. It is true that the circumstantial evidence could get no foothold unless the subject's beliefs were generally taken to be correct, just as the clairvoyants, in my analogy, could gain no credit unless their judgements were generally sustained by those of eyewitnesses. It is not just, as Pears puts it, that eyewitnesses are in general more likely to be right, but rather that it is not clear what either party's being right would consist in unless it were a matter of their making judgements which were finally confirmable by direct observation. Nevertheless, this does not exclude the possibility of there being particular instances in which the clairvoyants are right and the eyewitnesses wrong, if, for example, they are subject to some hallucination. So also, in the case of sense data, it may be that in some particular instance another person may, in his description of the content of my present sense experience, be right where I am wrong.

This leaves me perplexed, because I am still inclined to say that no amount of circumstantial evidence could show me to be factually mistaken in believing that I am now being presented at least with the appearance of leaves, or that they look green to me, or that I am not now suffering from a headache, or that I am thinking about philosophy. In these and many other such examples, I cannot see how my word can fail to be sovereign, once the possibility of purely verbal error is discounted. Yet what is to distinguish them, logically, from those in which it can fail?

I suppose that Pears would say that all there is to it is that in the examples I gave I am much more likely to be right. But what then would be the proof of my being right? I am afraid that his answer to this question might still leave me dissatisfied.

One mistake that I think I may have made is to confuse two levels of discourse. At the admittedly fictitious level where my solitary observer is supposed to be developing a primitive physical theory on the basis of his percepts, the question whether he identifies his percepts correctly hardly arises. It is enough that he be shown capable of following consistent meaning rules. If he can keep to the rules, he can also break them, but whether he breaks them is something that he decides. His word cannot be overridden, because there is nothing in this situation to override it. This does not obtain at the higher level, where percepts have been interpreted back into the theory, because there is then much more evidence that can be taken into account. The question about the fallibility of sense-datum statements has usually been posed, as it is by Pears, at the higher level, and I think that in dealing with it I may have wrongly assumed that the authority over its elements which the observer possesses before the theory is developed still holds when they have been absorbed within it. My trouble is that, even when I allow for this mistake, while I can believe that the area over which he is sovereign has diminished, I cannot believe that it has vanished altogether.

(5) The account, which I have sketched in *The Central Questions of Philosophy* and elsewhere, of the way in which an individual observer might arrive at something approaching what I have called the common-sense view of the physical world was not designed either as a work of fiction or as a contribution to genetic psychology, though I should naturally be gratified if the psychological evidence supported it. It was intended rather as a form of analysis of the common-sense view. Following the example of Russell and Carnap, I used the process of fictive construction to draw out the implications of our ordinary perceptual judgements. If our manifest image of the physical world could plausibly have been developed in the way I outlined, a corresponding light would be thrown upon its nature. On the assumption that the common-sense view can be treated as a theory with respect to the immediate data of perception, my purpose, as Strawson justly remarks, is to bring out those features of sensible experience which make it possible for us to employ the theory successfully and concurrently justify our acceptance of it.

Strawson raises no objection to the pursuit of this enterprise, and he also thinks that one both can and should accept its starting point, so long as it is suitably interpreted. He does not, however, think that it will be suitably interpreted unless the account of our sensible experience is sufficiently strict; and this means not only that it must not go 'beyond' the experience but also that it must faithfully portray the experience, not in the form in which it might be conjecturally ascribed to a newborn infant, but 'in the form which it takes in our mature life'. For it is only if this second condition is satisfied that the enterprise can at all plausibly pass for an exercise in analysis rather than genetic psychology. Strawson then suggests that the best way in which it could be satisfied would be for the person whose experience it was to use the perceptual claims that it would ordinarily lead him to make, without actually making those claims. Thus, he might say that his visual field is such as he would expect it to be if he were seeing the green-leaved branches of a tree, standing beside a low reddish stone wall, and then tailor this report to his experiences by making it clear that he is not committing himself in any way with regard to the actual existence of the physical objects which figure in it. There are other ways in which he could achieve the same effect, but they would all take the form of attenuating some perceptual judgement. If instead of saying that he saw what he took to be leaves on the branches of a tree, he had claimed to see green and brown forms in a network of spatial relations, his report would not have been faithful to his experience. It is not impossible to react to one's visual field in this purely aesthetic way, but it is an uncommon state of mind and one not easily attained.

From this Strawson draws the conclusion that it is 'quite inappropriate' for me to speak of our ordinary perceptual judgements as *interpretations* of the data of experience, or as involving inferences for which such data supply the premises, or as constituting a *theory* for which they provide *evidence*. His reason is that, 'in order for some belief or set of beliefs to be correctly described as a theory in respect of certain data, it must be possible to describe the data on the basis of which the theory is held in terms which do not presuppose the acceptance of the theory on the part of those for whom the data *are* data'. But, if Strawson is right in his account of the usual character of sensible experiences, this requirement is not met. Our experience is permeated by the concepts of objects which have, in Hume's phraseology, a continued existence, distinct from our perception of them, and our unreflective belief that these concepts are satisfied is 'a condition of that experience being what it is'.

What is substantially the same argument is used by Professor
Taylor to justify his rejection of the possibility of our having any
use for any such concept as that of a sense datum – a topic
which he treats as antiquarian, thereby showing himself, in my
view, to be a little behind the times. He is wrong in supposing
that it is essential, at least for my present purpose, to treat sense
data as objects, or sense-datum statements as incorrigible, but these
mistakes, for which indeed he has some historical warrant, do
not diminish the force of his objection to any attempt to detach
the contents of our sense experiences from the interpretations which
we put upon them. The objection is, as he puts it, that 'our phenomenal field, or the world as it appears to us, which is what our
sense-datum language is supposed to describe, is what I should
like to call a patterned activity'. He would like to call it so because
it is variously organised according to our present interests, past
experiences and future expectations and because its 'being organised
in a certain way is just our selecting, focusing, relating, identifying
the things before us in the way we do'. And this activity is not
aimless or subject to no criterion. The criterion is 'veridicalness'
and the activity directed not only by our desires and interests,
but also 'by our sense of what is real'.

Now I do not want to dispute any of these assertions, for which
I believe that Taylor could adduce good psychological evidence.
I do not deny that our sense fields are structured, or that their
character depends in part on our activity, if this term is used
to refer to our current interests and beliefs. There is a phenomenal
difference between seeing a Cubist picture as a portrait and seeing
it simply as a motley of colours; a sentence spoken in German
sounded differently to me before I had learned the language from
the way a repetition of it, uttered with the same intonation, sounds
to me now. The sounds have become, as it were, diaphanous,
and the same applies in the other cases where, as most often
happens, we have little or no interest in the appearances as such,
but bury them in the perceptual judgements which they prompt
us to make. I think that Taylor goes a little too far when he
denies the occurrence of any percepts 'which are not organised
at least partly by our sense of the real'. There are abnormal situations
in which a man's 'sense of the real' forsakes him and others perhaps
in which it is deliberately suspended. But it is enough for Taylor's
argument that these situations are abnormal.

So much I concede. Where I dissent both from Taylor and
from Strawson is in the conclusion that these facts invalidate the
distinction which I wish to draw between the contents of our sense
experiences and the interpretations which we put upon them, or

that they show me to be at fault in treating ordinary statements about physical objects as exhibiting a theory for which sense-datum statements supply evidence. It may seem that Strawson at least was doing no more than object to my terminology, since he allows that our perceptual judgements carry implications which would not be carried by what even he would regard as a strict account of the features of our sensible experience. That his disagreement with me goes deeper is shown by his saying, among other things, 'that the idea of our ordinary perceptual judgements as being invariably based upon, or invariably issuing from, awareness of such features is a myth'.

He is right, of course, to the extent that such judgements do not normally result from any conscious process of inference. I have to admit that the awareness in question is commonly no more than implicit. But where then do we disagree? I can best bring this out by examining his conclusion that 'the employment of our ordinary full-blooded concepts of physical objects is indispensable to a strict, and strictly veridical account of our sensible experience'. The employment of such concepts would not satisfy this description unless it incorporated such assumptions as that the objects were accessible to other observers, that they continued to exist unperceived, and, at least in Strawson's opinion, that they continued in possession of their phenomenal properties. But these assumptions surely are theoretical; and surely they are not indispensible to a veridical account of our sensible experience. Suppose that someone had been convinced by Berkeley that what we call physical objects do not exist unperceived, except, if this is intelligible, as ideas in the mind of God; suppose that he had been convinced by Locke or his followers that the properties which persistently characterise them bear at most a structural correspondence to anything that we actually see. Would it follow that their sense experiences were radically different in character from those of the ordinary man? I see no reason why it should. At one point Strawson quotes Mackie as saying that, 'even when we are trying to entertain a Lockian or scientific realism, "our language and our natural ways of thinking keep pulling us back" to a more primitive view'. No doubt this is true; but the more primitive view to which we are pulled back is surely not a different order of sensible experience but a different theory, a different manner of accounting for experiences of the same sort as those for which the scientific realist thinks that he can give a better account. The fact, which I do not deny, that our experience is 'permeated' by the more primitive view, the fact that our experience is originally organised in its favour, does not entail that they are not distinguishable. On the contrary, they need to be distinguished, if the primitive view is open, as Strawson admits, to being put in question.

I regard it as a further point in my favour that Strawson takes 'the idea of the presence of the thing as accounting for ... our perceptual awareness of it' as even an implicit feature of what he calls 'the pre-theoretical scheme'; for, as I have already remarked, it seems to me obvious that no strict description of the content of a sensory experience can carry any implication concerning its cause. I also adhere to my view that the insertion of a causal clause into our analysis of perceptual statements, whatever good reason there may be for it, is not a primitive procedure, since it is logically subsequent to the transformation of percepts into visuo-tactual continuants. It is true that, once I believe that a physical object is there in front of me, I am likely to accept the subjunctive conditional that, unless it really were there, I should not in these circumstances even be having the experience on which my perception of it is founded. But this by no means entails that the acceptance of any such conditional is a constituent of the belief that the physical object is there. On the contrary, unless the physical object were already posited, it would not be available to figure in the causal hypothesis. Neither can it be posited simply as the cause of the experience, for this would be consistent with its being anything whatsoever. It follows that Strawson is wrong in saying that in taking the enjoyment of an experience *y* to be a perception of a physical object *x*, 'we *are* implicitly taking it to be caused by *x*', though this may be an assumption that we do and should go on to make.

On this point Dummett is in agreement with me inasmuch as he disavows the belief 'that the notion of cause, as such, is integral to the notion of perception'. Where he thinks, perhaps rightly, that we come into conflict is in his maintaining that 'it does not follow from this that there must be more to our perceiving objects than their causing us to have certain perceptual experiences'. In fact I do not deny that we attain a level of theory at which this account of perception is acceptable. At the same time I maintain that in order to attain this level we must already have reason to believe in the existence of physical objects, that this reason must lie in the character of our sense experiences, and that it cannot simply consist in the attribution of causes to them.

(6) A more difficult problem arises when we try to estimate the influence that the causal account of perception, with which science provides us, has or should have upon our conception of the physical world. The central issue is most clearly put by Strawson. 'Can

we coherently identify the phenomenally propertied, immediately perceptible things which common sense supposes to occupy physical space with the configurations of unobservable ultimate particulars by which an unqualified scientific realism purports to replace them?' This is one of the main topics also of Dummett's and Armstrong's essays. Our responses to it are very varied. Strawson himself thinks that scientific realism is *prima facie* incompatible with the suppositions of common sense, but that there is a way of reconciling them. I agree with him on the first point, but am not satisfied with his treatment of the second. I am dubious also about the method of reconciliation which I myself have most recently put forward. Armstrong takes a serious view of the conflict, and resolves it in effect by sacrificing the common-sense standpoint. This leaves him, as we have seen, with a problem about the disposal of secondary qualities. Dummett, on the other hand, argues at length that the issue is spurious. He holds against the rest of us that *the* common-sense view is a myth. If we are talking of the contemporary man in the street, such a man does not think of immediately perceptible things as being phenomenally propertied, in the sense that Strawson attaches to this term. On the contrary, 'anyone accustomed to the use of observational predicates knows at least implicitly, and will recognise on reflection, that they stand for essentially dispositional properties'. The replacement which science seeks to effect is not the replacement of one set of objects by another but rather that of relative by absolute descriptions, where a relative description is one that characterises objects in terms which involve a reference 'to our own perceptual capacities' and an absolute description 'one that is independent of our modes of perception'. Philosophers such as myself have regarded it as at least a matter for debate whether merely relative descriptions capture objects as they really are, but here we have shown ourselves to be confused. The fact that a description is relative in this sense does not make it untrue, and absolute and relative descriptions can have the same extension.

I do not propose to take much space in discussing what views, if any, should be attributed to common sense. No doubt Dummett is right in saying that we have all been influenced, in some degree, by what we have learned of science, and perhaps this influence extends in many cases to the acceptance of something tantamount to the proposition that the properties, such as colour, for which observational predicates stand are essentially dispositional. At the same time, judging by my own observations, I think that many of us are inclined to treat properties such as shape and colour as persistently phenomenal. I dare say that the average man holds these two views in uneasy, perhaps inconsistent, combination.

However this may be, I now wish to argue that, if our average man does think of phenomenal properties as merely dispositional, he can be faced with a set of questions which Dummett has no right to ignore. What is the object which possesses these properties? How does he distinguish it from other objects? How does he visually locate it? It is no good his answering that it is the one and only object that satisfies such and such absolute descriptions, since the properties which answer to these descriptions are not phenomenal. If we knew nothing about an object except that it possessed these properties, we should not know where to look for it, nor should we have any means of recognising it if we did know where to look. Dummett tries to brush this objection aside by saying that, by hypothesis, the object is being observed. But here he conveniently forgets that all that its being observed amounts to, on his showing, is its producing a variety of sensible effects. It is these effects, not *its* visible colour and shape, for it has none, but the colour and shape of its sensory products that originally serve to distinguish it and to locate it in a space of which the other occupants are equally phenomenal. But how can it be conceived to occupy *this* position unless it is somehow identified with its effects or abstracted from them? If from the very outset it is set apart from them as their cause, we have nowhere to place it, indeed no object to place except an unknown somewhat of which *these* are the effects. We have to conceive of it, in Russell's way, as a wholly inferred entity; an unobservable occupant of an unobservable space. Dummett rejects this conclusion as firmly as I do, but it seems to me that his theory commits him to it.

Strawson is not open to this attack, since, although he takes what I have tried to show to be the mistaken view that the object of a perceptual experience is initially represented as its cause, he describes the object in phenomenal terms. I am inclined also to say that, even if he underrates the extent to which science impinges on what he calls 'the common consciousness', he gives a more accurate picture of it than Dummett allows. I agree with his contention that 'The lover who admires the curve of his mistress's lips or the lover of architecture who admires the lines of a building takes himself to be admiring features of these very objects themselves; but it is the visual shape, the visually defined shape, that he admires.' On the other hand, when it comes to his attempt to reconcile this view of the world with that of scientific realism, I think, as I have said, that he is less successful. He draws attention to the fact, which Dummett also stresses, that there is, as he puts it, 'an irreducible relativity, a relativity to what in the broadest sense may be called the perceptual point of view, built into our

ascriptions of visual properties to things'. Sometimes we treat a
particular point of view as privileged, in relation to certain others,
and consequently say that the colour which the object customarily
presents from that point of view is that which it really is. Sometimes
we shift our standards. The fact that blood looks mostly colourless
when seen through a microscope is not taken as conflicting with
the assertion that it is bright red. To insist that it is 'really' a
mainly colourless fluid would show a preference for one standard
over the other, but we are not required to choose between them.
In the same way, Strawson suggests, we can regard the adoption
of the standpoint of scientific realism as another illustration of
'the relativity of our "reallys"'. It is a shift to a different standard,
which is no more and no less valid than any of the others. '"This
smooth, green, leather table-top", we say, "is, considered scientifically, nothing but a congeries of electric charges widely separated
and in rapid motion."' These are two descriptions of the same
object, and the saving clause 'considered scientifically' renders them
compatible.

This is an ingenious suggestion which, if it were acceptable,
would neatly dispose of our problem. If I hesitate to accept it,
it is because I am not satisfied with the analogy between the shift
from one perceptual standpoint to another, the recognition of which
preserves us from inconsistency in our assignment of phenomenal
predicates, and the shift from any perceptual standpoint to one
that is not perceptual at all. For what is the force, in this context,
of the words 'considered scientifically'? If the analogy held, it would
be that the table looked quite different when seen through scientific
spectacles. But this would be merely to fall back on a metaphor.
The message delivered by 'considered scientifically' is that it is
no longer a question of how the table looks. In Dummett's terminology, we are to substitute an absolute for a relative description,
and the absolute description is abstract and not phenomenal. At
the same time the phenomenal standpoint has not wholly been
abandoned. For the 'congeries of electric charges' is supposed to
occupy the very same area of space as 'the smooth, green, leather
table-top'. The difficulty is to see how this is possible.

It was the attempt to meet this difficulty that prompted my
suggestion that the two standpoints might be fused by treating
the scientific particles as literally parts of the phenomenal table,
unobservable only because of their minuteness. But Strawson's arguments, among others, have convinced me that this is not satisfactory.
I am inclined to agree with him that 'no phenomenal properties
we seemed to perceive [these particles] as having would figure in
the physical explanation of our success' in perceiving them. Neither,

for the reasons which Dummett gives, am I any longer willing, as I once should have been, to dispense with scientific realism altogether by adopting a sufficiently radical form of instrumentalism. But then what possibility remains? It is not disputed that the scientist is able to explain the workings of our apparent objects of perception, as well as our perception of them, in terms of the workings of the imperceptible objects which figure in his theories. But then, if he is a realist, in the relevant sense of the term, he proceeds to expel the apparent objects from the places which they are needed to mark out, and allow his imperceptible objects to enjoy the vacant possession. The obvious objection to this procedure, as made by Russell and others, is that, when the appearances go, the places go with them; but perhaps this objection can be overruled. If it can be, and his procedure is consequently not incoherent, the scientific realist may be entitled to say that this is how things really are. But, for all the relativity of our 'reallys', in Strawson's happy phrase, I do not think that we can combine this conclusion with that which he attributes to the common consciousness. I do not see how such very disparate kinds of objects can each be regarded as 'really' occupying the same area of space.

Even so I may be wrong. This may not be a genuine difficulty. Perhaps I am underrating the relativity of my own last use of 'really'. If the criteria which are taken as justifying the scientist in regarding the place as occupied by a congeries of electric charges are satisfied, and if the criteria which justify us in seeing it as occupied by a smooth, green, leather table-top are also satisfied, the two propositions should not be in conflict. They come into conflict only when we put them on a par in arriving at a conception of what there is. But, as I said earlier, the question of what there is arises only at the level of some theory, and the materials in terms of which it is answered in one theory may not be given the same status in another. Thus, just as the sense data out of which the common-sense theory develops are treated in this theory as the effects on us of the visuo-tactual continuants which they have served to establish, so in the scientific theory which grows out of common-sense realism the visuo-tactual continuants are relegated in their turn to being the effects on us of the particles which are taken as accounting for them and, what is more, literally replace them.

In that case are we committed to scientific realism? I do not think that we are. We can admit the explanatory force of scientific theories without construing them instrumentally and still without letting them govern our conception of what there is. For that we can choose to remain at the level of theory which yields us a manifest picture of the world. This implies, I think rightly, that it is in the end a matter of choice. So long as the rival theories are intelligible and coherent, and can each within their own domains make good their claims to truth, there may, in Quine's terminology, be no further fact of the matter that would even give a sense to the question which one is correct. I see that this brings me back to something very close to Strawson's position, but it needed a consolidation which I hope that I have been able to supply.

II. INDUCTION

If there is such a thing as a set of common-sense beliefs about the world, it includes the belief that physical objects persist in time. It also includes the belief that they have causal powers. What these beliefs imply in both cases is the stability of the association of certain sets of properties. That such stabilities exist on a very wide scale is an assumption that permeates our language. In speaking of the house that I live in, the scenery that surrounds it, the clothes that I am wearing, the table at which I am writing, the pen with which I write, and, indeed, almost anything else that it might occur to me to mention, I am taking for granted not only a high degree of constancy in sets of complex patterns of appearances but the propensity for a number of possibilities to be realised. My pen would not be properly so called unless there were conditions, not difficult to bring about, in which it could be used to make marks on paper. The cigarette to which I have applied a lit match would not deserve the name unless in these actual circumstances it was gradually being transformed into smoke and ash. The conditions under which such possibilities are realised are not always easy to specify – indeed, we may not be capable of specifying them in detail if all the negative conditions which could prevent the effect from occurring have also to be listed – but the fact that we have a use not only for nouns such as 'pen' and 'match' and 'cigarette' but also for verbs such as 'write' and 'light' and 'burn' is a proof of our confidence that they frequently obtain.

Now, as Mr Mackie rightly points out, all such beliefs are inductive, in the sense that they involve an extrapolation from past to future experience. To quote his own example, 'The inductive question is not merely whether bread will continue to nourish us, but whether pieces of bread will continue, even for the next minute, to be bread.' Or, if their being pieces of bread is taken to entail this continuance, the same question can be rephrased by asking whether these objects satisfy this condition for being bread. It is important to stress the fact, as Mackie does, that induction is employed at this level because it is too often overlooked in philosophical discussions of the question. If there is a problem of induction, it is certainly not solved by the pretence that inductive reasoning does not occur, that what has been mistaken for it is the framing of hypotheses which we then attempt to falsify. Even if this were a correct account of scientific practice, at the level at which science searches for what Mackie calls deeper explanations, the question would still remain why the survival of a hypothesis should be thought to increase its credibility. What is more to the present purpose is that this scorning of induction is plainly in conflict with such elementary processes as our identification of the physical objects which we suppose ourselves to perceive, and the attribution to them of causal powers.

To say, however, that inductive reasoning undoubtedly occurs, is not to legitimise what has come to be known as the problem of induction. As frequently happens in philosophy, the problem has been thought to arise through the difficulty of meeting a sceptical argument. In this case, the argument goes back to David Hume and what it threatens to prove is that inductive reasoning cannot be rationally justified. As Mackie correctly summarises it, the steps in Hume's argument are, first, that inferences from one matter of fact to another are not deductively valid; secondly, that what is needed to validate them is the principle, which we do in fact assume, 'that the course of nature continues always uniformly the same'; and, thirdly, that this assumption is unwarranted. The principle of the uniformity of nature is not demonstrable, and any attempt to show it to be even probable must be circular, since, as Mackie puts it, 'probability always rests on causal relations, and therefore on the very presumption of uniformity which we are trying to establish'. It is to be remarked here that Hume uses the term 'causal relations' in a very weak sense, to cover any sort of factual regularity. But a principle which can neither be demonstrated nor shown to be probable has no warrant at all.

This argument has been challenged at every point. Some philosophers have made the futile attempt to show that factual inferences are deductive; others have appealed to a mythical relation of synthetic necessity; others have argued that the principle of the uniformity of nature is somehow demonstrable; and others that it can be shown to be probable without circularity. A second party admits the argument but denies that it forces a descent into scepticism. Obviously, there is no non-circular way of justifying inductive reasoning *in general*, any more than there is any non-circular way of giving a general justification of memory. It does not follow that anyone who relies on memory or induction in any particular instance is behaving irrationally. It is not as if it were necessary for a belief to be rational that it be guaranteed against error. We have criteria for deciding when a factual inference is warranted, and it should be enough for us that they are frequently satisfied: it would be illegitimate to ask for a justification of these criteria themselves.

A fact which has tended to escape the notice of both parties, though it tells more heavily against the first, is that Hume's argument is indeed invalid, but that what makes it invalid is that the second step fails. I doubt if we do rely on any such general principle as that of the uniformity of nature, except possibly in some such vague form as that every state of affairs is subject to some law or other, but the point is that, even if it were assumed, there is no tenable form of the principle which would validate inductive reasoning by making it deductive. This can be shown very simply by taking the example of the inference to a universal generalisation from a set of positive instances. Suppose that a number of objects of the kind A have been observed and all of them found to have the property f; then, if we add the premiss that nature is uniform, we are supposed to be able to deduce that every A has f. But what if we come upon an A which lacks f? In that case we shall have proved that nature is not uniform, since, if the conclusion of a valid deductive argument is false, one of the premisses must be false and in this case the only other premiss is true. But nobody in his senses who believes that the course of nature continues always uniformly the same can be construing this principle so narrowly that the discovery of any exception to a hitherto unviolated generalisation is sufficient to refute it.

This mistake in the form of Hume's argument is not, however, fatal to its purport. His contention that the principle of the uniformity of nature can neither be demonstrated nor shown without circularity to be probable will tell equally against any attempt to use such a principle to confer probability on the conclusion of a non-deductive argument, and, as I have argued elsewhere, a variant of his reasoning applies also to any attempt to achieve the same end without relying on a general principle of uniformity. A direct inference from one matter of fact to another cannot be demonstrated and any attempted proof of its probability will be circular, since, as I put it, 'the judgement of probability must have some foundation' and 'this foundation can lie only in our past experience'.

It is at this point that Mackie and I come into conflict. He

believes that there are logical, or at any rate *a priori*, relations
of probability on the basis of which we are entitled to assert,
independently of any previous evidence, that one proposition supports another. Having taken this vital step, he argues that such
a priori information when combined with knowledge drawn from
our past experience can serve to justify acceptance of a general
principle of uniformity. The use of this principle in conjunction
with 'specific observations and experiments' will then supply a respectable measure of support for 'particular generalisations and
extrapolations'. This position is not very different from that of
John Stuart Mill, except that Mill did not rely on *a priori* probabilities to save it from circularity.

Is Mackie entitled to rely on them? Many years ago, I advanced
an argument against the conception of probability as a logical
relation, to which I more recently said that I had not yet seen
any effective rejoinder. Put very briefly, my argument was that,
if all statements of probability are treated as necessary truths,
there can never be any reason for preferring one to another. In
particular, when two statements assign different degrees of probability to the same occurrence, on the basis of different amounts
of evidence, the one that is based on greater evidence can be
no 'better' than the one that is based on less. If the only 'facts
of the matter' are relational facts concerning the extent to which
one statement, or set of statements, probabilifies another, then,
provided that the relations have been correctly estimated in each
case, all statements of probability are equally valid; and if they
are equally valid what reason can we give for our failure to treat
them as equally reliable?

Mackie asserts that my argument has been met, but his own
way of meeting it, which he presents as typical, is simply to retreat
before it. He agrees that 'the logical-relation theory does not cover
the ground'. The reason why we should try to augment our evidence
is that the result will yield a better estimate of the 'epistemic
probability' of the conclusion. But what is this epistemic probability?
When he first introduces the term, Mackie treats it too as a logical
relation, differing from the others only in its being 'the probabilification by all the relevant evidence that someone has', which determines
'the degree of belief that it is rational for him to give to the
conclusion'. But giving a special name to a relation which satisfies
this condition achieves nothing to the purpose; it does not show
why it is rational to adjust one's degree of belief to this relation
of probability in preference to any of its equally valid competitors.
Mackie goes on to say that the reason why 'it is sensible, sometimes,
to look for more evidence' is that, 'in general, if you do so you

are more likely to be right in accepting or rejecting the conclusion, where this "likely" represents another epistemic probability'. But here he cannot simply be making the trivial point that an addition to the evidence may make the relation of probability greater or less. Whichever it was, we should still have no reason for preferring it to the one we had before. The greater 'likelihood' of our being right in accepting or rejecting the conclusion cannot consist in the substitution of one logical truth for another about the relation which the conclusion bears to different quantities of evidence. If such a likelihood is to be called an epistemic probability, then, as Mackie eventually acknowledges, epistemic probabilities are not relational. In other words, to say that an event is probable, in this sense, is not just an elliptical way of saying that its occurrence is probabilified logically by such and such items of evidence.

But what does it mean then? Mackie does not tell us, but he evidently takes it to imply that we are warranted in holding a corresponding degree of belief in the occurrence of the event in question; and one of the main points that he wishes to establish is that we can obtain this warrant *a priori*. This is the inference that we are supposed to draw from his example of the balls in the bag. If we know nothing but that the bag contains ten balls of equal size and weight, only one of which is white and the others black, it is rational to expect that a ball taken from the bag at random will be black. If the proportion of black to white were ninety-nine to one, the strength of this rational expectation would be correspondingly greater. Of course, it is taken for granted, as Mackie admits, that the black balls do not shrink or change colour once they have been put into the bag, and in general that there is nothing in the circumstances to favour the selection of the white ball. But these requirements are supposedly covered by the assumption that we are ignorant of everything except the dispro-portion in colour of the balls and their physical similarity.

As Mackie says, the reasoning seems cogent. The question is whether it is sustained by a valid *a priori* principle. Mackie claims that this is so, the principle in question being 'the principle of indifference or insufficient reason – say, that an incomplete body of information (a mixture of knowledge and ignorance) probabilifies equally each of a set of exclusive possibilities to which that incom-plete information is similarly related'. There are notorious difficulties about the selection of the range of possibilities, but let us suppose them to be overcome. We still need to ask what is meant by saying that each of the possibilities is equally probabilified. It seems to me that once we go beyond the purely mathematical calculus of chances – where to say, for example, that the probability of a tossed coin coming up heads three times in succession is $\frac{1}{8}$ is to say literally no more than that this is the ratio in which this sequence stands to the total number of possible sequences of three tosses each yielding either heads or tails – then all that we can sensibly be understood as claiming is that it is reasonable to expect that in the long run each of the possibilities will be realised with an approximately equal frequency; and it still seems to me obvious that a claim of this kind can be founded only upon past experience. Antecedently to experience, we have no reason in the case of any actual coin to suppose that it will turn up heads as often as tails. In the example of the balls in the bag, it is an inference from past experience that a mere difference in colour, as opposed to a difference in size or weight, will have no significant bearing upon the relative frequencies with which the balls are actually selected.

This is not to say that the principle of indifference cannot be put to any use at all. If we have reason to believe, or think that we have reason to believe, that an unexamined instance is covered by a strong statistical generalisation, then we should not expect it to belong to the relatively small minority of counter instances, unless we have grounds of a similar kind for assigning it to this class. This is the reason for assessing probabilities in the light of the total available evidence, which too often appears in the literature as a merely arbitrary principle. It is a matter of taking into account all those factors that have been shown to be relevant. The ground for not making exceptions where we have found no reason to make them is just that we have found no reason to make them. It is not that ignorance is a source of probability.

None of this takes us any further towards justifying induction. Mackie's invocation of Bayes's theorem merely illustrates the familiar point that, if we assign empirical counterparts to the ratios which figure in the calculus of chances, we can employ the calculus to derive empirical conclusions which inherit the truth that we have ascribed to the premises. Bayes's theorem assures us of the mathematical truism that, if the ratio of the possibilities which are favourable to a given occurrence is increased, for instance by the elimination of unfavourable alternatives, the ratio of the possibilities which are favourable to a distribution to which the event conforms is increased in the same proportion. For instance, if we are trying for three heads in succession and throw heads on the first occasion, the odds are doubled throughout. The half-chance on the first throw having been changed to unity, the chance of two successive heads advances from $\frac{1}{4}$ to $\frac{1}{2}$, and that of three from $\frac{1}{8}$ to $\frac{1}{4}$. It is a corollary of this sum that, if the number

of the adverse possibilities which are eliminated by a given occurrence is relatively large, the strengthening of the ratio in favour
of the more general outcome to which it conforms is correspondingly
great. That is, however, merely a matter of counting possibilities.
There is still a large step to be taken if we are to derive from
Bayes's theorem any such conclusion as that a hypothesis is likely
to be true if some event occurs which would be very improbable
if the hypothesis were false.

One way of taking this step is to correlate the possibilities with
actual frequencies on the basis of some set of assumptions about
the conditions under which past statistics can successfully be pro-
jected. Another is to make an *a priori* assessment of the actual
distribution of the possibilities throughout the universe, or some
portion of it, and hope that experience will bear it out. In fact,
a choice of the second option is almost bound to involve the
first. The assessment, though ostensibly *a priori*, will be made in
the light of past experience.

This seems to be true of Mackie's position. He represents himself
as relying on a principle of uniformity for which he claims initial
probability, but when we look into it we find that it resolves
itself into a set of rather vague descriptions of the arrangements
into which our observations have so far been contrived to fit:
'that individual things and goings-on tend to persist as they have
been'; 'that a confluence of two (or more) goings-on tends to
produce goings-on which partly continue each of the original ones';
'that most detectable events flow in this sort of way from detectable
neighbouring antecedents and likewise lead to detectable neighbouring sequels to which they are related by at least approximate generalisations'. This is, indeed, an improvement on a wholly general principle of uniformity, which would accommodate anything whatsoever,
but it remains doubtful whether these propositions are specific
enough to do the work required of them. The first two, in particular,
appear open to the objection that Nelson Goodman has raised.
There are many different views that can be taken of what is to
count as an 'individual thing' or a 'going on' or a 'partial continuance', and different decisions on these points bestow equal
favour on incompatible hypotheses. Mackie does indeed allude to
Goodman's argument, but his appeal to 'real resemblances' amounts
to no more than the adoption of Goodman's own proposal that
we should favour predicates which are entrenched, or, in other
words, persist in our linguistic habits and our reliance on the
inductions which are built into them. No new proof is offered
that this procedure is likely to be successful.

The third propostion, that lawlike connections are to be found between detectable neighbouring events, does have a useful content to the extent that, as Mackie claims, it supplies a basis for the employment of something like Mill's eliminative methods. This may itself be seen as a reason for adopting it, so long as the generalisations at which it helps us to arrive are found to hold good. I see no viciousness in the circle by which a more general principle is supported by more specific generalisations for which in its turn it provides support. Where I remain unconvinced is about the claim that any such principle can be shown to be probable *a priori*. It seems to me that at this level of specificity there is an indefinite number of directions that the course of nature could take, and I do not see that there can be any *a priori* ground for supposing that one is more likely to be realised than another. Indeed, unless one follows Carnap in constructing an artificial language, I do not see how one could draw up a list of *a priori* possibilities. The only possibility that Mackie offers, as an alternative to the conjunction of propositions which constitute his principle of uniformity, is 'that the world as a whole is purely random'. Since any describable world must exhibit some order, I do not know what would count as a purely random world, but I suppose it conceivable that we consistently failed to hit upon generalisations that we were able successfully to extrapolate. This is, however, clearly not the only alternative to the perpetuation of the degree and type of order that we believe currently to obtain.

I fail also to follow Mackie in his contrasting 'our ordinary way of thinking in terms of persisting things, and of what there is now producing what there will be' with what I have described as 'variations of scenery in a four-dimensional spatio-temporal con-tinuum'. It seems to me that the statements which conformed to this aspect of our ordinary way of thinking could all be rephrased in my terms and that the only significant difference is that, to the extent that my phrasing is more general, it admits a wider range of possibilities.

Mackie, to some extent echoing Harrod, has ingenious arguments which are designed to show, first, that even if the uniformity which he now believes to prevail lasts only for a limited time, it is unlikely to come to an end very soon, and, secondly, that its prevalence over a 100,000 years raises the probability that it holds over some period of a million years more than it raises the probability of its holding over some much shorter period. Once again these argu-ments depend upon the distribution of ratios throughout a finite list of logical possibilities, and it is not entirely clear to me in this instance how the list of alternative time-spans is to be compiled. It would seem that the number of items on the list must affect the outcome, and that the choice of this number must be arbitrary. Even so, let it be assumed that the list has been drawn up and that the ratios which Mackie relies on are exhibited in it. He still has to justify, and indeed to give something other than a purely numerical sense, to his contention that any two of these possibilities are equally probable. And this I still believe that he has been unable to do.

My conclusion is, then, that what Mackie calls his forward position is not tenable. I do not have the same objection to his 'second line of defence', and have indeed tentatively adopted a position which is very similar to it. The only difference here between us is that I dispensed with any general principle of uniformity, being satisfied with allowing particular inferences to be justified by the truth of the generalisations on which they severally relied. My reason for making no more general appeal to uniformity would not exclude Mackie's approach, since his principle is not devoid of specific content. It is unfortunate that he has been able to give us no more than an outline of it, but, going only by this outline, I doubt if its content is specific enough to carry the weight that he needs to rest upon it.

III. ESSENTIALISM

Professor Wiggins seeks to persuade me that there are necessary properties, which objects possess in virtue of being the objects that they are, and not merely in consequence of the way we choose to refer to them; that there are necessary connections between being an object of a given sort and having such and such an internal constitution; and that every relation of identity is a necessary relation. Thus, to use his own examples, he argues that Caesar is necessarily human, that whatever is human is necessarily generated in the way that human beings are, and that the evening and the morning stars are necessarily identical, although the proposition that they are necessarily identical may itself be contingent. It is characteristic of a necessary property, as Wiggins understands the term, that it belongs to its possessor *de re* and not merely to *de dicto*.

In spite of all that Wiggins says, I still find it difficult to make any sense of the notion of *de re* necessity. To take an example of my own, which he quotes, it still seems to me that the reason why my newspaper *must* contain news is not that it possesses the mysterious property of 'necessarily containing news' but just that if it did not contain news it would lack the property which I truly assign to it in calling it 'my newspaper'. I agree with him that it was a mistake for me to have said that the proposition 'my newspaper contains news' is analytic, since it contains the synthetic component that something is my newspaper, but it is sufficient for my purpose that the proposition that my newspaper does not contain news should be self-defeating.

Let me, however, examine his own examples. Caesar, he says, is necessarily human. Why should this be so? Obviously nothing of this sort can be deduced from the occurrence of the sign 'Caesar' in a grammatical English sentence, even if we make ourselves a present of the assumption that 'Caesar' is serving as a proper name. 'Cousin Theresa takes out Caesar, Fido, Jock, and the big borzoi.' Here the context makes it probable that what 'Caesar' names is a dog, but it might be an animal of any sort, or not even an animal: a book, for example, or, if the speaker or cousin Theresa herself is addicted to whimsy, a bicycle or a motor-car. It is certainly true that, if the sign is being used to name a human being, it is being used to name a human being, but this is no justification for any ascription of necessary properties.

What would be then? According to Wiggins, the question turns on our capacity to conceive of objects as having or lacking such and such a feature. 'X can be φ', he says, 'just in case it is possible to conceive of x that x is φ; x must be φ just in case it is not possible to conceive of x that x is not φ'. If the second of these conditions is fulfilled, φ is a necessary property of x. But now we need to be told something about the values that can be given to x. Consider the following example. I see what looks to me like a tortoise crawling among the flower beds. I decide to give the name 'Caesar' to this object, which I do not further identify. It seems to me that if I allow for the possibilities of illusion, including the imaginable effects of post-hypnotic suggestion, I can in this context conceive of Caesar as being almost anything whatsoever; since it is conceivable that I am undergoing a total hallucination, I cannot even exclude the possibility that 'Caesar' names nothing at all. I can, indeed, exclude the possibility of its naming a prime number or the quality of mercy but the reason for this is not that the Caesar to which I am referring has the necessary property of not being a prime number or not being the quality of mercy, but simply that the sentence that a prime number or the quality of mercy looks to me like a tortoise crawling among flower beds is not one to which in either case I am able to attach any meaning.

The position most favourable to Wiggins would be that in which my philosophical beliefs permitted me, as they in fact do, to interpret 'Caesar', in this usage, as naming a visual percept. For it does seem essential to its being that particular percept and no other that it be a tortoise pattern and that it be in the position which it actually occupies in my present visual field. The reason for this is that the existence of a visual percept simply consists, by definition, in there being such and such an appearance at such and such a point in a given visual field. If that constitutes an admission of *de re* modality, then I admit it. At the same time I see no call for any talk of necessity in this context. It is an entirely contingent fact that my sense experience at any given moment contains such and such features or, indeed, that it occurs at all.

What of the Julius Caesar to whom I presume that Wiggins was referring? Is Wiggins right in claiming that it is essential to this Caesar's identity that he was a human being? I find this question difficult, because I am not sure on what the answer to it depends. Certainly, there are many ways in which he can be identified that do not entail that he was human: for instance, as being whatever occupied such and such a position at a given time, or as being whatever so-and-so is currently thinking about. Not only that but everything that I believe to be true of him, except of course his actually being human and all that that entails, is logically consistent with his having been not a human being, but, let us say, a robot. It is true that the development of Roman technology was not such as to have made it causally possible for a robot then to have existed which accomplished all that I believe Caesar to have done, but that is again contingent. I can easily conceive of it as a possibility. On the other hand, if it were suggested to me that the Caesar whom I am taking it for granted that Wiggins and I both have in mind might conceivably have been a tortoise, or a chariot or a Gothic cathedral, I should be disposed to reject the suggestion. If it were asserted that our Caesar was a thing of one of these sorts, I should be inclined to say not just that the speaker was attributing to our Caesar properties that he did not in fact possess, but that he had mistaken our intentions: whatever the subject of his assertions might be, it was not the Julius Caesar to whom we were referring.

What does this prove? It may help if we begin by asking what makes me sure that I have captured Wiggin's reference. The answer lies in my belief, which is itself justified by my knowledge of Wiggins's habits, that, if I were to ask him who or what it was that he was intending to name, he would give such replies as that it was the author of *De Bello Gallico*, the conqueror of Pompey, the man who was stabbed by Brutus, and so forth. It is because I believe that these descriptions fit the object that I take him to be naming that I conclude that I have understood him correctly. This suggests that I associate a name such as 'Caesar', on a given occasion of its use, with some set of descriptions and that the reason why I regard the attribution of certain properties to the object named as evincing not just a factual error but also a failure to capture the reference is that the object's possession of them would be logically inconsistent with its satisfying those descriptions.

It does not follow from this, however, that the Caesar in question necessarily satisfies any one of these descriptions, or even any disjunction of them. One proof of this is that I can conceive of his having died in infancy. The fact that we can conceive of the history of any object as being curtailed to any extent we please has led some philosophers to conclude that everything necessarily comes into existence in the way that it does; in the case of a human being, that he is necessarily the offspring of such and such parents at such and such a place and time. I can see no warrant for paying such deference to horoscopes. If I were required to state Wiggins's exact age, or to furnish information about his parents, it is very unlikely that my guesses would be true, but their falsehood would certainly not entail that I have not been referring to him. It may be objected that the alleged necessity for things to originate in the ways that they actually do is not to be understood as implying that one cannot both be mistaken about a thing's origin and successfully refer to it, but, if it does not carry this implication, what such an attribution of necessity is supposed to mean is utterly obscure. I may add that the idea which has found favour in some circles, though not with Wiggins, that one can explain the nature of reference by saying that what makes A's use of a sign s a reference to an object O is its causal derivation from someone's original use of s to refer to O is a manifest absurdity. If one does not understand what it is for s to refer to O, one is none the wiser; and if one does, the causal flummery is otiose.

I wish that I could offer something more respectable. I once thought it necessary and sufficient for a reference to be made to a given object that one identified it by at least one item in its actual history or by at least one of its distinctive features, but, while I am still inclined to take this as a necessary condition of successful references, it no longer seems to me sufficient. It is true that, if I just see a stranger passing in the street, there seems to be no limit to the stories that I can make up about him. Even if I limit my freedom by supposing that he really is a man, which I have argued that I am not bound to do, I do not need to make all those stories consistent with his being where he was when I saw him. Having grasped him in this manner originally, I can keep my hold on him even when I relax this grasp. When I set him counterfactually at a different place and time, I rely on the safe hypothesis that he is otherwise identifiable. But suppose that the stories which I make up about this man are in the main true of someone else. Does it follow that I am unknowingly referring to this other person? I think not, so long as I am merely amusing myself with what I take to be counterfactual hypotheses. On the other hand, if I have actually mistaken my man, in the sense that I seriously attribute to him a set of properties which are in the main distinctive of some other person, then I think that I may legitimately be said to be referring to this other person, though possibly under the wrong name or under some false description. Such cases are not always clear-cut. In an article from which Wiggins quotes, I used the example of a schoolboy's writing an essay in which he so thoroughly confused the careers and the works of Dickens and Scott that there seemed to be no reason for saying that he was referring to one of them rather than the other, no matter which name he used, or indeed that he was making a successful reference to any one at all.

But are there no settled principles of individuation, as Wiggins puts it, by means of which we can decide between cases in which someone makes a false statement, or entertains a counterfactual hypothesis, about some particular to which he can properly be taken as referring, and those in which it must be held that the reference fails? I do not think that there are. So much depends upon the context of the speaker's utterance, the beliefs that he actually holds, even his position in time relatively to that of his referential target. For instance, it may seem obvious that, if Wiggins and I were to converse about a philosopher whom we agreed in describing as younger than ourselves, we could not conceivably be referring to the great David Hume. It enters into our common conception of David Hume that he lived in the eighteenth century. Yet a historian, writing hundreds of years hence, might very well give what we should regard as a substantially accurate account of the character and writings of David Hume, while placing his subject in the late twentieth century instead of the eighteenth. This would indeed be a serious mistake, but I should not infer from it that he could not be referring to the same person as we do. Living when I do, and knowing what I do, I feel debarred from conceiving of the Second World War as having not yet taken place. If it has not yet taken place, I am inclined to say, it cannot be the Second World War. At most it would be a third world war, which might resemble the second in its general features as closely as you please. Yet a believer in the foresight of Nostradamus might succeed in construing his sayings in such a way that they yielded accurate descriptions of the principal events of the Second World War, and the persons chiefly involved in it, with only the defect that they situated the whole episode a hundred years too late. His claim that Nostradamus had predicted the occurrence of the Second World War, but had made a mistake in his dating of it, would appear, to my mind at least, to make perfectly good sense.

These examples bring out the fatal weakness in the criteria which Wiggins offers for 'the elucidation of necessity *de re*'. The answer to the question what properties a thing can or cannot possibly be conceived of as having depends in part on the identity, the beliefs, and the imaginative power of the person to whom the question is put. But, if a property were necessarily attached to its owner, in the way that Wiggins wants, its detachment could not carry such relativity. It would have in all cases to lead to a failure of reference.

I do not therefore take my admission that intentions to refer to an object may sometimes properly be said to miss their mark as entailing that the object has any necessary properties. Nor has Wiggins persuaded me that the ascription to particular objects of necessary properties is sufficiently warranted on any other ground. But surely, it will be said, every object must at least have the necessary property of being identical with itself. And, if this is admitted, how can one refuse to accept Professor Ruth Barcan Marcus's proof that, if *x* is identical with *y*, it is so necessarily? As Wiggins so neatly put it, 'Hesperus is necessarily Hesperus, so if Phosphorus is Hesperus, Phosphorus is necessarily Hesperus'. 'The only conceivable point left to argue', he adds provocatively, 'is whether there is a *de re* use of "must" in English'. If this is true, the onus falls on his opponent. 'He has to dispel as illusion what seems to be fact that in English there exist many such *de re* uses.'

No doubt there do. There is no denying the fact that the English word 'must' and its rough equivalents in other languages are intelligibly used in a large variety of ways, and, while it is still not clear to me what Wiggins counts as a *de re* use, I am content to allow that some of them meet his requirements. He himself gives the example of the use of the word in acknowledgement of a moral or legal or social obligation, and it is also used in the expression of logical or scientific laws, or inferences which rely upon them; very often it represents no more than a choice between more or less probable explanations: 'I cannot find my umbrella. I must have left it on the bus.' What I cannot see is that any of these

uses commits one to a belief in natural necessity, if this is taken
to imply anything stronger than that the spatio-temporal relations
between the instances of different natural properties are in fact
found to exhibit a high degree of constancy.

But what of the property ascribed to some particular of being
necessarily identical with itself? All I can say is that I find it
mythical. This is not to deny that things are in fact identical with
themselves, or even that this fact can be stated in such a way
as to render the statement of it necessarily true. What makes the
property mythical, in my view, is that it is supposed to attach
to an object, independently of the way in which the object is
named or described. The proposition that Hesperus is identical
with Hesperus can be accounted necessarily true, under the presup-
position that Hesperus exists, so long as the sign 'Hesperus' in
each of its occurrences has not only the same reference but also
the same sense; or, if one demurs to saying that proper names
have a sense, so long as the name is associated in each case with
the same or with logically equivalent descriptions. In the case of
'Hesperus is identical with Phosphorus', the second condition is
not fulfilled. Consequently, Wiggins's argument fails, and its conclusion that 'Phosphorus is necessarily Hesperus', in the sense in which
I find it intelligible, is false.

I come now to the Crystal Palace and the Eiffel Tower. Let
it be granted that there are sets, and that the identity of a set
is derived from the identity of its members. Then it is plausible
to argue that the pair set consisting of these buildings has the
necessary property of having the Eiffel Tower for one of its members:
for surely any pair set which lacked the Eiffel Tower as a member
would necessarily be a different set. But this would be to overlook
the fact that the identity of a set is determinate only to the extent
that the identity of its members is determinate; and, as we have
already seen, and as Wiggins himself admits, the identity of an
object such as a building may be captured in many different ways,
not all of which necessarily yield the same result, though *ex hypothesi*
they all do so in fact. Thus, the pair set consisting of the Crystal
Palace and the Eiffel Tower is also the pair set consisting of the
largest building erected for the Great Exhibition in London in
1851 and the largest building erected for the Great Exhibition
in Paris in 1889. But it is obviously not necessary that these descriptions should be satisfied by the Crystal Palace and the Eiffel Tower.
There is therefore a sense in which the pair set consisting of the
Crystal Palace and the Eiffel Tower might not have contained
either of them. The sense is that the set can be uniquely identified
by a description which neither of them necessarily satisfies. Wiggins

indeed admits this possibility but contends that it does not affect his argument. He requires that the set be envisaged 'under a description which actually *excludes* the description "pair set consisting of Eiffel Tower and Crystal Palace"'. I confess that I do not follow his reasoning here. Evidently, no true description of a set which actually has these members is going to entail that it lacks them. For the removal of necessity, it is surely enough that the description be logically compatible with their failure to satisfy alternative descriptions, including the one that Wiggins selects, although this failure does not in fact occur.

I can deal at less length with Wiggins's third main example of what he takes to be *de re* necessity. The only reason that he gives for holding that there is a necessary connection between being an object of a given sort and having such and such an internal constitution is that, if we suppose 'that "man" (and every other natural-kind term, whether species or genus) has its sense fixed by reference to some hypothesised generic constitution', which in the case of 'man' he summarises as *G*, we can then draw such inferences as that anything 'is necessarily, if a man, then *G*'. But why should we suppose that senses are so fixed? It may be true, in the case of objects which we believe to share an internal constitution of some special kind that, when we take this constitution to have been discovered, we have a tendency to forge a conceptual link between it and the proper use of the term which is commonly used to collect objects of the sort in question. So, with the recent advance in our knowledge of genetics, it may be that the sense of the word 'man', and its counterparts in other languages, is already understood by scientists and may soon be generally understood as comprising *G*. It does not in the least follow that the words already had that sense before the knowledge to which they owe it was acquired, or even that we are bound to give it to them now. Neither is it necessary that men should have this constitution in order to possess their manifest properties. For, as Wiggins admits, other laws might have obtained. Wiggins's answer to this is that the existence of men is contingent on whatever laws of this sort actually do obtain, but this seems hardly to the purpose. The existence of men is contingent on many factors, including, for example, the fact that the temperature of the earth does not vary beyond certain limits, but surely no one wishes to incorporate references to facts of this sort in the concept of man. One could if one chose, since words have whatever senses one decides to give them, but the choice would not seem reasonable.

What makes one such choice more reasonable than another again depends on various factors, and I happily concede to Wiggins that our scientific beliefs are prominent among them. This is, however, a relatively slight concession and surely less than he sought to extract from me. I am sorry that I cannot make a better return for all the goodwill that he has shown me in his essay.

IV. PERSONAL IDENTITY

The problem of giving a wholly adequate account of the conditions that govern personal identity is one that has long troubled me, and I own that I am not entirely satisfied with any of my attempts to solve it. I remain a dualist in the sense that I maintain both a logical and factual distinction between physical and mental properties. I give primacy to the physical in that I believe that mental properties are causally dependent on them, at least to the extent that the possession of physical properties is causally necessary for anything to possess mental ones. This falls short of allowing that there is a perfect correlation between them, which I still regard as an open scientific question and I have not found any good reason to hold, as many philosophers now do, that the possession of a mental property of whatever sort is factually identical with being in some physical state. None of this would be inconsistent with taking the concept of a person to be primitive, in the sense that it is not susceptible of any further analysis than is contained in the statement that persons are persistent objects to which properties of both types are truly ascribable; but that does not content me either. The fact, on which Mr Foster and I are agreed, that Strawson failed in his attempt to prove this conclusion does not show it to be false, but does cast some suspicion on it; and I should in fact be surprised if it could be shown *a priori* that no further analysis was possible.

Even if we were to take the concept of a person to be primitive, as Professor Wollheim seems to do at least for the purposes of his essay, we should not be absolved from giving an account of personal identity; for, as Wollheim sees, we should still need to answer the question what it is that makes a person living at a given time the same person as one living at a different time: whether, for example, it is sufficient, or necessary, that the criteria for bodily identity be satisfied; whether memory, or the capacity for memory, is also a factor, and if so what weight should be attached to it. If we are to deal adequately with these questions we must also dispose of the problem, to which indeed Wollheim's essay is largely devoted, of the way in which memory itself is to be analysed.

The problems of giving an analysis of the concept of a person and of specifying the conditions of personal identity through periods of time would be solved together, if the attempt of William James and his followers to vindicate Hume's conception of the self as 'a bundle of perceptions' had been successful. For this would depend on our being able to discover relations between experiences occurring at the same or at different times, in virtue of which they could be held to belong to the same self. The self would then simply be identified with a series of experiences which were so related. In James's and Russell's version of this theory, some of the same elements, differently ordered, were made to compose physical objects, including human bodies, but, even if this treatment of physical objects were acceptable, which I no longer believe, it would not free us from the problem of matching selves with bodies; for the elements which were grouped to form a given body would themselves belong to different biographies. This is, indeed, a problem that confronts anyone who is not content to take the concept of a person as primitive. I am still inclined to think that the location of bodily sensations plays a part in its solution, but, as I admitted in my book *The Origins of Pragmatism*, where I made my most serious attempt to develop a Jamesian theory, I doubt if it can be made to bear the full weight.

Apart from this difficulty, which is not peculiar to it, there are serious objections to any theory of this type. To begin with, as Foster points out, any theory which both dispenses with a substance, a persistent Cartesian subject, and represents the continuity of the self as the product of relations which are only contingent seems forced to admit at least the logical possibility of there being experiences that are not anyone's. I find this consequence unpalatable, though I am not convinced by Foster that it is to be rejected on psychological grounds. I cannot agree with him that Hume would have spoken more truly if, instead of saying, 'I can never catch *myself* at any time without a perception, and never can observe anything but the perception', he had said, 'I never can catch a perception without myself'. Apart from the logical difficulty of deciding what would count in this context as 'catching myself', I do not think it empirically true that all of one's experiences are intrinsically labelled as one's own. The way in which I should now exclude the possibility of unowned experiences would be to accord them only an adjectival status in the theory which prescribed what there could be. This is not inconsistent with an attempt to construct persons out of them, if I am right in thinking that, once such a theory has been developed, the elements on which it is based can be reinterpreted into it.

The second main objection to an analysis of the sort that James attempts is that the relations of sensible continuity and sensible compresence, of which it is bound to make use, are covertly circular. This objection is raised by Wollheim with respect to sensible compresence: 'If,' he says, 'we ask what this relation of accompaniment is, the only satisfactory answer seems to be that it is the relation that holds between any two contemporary experiences just when they are parts of the total experience of one person at one time', and a little later he argues that 'it is quite unwarranted for someone, at any rate for an empiricist, who sets himself to solve the problem of personal identity over time, to find the problem of personal identity at a time quite unproblematic'.

The only answer that I can find to this objection is that, while the relation of sensible compresence does in fact hold between the contemporary features of a single person's experience, else it would not serve its purpose, it is not illegitimate to take it as a primitive. This is most clearly apparent in the case of single sense fields. For instance, I can see nothing objectionable in Goodman's use of a primitive relation of 'togetherness' to particularise his colour qualia by combining them with sensory qualia of place and time. The procedure becomes more dubious when the relation is understood to hold between the data of different senses, especially as it may also have to serve in turning qualia into particulars, but I am still inclined to think that it is defensible. The charge of circularity would also be weakened if provision could be made in these terms for co-consciousness, from which it would follow that experiences related by sensible compresence need not be only those of a single person. This would require that sensible compresence need not be transmissible through sensible continuity. At least two experiences which were sensibly compresent might each be sensibly continuous with different experiences which were not themselves sensibly compresent. If the series were divergent except at this one point, it might seem more natural to regard it as the sharing by two persons of a common portion of experience, rather than as the momentary fusion of two persons into one. It might be held against the theory which I developed in *The Origins of Pragmatism* that it excluded the possibility of any such intersections. I now think that the theory could be fairly easily modified so as to admit them, but there may well be complications which I have overlooked.

If we are going to accept the relations of sensible compresence and sensible continuity as primitive, and allow them to hold between any items of sense experience, in Foster's broad sense of the term, then I see no good reason why they should not also be allowed to range over propositional acts and attitudes to the extent that these consist, like thoughts and feelings, in mental episodes. To the extent that they do not so consist, the problem is shifted to that of the relation between mental states and bodily behaviour. Foster's motive for restricting the range of the relations on which he founds personal identity is to make room for his Cartesian subject. But the nature of this subject, considered apart from its experiences, remains obscure and we are not given any account of its ownership of its 'non-presentational states'. It might be thought to be needed to perform 'presentational acts' were it not that these presentational acts themselves appear superfluous, especially when we find that the relations which are intended to unite them are simply borrowed from those that obtain between the sensory patterns on which they are supposed to be directed.

Perhaps the most serious difficulty in the way of a Jamesian approach is that of finding a way to bridge the possible gaps in consciousness. Here memory comes into play, but, for reasons which Wollheim quotes me as giving and others that he adds to them, it proves unequal to the task. This does not imply that memory cannot in any way serve as a criterion of personal identity, but only that it cannot do the work on its own or with no stronger support than the relations of sensible compresence and continuity. As I showed in *The Origins of Pragmatism*, it needs to depend in some way upon a physical criterion.

Foster seems to me to come to the same conclusion, though by a very different route. In the first instance, he bridges the gap by use of the subjunctive conditional that, if the conscious 'streams' on either side of it were to be extended in the appropriate temporal direction, they would eventually merge. He sees, however, that this conditional needs some basis, otherwise there would be no guarantee that the right junctions would be made; and he looks for this basis to some natural law. The example which he gives is one that has the effect of tying presentations to the brain on which they are causally dependent, so that the gap is bridged by the continuity of the brain.

Foster regards himself as entitled to offer this example because he has given up what he calls a nomological – that is to say, a Humean – view of causation. He does not say with what he has replaced it. Had he not given it up, he would have fallen foul of his own previous objection, which I once accepted, that a view of causation which allows only a temporal mode of association between mental and physical states is not sufficient to secure the right pairings. I am now inclined to think that I gave way to Foster's objection too easily. It seems to me that one might be able to exclude the unwanted pairings by augmenting the causal generalisation that when a brain B is in state S an experience E occurs, in such and such a temporal relation to S, by a set of subjunctive conditionals to the effect that, if B were to be put in such and such other states, then such and such other experiences would occur which would be sensibly compresent or continuous with E. Admittedly, I tend to be dissatisfied with any analysis that terminates in subjunctive conditionals, but in this case there may be some mitigation in the fact that subjunctive conditionals are already implicit in the invocation of causality.

However this may be, the point I now wish to press is that, if Foster is willing to admit a unique causal dependence of particular mental phenomena upon the states of a particular brain, then much the simplest course for him to take would be to relate minds to bodies in this way and make the identity of persons depend on the identity of bodies – especially as he agrees with me, against Strawson, that such a procedure would not be circular. It would not even prevent him from admitting the possibility of fission and fusion, if he wished to, or allowing whatever weight he chose to the criterion of memory, since, while he would be bound to hold that the identity of a person at any given time depended on the identity of some body, he would not be bound to hold that one and the same person was necessarily tied throughout its existence to one and the same body. It is true that Foster does not commit himself to saying that the appeal to a form of bodily continuity is the only way of preserving personal identity through gaps in consciousness. He thinks that there may be 'persistence relations' which are sustained by laws of a purely mental kind, but he gives no examples and I very much doubt if he could find any. It is also true that the course which I am pressing on him, since it gives primacy to the body, would be out of tune with his claim that persons are essentially mental and only contingently corporeal. But for this claim, so far as I can see, he offers no argument whatsoever.

Since I have been mainly critical of Foster's views, I am happy to add that I accept his charge that my concept of a person has so far been too narrow and that he has convinced me that the association of 'functional role' with 'psychological character', which he outlines at the beginning of his essay, is most probably needed if we are to have adequate grounds for ascribing experiences to persons other than ourselves.

That functional role and psychological character are closely connected is maintained also by Wollheim, in particular with respect to memory, which forms the main topic of his essay. His way of putting it is that function is served by phenomenology and he suggests that the special function of memory is to place us under the influence of the past – not, of course, the past in general, but particular pieces of it. He goes on to argue that these particular pieces are not, as one might at first expect, the pieces that one remembers, in one way or another, but rather in each case 'that which currently satisfies the acquisition condition for the memory'. He provisionally explains his use of the term 'acquisition condition' by identifying it with a cognitive state of which it is true, first, 'that it is either that state of a person in which he first comes to know of what is remembered or a state in which he would have come to know of it if he had not already had knowledge of it', and, secondly, 'that the cognitive state is causally responsible for the rememberer's having that memory'.

This provisional explanation is later found to be inadequate, because it leaves out a factor which is of crucial importance for the claim, which Wollheim eventually makes, that memory, or at least a special form of it, is criterial of personal identity, where what he has told me that he means by its being criterial is that it is at least a sufficient condition, if not also a necessary condition. The factor in question is the 'affective tone' of the original cognitive state and that which it transmits with accretions to subsequent memories of what was cognised. It is his view of the development and power of this 'affective store' that enables Wollheim to say such things as that 'A partial explanation . . . of why it is that what we survey in memory is ours is not the absurd one . . . that surveying it makes it ours, but the profounder one, that surveying it makes us its', or that memory of the sort which he takes to be criterial of personal identity 'is so because it is creative of personal identity'.

I doubt if I fully understand everything that Wollheim has to say about the affective aspect of memory, and, to the extent that I do think that I understand it, I find some of it false, but before I enter into this question I have some comments to make on his account of memory in general. He criticises me, I think with good reason, for giving a one-sided analysis of memory, considering it only from the point of view of the contribution that it makes to knowledge, with the result that I have ignored its affective aspect, taken too little notice, in his view, of its causal filiation, and said next to nothing about its phenomenology. He himself classifies memory under the three separate headings of retention, recollection and experiential memory, distinguishing them both phenomenologically and causally. Retention is the memory of which the acquisition condition is knowledge obtained at second hand. It is 'to have been told some fact and not forgotten it'. It is not confined to events within one's own experience or even to the past. One can have retentive memory of something timeless, such as a theorem in mathematics, or even of the future: one can remember in this sense that something is going to happen. Recollection and experiential memory, on the other hand, are tied to the past and Wollheim seeks to show that when they are veridical they bear only on events that fall within one's own experience. In both cases the acquisition condition is knowledge at first hand. In the case of recollection it may be, and in that of experiential memory it must be, knowledge 'from the inside'. Otherwise the difference is phenomenological. Experiential memory is remembering an event 'from the inside' and recollecting it is not, even though its acquisition condition may have been inside knowledge. And what is characteristic of remembering, say, an action from the inside is, first, that 'I shall tend to remember, both systematically and literally, what I thought and what I felt in the doing and suffering of it', and, secondly, that 'I shall tend to rethink or refeel these very thoughts and feelings'. The distinction is later restated in the form, 'The function of recollection is to place us under the influence of the past as this was perceived. The function of experiential memory is to place us under the influence of some piece of the past as this was experienced.'

I have no fault to find with Wollheim's account of retention, except on a point of usage. It seems to me that when the episode of which one acquires second-hand knowledge is an action of one's own or an event of which one was oneself a witness, one does not normally say that one remembers it, even as a fact. For instance, it quite often happens to me that other people tell me that they well remember my doing or saying certain things, of which I have no recollection. In such cases, although I believe my informants, I should consider it incorrect to say that I remembered these episodes in any sense at all, even one which implied no more than that I remember the fact that they occurred. There are, however, examples that go the other way. I can properly speak of remembering the fact that I first went to my preparatory school at such and such a date, even though I do not recollect it. I do not know how to account for these vagaries of usage and see no harm in Wollheim's regimenting them.

The distinction between recollection and experiential memory seems to me very tenuous, especially when it is applied to one's memories of the day to day occurrences that make up the greater part of one's life. Do I recollect or experientially remember having sausages for breakfast, or going out to post a letter, or accepting an invitation to dinner, or staying up late last night to watch the dramatisation of an Agatha Christie novel on television, or writing the earlier part of this essay? In every case, except possibly that of the television play, where what stays in my memory is the story itself rather than any feelings that it aroused in me, the action would fall on the side of experience rather than perception, in so far as the two are contrastable; but I have no tendency to relive these experiences, or to revive the thoughts that I had when I underwent them. I have no sensation of eating a second breakfast, and no idea of what I was thinking about, if anything, when I walked to the pillar-box. Neither am I at all engaged in the re-creation of what I wrote yesterday, though I well remember writing it. In fact it seems to me that I have very few experiential memories, if one seriously applies Wollheim's criteria.

This would mean that I led an emotionally very impoverished life, and indeed hardly qualified as a person at all, as Wollheim understands the term, if he were right in his belief, or what appears to be his belief, that it is only experiential memory that causes affective tone. But this is surely false. I am more frequently and often more strongly affected by my memories of things that I have read about, or things that I have witnessed, than by 're-creations' of my own emotional experiences. Wollheim might try to answer that what carries the affective tone is not my retention or recollection of the facts in question but my experiential memory of my coming to learn about them, but this again seems to me false. For instance, I have strong feelings about the Sacco and Vanzetti case but no recollection at all of the occasion on which I first learned about it. Of course, there is a sense in which these feelings are causally derived from that occasion, whether I recollect it or not, inasmuch as I should not have them unless I had learned about the case; but that is trivial and beside the point.

I am the more confident that it is beside the point because I also think that Wollheim is wrong in claiming that the affective tone even of an experiential memory is causally dependent on the affective tone of one's original cognition of what is remembered. It seems to me entirely possible that an action which one performs with emotional indifference, or even with pleasure, should give rise to a very painful memory, either because of its unforeseen consequences, or because of a subsequent change in one's moral or religious beliefs. Indeed, I have no doubt that such things quite frequently happen.

This brings me to a wider issue on which we disagree. I cannot accept his assertion that memory is essentially causal. I briefly set out my main objection to any view of this kind at the end of my paper 'The Causal Theory of Perception'[5] and I think that

I cannot do better than quote what I said there.

> It has [I said] become fashionable in recent years to write a
> causal condition into the analysis of memory, the argument being
> that it is only by tracing the appropriate causal path between
> the event remembered and the remembering of it that we can
> distinguish the genuine memory of a past event from a true
> belief in its occurrence which is derived from some other source.
> It seems that the tracing of the path would have to go into
> scientific detail, so that it is questionable whether the causal
> condition should be held to enter into the meaning of the memory
> statement on which it bears. Nevertheless the argument for regard-
> ing it as a truth-condition is persuasive. Here too, however,
> it should be obvious that past events cannot be introduced as
> the otherwise unknown causes of our apparent memories of them.
> We cannot pick and choose among them in order to forge the
> right causal links, unless they have been independently identified.
> And how can this be originally achieved except through memory?
> The insertion of a causal clause into the analysis of some of
> our judgements of memory is therefore only a subsidiary refine-
> ment. It depends on our taking the experiences on which the
> judgements are initially based as pointing on their own to the
> occurrence of past events.

It is important to note that, if a causal clause is introduced,
it calls for scientific detail, since it is the way in which the original
experience is causally related to one's present belief in its occurrence
that makes the difference in the doubtful cases. I therefore consider
it a weakness in Wollheim's argument that he speaks of one or
other acquisition condition as being the reason for a memory without
giving any account, in physiological or even in psychological terms,
of what he takes 'being the reason' to consist in. I also wish
to argue that belief in the fulfilment of the 'right' causal condition
plays little or no part in what Wollheim calls the Goethe case,
at least from the point of view of Goethe himself. When something
that I had forgotten 'comes back' to me, or when I decide that
I really do remember something about which I was previously
unsure whether I really remembered it or only imagined it as the
result of believing what I had been told about it, it seems to
me just not true that the change consists in my acquiring a fresh
view of the causal provenance of my belief in the past occurrence
of the event in question. It consists in my passing into a different
phenomenological state: a state of which I am unable to give
an informative description, but one that is familiar to anyone who

has had the experience of having a memory 'flash' upon him.

As I see it, Wollheim's attempt to prove that experiential memory cannot run across persons is vitiated not only by what I take to be his mistaken view of the role of causality in memory but also by his misrepresenting the issue. Thus, one of the premisses of his argument is that the person who originally had the experience is *ex hypothesi* a different person from the one who claims to remember it from the inside. But the case presented, say in support of a belief in reincarnation, is one where someone claims to remember from the inside experiences which the use of a physical criterion of identity would lead us to assign to a different person, and the question at issue is whether they are to be accounted different persons or not. We have to decide whether the criterion afforded by the phenomenology of memory, and the truth of the beliefs about the past which are involved in it, supported perhaps by some similarities of character, are to be considered as overriding the criterion of physical continuity. Whatever the right answer, if there is one, the point of the problem is lost if it is considered only with respect to the use of the criterion of memory.

On the related question of fission, I admire the boldness but question the felicity of Wollheim's proposals. It is open to him to count what he assumes to be the elderly products of the fission of an elderly man as one and the same person, but I doubt if the similarity of the affective tones of their memories, even when backed by the telepathic understanding of one another with which he credits them, should be allowed to override the obvious objections to identifying what are to all other appearances two different persons, leading different lives. Where the fission takes place in youth, Wollheim's reason for saying that the products are different persons is that their common affective store is small and is likely to become increasingly divergent. But the trouble with this argument is that it threatens the personal identity of almost anyone who lives at all a long life. For instance, the affective tone of my present memories of my schooldays is very different from the intense feelings that I had about them at the time, and this is only one of the many ways in which my affective store has changed in the course of over sixty years. Yet I have no inclination to say that I have not remained the same person. Neither can I believe that I am unique in this respect.

A suggestion of a different kind which Wollheim makes is that the ancestral relation not of actual memories but of the capacity to remember might serve as a sufficient condition of personal identity. This would require that at every moment of a person's life, including periods of sleep and apparent unconsciousness, he was having at least one experience which he was subsequently capable of remembering. In default of a criterion for the capacity to remember, this proposition is hardly possible to decide, but on the face of it I see no compelling reason for supposing that it is empirically true.

The fact that I disagree with so much of the argument of Wollheim's paper does not diminish my admiration for the breadth of its range, its elegance and its ingenuity.

Professor Unger's proof that neither he nor any other composite object exists depends entirely, as he acknowledges, on Eubulides's 'paradox of the heap', more commonly known nowadays as the sorites paradox. If we regard everything as being composed of atoms, and think of Unger as consisting not of cells but of the atoms which compose the cells, then, as David Wiggins has pointed out to me, a similar argument could be used to prove that Unger, so far from being non-existent, is identical with everything that there is. We have only to substitute for the premiss that the subtraction of one atom from Unger's body never makes any difference to his existence the premiss that the addition of one atom to it never makes any difference either.

I do not pretend to be in a position to say all that needs to be said about the sorites paradox. In this particular application of it, the fallacy appears to lie in the false assumption that the relation of 'being the same X with one less element than on the previous count' is transitive. If B is the same X as A with one less element than A, and C is the same X as B with one less element than B, and D is the same X as C with one less element than C and so on, it does not follow that Z is the same X as A, since Z may not be an X at all. A crowd ceases to be one when it loses a sufficient number of members. The puzzle, as in the case of other vague terms, is that one cannot say what number is minimally sufficient. As in our previous instance of colour, the determination of the point at which the change takes place is in some degree arbitrary.

Unger's case is slightly easier than that of the heap because his existence depends not merely on the number of atoms which his body contains but on the structure which they form. Consequently the removal of a certain number of them, if suitably chosen, would put an end to him long before the number of remaining atoms came near to zero, and the addition of atoms to him, again if suitably chosen, would put an end to him very long before the number of atoms in the world was exhausted, even if we took it to be finite, and so exhaustible.

V. VERIFICATION AND METAPHYSICS

Both Professor Körner and Professor Williams are frequently justified in their criticisms of me. Williams, in particular, has hit
upon a serious flaw in the argument of my *Language, Truth and
Logic*, and indeed in the original standpoint of the members of
the Vienna Circle which *Language, Truth and Logic* was mainly
intended to reflect. In requiring that a proposition be verifiable,
at least in principle, if it was to have any factual content, and
in taking the further and much stronger step of equating the factual
content or 'cognitive meaning' of propositions which passed the
first test with the ways in which they could be verified, we failed
to make it clear, even to ourselves, whether 'the method of verification' had to lie within the possible resources of the person who
was interpreting the proposition or, to speak more accurately, the
sentence which was designed to express it, or whether the requirement of verifiability could be construed in a more impersonal and
therefore more liberal fashion.

In the first edition of *Language, Truth and Logic* I put forward
the verification principle only in its weaker aspect, as supplying
a means of demarcating sense from nonsense, but actually used
it in the stronger way when I attempted to give analyses of various
types of proposition. In both cases, I adopted the standpoint which
I think that Ryle was the first to criticise as that of 'verifiability
by me'. This was not made explicit in my unsuccessful attempt
to formalise the principle, where I required of 'a genuine factual
proposition' that 'experiential propositions' be derivable from it,
and defined an experiential proposition as one that recorded 'an
actual or possible observation'.[6] Though it was clear from the
remainder of the book that I took such observations as consisting
in the occurrence of sense data, or sense contents, as I then preferred
to call them, this need not have excluded the more liberal interpretation. I might have had in mind something along the lines of William
James's and Russell's neutral monism, later to be developed by
Nelson Goodman into a neutral 'language of appearance'. I was
strongly influenced at the time not only by Russell's work, in
the period of his phenomenalism, but even more by Carnap's book
Der Logische Aufbau der Welt, on which Goodman's *The Structure
of Appearance* was originally meant to be a commentary. That
I did not take this view, or at least that I was confused on this
point, as indeed Carnap also was, is shown, however, by my informal
rendering of the principle, where I speak of a sentence as being
'factually significant to any given person, if, and only if, he knows

how to verify the proposition which it purports to express – that is, if he knows what observations would lead him, under certain conditions, to accept the proposition as being true, or reject it as being false'.[7]

My use of the principle, in this narrow form, as a means of analysis determined my treatment, on which Williams comments, both of propositions about the past and of propositions about the experiences of others. In maintaining the view that propositions ostensibly about the past were reducible to propositions about the present or future evidence that was obtainable in their favour, I was following the example not of the Viennese positivists, who seem to have overlooked this problem, but that of the pragmatist C. I. Lewis, who advanced it in his book *Mind and the World-order*. Most probably Lewis derived the view from C. S. Peirce, whose work I had not yet read, though later I came greatly to admire it. This did not prevent me from coming to regard this conception of the past as excessively counter-intuitive, even if it was not inconsistent. What *was* inconsistent, I now think, was my attempt to combine a behaviouristic analysis of my attribution of experiences to others with a mentalistic analysis of my attribution of them to myself. For here I was not using the word 'my' as a constant: I was not making a factual claim to be the only creature to whom mental predicates could be attributed. The distinction was intended to hold good for anyone who referred to his own and to other persons' experiences. But, if I was bound to construe any reference to the experiences of another person behaviouristically, this would still remain true when the reference was made by him. The suggestion that he interpreted such propositions mentalistically should not have been intelligible to me, unless I violated my theory by interpreting these propositions also as referring to his behaviour.

No doubt my desire to escape from these consequences of my original use of the verification principle was partly responsible for my attempts to make it function neutrally in the ways that Williams criticises. I do not think, however, that this was my only motive. Independently of any views that one might hold about the connection between verification and meaning, it seemed clear to me that the factual content of a statement reporting a historical event must be the same, no matter when and no matter by whom the statement was made. The example I gave in my essay 'Statements about the Past',[8] to which Williams referred, was that of the coronation of George VI, and I argued that the only difference made by the use of the past, present or future tenses to situate this event in the year 1937 lay in the different 'indications' which it gave of the temporal relation of the utterance to that date.[9] I spoke

of the use of a particular tense as indicating rather than stating
the existence of this relation, in order to avoid the undesirable
consequence of making all tensed sentences self-referential, as they
would become if one construed the use of the different tenses
as actually stating that the reported event was earlier, or later,
than or contemporaneous with the utterance of the sentence which
contained the tensed verb. My example was, indeed, defective in
that I did not make it explicit that the name 'George VI' should
refer to the same person on each occasion of its use, and possibly
also be associated with the same descriptions, though this is a
point about which I remain uncertain.

The same considerations apply to statements about people's experiences. It seemed and still seems to me clear that a statement
which attributes an experience of a given sort to a particular person
at a particular time must have the same factual content, no matter
when or by whom the statement is made, at least so long as
the person in question is picked out by a demonstrative or identified
by the same description. If the person is identified by different
descriptions, and these descriptions are taken seriously as affecting
the truth value of the statements in which they occur, then clearly
their use in different statements may endow the statements with
different factual contents even though the descriptions are satisfied
by the same person. In the case where proper names are used,
the question whether more should be required for preservation
of factual content than that the names should agree in their reference
is here again open to dispute.

Though the need for a satisfactory account of our actual understanding of proper names will still remain, the problem can be
bypassed if we are able to carry out Quine's policy of eliminating
singular terms. As I see it, this calls for something more than
the ability to manoeuvre proper names and other singular terms
into the position of predicates. The introduction of predicates such
as 'being identical with Socrates', and their attachment to quantifiers,
though plainly feasible, seems to me of little philosophical interest
unless such expressions are taken as doing duty for some general
description which the individual in question happens in fact to
be the only one to satisfy. In such a case there will be no pretence
that the reformulation of the sentence containing a singular term
preserves synonymity; but it can be claimed that it provides an
adequate paraphrase of the sentence, in the sense that it supplies
all the same information with the addition of whatever else is
involved in fixing the reference of the proper name in general
terms, or in making explicit, again in general terms, what the
use of a demonstrative requires the interpreter of the sentence

to pick up from the context of its utterance.

I advanced this thesis on its merits, without taking it to bear on the question of verifiability – apart from discussing the difference which the introduction or omission of the claim that the descriptions employed were uniquely satisfied would make to the conditions under which the resultant propositions could be held true or false.[10] The question is whether the thesis is tenable. One objection to it, which I acknowledged, is that it implies the identity of indiscernibles, which has not been shown to be a necessary truth. Another, which Williams appears to favour, is that to assume that the supply of information consists only in the accumulation of predicates is to beg the question. I hope that I never seriously suggested that anything to the purpose would be achieved through replacing 'now' by 'at the same time as this utterance'. My present utterance could be taken as a point of temporal reference, as could any other contemporaneous event, but the thesis would require it to be explicitly dated, or identified by some general description. In that case Williams might argue that someone who knew that I was writing these words now would know something more than someone who knew only the truth of an 'eternal sentence' to the effect that someone answering uniquely to such and such a description writes such and such a series of words at a specified date. Of course, if we ask what more it is that the first of them knows, we can only be referred back to the context and to what the demonstratives indicate. He would know that *I* am the person who answers to the description, that *these* are the words in question, that the time at which they are written is *now*. If this does represent additional knowledge, then it will follow, though not quite in the way that Wittgenstein intended, that there are things that cannot be said, or at least not exhaustively said, but need to be shown.

I am impressed by this objection. On the other hand, if one can make sense of the notion of a recording angel and imagine his writing a history of the world, in which he was not himself included, one can envisage his employing a tenseless language and forgoing the use of any demonstratives. Would it follow on this ground that his record must be incomplete? Would there be anything known to us that he could not express? I am inclined to say that there would not be. But perhaps there is no more to this than that the knowledge which he would lack could *ex hypothesi* not be described. Yet, if the whole book of nature is open to him, it is hard to see why the mere fact that he does not figure in the story should in any way diminish his knowledge of it. Perhaps the right answer is that one who consciously participates in any section of the world's history is bound to see it differently from the way it is seen by one who finds or puts himself outside it; and it is this difference that the use of token-reflexive expressions is needed to mark out.

The adoption of a neutral standpoint, so far as this is feasible, affects scepticism only in the sense that it is a position in which a certain range of sceptical questions is ignored. It does not exclude them. Not only does it still allow us to raise doubts about the support which statements of one sort lend to those of another, but, even if I allow that statements about, say, the experiences of other persons, or events that happened long ago, can be adequately expressed without any references to myself, I can still be troubled by the question how I, being whom I am and occupying the spatio-temporal position that I do, can attach the right meaning to them, or what justification I can have for believing them to be true. It was my continuing interest in such problems that led to my attempts, which Williams criticises, to make it seem possible that events which occurred before I was born, or experiences which were in fact those of another person, might have been directly accessible to me. No doubt they were ill conceived. I think that Williams is right in saying that I was hovering in some confusion between the criteria of verifiability in general and verifiability by me. There was, however, a little more to it than that. Part of the point of my enlarging the range of descriptions which I might conceivably satisfy was to give a broader basis for the argument from analogy as a support for the attribution of experiences to others, and, as I have already shown in my remarks about essentialism, I was independently opposed to regarding my spatio-temporal position as a necessary fact about me.

Williams is surely right in saying that the notion of an optimal verification point is generally not independent of empirical theories. I have already conceded that there may be particular occasions on which the evidence of eyewitnesses can justifiably be overridden. If my idea was that the meaning of an indicative sentence could be identified with the honest report of whoever was in the best position to verify what it expressed, this would at most apply to someone's accounts of his current experiences. I have nothing to add to my rather inconclusive remarks on this topic in my discussion of David Pears's essay.

Professor Körner makes the familiar but substantial point that the status of the verification principle, in whatever form it is cast, is itself open to question. In the introduction to the second edition of *Language, Truth and Logic*, I treated it as a stipulative definition,[11] which admittedly blunted its use as a weapon for cutting off metaphysics. It then did no more in this way than throw the onus on the metaphysician to show how his assertions could have truth conditions of any sort, and how their fulfilment could be assessed. I think also that the power of the principle is further diminished by the substitution of verifiability in general for verifiability by me. The notion of an observation statement becomes less precise, and if one does not commit oneself to physicalism the limitations set to the extension of mental predicates may appear somewhat arbitrary.

Of the four examples that Körner gives of what he reckons to be metaphysical sentences, I think that I should never have wished to deny sense altogether to the three that he construes as expressing 'immanent' propositions. At the outset I think that I should have treated the principle of continuity as what I then called a disguised definition: I should have seen it as partly determining what was to count as a law of nature. Nowadays I should view it as contributing part of a possible framework for what, following Peirce, I call the arrangement of facts. The disagreement between those who accept and those who reject it I should treat as a disagreement of policy. The same would apply, in my view, to the dispute over the law of excluded middle, where I take the question at issue to be the utility of employing one or other set of logical constants. Once the decision is made – say, for the sake of argument, in favour of the interpretation of the sign for disjunction which yields the law of excluded middle – then I should still wish to claim, for what it is worth, that the law had been made analytically true. Körner is mistaken when he says that this puts me in no position to distinguish between contingent propositions and the necessary propositions of logic. It is indeed the case that the truth or falsehood of any proposition is partly dependent on the meaning which is conventionally attached to the signs which express it; what is thought to be distinctive of analytic propositions is that their truth depends upon this alone.

I have more difficulty with the principle that there are actually infinite sets. It could be represented as depending on the acceptance of a convention – in the case of integers, as a consequence of the rules that every number has to have a successor and no two numbers the same successor. But what sense is then to be made of the word 'actually'? This could be viewed as a proposal to take a realistic view of numbers, and so at least as raising the logical question of the possibility of reducing them to sets. This would, however, still leave us with what Körner might justifiably call the metaphysical but still significant question of the status of set-theory. I am puzzled also by the question whether it is possible that there should be an infinite number of physical objects of a given sort. Certainly the assertion of the existence of an infinity of any such instances would not be falsifiable, but it might perhaps enter into a confirmable theory. 'That is never just a single hypothesis which an observation confirms or discredits, but always a system of hypothesis' was a point that I acknowledged in the first edition of *Language, Truth and Logic*.[12]

At that time I dismissed as literally nonsensical all attempts to express 'transcendent' metaphysics, including the assertion that God exists when it was so interpreted as to fall into this class. I should still argue that there was no sense in attributing personal qualities to a 'necessary being'. On the other hand, in *The Central Questions of Philosophy* I did not exclude the possibility that the positing of a superior intelligence as the author of nature should serve as an explanatory hypothesis, though I also maintained that since it did not in fact fulfil this function there was no justification for it.[13]

Professor Körner appears to use the term '*a priori*' in an exceptionally wide sense. I should not agree that 'the primary system' which I developed in *The Central Questions of Philosophy* contains *a priori* concepts, unless one is to count any theoretical concept as *a priori*, which is not explicitly defined by the terms that one takes to be epistemologically primitive. On the contrary, I attempt to show in some detail how a theory which makes provision for the objective existence of a visuo-tactual continuant can be constructed on the basis not, as Körner wrongly says, of 'something only subjectively perceived', but of neutral qualia. It is only when the theory has been developed that the percepts into which qualia are concretised are annexed by the theory and contrasted as subjective states with the objects to which they have given rise.

I do, however, agree with Körner that my account of what I called 'the secondary system' was much too perfunctory. I should at least have said something about the different types of generalisations that it might include, and the problems raised by the occurrence within them of terms that stood at different removes from observation. At this point I find Körner's own suggestions helpful. I accept his view that, in many cases at least, 'making use of a scientific theory involves three sets of concepts': a set of concepts which apply to what could be observed; a set of ideal concepts which are not so directly applicable; and, thirdly, a linking set, though here I am not sure that the linking need always take so precise a form as that of making the extensions of concepts of the other two sets coincide. I also think that there may be more general principles, such as those setting out criteria of identity, which may be said to describe the framework of a theoretical system, though

I should not choose to call them metaphysical.

My answers to the questions that Körner explicitly puts to me are, first, that if I were to make a distinction between the scientific and metaphysical contributions to a secondary system, I should locate the metaphysical elements in the choice of the entities which the system countenanced and the conventions to which they were made subject. In this use, the word 'metaphysical' would not carry a pejorative force. Secondly, I do not take the propositions of a secondary system to be assertive, in Körner's sense. I speak of them as being acceptable or unacceptable arrangements of facts, rather than as being true or false. At the same time, I allow that what appears as a secondary system in one world-view might be accorded ontological primacy in another. I have already said that I do not exclude the option of scientific realism. Thirdly, it is surely not the business of science just to make explicit what is implicitly accepted. It could be the business of metaphysics in so far as it entered into the philosophy of science, but there seems no compelling reason why the use of the term should not be extended to cover the criticism of scientific theories, and proposals for conceptual revisions. I should, however, prefer to keep the term 'analysis' for the explication of current scientific theories. Finally, I suppose that some metaphysical propositions could be said to be necessary *a priori*, in that they spelled out conventions that were not envisaged within the system as capable of being violated. Nevertheless, in view of the possibility, which Körner himself acknowledges, of there being 'a plurality of categorial frameworks', I am more inclined to say that such an invocation of *a priori* necessity would be superfluous, if not misleading.

I have postponed my reply to Williams's query about the possibility of formulating a neutral sentence to express what he calls a 'core proposition': that is to say, a proposition which yields the common factual content of what is expressed by the members of a 'convergent set' of sentences. I take it that what is to be understood here by convergence is that the propositions which the members of the set express are all made true by the same concrete occurrence, or series of occurrences. Then the question is whether such an occurrence could, as it were, be uniquely pinned down. I think that it could, relatively to one's choice of a primary system. Assuming that one can find at least an indirect way of associating mental predicates with places as well as times, I think that a core proposition would be one that assigned to a determinate region of space–time the most specific property for which there was a corresponding predicate in a language in which the primary system could be fully described. If the primary system is one like my own, which requires the factual occurrence to be observable, then the character of the core propositions is relative not so much to any given language, which can always be enlarged, but to our admittedly contingent powers of sensory discrimination.

As for the question of whether 'an absolute representation of things' is possible, I have admitted the option of scientific realism only on condition that the theories of which the ideal constituents are reified are subject to empirical conditions of acceptance. The suggestion that the world is 'really' such that the entities of which it consists are not even capable of being conceptually linked to the possible objects of human observation is one that I continue to regard as devoid of any literal significance.

NOTES

N.B. With the exception of note 4, all notes refer to writings of A. J. Ayer.

1. 'Phenomenalism', *Proceedings of the Aristotelian Society*, XLVIII (1947–8); repr. in *Philosophical Essays* (London: Macmillan, 1954).
2. *The Central Questions of Philosophy*, (London: Weidenfeld and Nicolson, 1973).
3. *The Origins of Pragmatism* (London: Macmillan, 1968).
4. See H. H. Price, *Perception*, ch. I. (London, Methuen, 1932).
5. 'The Causal Theory of Perception', *Proceedings of the Aristotelian Society*, suppl. vol. LI (1977).
6. *Language, Truth and Logic*, 2nd edn (London: Gollancz, 1946) p. 38.
7. Ibid., p. 35.
8. 'Statements about the Past', *Proceedings of the Aristotelian Society*, LI (1950–1); repr. in *Philosophical Essays*.
9. *Philosophical Essays*, p. 186.
10. See 'Individuals', *Mind*, 1952; repr. in *Philosophical Essays*.
11. *Language, Truth and Logic*, p. 16.
12. *Language, Truth and Logic*, 1st edn, (London: Gollancz, 1936) p. 94.
13. *Central Questions*, pp. 222–3.

The Philosophical Works of A. J. Ayer

1930 Review of *The Art of Thinking* by Dimnet, in *Oxford Outlook*.
1933 'Atomic Propositions', *Analysis*, vol. I, no. 1, pp. 2–6.
1934 'The Genesis of Metaphysics', *Analysis*, vol. I, no. 4, pp. 55–8, repr. in M. Macdonald (ed.), *Philosophy and Analysis*.
'On Particulars and Universals', *Proceedings of the Aristotelian Society*, vol. XXXIV, pp. 51–62.
'Demonstration of the Impossibility of Metaphysics', *Mind*, vol. XLIII, no. 171, pp. 335–45, repr. in P. Edwards and A. Pap (eds), *A Modern Introduction to Philosophy* (Glencoe, Illinois Free Press; London: George Allen and Unwin, 1957).
1935 'Internal Relations', *Supplementary Proceedings of the Aristotelian Society*, vol. XIV, pp. 173–85.
'The Criterion of Truth', *Analysis*, vol. 3, nos 1 and 2, pp. 28–32.
'The Analytic Movement in Contemporary British Philosophy', in *Histoire de la logique et de la philosophie scientifique* (Paris: Hermann).
1936 *Language, Truth and Logic* (London: Gollancz).
'The Principle of Verifiability, *Mind*, vol. XLV, no. 178, pp. 199–203.
'Concerning the Negation of Empirical Propositions', *Erkenntnis*, vol. 6, pp. 260–3.
'Truth by Convention', *Analysis*, vol. 4, nos 2 and 3, pp. 17–22.
'Freedom of the Will', *The Aryan Path*.
Reviews of M. M. Lewis, *Infant Speech*; R. Aaron and A. Jocelyn Gibbs (eds), *An Early Draft of Locke's Essay*; Alfred Noyce, *Voltaire*; all in the *Spectator*.
1937 'Verification and Experience', *Proceedings of the Aristotelian Society*, vol. XXXVII, pp. 137–56.
'Does Philosophy Analyse Common Sense?', *Supplementary Proceedings of the Aristotelian Society*, vol. XVI, pp. 162–76.
Review of 'Die Sogennanten Definitionen durch Abstraction' by H. Scholtz and H. Schweitzen, in *Mind*, vol. XLVI, no. 182, pp. 244–7.

1938 'On the Scope of Empirical Knowledge: A Rejoinder to Bertrand Russell', *Erkenntnis*, vol. 7, pp. 267–74.
1940 *The Foundations of Empirical Knowledge* (London: Macmillan).
1944 'The Concept of Freedom', *Horizon*, vol. 9, no. 52, pp. 228–37.
1945 'The Terminology of Sense-Data', *Mind*, vol. LIV, no. 216, pp. 289–312, (repr. in *Philosophical Essays*, 1954).
      'Jean Paul Sartre', *Horizon*, vol. 12, no. 67, pp. 12–26.
      'Deistic Fallacies', *Polemic*, no. 1.
      'Secret Session' (on J.-P. Sartre), *Polemic*, no. 2, pp. 60–3.
1946 'Freedom and Necessity', *Polemic*, no. 5, pp. 36–44. (repr. in *Philosophical Essays*, 1954).
      'Other Minds', *Supplementary Proceedings of the Aristotelian Society*, vol. XX, pp. 188–97.
      'Contemporary British Philosophers', the *Listener*.
      'Albert Camus', *Horizon*, vol. 13, no. 75, pp. 155–68.
1947 'The Claims of Philosophy', in *Polemic*, no. 7, pp. 18–33. and *Reflections on Our Age* (Unesco).
      'Phenomenalism', *Proceedings of the Aristotelian Society*, vol. XLVII, pp. 163–96, (repr. in *Philosophical Essays*, 1954).
      Thinking and Meaning, University College London Inaugural Lecture (Athlone Press).
1948 'The Principle of Utility' in G. W. Keeton and G. Schwarzenberger (eds), *Jeremy Bentham and the Law* (repr. in *Philosophical essays*, 1954).
      'Portrait of a Victorian Liberal: J. S. Mill', the *Listener*.
      'Science and Philosophy', the *Listener*.
      'Some Aspects of Existentialism', *Rationalist Annual*.
      'Discussion: Philosophy without Science', *Philosophy*, vol. 23, no. 84, pp. 65–6.
      'What Can Logic Do for Philosophy', *Supplementary Proceedings of the Aristotelian Society*, vol. XXII, pp. 167–78.
1949 'On the Analysis of Moral Judgements', *Horizon*, vol. 20, no. 117, pp. 171–84.
      'Mr. Koestler's New System', the *New Statesman*.
      'Uber die Gedankenfreiheit', *Der Monat*.
      'Ockham's Razor and Modern Philosophy', the *Listener*.
      'There is no Mystery', the *Listener*.
1950 'Basic Propositions' in M. Black (ed.), *Philosophical Analysis* (Ithaca: Cornell University Press; repr. in *Philosophical Essays*, 1954), pp. 60–75.
      'J.-P. Sartre's Definition of Liberty', the *Listener*.
      'Religion and the Intellectual', *Partisan Revue*.
1951 'Statements About the Past', *Proceedings of the Aristotelian*

Society, vol. LII, pp. i–xx (repr. in *Philosophical Essays*, 1954).

'On What There Is', *Supplementary Proceedings of the Aristotelian Society*, vol. XXV, pp. 137–48 (repr. in *Philosophical Essays*, 1954).

'The Physical Basis of Mind', BBC talks (Oxford: Basil Blackwell).

'The Philosophy of Science', in A. Heath (ed.), *Scientific Thought in the 20th Century*.

1952 *British Empirical Philosophers*, ed. with R. Winch (London: Routledge and Kegan Paul).

'Individuals', *Mind*, vol. LXI, no. 244, pp. 441–57 (repr. in *Philosophical Essays*, 1954).

'Negation', *Journal of Philosophy*, vol. 49, no. 26, pp. 797–815 (repr. in *Philosophical Essays*, 1954).

1953 'Cogito Ergo Sum', *Analysis*, vol. 14, no. 2, pp. 27–31.

'To See the World Rightly', *20th Century*.

'The Identity of Indiscernibles', *Proceedings of XIth International Congress of Philosophy*, vol. III, pp. 124–9 (North Holland Pub. Co., Amsterdam; repr. in *Philosophical Essays*, 1954.

'L'Immutabilité du Passé', *Etudes Philosophiques*, no. 1, pp. 6–15.

'One's Knowledge of Other Minds', *Theoria*, vol. XIX, pp. 1–20 (repr. in *Philosophical Essays*, 1954).

'Truth', *Revue internationale de philosophie*, vol. 7, pp. 183–200 (repr. in *The Concept of a Person and Other Essays*, 1963).

1954 *Philosophical Essays* (London: Macmillan).

'Discussion of: "Sur la preuve en philosophie"', *Revue internationale de philosophie*, vol. 8, pp. 92–105, pp. 158–69.

'Can There be a Private Language', *Supplementary Proceedings of the Aristotelian Society*, vol. XXVIII, pp. 63–76, (repr. in *The Concept of a Person*, 1963).

'Beyond the Pleasure Principle', *Encounter*.

1955 'What is Communication', *Studies in Communication*, vol. I (London: Secker and Warburg).

'Philosophy at Absolute Zero', *Encounter* and *Jamtid Ock Framted*.

1956 'What is a Law of Nature', *Revue internationale de philosophie* vol. 10, pp. 144–65 (repr. in *The Concept of a Person*, 1963).

'The Vienna Circle', BBC Series: *The Revolution in Philosophy* (London: Macmillan).

'Philosophical Scepticism' in H. D. Lewis (ed.), *Contemporary*

British Philosophy (London: George Allen and Unwin Ltd.).
'The Philosophy of Bertrand Russell', the *Observer*.
'Mr. Wilson's Outsider', *Encounter*.
'Le Memoire exposé', *Bulletin de la société francaise de philosophie* (Paris).
The Problem of Knowledge (London: Macmillan; USA: St Martin's Press; UK Penguin Books).

1957 'In Defense of Reason', *Encounter*.
Reviews of: G. H. Von Wright, R. Rhees, G. E. M. Anscombe, *Ludwig Wittenstein: Remarks on the Foundations of Mathematics*; A. Wood, *Bertrand Russell: The Passionate Sceptic*; Colin Wilson, *Religion and the Rebel*, in the *Spectator*.
'Perception', C. A. Mace (ed.), *British Philosophy in the Mid-Century* (Allen and Unwin).
'Logical Positivism', debate with Father Copleston in P. Edwards and A. Pap (eds), *A Modern Introduction to Philosophy* (London: George Allen and Unwin Ltd).
'The Concept of Probability as a Logical Relation' in S. Körner (ed.), *Observation and Interpretation*, Proceeding of 9th Symposium of Colston Research Society (New York: Dover).

1958 'Meaning and Intentionality', *Proceedings of XIIth Congress of Philosophy*, vol. I, pp. 141–55 (Sansoni Editore: Firenze).
'Philosophie et langage ordinaire', *Dialectica*.
Biographies of Ernst Mach and Moritz Schlick, in *Encyclopedia Brittanica*.
Reviews in the *Spectator* of G. J. Warnock *English Philosophy Since 1900;* Ludwig Wittgenstein, *The Blue and Brown Books*; and Norman Malcolm, *Ludwig Wittgenstein: A Memoir*

1959 *Logical Positivism*, ed. A. J. Ayer (Glencoe, Illinois: Free Press; London: Allen and Unwin).
'Privacy', *British Academy Henriette Hertz Trust Lecture* (Oxford: University Press; repr. in *The Concept of a Person*, 1963).
'Critical Notice of P. F. Strawson's *Individuals*', *Indian Journal of Philosophy*.
'Phenomenology and Linguistic Analysis', *Supplementary Proceedings of the Aristotelian Society*, vol. XXXIII, pp. 111–24.
Reviews in the *Spectator* of K. Popper *The Logic of Scientific Discovery*; Bertrand Russell, *My Philosophical Development*; Stuart Hampshire, *Thought and Action*; Ernest Gellner, *Words and Things*.

1960 'The Philosophy of Bertrand Russell' in *Concise Encyclopedia of Philosophy and Philosophers* (London: Rainbird McLean Ltd).

'Philosophy and Language', Oxford University Inaugural Lecture (Oxford University Press).

'Professor Malcolm on Dreams', *Journal of Philosophy*, vol. LVII, no. 16, pp. 517–35 (repr. in *Metaphysics and Common Sense*).

1961   'The Concept of a Person', Royal Institute of Philosophy Lecture (repr. in *The Concept of a Person*, 1963).

'Reply to Mr. Stigen on Problem of Knowledge', *Inquiry*, vol. 4, pp. 291–304.

'Rejoinder to Professor Malcolm', *Journal of Philosophy*, vol. LXIII, no. 11, pp. 297–9.

Review in *Encounter* of P. Thody, *J.-P. Sartre*. Review in *Scientific American* of E. Nagel, *The Structure of Science*. 'On the Probability of Particular Events' in *Revue internationale de philosophie* vol. 15, pp. 336–75 (repr. in *The Concept of a Person*, 1963).

1962   'Breaching the Dialectical Curtain – Philosophy in Russia', *Observer*.

'A History of Logic. The Ghost Revives', the *New Statesman*.

1963   'Impressions of Contemporary Russian Philosophy', Willesden Public Library, lectured and taped.

'The Philosophy of Bertrand Russell', *Into the 10th Decade* (London: Allen and Unwin).

'Carnap's Treatment of Other Minds' in A. Schilpp (ed.) *The Philosophy of Rudolph Carnap* (Evanton, Illinois, USA: Northwestern University Press).

'Brain, Mind and Memory', the *Sunday Times*.

'Philosophy and Science' *Ratio*, vol. v, no. 2, pp. 156–67 (first published in Russian translation in *Voprosy Filosofi* 1962 and repr. in *Metaphysics and Common Sense*, 1969).

'Professor Popper's Work in Progress', the *New Statesman*.

'The Legacy of Hume', the *New Statesman*.

The Concept of a Person and Other Essays (London: Macmillan; USA: St Martin's Press).

1964   'On Making Philosophy Intelligible', British Association Granada Television Lecture, published in *Communication in the Modern World* (published by Granada Television) (repr. in *Metaphysics and Common Sense*).

'Reply to Mr. Getier on Personal Identity' (USA: Wayne State University).

'Freedom and Happiness', the *New Statesman*.

'Man as a Subject for Science', *Auguste Comte Memorial Lecture*, (University of London Athlone Press) (repr. in *Metaphysics and common Sense*, 1969).

'Knowledge, Belief and Evidence', Festschrift for Professor Jorgensen, published in Danish *Philosophical Yearbook* vol. 1 (Copenhagen: Munksgaard) (repr. in *Metaphysics and Common Sense*, 1969).

1965 Review in *Mind*, vol. LXXV, no. 299, pp. 444–7, *On the Nature of Meanings*, by N. E. Christensen.

Review of E. Gellner, *Thought and Change*, in the *Sunday Times*.

'Chance', *Scientific American* (October), vol. 213, no. 4 (repr. in *Metaphysics and Common Sense*, 1969).

1966 'Humanism and Reform', *Encounter*.

'What I Believe' in *What I Believe* (London: Allen and Unwin).

'The Relevance of Humanism: An Inquiry into Humanism' (BBC publications).

'Philosophy and Politics', Eleanor Rathbone Memorial Lecture (Liverpool: Liverpool University Press) (repr. in *Metaphysics and Common Sense*, 1969).

'Metaphysics and Common Sense' in W. Kennick and Morris Lazerowitz (eds), *Metaphysics* (USA: Prentice Hall) (repr. in *Metaphysics and Common Sense*, 1969).

Review of P. B. Medawar, *Scientific Thought: The Art of the Soluble*, in the *New Statesman*.

1967 'Reflections on Existentialism', Presidental Address to Modern Languages Association, published in *Modern Languages*, vol. XLVIII, no. 1 (repr. in *Metaphysics and Common Sense*, 1969).

Review of *The Autobiography of Bertrand Russell 1872–1914* in *Encounter*.

'Has Austin Refuted the Sense Datum Theory?', *Synthèse*, vol. XVIII, pp. 117–40 (repr. in *Metaphysics and Common Sense*, 1969).

'Induction and the Calculus of Probabilities', *Entretiens de Liège*.

1968 'Philosophy and Scientific Method', given to *Philosophical Congress* in Vienna.

'On what There Is', *Proceedings of the Israel Academy of Sciences and Humanities* (repr. as *On What Must There Be?* in *Metaphysics and Common Sense*, 1969).

'G. E. Moore on Propositions and Facts', in M. Lazerowitz

and A. Ambrose (eds), *G. E. Moore: Essays in Retrospect*
(London: Allen and Unwin).
The Origins of Pragmatism (London: Macmillan and Co.;
San Francisco: Freeman, Cooper and Co.).
Review of *The Autobiography of Bertrand Russell, vol. II,*
in the *Spectator*.
Review of D. Armstrong, *Mind and Matter. A Materialist
Theory of Mind*, in the *New Statesman*.
Review of *Correspondence of Jeremy Bentham vol. 1,
1752–1776, vol. II, 1777–1780*, ed. by T. L. S. Sprigge, in
the *Observer*.
Review of J.-P. Sartre, *Anti-Semite and Jew*, tr. by G. J.
Becher, and Paul Nizan, *Aden-Arabie*, in the *Spectator. The
Humanist Outlook*, ed. and introduced by A. J. Ayer (Lon-
don: Pemberton Books).

1969   'An Honest Ghost', Festschrift in honour of Professor Gilbert
       Ryle.
       'Qu' est'ce que la Communication?', *Revue internationale
       de philosophie*, vol. 23, pp. 385–403.
       Metaphysics and Common Sense (London: Macmillan; San
       Francisco: Freeman, Cooper and Co.).
1970   'Has Harrod Answered Hume', Festschrift in honour of Sir
       Roy Harrod in *Induction, Growth and Trade* (Oxford: Oxford
       University Press).
       'Pragmatism and Logic', *Times Literary Supplement*.
1971   *Russell and Moore: The Analytical Heritage* (London: Mac-
       millan; USA: Harvard University Press; 1970 William James
       Lectures at Harvard University).
       'Le Problème de la confirmation, *Revue internationale de philos-
       ophie*, vol. 25, pp. 1–31.
       Contribution to 'Conversations with Philosophers', published
       in *Modern British Philosophy* (London: Secker and Warburg).
       Contribution to 'Profiles and Discussion', published in
       Reflexive Water (London: Souvenir Press) ed. by Fons Elders.
1972   *Probability and Evidence* (London: Macmillan; Columbia
       University Press, USA, John Dewey Lectures for 1970 at
       Columbia University).
       Bertrand Russell (London: Fontana; USA: Viking Press).
       'Bertrand Russell', article in the *Evening Standard*.
       'Russell as a Philosopher', British Academy Lecture.
1973   'Wittgenstein on Certainty', Royal Institute of Philosophy
       Lecture, published in *Understanding Wittgenstein*, pp. 226–45
       (London: Macmillan Press, 1974).

'Dummett on Frege', Review of M. Dummett's *Frege: Philosophy of Language* in the *Listener*.

'Reflections on the Varna Congress', I.I.P. Proceedings.

The Central Questions of Philosophy (London: Weidenfeld; USA: Holt Reinhardt).

'On a Supposed Antimony', *Mind*, vol. LXXXII, no. 325, pp. 125–6.

'The Case for Materialism': Review of *The Nature of Things* by A. M. Quinton, *Encounter*.

1974　'Wittgenstein, the School Master', review of W. W. Bartley, *Wittgenstein*, III, in the *Observer*.

1975　'Self Evidence' in E. Pivcevic (ed), *Phenomenology and Philosophical Understanding* (Cambridge: Cambridge University Press).

'Identity and Reference' in *Philosophia*, vol. 5, no. 3, repr. in *Language in Focus*, ed. A. Kasher, a volume in honour of Y. Bar Hillel (Reidel, 1976).

'Philosophy' in *The Owl of Minerva*, edited by C. J. Bontemps and S. J. Odell, (USA: McGraw-Hill).

1977　*Part of My Life* (London: Collins).

'The Causal Theory of Perception', *Supplementary Proceedings of the Aristotelian Society*, vol. LI, pp. 105–26.

1978　'Introduction to William James' in W. James, *Pragmatism and Meaning of Truth* (Harvard University Press, paperback edn).

Contribution in *Men of Ideas*, BBC.

'Revival of Oxford Philosophy', *Guardian*.

1979　'Meaning and Truth', review of *Truth and Enigmas* by Michael Dummett.

'Weight of Evidence', review of *The Possible and The Probable* by Jonathan Cohen, *Books and Bookmen*.

'Geist und Körper' (Mind and Body) in *Seele und Leib: Geist und Materie* (Berne: Peter Lang).

Forthcoming

'Analytical Philosophy', Proceedings, IIP, Dusseldorf, 1978.

'Free Will and Rationality', *Festschrift* for Sir Peter Strawson.

Hume, (Oxford University Press).

Introduction to VI Book of John Stuart Mill's *System of Logic*.

Bibliography

ARTICLES CITED

G. E. M. Anscombe, 'The Intentionality of Sensation: A Grammatical Feature' in R. J. Butler (ed.) *Analytical Philosophy* (2nd series).
——— 'Memory "Experience" and Causation' H. D. Lewis (ed.) in *Contemporary British Philosophy* (4th ser.)
J. L. Austin, 'Other Minds' in *Philosophical Papers*, eds J. O. Urmson and G. Warnock.
N. J. Block, and J. A. Fodor, 'What Psychological States Are Not' in *Philosophical Review* LXXXI (1972).
R. Cartwright, 'Class and Attributes' in *Nous* I (1967).
——— 'Some Remarks on Essentialism' in *Journal of Philosophy* LXV (1968).
M. Deutscher, and C. B. Martin, 'The Causal Theory of Memory' in *Philosophical Review*, LXXV (1966).
A. Flew, 'Locke and the Problem of Personal Identity' in *Philosophy*, XXVI (1951).
J. A. Fodor, and N. J. Block, 'What Psychological States Are Not' in *Philosophical Review*, LXXXI (1972).
J. Foster, 'Psycho-physical Causal Relations' in *American Philosophical Quarterly*, Vol. 5, No. 1 (1968).
S. Freud, 'Screen Memories' in his *Complete Psychological Works*, J. Strachey, (ed.) Vol. III.
——— 'A Difficulty in the Path of Psycho-Analysis' in his *Complete Psychological Works*, ed. J. Strachey, Vol. XVII.
S. Kripke, 'Identity and Necessity' in *Identity and Individuation*, ed. M. K. Munitz.
J. L. Mackie, 'Locke's Anticipation of Kripke' in *Analysis*, Vol. 34, No. 6 (1974).
C. B. Martin, and M. Deutscher, 'The Causal Theory of Memory' in *Philosophical Review*, LXXV (1966).
T. Nagel, 'What Is It Like To Be a Bat?' in *Philosophical Review*, LXXXIII (1974).
D. Parfit, 'Personal Identity' in *Philosophical Review*, LXXX (1971) reprinted in *Personal Identity*, ed. J. Perry.
C. A. B. Peacocke, 'Appendix to David Wiggins "The De Re 'Must'"' in G. Evans and J. McDowell, *Truth and Meaning: Essays in Semantics*.
D. Pears, 'Hume's Account of Personal Identity' in *David Hume: A Symposium*, ed. D. Pears.
J. Perry, 'Can the Self Divide?' in *Journal of Philosophy*, LXIX (1972).
A. N. Prior, 'Opposite Number' in *Review of Metaphysics*, II (1957).
——— 'Time, Existence and Identity' in *Proceedings of the Aristotelian Society*, LXVI (1965–6).
H. Putnam, 'Is Semantics Possible' in *Languages, Belief and Metaphysics*, eds H. Kiefer and M. Munitz.
W. V. O. Quine, 'Quantifiers and Propositional Attitudes' in *Journal of Philosophy*, LIII (1955), reprinted in *Ways of Paradox and Other Essays*.
B. Russell, 'Knowledge by Acquaintance, Knowledge by Description' in *Mysticism and Logic*.
——— 'The Relation of Sense-Data to Physics' in *Mysticism and Logic*.

D. Sandford, 'Borderline Logic' in *American Philosophical Quarterly*, Vol. 12, No. 1 (1975).

W. Sellars, 'Empiricism and the Philosophy of Mind' in *Science, Perception and Reality*.

R. Sharvey, 'Why a Class Can't Change Its Members' in *Nous* II (1968).

S. Shoemaker (with R. Chisholm), 'The Loose and Popular and the Strict and Philosophical Senses of Identity' in *Perception and Personal Identity*, eds. N. S. Care and R. Grimm.

S. Shoemaker, 'Persons and Their Past' in *American Philosophical Quarterly*, Vol. 7 (1970).

S. C. Wheeler III. 'Reference and Vagueness' in *Synthèse*, Vol. 30, No's. 3–4 (1976).

D. Wiggins, 'Identity, Continuity and Essentialism' in *Synthèse*, Vol. 23 (1974).

―――― 'The *DeRe* "Must"; A Note on the Logical Form of Essentialist Claims' in G. Evans and J. McDowell, *Truth and Meaning: Essays in Semantics* (1976).

―――― 'Locke, Butler and the Stream of Consciousness: and Men as a Natural Kind' in *Philosophy*, LI (1976), reprinted in A. O. Rorty (ed.), *The Identities of Persons*.

B. Williams, 'Personal Identity and Individuation' in *Proceedings of the Aristotelian Society*, LVII (1956–7) also in *Problems of the Self*.

R. Wollheim, 'The Mind and the Mind's Image of Itself' in *International Journal of Psychoanalysis* 50 (1969).

―――― 'Imagination and Identification' in his *On Art and the Mind*.

―――― 'Identification and Imagination: The Inner Structure of a Psychic Mechanism', book cited in R. Wollheim (ed.), *Freud: A Collection of Critical Essays*.

C. Adam and P. Tannery, *Oeuvres de Descartes* (reissued Paris: Voin 1964–75).

Aristotle, *Metaphysics*.

J. L. Austin, *Sense and Sensibilia*, (Oxford: Clarendon Press, 1962).

―――― *Philosophical Papers*, eds. J. O. Urmson and G. Warnock (2nd ed, Oxford: Clarendon Press, 1970).

M. Black (ed.) *Philosophical Analysis* (Ithaca: Cornell University Press, 1950).

R. J. Butler, (ed.), *Analytical Philosophy*, (2nd ser., Oxford: Blackwell, 1965).

N. S. Care, and R. H. Grimm, (eds), *Perception and Personal Identity*, (Cleveland, Ohio, 1969).

R. Descartes, *Discourse on the Method*, in *Philosophical Writings*, (eds) G. E. M. Anscombe and P. T. Geach (Edinburgh: 1954).

M. Dummett, *Frege: Philosophy of Language*, (London: Duckworth, 1973).

A. Einstein, *Hedwig und Max Born – Briefwechsel 1916–1955* (Munich: 1969).

G. Evans, and J. McDowell, *Truth and Meaning: Essays in Semantics* (Oxford: Clarendon Press, 1976).

S. Freud, J. Strachey (ed.) *Complete Psychological Works*, (London: Hogarth Press.)

P. T. Geach, *Logic Matters* (Oxford: Blackwell, 1972).

C. I. Gerhardt, *Philosophische Schriften von G. W. Leibniz I–VII* (Berlin: 1875–90).

C. I. Gerhardt, *Mathematische Schriften von G. W. Leibniz I–VII*, Berlin–Halle: 1849–63.

J. W. von Goethe, *Warheit und Dichtung*,

N. Goodman, *Fact, Fiction and Forecast* (Cambridge, Mass: Harvard, 1955).

―――― *Problems and Projects* (Indianapolis: Bobbs-Merrill, 1972).

D. Hume, *A Treatise of Human Nature*, ed. L. A. Selby-Bigge (Oxford: 1888).

H. Ishiguro, *Leibniz: Philosophy of Logic and Language*, (London: Duckworth, 1972).

I. Kant, *Critique of Pure Reason*, translated by N. Kemp Smith (London: Macmillan & Co., 1929).

A. Kasher (ed.), *Language in Focus*, (Dordrecht: Reidel, 1976).

J. M. Keynes, *A Treatise on Probability* (London: Macmillan, 1921).
H. Kiefer and M. Munitz (eds), *Mind, Language and Reality* (Albany: State University of New York Press, 1970).
S. Körner (ed.), *Observation and Interpretation* (New York: Dover, 1957).
────── *Experience and Theory* (London: Routledge and Kegan Paul, 1966).
────── *Experience and Conduct* (Cambridge: Cambridge University Press, 1976).
Leibniz, *Discourse of Metaphysics*, trans. by P. Lucas and L. Grint. (Manchester: Manchester Univ. Press 1952).
H. D. Lewis (ed.), *Contemporary British Philosophy* (4th ser. London: Allen and Unwin, 1976).
Locke, Fraser (ed.), *An Essay Concerning Human Understanding*, (Oxford: 1894).
J. L. Mackie, *Truth, Probability and Paradox* (Oxford: Clarendon Press, 1973).
────── *The Cement of the Universe* (Oxford: Clarendon Press, 1974).
────── *Problems from Locke* (Oxford: Clarendon Press, 1976).
M. Merleau-Ponty, *Phénoménologie de la Perception* (Paris: Gallimard, 1945).
J. S. Mill, *A System of Logic* (8th edn. London: 1941).
M. K. Munitz, *Identity and Individuation* (New York: New York University Press, 1971).
D. Pears, *David Hume: A Symposium* (London: Macmillan, 1963).
────── *Questions in the Philosophy of Mind* (London: Duckworth, 1975).
J. Perry (ed.), *Personal Identity* (Berkeley and Los Angeles: Univ. of California Press 1975).
K. Popper, *The Logic of Scientific Discovery* (London: Hutchinson, 1959).
H. H. Price, *Perception* (London: Methuen, 1932).
W. V. O. Quine, *From A Logical Point of View* (Cambridge, Mass.: University of Harvard Press, 1953).
────── *Word and Object* (Cambridge, Mass: M.I.T. Press, 1960).
────── *Ways of Paradox and Other Essays* (New York: Random House, 1966, enlarged edn 1977).
A. O. Rorty, *The Identities of Persons* (Univ. of California Press: Berkeley and Los Angeles, 1976).
B. Russell, and A. N. Whitehead, *Principia Mathematica Vol 1* (Cambridge: Cambridge University Press, 1910).
B. Russell, *The Problems of Philosophy* (London: Oxford University Press, 1912).
────── *Mysticism and Logic* (2nd edn London; Allen and Unwin, 1917).
────── *The Analysis of Mind* (London: Allen and Unwin, 1921).
────── *An Enquiry into Meaning and Truth* (London: Allen and Unwin, 1940).
────── *Human Knowledge, Its Scope and Limits* (London: Allen and Unwin, 1948).
G. Ryle, *The Concept of Mind* (London: Hutchinson, 1949).
────── *Dilemmas* (Cambridge: Cambridge University Press, 1954).
P. A. Schlipp (ed.), *The Philosophy of Karl Popper* (La Salle, Illinois: The Open Court Publishing Co., 1974).
W. Sellars, *Science, Perception and Reality* (London: Routledge, 1963).
S. Shoemaker, *Self-Knowledge and Self-Identity* (Ithaca: Cornell University Press, 1963).
D. C. Stove, *Probability and Hume's Inductive Scepticism* (Oxford: Oxford University Press, 1973).
P. F. Strawson, *Individuals* (London: Methuen, 1959).
P. Suppes, *Introduction to Logic* (Princeton, N. J.: Van Nostrand, 1957).
R. G. Swinburne, *An Introduction to Confirmation Theory* (London: Methuen, 1973).
S. Themerson, *The Artifacts of Mind and Body* (London: Gaberbocchus, 1973).
D. Wiggins, *Identity and Spatio-Temporal Continuity* (Oxford: Blackwell, 1967).
B. Williams, *Problems of the Self* (Cambridge: Cambridge University Press, 1973).

———— *Descartes: The Project of Pure Enquiry* (Harmondsworth: Penguin, 1978).

R. Wollheim, *On Art and the Mind* (London: 1973).

R. Wollheim (ed.) *Freud: A Collection of Critical Essays* (New York: Anchor Books 1974).

M. J. Woods, *Substance and Quality*, B. Phil. Thesis (Oxford University, 1958, (unpublished).

Notes on the Contributors

D. M. ARMSTRONG. Challis Professor of Philosophy in the University of Sydney since 1964. He previously taught at Birkbeck College, University of London, and in the University of Melbourne. His publications include *Perception and the Physical World, A Materialist Theory of the Mind, Belief, Truth and Knowledge* and *Universals and Scientific Realism*. His main interests are in ontology, epistemology and the philosophy of mind.

MICHAEL DUMMETT. Succeeded, in 1979, Sir Alfred Ayer as Wykeham Professor of Logic in the University of Oxford, having since 1974 been Senior Research Fellow at All Souls College. From 1961 to 1974 he was Reader in the Philosophy of Mathematics in the University of Oxford, and in 1976 he was William James Lecturer at Harvard University. His publications include *Frege: Philosophy of Language, Elements of Intuitionism* and *Truth and Other Enigmas*.

JOHN FOSTER. Lecturer in Philosophy in the University of Oxford and Fellow of Brasenose College. A former pupil of Sir Alfred Ayer, his main interests are in epistemology, philosophy of mind and philosophical logic.

STEPHAN KÖRNER. Professor of Philosophy in the University of Bristol since 1952 and (jointly) in Yale University since 1970. His publications include *Conceptual Thinking, Kant, The Philosophy of Mathematics, Experience and Theory, Fundamental Questions in Philosophy, Categorical Frameworks* and *Experience and Conduct*.

GRAHAM MACDONALD (editor of this volume). A graduate of the University of Witwatersrand and gaining a B Phil. at Oxford, where he was a postgraduate pupil of Sir Alfred Ayer, he was appointed in 1974 Lecturer in Philosophy in the University of Bradford, having previously taught in the University of Witwatersrand. His publications include an introductory text (with R. Lindley and D. Fellows), *What Philosophy Does*.

J. L. MACKIE. Fellow and Tutor in Philosophy at University College, Oxford. He previously taught in the universities of Otago, Sydney and York. His publications include *Truth, Probability and Paradox, The Cement of the Universe: A Study of Causation, Problems from Locke* and *Ethics: Inventing Right and Wrong*. He is interested in the philosophy of science, of religion, and of law, as well as in epistemology, metaphysics and moral philosophy.

DAVID PEARS. Reader in Philosophy in the University of Oxford and Tutor in Philosophy at Christ Church College. His publications include *Bertrand Russell and the British Tradition in Philosophy, Wittgenstein* and *Some Questions in the Philosophy of Mind*. His main interests are in the philosophy of mind and in the work of Aristotle, Russell and Wittgenstein.

P. F. STRAWSON. Waynflete Professor of Metaphysical Philosophy in the University of Oxford and Fellow of Magdalen College. From 1948 to 1968 he was Fellow of University College, Oxford. His publications include *Introduction to Logical Theory*, *Individuals*, *The Bounds of Sense* and *Subject and Predicate in Logic and Grammar*.

CHARLES TAYLOR. Chichele Professor of Social and Political Theory in the University of Oxford. He was previously Professor of Philosophy and Political Science in McGill University, Montreal. His publications include *The Explanation of Behaviour* and *Hegel*. His main interests are in philosophy of mind and political theory.

PETER UNGER. Professor of Philosophy in New York University. Working under Sir Alfred Ayer, he received his D Phil. from Oxford in 1966. His publications include *Ignorance: A Case for Scepticism*. His main interests are in epistemology, metaphysics and the philosophy of language.

DAVID WIGGINS. Professor of Philosophy at Bedford College in the University of London. From 1959 to 1967 he was Lecturer and Fellow of New College, Oxford. His publications include *Identity and Spatio-Temporal Continuity* and *Truth, Invention and the Meaning of Life* (the British Academy's Henrietta Hertz Lecture, 1977).

BERNARD WILLIAMS. Knightsbridge Professor of Philosophy in the University of Cambridge since 1967, and Fellow of King's College. He earlier taught at Oxford, at University College, London (appointed by Sir Alfred Ayer), and at Bedford College, London. His publications include *Morality*, *Problems of the Self*, *A Critique of Utilitarianism* and *Descartes: The Project of Pure Enquiry*.

RICHARD WOLLHEIM. Grote Professor of Philosophy of Mind and Logic in the University of London. He has taught at University College, London since 1949 (until 1959 under Sir Alfred Ayer). His publications include *F. H. Bradley*, *Art and its Objects*, *Freud* and *Art and the Mind*. His main interests are in the philosophy of mind and in aesthetics.

A. J. AYER. From 1959–1978 Wykeham Professor of Logic in the University of Oxford and a Fellow of New College. He was previously Grote Professor of the Philosophy of Mind and Logic in the University of London, at University College. He is a fellow of the British Academy, Honorary Fellow of Wadham College, Oxford, Doctor *honoris causa* of the University of Brussels, Honorary D.Litt. of the University of East Anglia, Honorary Doctor of the Danish Academy of Sciences and Letters, Chevalier de la Legion d'Honneur and Member of the Bulgarian Order of Cyril and Methodius, 1st class. He was knighted in 1970.

Name Index

Chapter references are printed in bold type.

Albert Einstein – Hedwig und Max Born – Briefweschel 1916–1955 276
Alexander the Great 234
Analysis of Mind, The 61, 82
Analytical Philosophy 98
Anderson, John 84
Anscombe, G. E. M. 98, 233
Aquinas, Thomas 18, 263
Aristotle 146, 152, 156, 263
Armstrong, D. M. 84, 278, 281, 282, 294
Arnauld 136, 137, 154, 156
Artifacts of Mind and Body, The 157
Austin, J. L. 61, 64, 65, 70ff, 82, 158, 287
Ayer, A. J. **1** *passim*; **2** *passim*; **3** *passim*; **4**, 84, 85, 90, 91, 97, 98; **5** 100–2, 111, 112; **6** *passim*; **7** *passim*; **8** 163, 167, 170, 171, 178, 184; **9** 186, 195ff, 210, 223, 232, 233, 234; **10** 235; **11** *passim*; **12** *passim*; **13** 277, 333

Barcan Marcus, Ruth 141, 142, 311
Bayes 121, 128, 303
Berkeley, George 21, 87, 92, 282, 329
Bergson, H. 13
Black, Max 82
Block, N. J. 234
Bohr, N. 263
Born, Max 275
Brutus 308
Butler, Bishop 223
Butler, R. J. 98

Caesar, Julius 140, 145ff, 156, 306ff
Cambridge 131
Care, Norman S. 234
Carnap, R. 116, 126, 289, 305, 325
Cartwright, Richard 154, 155, 156
Categories 156
Cement of the Universe, The 129, 130
Central Questions of Philosophy, The 1–7, 12, 21, 29, 35, 36, 41ff, 60, 84ff, 97, 98, 154, 155, 160, 233, 267, 276, 277, 280, 281, 289, 331, 333
Chisholm, Roderick 234
Christie, Agatha 321
Cicero 149, 249
Complete Psychological Works 233, 234
Concept of a Person and Other Essays, The 129, 154, 184, 186, 233
Concept of Mind, The 101, 111
Contemporary British Philosophy, 4th ser. 233
Crick, F. 157
Crippen 255
Critique of Pure Reason 60, 112, 276

Davidson, Donald 6
David Hume: A Symposium 234
De Bello Gallico 308
Der Logische Aufbau der Welt 325
Descartes, René 99, 156, 163, 172ff, 183, 235, 242, 244, 245, 249
Descartes: The Project of Pure Enquiry 261
Deutscher, Max 82, 233
Dickens, Charles 141, 310
Dilemmas 102, 111
Discourse of Metaphysics 157
Discourse on the Method 184
Dummett, M. 1, 261, 277ff, 293ff

Einstein, A. 275
Essay Concerning Human Understanding, An 29, 30, 157, 158
Eubulides 248ff
Evans, Gareth 154, 160
Evening Star 140, 141, 155, 306
Experience and Conduct 276
Experience and Theory 276

Fact, Fiction and Forecast 129
Fann, K. T. 82
Feyerabend, Paul 92
Flew, Anthony 233

Fodor, J. A.   234
Foster, John   36, 161, 184, 280, 314ff
Foundations of Empirical Knowledge,
* The*   131, 186, 233
Frege: Philosophy of Language   261
Freud: A Collection of Critical
* Essays*   233
Freud, S.   13, 216, 221–2, 233, 234
From a Logical Point of View   154. 155

Geach, P. T.   154
George VI   326, 327
Gerhardt   153, 154, 157
Gödel   263
Goethe, J. W. von   198ff, 206, 233, 322
Goodman, Nelson   12, 119, 120, 129,
  155, 157, 278, 283, 304, 316, 325
Grimm, Robert H.   234

Hamlet   134–5
Harrod, R.   115, 120, 128, 129, 305
Hesperus   140, 141
Howarth, Jane   234
Human Knowledge, Its Scope and
* Limits*   66
Hume, David   36, 48, 110, 114ff, 168,
172ff, 183, 232, 234, 235, 290, 299, 300,
310, 314, 315

Identity and Individuation   154, 234
Identity and Spatio-Temporal
* Continuity*   153, 234
Identities of Persons, The   234
Individuals   156, 183
Introduction to Confirmation Theory,
* An*   129
Introduction to Logic   155
Inquiry into Meaning and Truth, An   66,
  67, 82
Ishiguro, Hide   153, 157, 158, 234

Jackson, Frank   87, 98
James, W.   178, 315, 325
Joske, W. D.   93, 94

Kant, I.   53, 55, 60, 99, 110, 111, 112,
  263, 267, 268, 271, 272, 274, 276
Kasher, A.   154
Kemp Smith, N.   112
Keynes, J. M.   116, 129
Kiefer, H.   234
Körner, S.   129, 262, 276, 325, 329ff
Kripke, S.   141, 157, 232, 234

Languages, Belief and Metaphysics   234
Language in Focus   154
Language, Truth and Logic   67, 82, 131,
  133, 135, 252, 261, 262, 276, 277, 325,
  329, 331, 333
Leibniz, G.   133, 135ff, 146–60 passim,
  263, 271
Leibniz–Arnauld Correspondence   154
Leibnizens Mathematischen Schriften   157
Leibniz's Philosophy of Logic and
* Language*   153, 157, 158
Lewis, C. I.   278, 326
Lewis, H. D.   233
Locke, John   8, 21, 29, 30, 31, 33, 41,
  48, 99, 110, 116, 148, 157, 158, 159,
  173, 174, 184, 194, 292
Logic of Scientific Discovery, The   129
Logical Syntax of Language   265
London   131

Macbeth   89, 134
Macdonald, Graham   277
Mackie, J. L.   41, 48ff, 60, 113, 129,
  130, 158, 292, 298ff
Malebranche   35
Marcus, Ruth Barcan   141, 142, 311
Martin, C. B.   82, 233
McDowell, John   154, 160
Merceau-Ponty, M.   110, 112
Metaphysics   156
Midwest Studies in Philosophy, Vol. IV:
* Studies in Metaphysics*   251
Mill, J. S.   123, 128, 129, 130, 168, 301,
  305
Mind and the World-order   326
Mind, Language, and Reality   234
Moore, G. E.   97, 240
Munitz, Milton K.   154, 234
Mysticism and Logic   82

Nagel, Thomas   234
Nostradamus   310, 311
Nouveaux Essais   133, 156, 157, 159

Observation and Interpretation   129
Oeuvres de Descartes   156
On Art and The Mind   233, 234
Origins of Pragmatism, The   184, 186,
  233, 315, 316, 317, 333
Oxford Philosophy   131

Parfit, Derek   234
Pears, David   61, 234, 285ff

Peacocke, C. A. B. 154
Peirce, C. 267, 273, 326, 330
Perception 333
Perception and Personal Identity 234
Perry, John 234
Personal Identity 234
Phénoménologie de la perception 110, 112
Philosophical Essays 82, 157, 260, 261, 333
Philosophical Investigations 110
Philosophical Papers 82
Philosophy of Karl Popper, The 129
Plato 263
Popper, Karl 113, 115, 117, 129
Price, H. H. 286, 333
Principia Mathematica 63, 65, 82, 266
Prior, A. N. 234, 254
Probability and Evidence 115, 117, 129, 130
Probability and Hume's Inductive Scepticism 129
Problem of Knowledge, The 75, 76, 82, 100, 111, 112, 186, 195, 197, 233, 234, 251, 260, 261
Problems and Projects 155, 157
Problems of Analysis (ed. M. Black) 82
Problems of Philosophy, The 62, 63, 65, 82
Problems of the Self 233, 234
Problems from Locke 60, 130
Putnam, H. 157, 232, 234

Questions in the Philosophy of Mind 234
Quine, W. V. 134, 138, 139, 142, 143, 154, 155, 253, 298, 327

Ramsey, F. P. 1, 16, 97
Reid, T. 223
Robinson, H. M. 183
Rorty, Amélie Oksenberg 234
Rorty, Richard 92
Russell, B. 61ff, 82, 97, 135, 155, 160, 278, 279, 287, 289, 295, 297, 315, 325
Russell and Moore: The Analytical Heritage 82
Ryle, Gilbert 101, 102, 111, 132

Sacco 321
Sainsbury, R. M. 184
Sameness and Substance 153
Sanford, David H. 251
Schlick, M. 67
Schilpp, P. A. 129
Science, Perception, and Reality 98

Self-Knowledge and Self-Identity 234
Sellars, Wilfred 91, 92, 98, 281
Sense and Sensibilia 82
Shakespeare, W. 134
Sharvey, R. 156
Shoemaker, Sidney 233, 234
Silverman, Ralph 251
Slote, Michael 234
Smart, J. T. C. 91
Socrates 327
Stout, G. F. 91
Stove, D. C. 129
Strachey, James 233
Strawson, P. F. 41, 148, 156, 157, 163ff, 171, 182, 183, 277, 281, 282, 289ff
Structure of Appearance, The 325
Substance and Quality 158
Suppes, Patrick 155
Swinburne, R. G. 129
Symposium on J. L. Austin 82
System of Logic, A 129, 130

Tarski, A. 155
Taylor, Charles 99, 291
Themerson, Stefan 157
Transcendental Dialectics 267
Treatise of Human Nature, A 116–17, 129, 184, 234
Treatise on Probability, A 129
Truth and Meaning: Essays in Semantics 154, 160
Truth, Probability and Paradox 129, 130

Unger, Peter 235, 236, 324

Valberg, Jerry 234
Van Straaten, Z. 157
Vanzetti 321
Von Juhos, B. 67

Wahrheit und Dichtung 233
Watling, John 234
Watson, J. 157
Ways of Paradox and Other Essays 154
Wheeler, Samuel 236, 249, 251
Wiggins, D. 131, 154, 156, 160, 234, 306ff, 324
Williams, Bernard 190, 233, 234, 252, 325, 326, 328ff
Wittgenstein, L. 3, 110, 328
Wollheim, Richard 186, 233, 234, 314ff
Woods, M. J. 158
Word and Object 155

Subject Index

Chapter references are printed in bold type.

abstraction operator   139
absurdity, reduction to   237, 243, 264, 265
acquaintance, knowledge by   61ff, 82
acquisition condition   203ff, 219, 233, 319, 320, 322
affective adequacy   215, 216; impact 209; influence   211ff, 229, 230; store 209, 212ff, 230, 231, 319, 320, 323; tendency   208; tone   208, 209, 212, 215, 216, 220, 222, 229ff, 319, 321, 323
alternation   269
analogy, argument from   164, 329
analytic   154; propositions   134, 135, 307, 330; truth   115–16, 149, 330,
analyticity   134, 135
ancestral   187
atom   **10** *passim*
attitudes, propositional   166, 175, 184, 316
attribute   142, 149, 155, 156, 163, 165, 182, 272; non-observable   271; fictitious   273; individuating   274

basic propositions   66ff, 82
Bayes's theorem   121, 128, 303
behaviour, bodily   317
Biography(ies)   187, 188, 192, 202ff, 315
bivalence, principle of   4, 5, 7, 278
bodily behaviour   317; continuity   178, 318; identity   314, 318; sensation 178
body   **8** *passim*, 226, 315
brain, continuity of   317

Cartesian   167, 172ff, 317
categorial framework   272, 274, 332
Categories   268
causal chain   85, 222; clause   322; condition   322; connection   52, 97; definition   157; dependence   51, 180, 314, 317, 318; explanation   31, 48; generalisation   151, 317–18; history

194, 197ff, 215ff; influence ʹ2ʋ3, ʑʋ3, 211; law   114; mechanism   58, 122; origin   229, 230; powers   298, 299; property   1; relation   51, 52, 86ff, 115, 164, 167, 168, 169, 184, 299; sequences   122, 124
causality   36, 37, 84, 110, 166, 272, 318, 323
causation   169, 191, 207, 217, 228; of memory   197ff, 321
cause   35, 293, 295
cell   242ff
circular(ity)   115, 116, 119, 167, 168, 170, 174, 186, 189, 192, 299, 300, 316
class   142; of propositions   271
cognitive   210, 215, 220, 223, 262; impact   209; influence   211; meaning   325; principles   270, 271; supremacy   272ff; state   203ff, 318; store   209
common sense   1, 14, 16ff, 27, 41, 42, 47, 49ff, 110, 120, 240, 249, 263, 273, 274, 289, 294, 298
communication, interpersonal   227, 228
compresence, sensible   316ff
concept, individual   153
concept of a mind   166; of a person 162ff, 182, 227, 232, 314ff; of a subject   179
concepts   37, 38, 54, 153, 156, 159, 165, 184; *a priori*   111, 268, 270, 271ff, 331; fundamental   145; ideal   272, 273, 275, 331; interpretative   270ff; interpreted   270ff; linking   331; natural – kind-   146; physical   32, 46; sortal   145; theoretical   331
Concepts of objects   46, 53, 290, 292
conditionals, subjunctive   3, 6, 7, 268, 269, 281, 293, 317, 318; unfulfilled   84
conditions   298; acquisition   203ff, 219, 233, 319, 320, 322; background 124; causal   322; identity   155; necessary   76, 86, 123, 186, 187, 192ff,

conditions – *continued*
285, 309, 314, 319; normal 24ff, 57;
persistence 145, 146, 150, 151, 159;
sufficient 80, 86, 123, 186, 194ff, 222,
261, 285, 309, 314, 319; truth 38, 39,
74, 78, 151, 322, 328
conjunction 269, 272, 305
co-consciousness 316
conscious 106
consciousness 54, 162, 163, 173, 183,
184, 194, 244, 318; unity of 110; *see
also* unconsciousness
continuity sensible- 316ff;
physical 323; principle of 266, 271,
275, 330; *see also* brain; self
continuous functions 263, 264
contradiction 282; self- 187, 224;
contradictory, self- 49, 226ff
conventional(-al, -alism) 187, 258, 330
corrigibility 95
counterfactually 137, 148, 179, 241,
244, 310
criterion of identity 146, 152, 323, 331

death 185, 245
decomposition 241, 243; arguments
242; *see also* sorites, arguments
de dicto 171, 306; necessity 134, 135;
translation 139
deduction 115ff
deductive validity 299, 300
definition 147, 149, 156, 157, 180;
causal 157; disguised 330;
nominal 158; stipulative 265, 266,
329; *see also* stream
demonstrative 327, 328; symbols 67
de re 171; conceivings 148; modal
assertion 143, 148, 151, 154;
modality 143, 308; necessary
properties 145; necessity 138, 139,
141, 142, 149, 150, 155, 156, 179, 306,
311, 313; 'possibly' 139; predicates
139
descriptions 308ff; absolute (cf.
representation, absolute) 16, 25, 33ff,
294ff; definite 135; identifying 164,
327; logically equivalent 312;
relative 16, 25, 33, 36, 37, 294ff;
state- 126; theory of- 155; vague
144, 304
disembodied 171
dispositional manner 30; properties
29, 31, 114, 294, 295

dispositions 192, 193
dualist 168, 174, 314; orthodox 167,
171, 172
dualistic 162, 163, 164, 166, 182, 183

ego 163, 164
egocentric predicament 258
embodiment 168; causal 182
emotion(al) 219, 321
empirical, conclusions 303;
conditions 333; discourse 263;
hypothesis 263, 264; knowledge
287; meaning 252, 259; probability
119; realism 55; theory 329
empiricism 110, 136, 259; British 186;
verificationist 260
empiricist 169, 189ff, 210, 258;
classical- 185, 195, 232
entelechies 245
entrenched predicates 301
epistemic probability 116ff, 301, 302;
situation 199ff
epistemological considerations 100;
intermediates 97; status 37; point
103
epistemologically based 281;
primitive 331; privileged 109
epistemology 210, 249; empiricist 191
essence 131, 133, 147ff, 246;
individual 137, 148, 245;
nominal 148, 158
essentialism 133, 136, 143, 147ff, 306,
329
essentialist 141, 152, 153
excluded middle, principle of 263, 275,
330
existential proposition 135;
quantification 269
experience 23, 24, 26ff, 31, 37, 39, 68,
74, 78, 101ff, 119, 164ff, 176, **9** *passim*,
259, 272, 287ff, 298ff, 315ff;
auditory- 175; memory- 193;
subjectless 171; perceptual 99ff;
perceptible 66; sense **2** *passim*, 101,
175, 176, 280, 286ff; visual 102
experiential memory 186, 194ff, 319ff
explanation 1, 34, 35, 114, 115, 118,
127, 144ff, 161, 164, 262, 274, 296,
299; causal 31, 48; philosophical
259; physical 58; second-level 139
explanatory account 224; adequacy
221; function 276; power 267ff;
theories 114

extensional(ly) 62, 64, 65, 67, 71, 136, 155, 156, 158, 180
extensional positions 141; principle 143
extentionalism 136; extensionalist 138
extensionality 152; axiom of 142, 144

fact 65, 329; complex 63, 65; hard 1, 2; physical 163; psychological 163, 211; relational 301; soft 2
factual content 253, 258, 325ff, 332; error 69ff, 287, 288, 309; inferences 130, 299, 300; proposition 267, 268, 270; regularity 299
factually false 286
fission 179, 180, 224ff, 234, 318, 323
fregian 135
frequency 117, 120
function 218, 219; of memory 218ff, 319; of metaphysical principles 262, 264; *see also* explanatory function
functional adaptation 221; role 161ff, 182, 318
fusion 174, 179, 180, 234, 318

generic constitution 146, 313
genetic 139; feature 147
genus 146, 178, 313
God 30, 31, 136, 246, 263, 264, 278, 292, 331
'Goethe case' 198ff, 322

habit-memory 195
helix, double 157
Humian 52, 97, 122, 156, 167, 172ff

idealism 278
identical, necessarily 140, 306
identification 31, 34, 35, 74, 103, 106, 107, 144, 164ff; of effects and causes 123; of perception and sense datum 94; of physical objects 46, 299; of secondary qualities with physical correlates 90; *see also* self-identification
identifiable 145, 310
identify 75ff, 163, 164, 170, 309
identifying 282, 291; -descriptions 164, 327
identity 137, 147, 156, 172ff, 244, 308; bodily 314, 316; criterion of 146, 152, 323, 331; necessity of 141, 311, 312; numerical 176; personal 186ff, 210, 224, 228, 232, 314ff, 327; criterion

identity – *continued*
of 189ff, 209, 215, 223ff; relative 145; self- 147, 311, 312; set- 142, 143, 312; subject 168, 173ff; *see also* conditions; indiscernibles; link; memory path; time; statement
illusion, argument from 2, 97; metaphysical 246
image, manifest 91, 282, 289; scientific 91
images 184
imagining, centrally 195, 208, 211, 216, 217
imaginary situation 224ff
imagination 216, 219, 221
indifference, principle of 120, 121, 125, 126, 128, 129, 302, 303
indiscernibles, identity of 328
indiscernibility 282, 283; condition 9, 10
indiscriminability 10ff
individuation 149, 272, 273; autonomous 151; conception of 145, 146; principle of 138, 150ff, 159, 191; theory of 147, 150, 159
individuation of classes 142ff
individuative, sortal 150, 151
incorrigibility 61, 69, 78, 100, 286
induction 6 *passim*, 298ff; eliminative methods of 123, 305; new riddle of 119, 120
infallible 47
infallibility 61ff, 69, 78, 286ff
infinite sets 263, 330
infinities 264
infinity 331; mathematical 275
instrumentalism 1, 7, 37ff, 91, 297
intensional 62, 64, 65
intentional 165, 166; object 96
interpretative(-ed) concepts 270ff
interpretation 107; of experience 111, 290, 291; of movement 165, 166
intersubjective 274
intersubjectivity 268, 271, 272
introspective awareness 172
irreducibility 5, 90, 93; thesis 4

knowledge 18, 19, 27, 31, 34, 71, 77, 118, 130, 132, 170, 199, 200, 210, 257, 301, 313, 319, 320, 328; authoritative 129, 130; causation of 199; claims to 196, 198; empirical 287; indistinct 157; *see also* acquaintance
lambda 141

language, philosophy of 249
law 6, 24, 38, 39, 146, 147, 168ff, 300, 313; bridge 91; causal 114; excluded middle 330 (cf. principle of); logical 311; natural 179, 181, 317; scientific 311
lawlike connections 304
link, identity 144
logic, alternative 239; classical 263, 268, 273, 275; predicate 269, 273; truth – functional 268, 269; *see also* philosophers of logic
logical atomism 92; connection 52; connectives 268, 269; constants 149, 156, 330; corrigibility 95; form 139; impossibility 166; necessity 149, 156, 266, 269; possibility 98, 156, 171, 181, 187, 203, 245, 246, 272, 315, 330; truth 156, 302; vocabulary 254
logically independent 161, 162, 172, 173; primitive 163, 164; prior 164, 166

meaning 21, 22, 31–3, 39, 65, 66, 77, 78, 149, 156, 158, 253, 256, 259, 263, 267, 285ff, 326, 330; theory of 39; *see also* cognitive and pragmatic theory of meaning
meaningless 262, 264
memory 52, 71, 178, **9** *passim*, 257, 286, 300, 314, 317ff; as recollection 200, 204, 209, 219, 220, 319ff; as retention 200, 204, 219, 319ff; *see also* causation; experiential memory; function; habit-memory; phenomenology; screen memory
memory path, identity of
mental attribute 163; image 184; items 166ff; phenomenon 209, 217ff, 252, 318; predicates 326, 332; state 3, 4, **8** *passim*, 196, 207, 317; substance 173, 174
mergological 150, 155
metaphysical conception 129; enquiry 2, 3; hypotheses 124; illusion 246; necessity 273; possibility 273; principles 270, 274, 275, 276; propositions 263ff; truth 127, 128
metaphysically misleading 259
metaphysics 158, **12** *passim*, 329ff
mind **8** *passim*, 278; philosophy of 162, 200, 218, 249; states of 92; *see also* other minds

modal 151, 152, 155, 158; involvement 134, 142, 154; translation 139
modality 140; *de re* 143, 308; theory of 142
molecules 240, 242, 247
monism 131, 133, 153

nature, law of 255, 263, 264, 330
natural kind 145ff, 158, 232, 313
NEC 139ff, 155
necessary, *a priori* 332; being 331; connection 95, 96, 306, 313; fact 329; identity 141, 311, 312; properties 133, 135, 145, 147, 306, 307, 311; propositions 93, 265, 266; truths 95, 180, 181, 192, 255, 266, 301, 312
necessity 95, 269, 308ff; category of 141; conceptual 148; *de dicto* 134, 135; *de re* 138, 139, 141, 149, 155, 156, 179, 306, 311, 315; logical 149, 156, 266, 269; metaphysical 272, 273; physical 32; *see also* origin, necessity of
negation 4; predicate 155; sentence 155
neurons 242, 245
neuro-physiological 4, 6; -physiologist 225
neutral monists 94
nihilism 236, 248, 251
nominalism 136
nominalist 138
nomological 168ff, 180, 184, 317
non-embodied 169, 180
no-ownership theory 166, 167, 169ff, 182, 184

ontology 152, 160
ontological status 37, 281
opaque context 141
origin, necessity of 309
other minds 257, 259

paradigm-case argument 17
particles 240; elementary 237; extensionless 274; physical 2, 3, 91, 98; scientific 296; sub-atomic 16; ultimate 58
perception **1, 2, 3, 4** *passim*, pp. 259, 278ff, 315, 321; causal theory of 35ff, 293; direct realist theory of 84, 94, 96, 279; problem of 41, 277;

perception – *continued*
  relations of 85ff; representative
  theory of 49, 84ff, 97, 279, 281
percepts 107, 278, 281, 289, 293, 307,
  308, 331
perceptual claims 290; judgements
  290ff; point of view 295;
  statements 286, 287
person **9** *passim*, 314ff, 323; concept
  of 162ff, 182, 227, 232, 314ff
personality 228
personal identity 186ff, 210, 224, 228,
  232, 314ff, 327; criterion of 189ff,
  209, 215, 223ff
phenomenal field 104, 291; objects
  175; pattern 175; predicates 296;
  property 54, 58, 292, 294ff;
  resemblance 181
phenomenalism 41, 84, 85, 99, 105,
  255, 277, 325
phenomenalist 84, 279
phenomenological 90ff, 184, 320
phenomenology, of memory 195ff,
  206ff, 218, 318, 319, 323; of mental
  states 207
philosophy 31, 36; English-language
  111; linguistic 132; natural 157;
  nature of 133; Oxford 131; school
  of 131, 132; *see also* language
philosophers of logic 263
phosphorus 140, 141
physical, attribute 163; laws 146;
  objects 1, 2, 5ff, 46, 48ff, 62ff, 85ff,
  241, 267, 268, 274, 278ff, 298ff, 315,
  330–1; particles 2, 3, 91, 98;
  properties 314; science 42, 59;
  state 162, 163, 317; system 161;
  theory 1ff, 23, 24, 48, 91, 289;
  world 289
physicalism 330
physicalist 161, 171, 264
pluralism 133, 153
positivism 256, 258, 260, 262, 267
positivist 154, 264, 265, 269, 272,
  275
POSS 139ff, 155
possibilia 136
possibilities 304; *a priori* 305;
  logical 305; range of 302; ratio of
  303
possibility 138, 203, 269, 302, 308;
  conceptual 137, 138, 156;
  contrary-to-fact- 256; logical 98,

possibility – *continued*
  156, 171, 181, 187, 203, 245, 246, 269,
  272, 315, 330; metaphysical 273
possible 268; causally 308
possible-worlds 136, 139
pragmatic theory of meaning 264
pragmatism 264
predicate, truth 154
presentational unity, principle of
  177
presentational acts 175ff, 317
pre-theoretical description 226, 227;
  realism 51; scheme 48, 50, 51
principle of continuity 266, 271, 275,
  330
probability 115ff, 125, 299, 300ff, 306;
  antecedent 121; *a priori* 301, 305;
  empirical 119; epistemic 116ff, 301,
  302; equi- 169; inverse 124ff
  logical 116ff, 301; relations of 301,
  302; subjective 116
project 268
projectible 6, 7
proofs, apogogic 276
proofs of probability 300
propensity 117, 120, 121
properties 58, 87, 91ff, 133, 138ff, 157,
  284, 294, 298, 306ff, 332; disjunctive
  150, 158; dispositional 29, 31, 114,
  294, 295; essential 147, 148, 150;
  internal 134; intrinsic 37; mental
  314; necessary 133, 135, 145, 147,
  306, 307, 311; observable 268;
  phenomenal 54, 58, 292, 294ff;
  physical 34, 54, 314; relational 153;
  sortal 146, 148; tactile 53;
  unanalysable 92, 282; visual 53,
  296
propositions 43, 155, 252, 326;
  analytic 134, 135, 307, 330; *a priori*
  265ff; basic 66, 68, 69, 82;
  consistent 271; contingent 266,
  330; core 253, 332, 333;
  dominating 270, 271; empirical
  286; existential 135; experiential
  325; factual 1, 267, 268, 270, 325;
  hypothetical 279; metaphysical
  263ff, 332; necessary 93, 265, 266,
  330; subsistent 96; verifiable 69
propositional, attitudes 166, 175, 184,
  316; form 63
psychology, genetic 289, 290;
  mechanistic 100

psychological 42, 161ff; character
  161ff, 166, 168, 182, 318; evidence
  289, 291; facts 163, 211; laws 211;
  phenomenon 195; statements 6;
  states 258; theory 232; words 232
psycho-physical, causal relations 168,
  184; laws 168

'quale' 278
qualia 316, 331
qualities, observational 282ff;
  perceptible 7ff; personal 331;
  primary 50; secondary 90ff, 281,
  282, 294; sensible 49, 59, 89, 175;
  sensory 77; tactile 49, 50, 56, 58;
  visual 49, 50, 56, 58
quantification 269
quantifier 327

rational 161, 162, 166, 302;
  justification 299, 300
rationality 113ff, 274
realism 2ff, 16, 38ff, 41ff, 277ff, 333;
  anti- 5, 6, 170; common-sense 49ff;
  direct 84, 94, 279; lockian 48ff;
  naïve 2ff, 48, 278, 279;
  pre-theoretical 51; scientific 48ff,
  292, 294ff, 332; sophisticated 5ff,
  277ff
'realistic reduction' 90
recollection 200, 204, 209, 219, 220, 222
recollectively adjacent 178; linked 178
reducibility 172
reducible 163, 280
reducing 330
reduction-ist 3ff, 5, 6, 252, 278
reductive thesis 4ff, 16, 39, 280;
  verificationism 259
reference 78, 146, 149, 232, 252, 267,
  308, 309ff, 327; causal theory of 52,
  cf 309; theory of 137
referring expressions 102
relations, ancestral 323; causal 51, 52,
  86ff, 115, 164, 167ff, 184, 299; direct
  62; equivalence 177, 179ff; logical
  117, 301; memory 187, 188, 190ff;
  observational 8ff, 283; persistence
  179ff; psycho-physical 168;
  sensible 89, 316; spatial 290;
  spatio-temporal 312; structural
  270; subject-body 164;
  syntactical 266; temporal 318, 326;

relations – *continued*
  three-place 151; time 175;
  transitive 282ff, 324; triadic 138;
  two-term 63; unifying 172ff; *see
  also* probability, relations of and
  perception, relations of
relational facts 301
relative identity 145
representation, absolute 260, 333;
  subjective 54
rules 269, 270, 274, 330; linguistic
  262, 265ff; meaning 78, 285, 287, 289

sceptic 44, 45, 47, 115, 255
sceptical argument 115, 128, 299
scepticism 114, 118, 255, 299, 329
science 18, 20, 31, 33, 35, 37, 39, 42, 59,
  113, 114, 158, 221, 240, 258, 263, 269,
  274, 294, 299, 332; philosophy of 332
scientific: account 147; beliefs 314;
  detail 322; discoveries 150;
  explanation 34–5; image 91, 282;
  knowledge 18, 19, 27, 31, 53; law
  38, 311; particles 296; perspective
  236, 237, 242, 243, 245, 249; realism
  48ff, 292, 294ff, 332; theory 16, 18,
  20, 21, 232, 273, 297, 330ff;
  understanding 259; view 1, 50, 58,
  259, 260
'screen memory' 216, 217, 221, 222
self 161, 172ff, 315; -referential 327;
  -identification 164; -identity 147,
  311, 312
self, continuity of 315
semantics 38, 150, 155, 232, 265;
  model-theoretic 142
semantic-status 37
sense, cf experience 63, 175, 280; cf
  meaning 146, 149, 312, 313, 325,
  330; data 3 *passim*, 84, 88ff, 99ff,
  278, 279, 281, 284ff, 325; -datum
  statements 3 *passim*, 279, 280, 285ff;
  impressions 7
sentences, convergent set of 252ff, 332,
  eternal 253, 328; indicative 329;
  metaphysical 262ff, 330; neutral
  253, 254, 258ff, 332; token 248,
  252ff; type 248, 252, 253;
  well-formed 266
set, ideal- 274; identity 142ff, 143,
  312; linking 274; pair 143, 144,
  312, 313
set-theorist 263; -theory 142, 330

sets   142ff, 312; convergent-   252ff,
    332; infinite   263, 330
sets of properties   298, 310
singular terms   327
sorites, arguments   241, 249, 250; of
    accumulation   241, 242; of
    decomposition   236, 241ff; paradox
    324
sortal   77, 145, 146, 148, 150ff, 156
species   159, 313
species, infima   146
statement, identity   253, 261
stream (of awareness)   176ff; definition
    of   177
subject identity   168, 173ff
substance   272, 315; immaterial   174;
    mental   173, 174; possible   136;
    spiritual   190; thinking   172;
    unchanging   232
'substratum'   145, 153
supervenient   163
syntactically   265, 266
syntax   155
system, metaphysical   262, 269;
    physical   161; primary   1, 22, 97,
    267ff, 331, 332; scientific   269;
    secondary   1, 7, 16, 17, 37, 267ff, 275,
    331; spatial   2

tautology(-ies)   263, 264
temporal equivalence, principle of   177ff
theorem   155, 266, 320; Barcan's   141,
    142; Bayes's   121, 128, 303; modal
    140
theoretical concept   331; entities   37;
    material   254; statements   37ff;
    system   331
theory   16, 19, 38, 41, 42, 45, 47, 51, 62,
    81, 156, 174, 267, 275, 281, 289, 290,
    292, 293, 297, 298, 315, 331, 333;
    empirical   329; explanatory   114;
    metaphysical   267; physical   1ff, 23,
    24, 40, 48, 58, 91, 289; scientific   16,
    18, 20, 21, 232, 273, 297, 330ff;

theory – *continued*
    sense-datum   101, 109–10; set   142,
    330; *see also* individuation; meaning
    and modality
time   168, 173, 175, 252; identity over
    190; phenomenal   175, 176;
    presentational   175, 176
token reflexive devices   252, 253;
    expressions   254, 329; reflexives
    258, 261; sentences   252, 253
transparent contexts   142
truth   4ff, 20, 37, 38, 43, 47, 63, 80, 81,
    113, 187, 198, 233, 265, 266, 280, 286,
    287, 298, 303, 306, 330; absolute   264;
    analytic   115–16, 149, 330; *a priori*
    119; conditions   38, 39, 74, 78, 151,
    322, 328; empirical   119; functional
    268; indubitable   205; logical   156,
    302; metaphysical   127, 128; necessary
    95, 180, 181, 192, 215, 255, 266, 301,
    312; scientific   39; theory of   155;
    see also conditions, predicate and
    value

unconsciousness   178, 179, 209, 317, 323
uniformity, principle of   115, 116, 118,
    124, 128, 129, 301, 304, 306
uniformities of coexistence   123; of
    succession   123; of nature   299
universals   175, 176

vagueness   151, 251, 279; of
    descriptions   144, 304; of
    expressions   9; of terms   324; of
    qualities and relations   9ff
value, truth   247, 251, 253, 279, 281, 327
variable, free   139; of quantification
    142
verifiable(-ility)   68, 325, 328ff
verification   254ff, 325, 326, 327;
    principle of   325, 326, 329
verificationist   61, 171

worlds, possible   136, 139